LOGIC PROGRAMMING

A Classified Bibliography

LOGIC PROGRAMMING

A Classified Bibliography

by

Isaac Balbin

and

Koenraad Lecot

Isaac Balbin,
Department of Computer Science,
University of Melbourne,
Parkville, Victoria 3052,
AUSTRALIA.
electronic mail: munnari!isaac@seismo.ARPA

Koenraad Lecot,
Computer Science Department,
University of California,
Los Angeles, California 90024,
U.S.A.
electronic mail: koen@ucla-locus.ARPA

WILDGRASS BOOKS Pty Ltd.
289A Smith St., Fitzroy, Victoria 3065, AUSTRALIA

NATIONAL LIBRARY OF AUSTRALIA
CATALOGUING-IN-PUBLICATION

Balbin, Isaax, 1959-
    Logic programming.

    Includes index.
    ISBN 0 908069 15 4

    1. Programming languages (Electronic computers) –
    Semantics – Bibliography. 2. Prolog (Computer
    program language) – Bibliography. 3. Electronic
    digital computers – Programming – Bibliography.
    4. Logic, Symbolic and mathematical – Bibliography.
    I. Lecot, Koenraad. II. Title.

016.00164'24

ACKNOWLEDGEMENTS

Isaac Balbin would like to acknowledge the encouragement of his wife, Leonie, without whom this effort might have never been completed. The continued support of his parents, Mr & Mrs S. Balbin, and family - Sara & Daniel, Gila & Rommy, and Adina - were very much appreciated.

Thanks are due to Larry Overbeek and Randy Goebel for contributions from their personal bibliographies as well as Alan Bundy, Maarten Van Emden, Bernard Silver, Ivan Futo, Mehmet Dincbas and Jack Minker for their additions, corrections and comments.

Last, but not least, acknowledgement is due to the Digital Equipment Engineering Group which supported **mulga's** link to **decvax** thereby initially facilitating the electronic link between the two authors.

Koenraad Lecot would like to acknowledge contributions from Luis Pereira, Oskar Fuhlrott, and Michael Poe from their personal bibliographies.

FOREWORD

Logic Programming was effectively defined as a discipline in the early seventies. It is only during the early to mid eighties that books, conferences and journals devoted entirely to Logic Programming began to appear. Consequently, much of the work done during this first crucial decade in Marseilles, Edinburgh, London, Budapest and Stockholm (to name a few) is often overlooked or difficult to trace. There are now two main regular conferences on Logic Programming, and at least five journals: The Journal of Logic Programming, New Generation Computing, Automated Reasoning, The Journal of Symbolic Computation, and Future Generation Computer Systems.

Logic Programming, however, has its roots in Automated Theorem Proving and via the expanding area of expert systems, strongly influences researchers in such varied fields as Civil Engineering, Chemistry, Law, etc. Consequently, many papers related to Logic Programming appear in a wide variety of journals and proceedings of conferences in other disciplines. This is particularly true of Computer Science where a revolution is taking place in hardware design, programming languages, and more recently databases.

One cannot overestimate the importance of such a bibliography.

Jean-Louis Lassez, June, 1985, Melbourne, Australia.

INTRODUCTION

This bibliography evolved to provide a comprehensive source for literature related to the field of Logic Programming. Logic Programming is such an explosive area of Computer Science research that we felt a proper effort to collect and categorise most of the relevant papers was highly desirable. It is well known that the problem of accurately categorising each reference so as to satisfy both the authors and the readers is a difficult task. We have, however, made an attempt in this direction with the full knowledge that there will be inaccuracies and omissions, recognising the value of even partial correctness.

Chapter 1 deals with those papers and books devoted to introductory material regarding Logic Programming and its most prominent language, Prolog. We have devoted Chapter 2 to the general theoretical issues of Logic Programming, as well as relevant literature from automatic theorem proving and rewriting systems. Currently, much of the theory of Logic Programming is based around the concept of *Horn Clause* programs and their associated implementation using resolution and unification. Consequently, we have separately placed references to unification in Chapter 3. Papers devoted to the semantics of Logic Programming languages form the basis of Chapter 4.

Prolog eventually emerged as "the language of the eighties" - or in another parlance, the fifth generation *assembly* language. This has been partly because of the continuing research of the specialised implementation techniques required, which we survey in Chapter 5.

Owing to the wider exposure that Logic Programming has had over the the last few years, a whole new vista of programming techniques and methodologies is slowly crystallising. Whilst many of the more classical themes have been reincarnated in the new point of reference which is Logic Programming, new and exciting concepts have also been researched and developed. We present literature relevant to this subject area in Chapter 6.

Prolog is not, however, the only approach to Logic Programming, nor is it the only approach that incorporates *definite clauses*, and the techniques of resolution and unification. Chapter 7 comprises of references to these alternative approaches.

The excitement and promise that Logic Programming offers due to its simple stateless (or declarative) semantics, varied application areas, and firm theoretical foundation, encouraged the Japanese to launch their *fifth generation project* - the associated literature of which is listed in Chapter 8.

One of the problems regarding Logic Programming was the seeming inability of classical von Neumann architectures to cope with the demands of efficient implementation. New architectures, the literature of which appears in Chapter 9, were devised. Most solutions seem to incorporate parallelism in one form or another. Literature describing this technique is listed in Chapter 10. Of the more popular languages utilising a form of non determinism, and parallelism is *Concurrent Prolog* which also formed the basis of the Japanese fifth generation project, and is covered in Chapter 11.

Traditionally, Lisp has been the language used in artificial intelligence applications. Whilst this form of programming, also known in some quarters as *functional programming*, has enjoyed continued popularity, its protagonists as well as the Logic Programming "community", have attempted to amalgamate features of the two approaches with some success. These results, both in theory and in practice, are listed in Chapter 12.

Logic Programming has found application to many wide and varied fields; which are described by the literature listed in Chapter 13. Some specific areas, because of their importance and suitability, have merited separate chapters. These include: Expert Systems in Chapter 14; Databases in Chapter 15; Natural Language processing and Grammar formalisms in Chapter 16; Knowledge Engineering and Representation in Chapter 17; and, systems which *learn*, in Chapter 18. Often, an implementation of these applications warrants the amalgamation of a meta-level that is closer to the problem area, and the default object level that Logic Programming languages provide. Research dealing with this amalgamation is featured in Chapter 19.

CONTENTS

Chapter 1 1
Introductory Papers to Logic Programming and Prolog

Chapter 2 10
Theoretical Issues of Logic Programming

Chapter 3 61
Unification - Theory and Practice

Chapter 4 70
Semantics of Prolog and Logic Programming in General

Chapter 5 76
Implementation Issues of Logic Programming Languages

Chapter 6 101
Programming Concepts in Logic Programming

Chapter 7 120
Alternatives to Prolog as a Logic Programming Language

Chapter 8 137
Papers Related to Fifth Generation Computer Systems

Chapter 9 143
Harware Architectures for Logic Programming

Chapter 10 152
Parallelism and Logic Programming

Chapter 11 167
    Concurrent Prolog

Chapter 12 172
    Functional Programming and Equality: their
    Relationship with Logic Programming

Chapter 13 178
    Various Application Areas of Logic Programming

Chapter 14 219
    Application of Logic Programming to Expert Systems

Chapter 15 236
    Databases - Relationship with Logic Programming

Chapter 16 257
    Grammar Formalisms for Natural Language Processing

Chapter 17 277
    Knowledge Representation Issues in Logic Programming

Chapter 18 287
    Logic Programming in Learning Systems

Chapter 19 292
    Amalgamation of Object and Meta Level

Permuted Subject Index 295

Author Index 345

CHAPTER 1

Introductory Papers to Logic Programming and Prolog

1. Prolog Programming Language, Publication PB84-874775, National Technical Information Service, Springfield, Virginia, 1984.

2. AMSTERDAM, J., Forth, APL, LISP, MODULA-2, Smalltalk, Prolog: Computer Languages for the Future, *Popular Computing*, September 1, 1983, 136-150.

3. BECKER, J. M., AQ-Prolog User's Guide and Program Description, Technical Report, Department of Computer Science, University of Illinois, December 1983.

4. BELL, W., Prolog: Tomorrows Language For The Classroom, *Sixth European Conference On Artificial Intelligence*, Pisa, September, 1984.

5. BIEN, J. S., *Opis Systemu Prolog*, Maszynopis Powielony, Warsaw University, Poland. In Polish.

6. BOBROW, D. G., If Prolog Is The Answer, What Is The Question?, *International Conference On Fifth Generation Computer Systems*, November 1984.

7. BOWEN, D. L., BYRD, L., PEREIRA, F. C. N., PEREIRA, L. M. and WARREN, D. H. D., Decsystem-10 Prolog User's Manual, Occasional Paper 27, Department of Artificial Intelligence, University of Edinburgh, Scotland, November, 1982.

8. BOWEN, K. A., Prolog, *Proceedings of the Annual Conference of the ACM*, 1979, 14-23.

9. BUNDY, A., My Experience with Prolog, Technical Report, Department of Artificial Intelligence, University of Edinburgh, 1976.

10. BUNDY, A., What Stories Should We Tell Prolog Students?, Working Paper 156, Department of Artificial Intelligence, University of Edinburgh, 1984.

11. VAN CANEGHEM, M., Prolog II - Manual d'Utilisation, Technical Report, Groupe d'Intelligence Artificielle, Universite d'Aix-Marseille II, Marseille, France, 1982.

12. CARLSSON, M. and KAHN, K. M., LM-Prolog User Manual, UPMAIL Technical Report 24, Computer Science Department, Uppsala University, 1983.

13. CHIKAYAMA, T., ESP reference manual, ICOT TR-044, February, 1984.

14. CLARK, K. L., An Introduction to Logic Programming, Technical Report, Imperial College, London, 1981. Also in Introductory Readings in Expert Systems, (ed) D. Michie, Gordon and Breach, 1981.

15. CLARK, K. L. and McCABE, F. G., *Micro-Prolog Reference Manual*, Logic Programming Associates, London, England, 1981.

16. K. L. CLARK and F. G. McCABE, eds., *Micro-Prolog: Programming in Logic*, Prentice Hall, 1984.

17. CLOCKSIN, W. F. and MELLISH, C. S., *Programming in Prolog*, Springer Verlag (2nd Edition), New York, 1984.

18. CLOCKSIN, W. F. and YOUNG, J. D., Prolog, *Computerworld 17*, 31 (August, 1983).

19. CORTESI, D. E., Tour of Prolog, *Dr. Dobbs Journal*, March, 1985, 43-63.

20. DAVIS, R. E., Logic Programming is NOT Circuit Design, *Proceedings of COMPCON 84*, Spring 1984.

21. DEMOEN, B., How To Obtain A Prolog System With Your Preferred Syntax, *Sixth European Conference On Artificial Intelligence*, Pisa, September, 1984.

22. DUNIN-KEPLICZ, B. and SZPAKOWICZ, S., The Prolog Programming Language, ICS PAS Report 374, Department of Computer Science, Warsaw University, 1979. In Polish.

23. ENNALS, J. R., Logic as a Computer Language for Children: A One Year Course, Technical Report 81-6, Imperial College, London, 1981.

24. ENNALS, J. R., Prolog: An Introduction for Teachers, Technical Report, Imperial College, London, 1981.

25. ENNALS, J. R., *Beginning Micro-Prolog*, Ellis Horwood and Heinemann, Chichester, England, 1983.

26. ENNALS, J. R. and BRIGGS, J. H., Micro-Prolog Across The Curriculum: Collected Papers 1982-84, Doc 84/17, Department of Computing, Imperial College, 1984.

27. ENNALS, J. R. and BRIGGS, J. H., Logic and Programming, in *The Mind and the Machine*, S. TORRANCE, (ed.), Ellis Horwood Publishing, 1984.

28. FUTO, I. and SZEREDI, J., AI Languages: The Prolog Language, *Informacio-Elektronika XII*, 2-3 (1977), 108-113. In Hungarian.

29. FUTO, I. and SZEREDI, J., Prolog Reference Manual, *Szamologep VII*, 3-4 (1977), 5-130. In Hungarian.

30. FUTO, I. and SZEREDI, J., T-Prolog User Manual, Technical Report, Institute for the Coordination of Computer Techniques, Budapest, Hungary, 1981. In Hungarian.

31. FUTO, I. and SZEREDI, J., TPROLOG User Manual Version 4.2, Technical Report, Institute for Coordination of Computer Techniques, Hungary, 1983.

32. GALLAIRE, H., A Study of Prolog, *Proceedings of the NATO Summer School on Automatic Programming Systems*, 1981.

33. GOEBEL, R. G., Prolog/MTS User's Guide, Technical Manual TM80-2, UBC, Department of Computer Science, December, 1980.

34. GOEBEL, R. G. and CHENG, M. H. M., *Waterloo Unix Prolog Reference Manual*, University of Waterloo, Logic Programming Group, Waterloo, Ontario, 1983.

35. GOEBEL, R. G. and VAN EMDEN, M. H., *Waterloo Unix Prolog Tutorial*, University of Waterloo, Logic Programming Group, Waterloo, Ontario, 1983.

36. GOODALL, A., Prolog: The Rules to Become an Expert, *New Electronics 17*, 19 (October, 1982), 79-82.

37. GREEN, T. R., Reactions to Micro-Prolog, *SWURCC Microcomputer Software Quarterly 8*, (1982).

38. GUST, H., Logisches Programmieren fur Anfanger, *Elektronik*, November, 1984, 64-69.

39. HOGGER, C. J., *Introduction To Logic Programming*, Academic Press, 1985.

40. KAHN, K. M. and CARLSSON, M., LM-Prolog User Manual, 24, Uppsala Programming Methodology and Artificial Intelligence Laboratory, November 22, 1983.

41.   KLUZNIAK, F. and SZPAKOWICZ, S., *Prolog*, Wydawnicta Naukowo-Technicze, Warsaw, Poland. In Polish.

42.   KLUZNIAK, F. and SZPAKOWICZ, S., A Note on Teaching Prolog, in *Workshop on Logic Programming*, S. TARNLUND, (ed.), Debrecen, Hungary, July 1980.

43.   KLUZNIAK, F. and SZPAKOWICZ, S., Prolog: A Panacea?, in *Implementations of Prolog*, J. A. CAMPBELL, (ed.), Ellis Horwood, 1984.

44.   KOVES, P., BS2000 Prolog User's Reference Manual V2.4, SZKI Technical Report, SZKI Insititute, Budapest, Hungary, 1978. In Hungarian.

45.   KOWALSKI, R. A., Predicate Logic as a Programming Language, *Proceedings of the IFIP Congress*, Amsterdam, 1974, 569-574. Also DAI Research Report 74, University of Edinburgh.

46.   KOWALSKI, R. A., *Logic for Problem Solving*, Elsevier North-Holland, New-York, 1979.

47.   KOWALSKI, R. A., Algorithm = Logic + Control, *Communications of the ACM 22*, 7 (July 1979), 424-436.

48.   KOWALSKI, R. A., Prolog as a Logic Programming Language, Technical Report 81-26, Computer Science Department, Imperial College, London, 1981. Presented at the AICA Congress, Pavia, Italy, 1981.

49.   KOWALSKI, R. A., Logic as a Database Language, *Workshop on Logic Programming*, Long Beach, Los Angeles, September 1981. Also available as Technical Report from Imperial College, London; and in Proceedings of Advanced Seminar on Theoretical Issues in Data Bases, Cetraro, Italy..

50. KOWALSKI, R. A., Logic as a Computer Language for Children, Technical Report 82-23, Computer Science Department, Imperial College, London, 1982. Also Published in New Horizons in Educational Computing, M. Yazdani (ed), Ellis Horwood, 1984.

51. KOWALSKI, R. A., Logic Programming for the Fifth Generation, *International Conference of Fifth Generation Systems*, 1982.

52. KOWALSKI, R. A., Logic as a Computer Language, in *Logic Programming*, K. L. CLARK and S. TARNLUND, (eds.), Academic Press, New York, 1982. A.P.I.C. Studies in Data Processing No. 16 (Also available as Technical Report from Imperial College, London).

53. KOWALSKI, R. A., Logic Programming, *Proceedings of the IFIP-83 Congress*, Amsterdam, 1983, 133-145.

54. KOWALSKI, R. A. and SERGOT, M. J., Micro-Prolog For Problem Solving, in *Micro-Prolog: Programming In Logic*, K. L. CLARK and S. A. TARNLUND, (eds.), Prentice Hall, 1984.

55. LASSEZ, J. L. and MAHER, M. J., Begriffschrift - a Fifth Generation Language, Internal Note, Dept. of Computer Science, University of Melbourne, 1983.

56. MALPAS, J., Programming in Logic, *Dr. Dobbs Journal*, March, 1985, 36-43.

57. MCCABE, F. G., *Micro-Prolog, Programmer's Reference Manual*, Logic Programming Associates Ltd., 1981.

58. MCDERMOTT, D. V., The Prolog Phenomenon, *SIGART Newsletter*, July 1980, 16-20.

59. NAISH, L., An Introduction to MU-Prolog, Technical Report 82-2, Department of Computer Science, University of Melbourne, 1982. Revised in 1983.

60. NAKASHIMA, H., Prolog/KR User's Manual, Technical Report
     METR-82-4, Department of Computer Science, University of
     Tokyo, Japan, 1981.

61. O'KEEFE, R. A., Prolog Compared with LISP ?, *ACM Sigplan
     Notices*, August 1983. Also available as a Research Paper from
     Artificial Intelligence Department, University of Edinburgh.

62. PEREIRA, F. C. N., *C-Prolog User's Manual Version 1.1*,
     EdCAAD, Department of Architecture, University of Edinburg,
     1981.

63. PEREIRA, F. C. N., WARREN, D. H. D., BYRD, L. and PEREIRA,
     L. M., *C Prolog User's Manual Version 1.2*, SRI International,
     Menlo Park, California, 1983.

64. PEREIRA, L. M., PEREIRA, F. C. N. and WARREN, D. H. D.,
     User's Guide to DECsystem-10 Prolog, Technical Report,
     Department of Artificial Intelligence, University of Edinburgh,
     Scotland,, 1978.

65. POUTAIN, D., Prolog on Microcomputers, *Byte 9*, 13 (December
     1984), 335-358.

66. POWERS, D. M. W., Prolog - The wood for the trees, *Electronics
     Today International (Australia)*, R. HARRISON, ed., September
     1984, 132-136.

67. RIET, R. P. V., Knowledge Bases: De Databanken van de
     Toekomst, *Informatie 25*, 5 (1983), 16-23. In Dutch.

68. ROACH, J. W. and FOWLER, G. S., The HC Manual: Virginia
     Tech prolog, Technical Report, Department of Computer
     Science, Virginia Institute of Technology, 1982.

69. ROBINSON, J. A., Logic Programming: Past, Present and
     Future, *New Generation Computing 2*, (1983), Springer Verlag.
     Also available as ICOT Technical Report TR-015.

70. SAMMUT, R. A. and SAMMUT, C. A., Prolog: A Tutorial Introduction, *The Australian Computer Journal 15*, 2 (May 1983).

71. SCHNUPP, P., Was ist Prolog?, *Elektronische Rechenanlagen 29*, 4 (1984), 194-200.

72. SOWA, J. F., A Prolog to PROLOG, Technical Report, IBM System Research Institute, 1981.

73. SPACEK, L., *An Introduction to Prolog*, Ellis Horwood Series In Artificial Intelligence, Ellis Horwood, 1984.

74. SWINSON, P. S. G., An Introduction to Prolog, Technical Report TR-82-02, EdCaad Department, University of Edinburgh, 1983.

75. SZEREDI, J., On a High Level Programming Language Based on Logic, *Proceedings of the Conference on Programming Systems*, Szeged, Hungary, 1975, 191-209. In Hungarian.

76. SZEREDI, J., Prolog: A Very High Level Language Based on Predicate Logic, *Proceedings of the Second Hungarian Computer Science Conference*, Budapest, Hungary, 1977, 853-856. In Hungarian.

77. TAYLOR, J., Why Novices Will Find Learning Prolog Hard, *Sixth European Conference On Artificial Intelligence*, Pisa, September, 1984.

78. VERITY, J. W., Prolog versus LISP, *Datamation*, January, 1984, 50-54.

79. WALLER, L., Prolog Compiler Due for Microcomputers, *Electronics*, November 3, 1983, 55-61.

80. WALLER, L., New Prolog Runs on LISP Machine, *Electronics*, January 12, 1984, 56-62.

81. WARREN, D. H. D., Guest Private View: What is Prolog ?, *Computer Weekly 615*, (August 24, 1978).

82. WELHAM, R., Prolog, *Computer Age*, July, 1980.

83. WILK, P. F., Prolog Benchmarking, Technical Report, Department of Artificial Intelligence, University of Edinburgh, 1983.

84. WISE, M. J., Derivation of Prolog From First Order Predicate Calculus: A Tutorial, DCS Report 8315, University of New South Wales, June, 1982.

85. YAZDANI, M., *Micro-Prolog Programming*, Addison-Wesley, 1984.

CHAPTER 2

Theoretical Issues
of Logic Programming

86. ABRAMSON, H., Unification-Based Conditional Binding Constructs, *Proceedings of the First International Logic Programming Conference*, Marseille, France, September, 1982.

87. AHMAD, S., Logic Program Control in Logic, Technical Report, Department of Computer Science, Imperial College, London, 1982.

88. AIDA, H., TANAKA, H. and MOTO-OKA, T., A Prolog Extension for Handling Negative Knowledge, *New Generation Computing 1*, (1983), Springer Verlag.

89. AIELLO, L., Evaluating Functions Designed in First Order Logic, *Workshop on Logic Programming*, Debrecen, Hungary, July 1980.

90. AIELLO, L., ATTARDI, G. and PRINI, G., Towards a More Declarative Programming Style, in *Formal Description of Programming Concepts*, J. NEUHOLD, (ed.), North-Holland, New-York, 1978.

91. ALLISON, L., An Executable Prolog Semantics, *Algol Bulletin 50*, (December, 1983).

92. ANDERSON, R. and BLEDSOE, W. W., A Linear Format for Resolution with Merging and a New Technique For Establishing Completeness, *Journal of the ACM 30*, (1983), 525-534.

93. ANDREKA, H. and NEMETI, I., The Generalized Completeness of Horn Predicate Logic as a Programming Language, DAI Report 21, Department of Artificial Intelligence, University of Edinburgh, 1976.

94. APONTE, M. V. and FERNANDEZ, J. A., EDILOG: Sistema de Edicion de Teoremas en Logica, Technical Report, Computer Science Department, Simon Bolivar University, Venezuela, 1982.

95. APT, K. R. and VAN EMDEN, M. H., Contributions to the Theory of Logic Programming, *Journal of the ACM 29*, 3 (July 1982), 841-862. Also available as a Technical Report CS-80-13 from the University of Waterloo, Canada.

96. ARONSON, A., JACOBS, B. and MINKER, J., Remarks on Fuzzy Resolution, Technical Report 687, Department of Computer Science, University of Maryland, 1978.

97. ARONSON, A., JACOBS, B. and MINKER, J., A Note on Fuzzy Deduction, *Journal of the ACM 27*, 4 (October, 1980), 599-603.

98. ASHCROFT, E. and WADGE, B., A Logical Programming Language, Technical Report DCS-79-20, Department of Computer Science, University of Waterloo, 1980.

99. ASIRELLI, P., Some Aspects of the Static Semantics of Logic Programs with Monadic Functions, *Proceedings of 2nd Workshop on Logic Programming*, Algarve, Portugal, 1983, 485-505.

100. ASIRELLI, P., BARBUTI, R. and LEVI, G., Types and Declarative Static Type Checking in Logic Programming, Research Report, Dipartimento di Informatica, University of Pisa, 1984.

101. BABB, E., Finite Computation Principal - An Alternative Method of Adapting Resolution for Logic Programming, *Proceedings of Workshop on Logic Programming*, Algarve, Portugal, 1983.

102. BALOGH, K., FUTO, I. and LABADI, K., On an Interactive Program Verifier for Prolog Programs, *Proceedings of a Colloqium on Mathematical Logic in Programming*, 1978.

103. BALOGH, K., FUTO, I., SZEREDI, P. and LABADI, K., On the Implementation Methods and the Theoretical Foundations of the Prolog Language, SZKI Technical Report, SZKI Institute, Budapest, Hungary, 1979. In Hungarian.

104. BARBUTI, R., BELLIA, M., LEVI, G. and MARTELLI, M., LEAF: a language which integrates logic, equations and functions, in *Functional Programming and Logic Programming*, D. DEGROOT and G. LINDSTROM, (eds.), Prentice Hall, June 1985.

105. BARBUTI, R., DEGANO, P. and LEVI, G., Towards an Inductionless Technique for Proving Properties of Logic Programs, *Proceedings of the First International Logic Programming Conference*, Marseille, France, September, 1982.

106. BARBUTI, R., DEGANO, P. and LEVI, G., Proving Properties of Logic Programs, *Sottoposto a Logic Programming 2*, M. VAN CANEGHEM and D. H. D. WARREN, eds., 1984.

107. BARBUTI, R., DEGANO, P. and LEVI, G., On Applying an Inductionless Technique to Prove Properties of Restricted Prolog Programs, *Logic Programming Newsletter*, Winter 82/83, 2-3.

108. BAXTER, L. D., An Efficient Unification Algorithm, Technical Report CS-73-23, Applied Analysis and Computer Science Department, University of Waterloo, 1973.

109. BAXTER, L. D., A Practical Linear Algorithm, Technical Report CS-76-13, Applied Analysis and Computer Science Department, University of Waterloo, 1976.

110. BAXTER, L. D., The Versatility of Prolog, *SIGPLAN Notices 15*, 12 (1980).

111. BELLIA, M., DAMERI, E., DEGANO, P., LEVI, G. and MARTELLI, M., A Formal Model for Lazy Implementations of a Prolog compatible Functional Language, in *Issues in Prolog Implementations*, J. A. CAMPBELL, (ed.), Ellis Horwood, 1984.

112. BELLIA, M., DEGANO, P. and LEVI, G., A Functional plus Predicate Logic Programming Language, *Workshop on Logic Programming*, Debrecen, Hungary, July 1980.

113. BELLIA, M., DEGANO, P. and LEVI, G., The Call by Name Semantics of a Clause Language with Functions, in *Logic Programming*, K. L. CLARK and S. TARNLUND, (eds.), Academic Press, New York, 1982, 281-298. A.P.I.C. Studies in Data Processing No. 16.

114. BELLIA, M., DEGANO, P., LEVI, G., DAMERI, E. and MARTELLI, M., Applicative Communication Processes in First-Order Logic, *Proceedings of the 5th International Symposium on Programming, Lecture Notes in Computer Science 137*, Torino, 1982. Also Technical Report, University of Pisa, Italy.

115. BELLIA, M., LEVI, G. and MARTELLI, M., On the Transformation of Kahn-Macqueen Processes into Applicative Communicating Processes: A Case Study on Language Homomorphic Mappings, *Colloqia su Logica, Semantics, Informatica*, Rende 1983.

116. BERGMAN, M., Algebraic Specifications: A Constructive Methodology In Logic Programming, *Proceddings of EUROCAM*, 1982. Also Lecture Notes in Computer Science no. 82.

117. BERGMAN, M. and DERANSART, P., Abstract Data Types And Rewriting Systems: Application To The Programming Of Algebraic Abstract Data Types In Prolog, *CAAP'81 Trees In Algebra And Programming, 6th Colloqium*, March 1981. Also Lecture Notes in Computer Science no. 112.

118. BIBEL, W., Predicative Programming, Technical Report, Department of Computer Science, Technical University Munchen, January, 1975.

119. BIBEL, W., On Strategies for the Synthesis of Algorithms, *Proceedings of the AISB Conference on Artificial Intelligence,* Hamburg, 1978.

120. BIBEL, W., Logical Program Synthesis, in *Fifth Generation Computer Systems,* T. MOTO-OKA, (ed.), North-Holland, New York, 1981. Proceedings of the First International Conference on Fifth Generation Computer Systems.

121. BIBEL, W., Knowledge Representation from a Deductive Point of View, Technical Report ATP-19-V-83, University of Munchen, Germany, 1982. Also published in Proceedings of IFAC Symposium on Artificial Intelligence, Pergamon Press, 1983.

122. BIBEL, W., *Automated Theorem Proving,* Vieweg und Sohn, Braunschweig, 1982.

123. BIBEL, W. and KOWALSKI, R. A., *Proceedings of the 5th Conference on Automated Deduction - Lecture Notes in Computer Science 87,* Springer-Verlag, New York, 1980.

124. BILLAUD, M., Une Formalisation des Structures du Controle de Prolog, These du Troisieme Cycle, Department of Computer Science, Universite de Bordeaux, France, 1985.

125. BLAIR, H. A., The Recursion-Theoretic Complexity of the Semantics of Predicate Logic as a Programming Language, Technical Report, Iowa University, 1982. Also Appeared in Information and Control, 54, 25-47, 1982.

126. BLAIR, H. A., The Undecidability of Two Completeness Notions for the Negation By Failure Rule in Logic Programming, *Proceedings of the First International Logic Programming Conference*, Marseille, France, September, 1982.

127. BLEDSOE, W. W., Non-Resolution Theorem Proving, *Artificial Intelligence 9*, 1 (1979), 1-35. Also in Readings in Artificial Intelligence, edited by Webber and Nilsson, published by Tioga, 1981.

128. BLEDSOE, W. W. and HINES, L. M., Variable elimination and chaining in a resolution-based prover for inequalities, in *Proceedings of the Fifth Conference on Automated Deduction*, Springer-Verlag Lecture Notes in Computer Science, vol. 87, R. A. KOWALSKI and W. BIBEL, (eds.), Springer-Verlag, New York, July 1980.

129. BOIZUMAULT, P., Sur la Transformation de l'Appel Terminal en Iteration dans un Interprete Prolog, Technical Report, Institut de Mathematiques Appliquees, Angers, France, 1984.

130. BOSSU, G. and SIEGEL, P., Non Monotonic Reasoning and Databases, *Proceedings of Workshop on Logical Bases for Databases*, Toulouse, France, 1982.

131. BOWEN, K. A., A Note on Cut Elimination and Completeness in First Order Theories, *Zeitschrift fur Mathematische Logik und Grundlagen der Mathematik 18*, (1972), 173-176.

132. BOWEN, K. A., Reasoning about Programs in Amalgamated Logic, *Proceedings of the Prolog Programming Environments Workshop*, Linkoping University, Sweden, 1982.

133. BOWEN, K. A., Programming with Full First-Order Logic, *Presented at Workshop on Logic Programming for Intelligent Systems*, Long Beach, California, 1982. Published in Machine Intelligence 10, 1982, 421-440.

134. BOWEN, K.˙A. and KOWALSKI, R. A., Amalgamating Language and Metalanguage in Logic Programming, in *Logic Programming*, K. L. CLARK and S. TARNLUND, (eds.), Academic Press, New York, 1982, 153-173. A.P.I.C. Studies in Data Processing No. 16 (Also available as Technical Report from Syracuse University).

135. BOWEN, K. A. and WEINBERG, T., A Meta-Level Extension of Prolog, *Proceedings of the 2nd IEEE International Symposium on Logic Programming*, Boston, USA, July, 1985.

136. BOYER, R. S., *Locking: a restriction of resolution*, Univ. of Texas at Austin, 1971. Ph.D. Thesis.

137. BOYER, R. S. and MOORE, J. S., The Sharing of Structure in Theorem-Proving Programs, DAI Research Report 47, Department of Artificial Intelligence, University of Edinburgh, 1972.

138. BOYER, R. S. and MOORE, J. S., A Lemma Driven Automatic Theorem Prover for Recursive Function Theory, *Proceedings of the Fifth International Conference on Artificial Intelligence*, Cambridge, 1977, 511-519.

139. BOYER, R. S. and MOORE, J. S., *A Computational Logic*, Academic Press, 1979.

140. BRODA, K., The Relation between Semantic Tableaux and Resolution Theorem Provers, *Proceedings Workshop on Logic Programming*, Debrecen, Hungary, 1981. Also available as Technical Report 80-20 from Imperial College, London.

141. BROUGH, D. R., Loop Trapping in Logic Programs, Technical Report 79-9, Computer Science Department, Imperial College, London, 1979.

142. BROUGH, D. R. and VAN EMDEN, M. H., DataFlow, Flowcharts and LUCID Style Programming in Logic, *Proceedings of the International IEEE Conference on Logic Programming*, Atlantic City, 1984.

143. BROUGH, D. R. and WALKER, A., Some Practical Properties of Logic Programming Interpreters, *Proceedings of the 1984 Conference on Fifth Generation Computer Systems*, Tokyo, Japan, November, 1984.

144. BROWN, F. M., A Semantic Theory for Logic Programming, DAI Report 51, Department of Artificial Intelligence, University of Edinburgh, 1978.

145. BRUYNOOGHE, M., The Inheritance of Links in a Connection Graph, Technical Report CW2, Departement Toegepaste Wiskunde en Programmatie, Katholieke Universiteit Leuven, Belgium, 1975.

146. BRUYNOOGHE, M., Naar een Betere Beheersing van de Uitvoering van Programma's in de Logika der Horn-Uitdrukkingen, Doctoral Dissertation, Departement Toegepaste Wiskunde en Programmatie, Katholieke Universiteit Leuven, Belgium, 1979. In Dutch.

147. BRUYNOOGHE, M., A Control Regime for Horn Clause Logic Programs, Draft Report, Departement Toegepaste Wiskunde, Katholieke Universiteit Leuven, 1979.

148. BRUYNOOGHE, M., Analysis of Dependencies to Improve the Behaviour of Logic Programs, *Lecture Notes in Computer Science 87: 5th Conference on Automated Deduction*, Berlin, Germany, July 1980, 293-305.

149. BRUYNOOGHE, M., Solving Combinatorial Search Problems by Intelligent Backtracking, *Information Processing Letters 1*, (1981).

150. BRUYNOOGHE, M. and PEREIRA, L. M., Revision of Top-Down Logical Reasoning Through Intelligent Backtracking, Technical Report CIUNL-8/81, Universidade Nova de Lisboa, 1981.

151. BRUYNOOGHE, M. and PEREIRA, L. M., Deductive Revision by Intelligent Backtracking, UNL-10/83, Universidade Nova Lisboa, Lisbon, Portugal, 1983. Also in "Issues in Prolog Implementation", J. Campbell (ed).

152. BUNDY, A., *The Computer Modelling of Mathematical Reasoning*, Academic Press, 1983.

153. BUNDY, A., Computer Modelling of Mathematical Reasoning, *Proceedings of the Annual Conference of The British Society For The Psychology of Learning Mathematics*, 1983. Also Research Paper 200, Department of Artificial Intelligence, Edinburgh, October 1983.

154. BUNDY, A., Incidence Calculus: A Mechanism For Probabilistic Reasoning, *International Conference On Fifth Generation Computer Systems*, November 1984.

155. CAFERRA, R., EDER, E., FRONHOEFER, B. and BIBEL, W., Extension of Prolog Through Matrix Reduction, *Sixth European Conference On Artificial Intelligence*, Pisa, September, 1984.

156. CAMPBELL, J. A. and HARDY, S., Should Prolog be List or Record Oriented ?, in *Implementations of Prolog*, J. A. CAMPBELL, (ed.), Ellis Horwood, 1984.

157. M. VAN CANEGHEM, ed., *Proceedings of the First International Logic Programming Conference*, Marseille, France, September, 1982.

158. CERRO, L. F., A Resolution Principle in Modal Logic, *RAIRO Informatique Theorie 18*, 2 (1984), 161-170.

159. DEL CERRO, L. F., Deduction Automatique en Logique Modale, Technical Report, Groupe d'Intelligence Artificielle, University de Paris VII, 1975. Thesis.

160. CHANDRA, A. and HAREL, D., Horn Clause Queries and Generalizations, *Proceedings of Symposium on Principles of Database Systems*, 1982.

161. CHANG, C. L. and LEE, R., *Symbolic Logic and Mechanical Theorem Proving*, Academic Press, New York, 1973.

162. CHANG, C. L. and SLAGLE, J., Using Rewriting Rules for Connection Graphs to Prove Theorems, *Artificial Intelligence 12*, 2 (1979), 159-178. Also in Readings in Artificial Intelligence, edited by Webber and Nilsson, published by Tioga, 1981.

163. CIANCARINI, P. and DEGANO, P., An Approach to Proving Properties of Non-Terminating Logic Programs, *Proceedings Janos Bolyai Mathematical Society, Colloquim on Algebra, Combinatorics and Logic in Computer Science*, Gyor, Hungary, 1983.

164. CLARK, K. L., Negation as Failure, in *Logic and Databases*, H. GALLAIRE and J. MINKER, (eds.), Plenum Press, 1978.

165. CLARK, K. L., The Control Component of a Logic Program, *In AISB Summer School on Expert Systems*, July, 1979.

166. CLARK, K. L., The Synthesis and Verification of Logic Programs, Technical Report 81-36, Imperial College, London, 1981.

167. CLARK, K. L. and SICKEL, S., Predicate Logic: A Calculus for Deriving Programs, *Proceedings of the Fifth International Joint Conference on Artificial Intelligence*, Cambridge , Massachusetts, August , 1977.

168. CLARK, K. L. and TARNLUND, S. A., A First Order Theory of Data and Programs, *Proceedings IFIP 77*, 1977. North Holland.

169. K. L. CLARK and S. A. TARNLUND, eds., *Logic Programming*, Academic Press, 1982. A.P.I.C. Studies in Data Processing No. 16.

170. COHEN, S., The APPLOG language , in *Functional Programming and Logic Programming*, D. DEGROOT and G. LINDSTROM, (eds.), Prentice Hall, June 1985.

171. COLMERAUER, A., Total Procedure Relations, *Journal of the ACM 17*, 1 (January, 1970).

172. COLMERAUER, A. and OTHERS, Etude et Realization d'un Systeme Prolog, Technical Report 77030, Convention de Reserche IRIA-Sesori, 1973.

173. COLMERAUER, A., Les Bases Theoriques de Prolog, Technical Report, Groupe d'Intelligence Artificielle, Universite d'Aix-Marseille II, 1979. Also in AFCET Groplan Bulletin, No. 9, 1979.

174. COLMERAUER, A., Prolog-II Manuel de Reference et Modele Theorique, Groupe Intelligence Artificelle, Univerisite d'Aix-Marseille II, 1982.

175. COLMERAUER, A., Equations and Inequations on Finite and Infinite Terms, *Proceedings of the 1984 Conference on Fifth Generation Computer Systems*, Tokyo, Japan, November, 1984.

176. CONSTABLE, R. L., Programs as Proofs : A Synopsis, *Information Processing Letters 16*, 3 (April, 1983), 105-112.

177. COX, P. T., Deduction Plans: A Graphical Proof Procedure for the First Order Predicate Calculus, Technical Report CS-77-28, Department of Computer Science, University of Waterloo, 1977.

178. COX, P. T., On Determining the Clauses of Non Unifiability, Technical Report, Department of Computer Science, Auckland University, 1982.

179. COX, P. T., Finding Backtrack Points for Intelligent Backtracking, in *Implementations of Prolog*, J. A. CAMPBELL, (ed.), Ellis Horwood, 1984.

180. COX, P. T. and PIERTRZYKOWSKI, T., Surface Deduction: a uniform mechanism for logic programming, Technical Report 8405, School of Computer Science, Technical University of Nova Scotia, October 1984.

181. COX, P. T. and PIETRZYKOWSKI, T., Deduction plans: A Basis for Intelligent Backtracking, *IEEE Transactions on Pattern Analysis and Machine Intelligence PAMI-3*, 1 (1981), 52-65. Also available as a Technical Report from Auckland University, 1981.

182. DAHL, V., Two Solutions for the Negation Problem, in *Workshop on Logic Programming*, S. A. TARNLUND, (ed.), Debrecen, Hungary, July 1980.

183. DAHL, V., A Short Cut to More Informative Answers, *Logic Programming Newsletter*, December, 1982.

184. DARLINGTON, J. and BURSTALL, R. M., A transformational system for developing recursive programs, *JACM 29*, 1982.

185. DARLINGTON, J., FIELD, A. J. and PULL, H., The Unification of Functional and Logic Languages, in *Logic Programming: Relations, Functions, and Equations*, D. D. G. LINDSTROM, (ed.), Prentice-Hall, Inc., Inglewood Cliffs, 1985.

186. DAVIS, R. E., GALLAIRE, H. and LASSERRE, C., Controlling Knowledge Deduction in a Declarative Approach, *Proceedings Sixth Joint Conference on Artificial Intelligence*, 1979. International Joint Conference on Artificial Intelligence.

187. *Functional Programming and Logic Programming*, D. DEGROOT and G. LINDSTROM, (eds.), Prentice Hall, June 1985.

188. DERANSART, P., Derivations de Programmes Prolog a Partir de Specifications Algebriques, Tecnical Report, INRIA, France, 1982.

189. DERANSART, P., An Operational Algebraic Semantics of Prolog Programs, *Proceedings of Workshop on Logic Programming*, Algarve, Portugal, 1983.

190. DERANSART, P. and MALUSZYNSKI, J., Relating Logic Programs and Attribute Grammers, Technical Report, Institut National de Recherche en Informatique et en Automatique, France, 1984.

191. DERSHOWITZ, N. and PLAISTED, D., Logic Programming Cum Applicative Programming, *Proceedings of the 2nd IEEE International Symposium on Logic Programming*, Boston, USA, July, 1985.

192. DIGRICOLI, V. J., Resolution by Unification and Equality, *Proceedings of the 4th Workshop on Automated Deduction*, Austin, Texas, 1979, 43-52.

193. DILGER, W. and JANSON, A., Unification Graphs for Intelligent Backtracking in Deduction Symbols, *Proceedings of GWAI 83*, Dassel, Germany, 1983. Informatik-Fachbericht series.

194. DILGER, W. and MULLER, J. P., PUNIFY: An AI-Machine for Unification, in *Proceedings of the 6th European Conference on Artificial Intelligence*, T. O'SHEA, (ed.), Elsevier Publishing Company, Pisa, Italy, 1984.

195. DINCBAS, M. and LE PAPE, J. P., Nouvelle Implementation de MetaLog, *CNET*, Lannion, France, 1984.

196. DOWLING, W. and GALLIER, J. H., Linear-Time Algorithms for Testing the Satisfiability of Propositional Horn Formulae, *The Journal of Logic Programming 1*, 3 (October, 1984).

197. DURAND, J., Une Strategie de Reecriture pour les Programmes Logiques, Technical Report, Department of Computer Science, Universite de Nancy, France, 1984. In French.

198. DWORK, C., KANELLAKIS, P. C. and MITCHELL, J. C., On The Sequential Nature Of Unification, *The Journal Of Logic Programming 1*, 1 (June 1984), 35-50.

199. EDER, E., Properties of Substitutions and Unifications, *Proceedings of GWAI 83*, Dassel, Germany, 1983. Informatik-Fachbericht series.

200. EDER, G., A Prolog-Like Interpreter for Non-Horn Clauses, Working Paper 26, Department of Artificial Intelligence, University of Edinburgh, 1976.

201. ELCOCK, E. W., Goal Selection Strategies in Horn Clause programming, *Proceedings of the 4th National Conference of the Canadian Society for Study in Artificial Intelligence*, 1982.

202. ELCOCK, E. W., The Pragmatics of Prolog: Some Comments, *Proceedings of Workshop on Logic Programming*, Algarve, Portugal, 1983.

203. ELSINGER, N., A Technical Note on Splitting and Clausal Normal Form Algorithms, *Proceedings of GWAI 83*, Dassel, Germany, 1983. Informatik-Fachbericht series.

204. VAN EMDEN, M. H., First-Order Predicate Logic as a High-Level Programming Language, Technical Report MIP-R-106, Department of Artificial Intelligence, University of Edinburgh, 1974.

205. VAN EMDEN, M. H., Programming with Resolution Logic, Technical Report CS-75-30, Department of Computer Science, University of Waterloo,Canada, November 1975.

206. VAN EMDEN, M. H., Verification Conditions as Representations for Programs, Technical Report CS-76-03, Department of Computer Science, University of Waterloo,Canada, 1976. Published in Automata, Languages and Programming, Edinburgh University Press, 1976.

207. VAN EMDEN, M. H., A Proposal for an Imperative Complement to Prolog, Technical Report CS-76-39, Department of Computer Science, University of Waterloo,Canada, 1976.

208. VAN EMDEN, M. H., Computation and Deductive Information Retrieval, Technical Report CS-77-16, Department of Computer Science, University of Waterloo,Canada, 1977. Published in the Proceedings of the IFIP Working Conference, St. Andrews, Canada, 1977. Was also published in Formal Descriptions of Programming Concepts, E.J. Neuhold (ed), North-Holland, 1978.

209. VAN EMDEN, M. H., Relational Equations, Grammars and Programs, Technical Report CS-77-17, Department of Computer Science, University of Waterloo,Canada, 1977. Published in the Proceedings of the Conference on Theoretical Computer Science, University of Waterloo, 1977.

210. VAN EMDEN, M. H., Programming in Resolution Logic, *Machine Intelligence 8*, (1977), 266-299.

211. VAN EMDEN, M. H., Computation and Deductive Information Retrieval, in *Formal Description of Programming Concepts*, E. NEUHOLD, (ed.), North-Holland, New York, 1978, 421-440.

212. VAN EMDEN, M. H., Programming with Verification Conditions, *IEEE Transactions on Software Engineering SE-5*, (1979), 148-159.

213.   VAN EMDEN, M. H., An Algorithm for Interpreting Prolog Programs, Technical Report CS-81-28, Department of Computer Science, University of Waterloo,Canada, 1981. Also appeared in Implementation Issues of Prolog Systems, by John Campbell, Ellis Horwood, 1984.

214.   VAN EMDEN, M. H., An Interpreting Algorithm for Prolog Programs, *Proceedings of the First International Logic Programming Conference,* M. VAN CANEGHEM, ed., Marseille, France, September 14-17, 1982, 56-64.

215.   VAN EMDEN, M. H. and KOWALSKI, R. A., The Semantics of Predicate Logic as a Programming Language, *Journal of the ACM 23,* 4 (1976), 733-742.

216.   VAN EMDEN, M. H. and LLOYD, J. W., A Logical Reconstruction of Prolog II, *Proceedings of the 2nd International Logic Programming Conference,,* Uppsala, Sweden, July, 1984, 35-40. Also Technical Report CS-83-35, Department of Computer Science, University of Waterloo.

217.   VAN EMDEN, M. H. and LUCENA, G. J., Predicate Logic as a Language for Parallel Programming, Technical Report CS-77-15, Department of Computer Science, University of Waterloo,Canada, 1980. Also in Logic Programming, Clark and Tarnlund, Academic Press, 1982.

218.   VAN EMDEN, M. H. and NAIT-ABDALLAH, M. A., Top-Down Semantics of Fair Computations of Logic Programs, Technical Report CS-84-27, Department of Computer Science, University of Waterloo, Canada.

219.   ERIKSSON, L., Synthesis Of A Unification Algorithm In a Logic Programming Calculus, *The Journal Of Logic Programming 1,* 1 (June 1984), 3-18. Also available as UPMAIL Technical Report 22B.

220. FAGES, F., Note Sur L'unification Des Termes De Premier Ordre Finis Et Infinis, *Actes du Seminaire Programmation En Logique*, M. DINCBAS, ed., March, 1983.

221. FAGES, F., Note sur l'Unification des Tremes de Premier Ordre Finis et Infinis, Technical Report, Institut National de Recherche en Informatique et en Automatique, France, 1984.

222. FAGES, F., Associative-Commutative Unification, Technical Report No. 287, Institut National de Recherche en Informatique et en Automatique, 1984.

223. FAGIN, R., Functional Dependencies in a Relational Database and Propositional Logic, *IBM Journal of Research and Development 21*, 6 (November 1977), 534-544.

224. FAGIN, R., Horn Clauses and Database Dependencies, *Journal of the ACM 29*, 4 (October 1982), 952-985.

225. FAHMI, A., Controle de Systemes de Deduction Automatique Fondes sur la Logique, These de Docteur-Ingenieur, ENSAE-CERT, 1979.

226. FALASCHI, M., LEVI, G. and PALAMIDESSI, C., On the Fixed Point Semantic of Horn Clauses with Infinite Terms, *Proceedings of 2nd Workshop on Logic Programming*, Algarve, Portugal, 1983, 474-484.

227. FALASCHI, M., LEVI, G. and PALAMIDESSI, C., A Synchronization Logic: Axiomatics and Formal Semantics of Generalized Horn Clauses, *Proceedings Janos Bolyai Mathematical Society, Colloquim on Algebra, Combinatorics and Logic in Computer Science*, Gyor, Hungary, 1983.

228. FARINAS, L. and ORLOWSKA, E., DAL- A Logic For Data Analysis, *International Conference On Fifth Generation Computer Systems*, November 1984.

229. FAY, M. J., First-order unification in an equational theory, M.S. Thesis, Information Sciences Board, University of California at Santa Cruz, May 1978.

230. FAY, M. J., First-order unification in an equational theory, *Proceedings of the Fourth Workshop on Automated Deduction*, February 1979, 161-167.

231. FILE, G., Tree Automata and Logic Programs, *Proceedings of the 2nd Annual Symposium on Theorietical Aspects of Computer Science*, Berlin, 1984. Lecture Notes in Computer Science 182.

232. FILE, G., Tree Automata and Logic Programs, These du Troisieme Cycle, Department of Computer Science, Universite de Bordeaux, France, 1985.

233. FRIBOURG, L., Oriented Equational Clauses as a Programming Language, *The Journal Of Logic Programming 1*, 2 (August 1984), 165-178.

234. FRISCH, A. M., An Investigation into Inference with Restricted Quantification and a Taxonomic Representation, *Logic Programming Newsletter*, Universidade Nova de Lisboa, Winter 1984.

235. FUCHI, K., Logical Derivation Of Prolog Interpreters, *International Conference On Fifth Generation Computer Systems*, November 1984.

236. FUHLROTT, O., Prolog als Databank- und Programmiersprache, Technical Report, University of Hamburg, Germany, 1982.

237. FUTUMURA, Y., Partial Computation of Programs, in *Proceedings of the RIMS Symposia on Software Science and Engineering*, S. GOTO, (ed.), Springer Verlag, 1983. Lecture Notes in Computer Science - 147.

238. GABBAY, D., Theoretical Foundations For Non-Monotonic Reasoning In Expert Systems, Doc 84/11, Department of Computing, Imperial College, 1984.

239. GABBAY, D., What Is Negation In A System And When Is Failure A Negation, Doc 84/10, Department of Computing, Imperial College, 1984.

240. GABBAY, D. and KOWALSKI, R. A., Prolog With A Dema Predicate, Doc 84/9, Department of Computing, Imperial College, 1984.

241. GABBAY, D. and SERGOT, M. J., Negation As Inconsistency, Doc 84/7, Department of Computing, Imperial College, 1984.

242. GALLAIRE, H. and LASSERRE, C., A Control Metalanguage for Logic Programming, *Workshop on Logic Programming*, Debrecen, Hungary, 1980, 123-132. Also in Logic Programming, Clark and Tarnlund, Academic Press, 1982.

243. GALLAIRE, H. and LASSERRE, C., Metalevel Control for Logic Programming, *Proceedings Logic Programming Workshop*, Long Beach, CA, September 1981.

244. GALLAIRE, H. and MINKER, J., *Logic and Databases*, Plenum Press, 1978. Editors.

245. GALLIER, J. H., HORNLOG: A First-Order Theorem Prover for Negations of Horn Clauses Based on Graph-Rewriting, Technical Report, Department of Computer Science, University of Pennsylvania, 1984.

246. VAN GELDER, A., A Satisfiability Tester for Non-Clausal Propositional Calculus, Technical Report STAN-CS-83-1002, Department of Computer Science, Stanford University, 1984.

247. GERGELY, T. and SZOTS, M., Cuttable Formulas for Logic Programming, *Proceedings of the International IEEE Conference on Logic Programming*, Atlantic City, 1984.

248. GERGELY, T. and SZOTS, M., Some Features of A New Logic Programming Language, *Workshop and Conference on Applied AI and Knowledge-Based Expert Systems*, Stockholm, November, 1984.

249. GIANNESINI, F. and COHEN, J., Parser Generation and Grammar Manipulation Using Prolog's Infinite Trees, *The Journal of Logic Programming 1*, 3 (October, 1984).

250. GOEBEL, R. G., *Using Hilbert terms to embed descriptions in Prolog*, Syracuse University, Logic Programming Workshop, April 8-10, 1981.

251. GOGUEN, J. A. and MESEGUER, J., Equality, Types, Modules and Generics for Logic Programming, *Proceedings of the Second International Logic Programming Conference*, S. TARNLUND, ed., Uppsala University, Uppsala, Sweden, July 2-6, 1984, 115-126. Also as Technical Report, SRI, Stanford.

252. GOLDREICH, O., DERANSART, P. and MALUSZYNSKI, J., Modelling Data Dependencies in Logic Programs by Attribute Schemata, Technical Report No. 323, Institut National de Recherche en Informatique et en Automatique, July 1984.

253. GREEN, C. C., Application of Theorem Proving to Problem Solving, *Proceedings of the First International Joint Conference on Artificial Intelligence*, 1969, 219-239. Also in Readings in Artificial Intelligence, edited by Webber and Nilsson, published by Tioga, 1981.

254. GREEN, C. C., Theorem proving by resolution as a basis for question-answering systems, in *Machine Intelligence*, vol. 4, B. MELTZER and D. MICHIE, (eds.), American Elsevier, New York, 1969, 183-205.

255. GREEN, C. C., *Application of Theorem Proving to Question-Answering Systems*, Garland, New York, 1980.

256. HABEL, C. U., Logical Systems and Representation Problems, *Proceedings of GWAI 83*, Dassel, Germany, 1983. Informatik-Fachbericht series.

257. HAGIYA, N., Logic Programming and Inductive Definition, Research Report RIMS-420, Research Institute for Mathematical Studies, Kyoto University, Japan, 1983.

258. HAGIYA, N. and SAKURAI, T., Foundation Of Logic Programming Based on Inductive Definition, *New Generation Computing 2*, 1 (1984).

259. HANSSON, A., A Formal Development of Programs, Technical Report (Ph.D. Dissertation), Computer Science Department, Royal Institute of Technology, University of Stockholm, 1980.

260. HANSSON, A. and HARIDI, S., Programming in a Natural Deduction Framework, *Proceedings of Conference on Functional Languages and their Implications for Computer Architecture*, Goteborg, Sweden, 1981.

261. HANSSON, A., HARIDI, S. and TARNLUND, S. A., Properties of a Logic Programming Language, in *Logic Programming*, K. L. CLARK and S. TARNLUND, (eds.), Academic Press, New York, 1982. A.P.I.C. Studies in Data Processing No. 16.

262. HANSSON, A. and JOHANSSON, A. L., A Natural Deduction System For Program Reasoning, in *Workshop on Logic Programming*, S. A. TARNLUND, (ed.), Debrecen, Hungary, July 1980.

263. HANSSON, A. and TARNLUND, S. A., A Natural Programming Calculus, *Proceedings Sixth Joint Conference on Artificial Intelligence*, 1979.

264. HANSSON, A. and TARNLUND, S. A., Program Transformation by a Function that Maps Simple Lists into D-Lists, in *Workshop on Logic Programming*, S. A. TARNLUND, (ed.), Debrecen, Hungary, July 1980.

265. HANSSON, A. and TARNLUND, S. A., Program Transformation by Data Structure Mapping, in *Logic Programming*, K. L. CLARK and S. A. TARNLUND, (eds.), Academic Press, New York, 1982. A.P.I.C. Studies in Data Processing No. 16.

266. HARANDI, M. T. and SCHOPPERS, M. J., *Incorporating non-logical components into a logic-based system*, University of Illinois at Urbana-Chanpaign, Department of Computer Science, Urbana, Illinois, October, 1983.

267. HARIDI, S., Logic Programming Based on a Natural Deduction System, TRITA-CS-8104, The Royal Institute of Technology, Stockholm, Sweden, 1981. Ph.D Thesis.

268. HARIDI, S. and SAHLIN, D., Evaluation of Logic Programs Based on Natural Deduction, *Proceedings of Workshop on Logic Programming*, Algarve, Portugal, 1983.

269. HARIDI, S. and SAHLIN, D., Efficient Implementation of Unification of Cyclic Structures, in *Implementations of Prolog*, J. A. CAMPBELL, (ed.), Ellis Horwood, 1984.

270. HENSCHEN, L. J. and NAQVI, S. A., An Improved Filter for Literal Indexing in Resolution Systems, *Proceedings of the 7th International Joint Conference on Artificial Intelligence*, Vancouver, August, 1981, 528-529.

271. HENSCHEN, L. J. and NAQVI, S. A., Representing Infinite Sequences of Resolvents in Recursive First-Order Horn Databases, *Proceedings of the 6th Conference on Automated Deduction*, 1982.

Theoretical

272. HENSCHEN, L. J. and NAQVI, S. A., Synthesizing Least Fixed Point Queries into Iterative Programs, *Proceedings International Joint Conference on Artificial Intelligence*, Karlsruhe, Germany, 1983.

273. HEUSCHEN, L. J., Semantic Resolution For Horn Sets, *IEEE Transactions On Computers 25*, 8 (1976).

274. HILL, R., LUSH-Resolution and Its Completeness, DCS Memo, No. 78, Department of Artificial Intelligence, University of Edinburgh, 1974.

275. HIRSCHMAN, L., MCKAY, D. P., NORTON, L. M. and PALMER, M., Selective Depth-First Search in Prolog, *Proceedings of the First IEEE/AAAI Conference on Artificial Intelligence Applications*, Denver, Colorado, December, 1984.

276. HOGGER, C. J., Deductive Synthesis of Logic Programs, DoC Report, Department of Computing, Imperial College, 1977.

277. HOGGER, C. J., Goal-Oriented Derivation of Logic Programs, *Proceedings of a Conference on the Mathematical Foundations of Computer Science*, 1978. Lecture Notes in Computer Science No. 64.

278. HOGGER, C. J., Program Synthesis in Predicate Logic, *Proceedings AISB-79 Conference On Artficial Intelligence*, Hamburg, 1978.

279. HOGGER, C. J., Logic Representation of a Concurrent Algorithm, in *Workshop on Logic Programming*, S. A. TARNLUND, (ed.), Debrecen, Hungary, July 1980.

280. HORN, A., On Sentences Which are True of Direct Unions of Algebras, *Journal of Symbolic Logic*, 1951.

281. HSIANG, J. and SRIVAS, M., On Proving First Order Inductive Properties in Horn Clauses, Technical Report 84/075, State University of New York, Stony Brook, 1984.

282. HUAI-MIN, S. and LI-GUO, W., A Model Theory of Programming Logic, *Internal Note, Beijing Institute of Aeronautics and Astronautics*, Beijing, China, 1983.

283. HUET, G., Algebraic Aspects of Unification, *Proceedings of Workshop on Automated Theorem Proving*, Oberwolfach, Germany, 1976.

284. HUET, G., In Defense of Programming Language Design, *Proceedings of the European Conference on Artificial Intelligence*, 1982, 19-27.

285. IDA, T. and OTHERS, Higher Order: Its Implications to Programming Languages and Computational Models, Technical Memorandum TM-0029, ICOT - Institute for New Generation Computer Technology, Tokyo, Japan, 1983. In Japanese.

286. ISHIZUKA, M., Inference Methods Based On Extended Dempster and Shafer's Theory For Problems With Uncertainty/Fuzziness, *New Generation Computing 1*, 2 (1983).

287. ITAI, A. and MAKOWSKY, J. A., Unification as a Complexity Measure for Logic Programming, Technical Report 301, Technion - Israel Institute of Technology, November 1983.

288. JAFFAR, J., Efficient Unification Over Infinite Terms, *New Generation Computing 2*, 3 (January 1984). Also, Technical Report, Monash University, Clayton, Victoria, Australia.

289. JAFFAR, J., LASSEZ, J. L. and LLOYD, J. W., Completeness of the Negation As Failure Rule, *Proceedings of the International Joint Conference on Artificial Intelligence*, Karlsruhe, Germany, 1983, 500-506. Also available as Technical Report 83/1, Department of Computer Science, University of Melbourne, Australia.

290. JAFFAR, J., LASSEZ, J. L. and MAHER, M. J., A Theory of Complete Logic Programs With Equality, Technical Report , Monash University, Clayton, Victoria, Australia, May, 1984. Also FGCS Conference Proceedings, 1984.

291. JAFFAR, J., LASSEZ, J. L. and MAHER, M. J., A Logical Foundation For Prolog II, Technical Report , Monash University, Clayton, Victoria, Australia, September, 1984.

292. JAFFAR, J., LASSEZ, J. L. and MAHER, M. J., A Logic Programming Language Scheme, in *Functional Programming and Logic Programming*, D. DEGROOT and G. LINDSTROM, (eds.), Prentice Hall, June 1985.

293. JONES, N. D. and MYCROFT, A., Stepwise Development of Operational and Denotational Semantics for Prolog, *Proceedings of the International IEEE Conference on Logic Programming*, Atlantic City, 1984.

294. KAHN, G., The Scope of Symbolic Computation, in *Fifth Generation Computer Systems*, T. MOTO-OKA, (ed.), North-Holland, New York, 1981. Proceedings of the First International Conference on Fifth Generation Computer Systems.

295. KAHN, K. M., Intermission - Actors in Prolog, in *Workshop on Logic Programming*, S. TARNLUND, (ed.), Debrecen, Hungary, July 1980. Also in Logic Programming, Clark and Tarnlund, Academic Press, 1982.

296. KAHN, K. M., A Primitive for the Control of Logic Programs, *Proceedings of the International IEEE Conference on Logic Programming*, Atlantic City, 1984.

297. KALE, L. V., Control Strategies for Logic Programming, Technical Report, Department of Computer Science, State University of New York at Stony Brook, May, 1984.

298. KANOUI, H. and BERGMAN, M., Generalized Substitutions, Technical Report, Groupe d'Intelligence Artificielle, Universite d'Aix-Marseille II Marseille, France, 1977.

299. KAPUR, D., KRISHNAMOORTY, M. S. and NARENDRAN, P., A New Linear Algorithm for Unification, Technical Report, General Electric, Schenectady, New York, 1982.

300. KARATSU, H., What is Required of the Fifth Generation Computer - Social Needs and Impact, in *Fifth Generation Computer Systems*, T. MOTO-OKA, (ed.), North-Holland, New York, 1981. Proceedings of the First International Conference on Fifth Generation Computer Systems.

301. KELLOG, C. and TRAVIS, L., Reasoning with Data in a Deductively Augmented Data Base Management System, in *Advances in Database Theory*, H. GALLAIRE, J. MINKER and J. M. NICOLAS, (eds.), Plenum Press, 1981.

302. KIBLER, D. F., Boolean Satisfiability, *Logic Programming Newsletter*, February, 1982.

303. KLAHR, P., Planning Techniques for Rule Selection in Deductive Question-answering, in *Pattern Directed Inference Systems*, D. A. WATERMAN and R. HAYES-ROTH, (eds.), Academic Press, 1978, 223-229.

304. KLEENE, S. C., Permutability of Inferences in Gentzen's Calculi LK and LJ, *Memoirs of the American Mathematical Society,,* Providence, Rhode Island., 1952, 1-26. 3rd printing, 1972.

305. KLEENE, S. C., Two papers on the Predicate Calculus, *Memoirs of the American Mathematical Society,,* Providence, Rhode Island., 1952. 3rd printing, 1972.

306. KOHLI, M. and MINKER, J., Intelligent Control Using Integrity Constraints, *Proceedings of the National Conference on Artificial Intelligence,* Washington D.C., August, 1983. Also in Proceedings of Workshop on Logic Programming, Algarve, Portugal, 1983.

307. KOMOROWSKI, H. J., Partial Evaluation as a Means for Inferencing Data Structures in an Applicative Language: a Theory and Implementation in the Case of Prolog, *Conference Record of the Ninth Annual ACM Symposium on Principles of Programming Languages,* 1982, 255-268.

308. KOMOROWSKI, H. J. and MALUSZYNSKI, J., Unification-Free Execution of Logic Programs, *Proceedings of the 2nd IEEE International Symposium on Logic Programming,* Boston, USA, July, 1985.

309. KORNFELD, W. A., Equality for Prolog, *Proceedings of the International Joint Conference on Artificial Intelligence,* Karlsruhe, Germany, 1983.

310. KOWALSKI, R. A., Studies in the Completeness and Efficiency of Theorem Proving by Resolution, Ph.D. Dissertation, Computer Science Department, University of Edinburgh, 1970.

311. KOWALSKI, R. A., An Improved Theorem-Proving System for First-Order Logic, Working Paper 65, Department of Artificial Intelligence, University of Edinburgh, 1973.

312. KOWALSKI, R. A., A Proof Procedure Using Connection Graphs, Working Paper 74, Department of Artificial Intelligence, University of Edinburgh, 1974.

313. KOWALSKI, R. A., *Logic for Problem Solving*, Elsevier North-Holland, New-York, 1979.

314. KOWALSKI, R. A., The Case For Using Equality Axioms In Automatic Demonstration, in *Anthology Of Automated Theorem-Proving Papers, Vol. 1*, Springer Verlag, 1982. Symposium On Automatic Demonstration.

315. KOWALSKI, R. A., The Use of Metalanguage to Assemble Object Level Programs and Abstract Programs, *Proceedings of the Prolog Programming Environments Workshop*, Linkoping University, Sweden, 1982.

316. KOWALSKI, R. A. and KUEHNER, D., Linear Resolution with Selection Function, *Artificial Intelligence 2*, (1971), 227-60.

317. KUEHNER, D., Some special purpose resolution systems, in *Machine Intelligence*, vol. 7, B. MELTZER and D. MICHIE, (eds.), American Elsevier, New York, 1972, 117-128.

318. KUNIFUJI, S., ASOU, M., TAKEUCHI, A., MIYACHI, T., KITAKAMI, H., YOKOTA, H., YASAKUWA, H. and FURUKAWA, K., Amalgamation of Object Knowledge and Meta Knowledge by Prolog and Its Applications, *Knowledge Engineering and Artificial Intelligence Working Group of the Information Processing Society of Japan*, June, 1983. preprint 30-1, TR-009.

319. KUNIFUJI, S., TAKEUCHI, A., FURUKAWA, K., UEDA, K. and KURUKAWA, T., A Logic Programming Language for Knowledge Utilization and Realization, *Proceedings of the Prolog Conference*, Tukuba, Japan, 1982. In Japanese.

320. LASSERRE, C. and GALLAIRE, H., Controlling Backtrack in Horn Clause Programming, *Workshop on Logic Programming*, Debrecen, Hungary, July 1980.

321. LASSEZ, J. L. and MAHER, M. J., *The Semantics of Logic Programs*, Oxford University Press, . In Preparation.

322. LASSEZ, J. L. and MAHER, M. J., Chaotic Semantics of Programming Logic, Technical Report, University of Melbourne, Department of Computer Science, Australia, 1982.

323. LASSEZ, J. L. and MAHER, M. J., Optimal Fixedpoints of Logic Programs, in *Proc. 3rd Inter. Conf. on the Foundations of Software Technology and Theoretical Computer Science*, Bangalore, India, December 1983.

324. LASSEZ, J. L. and MAHER, M. J., Closures and Fairness in the Semantics of Programming Logic, *Theoretical Computer Science 29*, (1984), 167-184. Also as Technical Report 83/3, Department of Computer Science, University of Melbourne.

325. LASSEZ, J. L. and MAHER, M. J., Antiunification, Technical Report 84-5, Department of Computer Science, University of Melbourne, Australia, 1984.

326. LEE, R. C. T., Fuzzy Logic and the Resolution Principle, *Journal of the ACM 19*, (1972), 109-119.

327. LEWIS, H. R., Renaming a Set of Clauses as a Horn Set, *Journal of the ACM 25*, 1 (January, 1978), 134-135.

328. LINGAS, A., A Note on the Computational Complexity of Logic Programs, *Proceedings of Workshop on Logic Programming*, Algarve, Portugal, 1983.

329. LLOYD, J. W., Foundations of Logic Programming, Technical Report 82-7, Department of Computer Science, University of Melbourne, Australia, 1982.

330. LLOYD, J. W., An Introduction To Deductive Data Base Systems, Technical Report, Department of Computer Science, University of Melbourne,Australia, 1982. Also in the Australian Computer Journal, 15, 2, 1983.

331. LLOYD, J. W., *Foundations Of Logic Programming*, Springer Verlag, 1984.

332. LLOYD, J. W. and TOPOR, R. W., Making Prolog More Expressive, Technical Report 84/8, Department Of Computer Science, University Of Melbourne, 1984. To appear in the Journal of Logic Programming, 1984.

333. LOVELAND, D. W., Theorem Provers Combining Model Elimination And Resolution, in *Machine Intelligence*, Volume 4B, B. MELTZER and D. MICHIE, (eds.), American Elsevier, New York, , 73-86.

334. LOVELAND, D. W., Mechanical Theorem Proving by Model Elimination, *Journal of the ACM 15*, 2 (1968).

335. LOVELAND, D. W., A linear format for resolution, *Proceedings of the IRIA Symposium on Automatic Demonstration*, Versailles, France, 1968, 147-162.

336. LOVELAND, D. W., *Automated Theorem Proving: A Logical Basis*, North-Holland, New York, 1978.

337. LOVELAND, D. W., *Proceedings of the 6th Conference on Automated Deduction - Lecture Notes in Computer Science 138*, Springer-Verlag, New York, 1982. Editor.

338. LOVELAND, D. W., Automated Theorem Proving: A Quartercentury Review, Technical Report CS-1983-9, Department of Computer Science, Duke University, 1983.

339. LOVELAND, D. W. and STICKEL, M. E., A Hole in Goal Trees: Some Guidance from Resolution Theory, *IEEE Transactions on Computers C-25*, 4 (April 1976), 335-341.

340. LUNDBERG, B., Information Modeling and the Axiomatic Method, *Proceedings of the First International Workshop on Expert Database Systems*, Kiawah Island, South Carolina, October 24-27, 1984.

341. LUSK, E. L. and OVERBEEK, R. A., Experiments With Resolution-based Theorem-proving Algorithms, *Computers and Mathematics with Applications 8*, 3 (1982), 141-152.

342. LUSK, E. L. and OVERBEEK, R. A., An LMA-based Theorem Prover, ANL-82-75, Argonne National Laboratory, December, 1982.

343. LUSK, E. and OVERBEEK, R. A., Non-Horn Problems, *Journal of Automated Reasoning 1*, 1 (February, 1985), 103-114.

344. MACLENNAN, B. J., Introduction to Relational Programming, *Proceedings of ACM Conference on Functional Programming Languages and Computer Architecture*, Wentworth-by-the-Sea, October, 1981, 213-222.

345. MACLENNAN, B. J., Overview of Relational Programming, *ACM SIGPLAN Notices 18*, 3 (March, 1983), 36-45.

346. MAHER, M. J., Semantics of Logic Programs, PhD Thesis, University of Melbourne, Department of Computer Science, 1985.

347. MAKOWSKY, J. A., Why Horn Formulas Matter in Computer Science: Initial Structures and Generic Examples, Technical Report, Department of Computer Science, Technion, Haifa, Israel, 1985.

348. MALUSZINSKI, J. and FULLSON, J. F., A Notion of Grammatical Unification Applicable to Logic Programming Languages, Technical Report, University of Denmark, 1981.

349. MALUSZINSKI, J. and FULLSON, J. F., A Comparison of the Logic Programming Language Prolog with Two-Level Grammars, *Proceedings of the First International Logic Programming Conference*, M. VAN CANEGHEM, ed., Marseille, France, September 1982.

350. MALUSZINSKI, J. and NILSSON, J. F., A Version of Prolog Based on the Notion of Two-Level Grammars, *Proceedings of the Prolog Programming Environments Workshop*, Linkoping University, Sweden, 1982.

351. MANNA, Z. and WALDINGER, R., A deductive approach to program synthesis, *ACM TOPLAS 2*, 1 (January 1980), 92-121.

352. MANNA, Z. and WALDINGER, R., Special Relations in Program-synthetic Deduction, *Logic and Computation Proceedings of a Conference 1*, J. N. CROSSLEY and J. JAFFAR, eds., (1983).

353. MARQUE-PUCHEU, G., Relational Set of Trees and the Algebraic Semantics of Logic Programming, *Acta Informatica 20*, (1983), 249-260.

354. MARTELLI, A. and MONTANARI, U., Unification in Linear Time and Space, Technical Report B76-16, University of Pisa, Italy, 1976.

355. MARTELLI, A. and MONTANARI, U., An Efficient Unification Algorithm, *ACM Transactions on Programming Languages & Systems 4*, 2 (1982), 258-282.

356. MARTELLI, A. and ROSSI, G., Efficient Unification With Infinite Terms In Logic Programming, *International Conference On Fifth Generation Computer Systems*, November 1984.

357. MARTINS, J., McKAY, D. P. and SHAPIRO, S. C., Bi-directional Inference, Technical Report 174, Dept. of Comp. Sci. SUNY/Buffalo, March 1981.

358. MATWIN, S. and PIETRZYKOWSKI, T., Intelligent Backtracking for Automated Deduction in FOL, *Proceedings of Workshop on Logic Programming*, Algarve, Portugal, 1983.

359. MAYOR, B., The Meaning of Logical Programs, in *Workshop on Logic Programming*, S. A. TARNLUND, (ed.), Debrecen, Hungary, July 1980.

360. McCABE, F. G., Lambda Prolog, *Proceedings of the Logic Programming Workshop*, Algarve, Portugal, 1983.

361. McCARTHY, J., Representation of Recursive Programs in First Order Logic, Research Report, Artificial Intelligence Department, Stanford University, 1977.

362. McCARTHY, J., Coloring Maps and the Kowalski Doctrine, Technical Report, Department of Computer Science, University of Stanford, 1982.

363. McCORD, M. C., Semantic Interpretation for the Epistle System, *Proceedings of the Second International Logic Programming Conference*, S. A. TARNLUND, ed., Uppsala University, Uppsala, Sweden, July 2-6, 1984, 65-76.

364. McCUME, W. W., An Inference Mechanism For Resolution-style Theorem Provers, Master's Thesis, Northwestern University, 1981.

365. McDERMOTT, D. V., Data Dependencies on Inequalities, *Proceedings of the National Conference on Artificial Intelligence*, Washington D.C., August, 1983, 266-269. AAAI-83.

366. McKay, D. P. and Shapiro, S. C., Using Active Connection Graphs for Reasoning with Recursive Rules, *Proceedings of the Seventh International Joint Conference on Artificial Intelligence*, 1981, 368-374.

367. Mellish, C. S., Controlling Inference in the Semantic Interpretation of Mechanics Problems, *Workshop on Logic Programming*, Long Beach, Los Angeles, September 1981.

368. Merret, T. H., The Relational Algebra as a Typed Language for Logic Programming, *Proceedings of the First International Workshop on Expert Database Systems*, Kiawah Island, South Carolina, October 24-27, 1984. Also Technical Report, Department of Computer Science, McGill University, Canada, 1984.

369. Minker, J., A Set-Oriented Predicate Logic Programming Language, Technical Report, Computer Science Department, University of Maryland, 1975. Also Published in Proceedings Logic Programming Workshop, Debrecen, 1981.

370. Minker, J., Control Structure of a Pattern Directed Search System, Technical Report TR-503, University of Maryland, Computer Science Technical Report Series, 1977.

371. Minker, J., Search Strategy and Selection Function for an Inferential Relational System, *ACM Transactions on Database Systems 3*, 1 (March, 1978), 1-31.

372. Minker, J., On Indefinite Databases and the Closed World Assumption, *Proceedings of the First International Logic Programming Conference*, Marseille, France, 1981. Also in 6th Conference on Automated Deduction, 1982.

373. Minker, J., On Deductive Relational Databases, in *Proceedings of the Fifth International Conference on Collective Phenomena*, Annals of the New York Academy of Sciences, Vol. 10, J. L. Lebowitz, (ed.), 1982, 181-280.

374. MINKER, J., On Theories of Definite and Indefinite Databases, Technical Report TR-1250, Department of Computer Science, University of Maryland, 1983.

375. MINKER, J. and PERLIS, D., On the Semantics of Circumscription, Technical Report, University Of Maryland, 1983.

376. MINKER, J. and PERLIS, D., Applications of Protected Circumscription, *Proceedings of the Conference on Automated Deduction 7*, Napa, California, May, 1984, 414-425.

377. MINKER, J. and ZANON, G., An Extension to Linear Resolution with Selection Function, *Information Processing Letters 14*, 4 (June, 1982), 191-194.

378. MISHRA, P., Towards a Theory of Types in Prolog, *Proceedings of the International IEEE Conference on Logic Programming*, Atlantic City, 1984.

379. MONTEIRO, L. F., A Mathematical Formalism for Logic Programming Based on the Theory of Relations, Technical Report CIUNL-2/80, Universidade Nova de Lisboa, 1980.

380. MOORE, J. S., Computational Logic: Structure Sharing and Proof of Program Properties - Parts I and II, Working Paper 67, Department of Artificial Intelligence, University of Edinburgh, 1973.

381. MOORE, R. C., Problems in Logical Form, SRI Technical Report, Stanford Research Institute, Menlo Park, California, 1981.

382. MOROKHOVETS, M. K., A Modified Unification Procedure, *Cybernetics 20 20*, 1 (1984), 147-152 .

383. MORRIS, J. B., E-resolution: Extension of Resolution to Include the Equality Relation, *Proceedings of the International Joint Conference on Artificial Intelligence*, Washington, D.C., May 7-9, 1969, 287-294.

384. MORRIS, P. H., A Dataflow Interpreter for Logic Programs, in *Workshop on Logic Programming*, S. A. TARNLUND, (ed.), Debrecen, Hungary, July 1980.

385. MORRIS, P. H., A Forward Chaining Problem Solver, *Logic Programming Newsletter*, February, 1982.

386. MOSS, C. D., The Formal Description of Programming Languages Using Predicate Logic, Technical Report, Imperial College, London, 1981. P.H. Dissertation.

387. MOSS, C. D., How to Define a Language Using Prolog, *Proceedings of the 1982 ACM Conference on LISP and Functional Programming*, Pittssburgh, 1982, 67-73.

388. MOSS, C. D., Computing with Sequences, *Proceedings of Workshop on Logic Programming*, Algarve, Portugal, 1983.

389. MUKAI, K., A Unification Algorithm for Infinite Trees, *Proceedings of the International Joint Conference on Artificial Intelligence*, Karlsruhe, Germany, 1983.

390. MUKAI, K. and FURUKAWA, K., An Ordered Linear Resolution Theorem Proving Program in Prolog, Technical Memorandum TM-0027, ICOT - Institute for New Generation Computer Technology, Tokyo, Japan, 1983.

391. MYCROFT, A., Logic Programs and Many-Valued Logic, *Proceedings of Symposium on Theoretical Aspects of Computer Science*, Paris, 1984.

392. NAISH, L., Heterogeneous SLD Resolution, Technical Report 84/1, Department of Computer Science, University of Melbourne, January, 1984. To Appear in the Journal Of Logic Programming, Vol 3, 1984.

393. NAISH, L., Negation and Control in PROLOG, Ph.D. Thesis, Department of Computer Science, University of Melbourne, 1985.

394. NAISH, L. and LASSEZ, J. L., Most Specific Logic Programs, Technical Report 84/9, 1984.

395. NAQVI, S. A. and HENSCHEN, L. J., Performing Inferences over Recursive Data Bases, *Proceedings NCAI*, 1980.

396. NICOLAS, J. M., Logic for Improving Integrity Checking in Relational Databases, *Acta Informatica 18*, 3 (1979).

397. NILSSON, J. F., Formal Vienna Definition Method Models of Prolog, in *Implementations of Prolog*, J. A. CAMPBELL, (ed.), Ellis Horwood, 1984.

398. NORDSTROM, B. and PETERSSON, K., Types and Specifications, *Information Processing 83*, R. E. A. MASON, ed., 1983.

399. O'KEEFE, R. A., Towards an Algebra for Constructing Logic Programs, *Proceedings of the 2nd IEEE International Symposium on Logic Programming*, Boston, USA, July, 1985.

400. OHLBACH, H. J., A Rule-Based Method of Proof Using Clausal Graphs, *Proceedings of GWAI 83*, Dassel, Germany, 1983. Informatik-Fachbericht series.

401. OVERBEEK, R. A., A New Class of Automated Theorem-proving Algorithms, Ph.D Thesis, Penn. State Univ, 1971.

402. OVERBEEK, R. A., A New Class of Automated Theorem-proving Algorithms, *Journal of the ACM 21*, (1974), 191-200.

403. OVERBEEK, R. A., An Implementation of Hyper-resolution, *Computers and Mathematics with Applications 1*, (1975), 201-214.

404. PAGELLO, E. and VALENTINI, S., Computing Algorithms and Proving Properties by Computing Terms, in *Workshop on Logic Programming*, S. A. TARNLUND, (ed.), Debrecen, Hungary, July 1980.

405. PALMER, M., McKAY, D. P., NORTON, L. M., HIRSCHMAN, L. and FREEMAN, M. W., Selective Depth-First Search in Prolog, *Proceedings of the First IEEE Conference on Artificial Intelligence Applications*, Denver, Colorado, December, 1984.

406. PATERSON, M. S. and WEGMAN, M. N., Linear Unification, *Proceedings of the 8th ACM Symposium on the Theory of Computing*, 1978. Also in Computer and System Sciences, Vol 16, 1978.

407. PEREIRA, L. M., Backtracking Intelligently in AND/OR Trees, Research Report CIUNL No. 1, Departemento de Informatica, Universidade Nova de Lisboa, Portugal, 1979.

408. PEREIRA, L. M., Logic Control with Logic, Technical Report, Departemento de Informatica, Universidade Nova de Lisboa, Portugal, 1982. Also in Proceedings of the First International Logic Programming Conference Marseille, France September, 1982.

409. PEREIRA, L. M., A Prolog Demand Driven Computation Interpreter, *Logic Programming Newsletter*, 1982, 6-7. Issue of Winter 82/83.

410. PEREIRA, L. M., Logic Control with Logic, in *Implementations of Prolog*, J. A. CAMPBELL, (ed.), Ellis Horwood, 1984.

411. PEREIRA, L. M. and MONTEIRO, L. F., The Semantics of Parallelism and Coroutining in Logic Programming, *Colloquium on Mathematical Logic in Programming*, Hungary, 1978. Published by North-Holland in 1981.

412. PEREIRA, L. M. and PORTO, A., Intelligent Backtracking and Sidetracking in Horn Clause Programs: The Theory, Research Report CIUNL No. 2, Departemento de Informatica, Universidade Nova de Lisboa, Portugal, 1979.

413. PEREIRA, L. M. and PORTO, A., Selective backtracking for logic programs, *5th Conference on Automated Deduction*, Les Arcs, France, 1980, 306-317.

414. PEREIRA, L. M. and PORTO, A., An Interpreter of Logic Programs Using Selective Backtracking, Research Report CIUNL No. 9/80, Departemento de Informatica, Universidade Nova de Lisboa, Portugal, 1980. Also in the Proceedings of the Workshop on Logic Programming Debrecen, Hungary July 1980.

415. PEREIRA, L. M. and PORTO, A., Selective Backtracking, in *Logic Programming*, K. L. CLARK and S. TARNLUND, (eds.), Academic Press, 1982.

416. PERROT, E., Etude et Realisation en Prolog de Problemes de Logique, Technical Report 077, Department of Computer Science, Universite de Nancy, France, 1985.

417. PIETRZYKOWSKI, T. and MATWIN, S., *Exponential Improvement of Exhaustive Backtracking: A Strategy for Plan-based Deduction*, School of Computer Science, Acadia University, 1982.

418. PLAISTED, D. A., The Occur-Check Problem in Prolog, *Proceedings of the International IEEE Conference on Logic Programming*, Atlantic City, 1984.

419. PLAISTED, D. A., Complete Problems in the First-Order Predicate Calculus, *Journal of Computer and System Sciences 29*, (1984), 8-35.

420. PLAISTED, D. A. and GREENBAUM, S., Problem Representations for Back Chaining and Equality in Resolution Theorem Proving, *Proceedings of the First IEEE/AAAI Conference on Artificial Intelligence Applications*, Denver, Colorado, December, 1984.

421. POOLE, D. L., The Theory of CES: A Complete Expert System, Ph.D. Dissertation, Department of Computer Science, University of Waterloo, Canada, 1982.

422. POOLE, D. L., A Computational Logic of Default Reasoning, Technical Report, Department of Computer Science, University of Waterloo, Canada, 19824.

423. PORTO, A., Logical Action Systems, *Proceedings of Workshop on Logic Programming*, Algarve, Portugal, 1983.

424. PORTO, A., Controlo Sequencial de Programas em Logica, Ph.D. Dissertation, Department of Computer Science, Universidade Nova de Lisboa, Lisbon, Portugal, 1984. In Portuguese.

425. PRAWITZ,, D., *Natural Deduction, Proof Theoretical Study*, Almqvist and Wiksell, Stockholm, 1965.

426. RAMANUJAM, R. and SHYAMASUNDAR, R. K., Process Specification Of Logic Programs, *Fourth Conference On The Foundations Of Software Technology And Theoretical Computer Science*, December, 1984.

427. RAULEFS, P., SIEKMANN, J., SZABO, P. and UNVERICHT, E., A Short Survey on the State of the Art in Matching and Unification Problems, *AISB Quarterly 32*, (December, 1978), 17-21.

428. REDDY, U., Narrowing as the Operational Semantics of Functional Languages, *Proceedings of the 2nd IEEE International Symposium on Logic Programming*, Boston, USA, July, 1985.

429. REITER, R., Two Results On Ordering For Resolution with Merging and Linear Format, *Journal of the ACM 18*, 4 (1971), 630-646.

430. REITER, R., On Closed World Databases, in *Logic and Databases*, H. GALLAIRE and J. MINKER, (eds.), Plenum Press, 1978, 55-76. Also in Readings in Artificial Intelligence, edited by Webber and Nilsson, published by Tioga, 1981.

431. REITER, R., Deductive Question-answering on Relational Databases, in *Logic and Databases*, H. GALLAIRE and J. MINKER, (eds.), Plenum Press, 1978, 149-178.

432. REITER, R., Equality and Domain Closure for first order databases, *Journal of the ACM 27*, 2 (April 1980), 235-249.

433. REITER, R., On the Integrity of Typed First Order Databases, in *Advances in Data Base Theory*, H. GALLAIRE, J. MINKER and J. M. NICOLAS, (eds.), Plenum Press, 1981.

434. REITER, R., Circumscription Implies Predicate Completion (sometimes), *Proceedings AAAI Conference*, Pittsburgh, August, 1982, 418-420.

435. REITER, R., Towards a Logical Reconstruction of Relational Database Theory, in *Perspectives on Conceptual Modelling*, M. L. BRODIE, J. MYLOPOULOS and J. W. SCHMIDT, (eds.), Springer Verlag, 1983.

436. ROBINSON, G. and WOS, L., Paramodulation and Theorem Proving in First Order Theories with Equality, *Machine Intelligence 4*, (1969), 135-150, American Elsevier.

437. ROBINSON, J. A., Automatic Deduction with Hyper-resolution, *International Journal of Computer Mathematics 1*, (1965), 227-234.

438. ROBINSON, J. A., A Machine-Oriented Logic Based on the Resolution Principle, *Journal of the ACM 12*, (January 1965), 23-44.

439. ROBINSON, J. A., A review of automatic theorem proving, *Proc. of the Symposia in Applied Mathematics 19*, (1969), 1-18, American Mathematical Society.

440. ROBINSON, J. A., Computational Logic: the Unification Computation, *Machine intelligence 6*, (1971), 63-72.

441. ROBINSON, J. A., Fast Unification, *Proceedings of Workshop on Automated Theorem Proving*, Oberwolfach, Germany, 1976.

442. ROBINSON, J. A., *Logic: Form and Function - The Mechanization of Deductive Reasoning*, North-Holland, New York, 1979. Also available from Edinburgh University Press.

443. ROBINSON, J. A., The Logical Basis of Programming by Assertion and Query, in *Expert Systems in the Microelectronic Age*, D. MICHIE, (ed.), University of Edinburgh, Scotland, 1979, 153-167.

444. ROBINSON, J. A., Fundamentals of Machine-Oriented Deductive Logic, in *Introductory Readings in Expert Systems*, D. MICHIE, (ed.), Gordon and Breach, New York, 1982, 81-92.

445. DE ROUGEMONT, M., From Logic to Logic Programming, *Proceedings of AIMSA-84*, Varna, Bulgaria, September, 1984.

446. SAGIV, Y. and ULLMAN, J. D., Complexity of a Top-Down Capture Rule, Technical Report STAN-CS-84-1009, Department of Computer Science, Stanford University, July, 1984.

447. SAKURAI, T., Prolog and Inductive Definition, Technical Report 83-10, Information Science Department, University of Tokyo, 1984.

448. SANDEWALL, E., PCF-2, A First-Order Calculus for Expressing Conceptual Information, Technical Report, Computer Science Department, Uppsala University, 1972.

449. SANDFORD, D. M., *Using Sophisticated Models in Resolution Theorem Proving - Lecture Notes in Computer Science 90*, Springer-Verlag, New York, 1980.

450. SATO, M., Negation and Semantics of Prolog Programs, *Proceedings of the First International Logic Programming Conference*, Marseille, France, September, 1982.

451. SATO, M. and SAKURAI, T., QUTE: A Functional Language Based on Unification, in *Logic Programming: Relations, Functions, and Equations*, D. D. G. LINDSTROM, (ed.), Prentice-Hall, Inc., Inglewood Cliffs, 1985.

452. SATO, T., An Algorithm for Intelligent Backtracking, in *Proceedings of the RIMS Symposia on Software Science and Engineering*, S. G. AL, (ed.), Springer Verlag, 1983. Lecture Notes in Computer Science - 147.

453. SATO, T. and TAMAKI, H., Transformational Logic Program Synthesis, *International Conference On Fifth Generation Computer Systems*, November 1984.

454. SATO, T. and TAMAKI, H., Enumeration of Success Patterns in Logic Programs, *Theoretical Computer Science 34*, 1-2 (Feb 1985).

455. SCHULTZ, J. W., The Use Of First-order Predicate Calculus As A Logic Programming System, M.Sc Thesis, Department Of Computer Science, University Of Melbourne, 1984.

456. SCHWIND, C. B., Un Demonstrateur de Theoremes pour des Logiques Modales et Temporelles en Prolog, *Proceedings of the 5th Congres AFCET on Reconnaissances des Formes en Intelligence Artificielle*, Grenoble, France, November, 1985.

457. SEBELIK, J. and STEFANEK, P., Horn Clause Programs Suggested by Recursive Function, in *Workshop on Logic Programming*, S. A. TARNLUND, (ed.), Debrecen, Hungary, July 1980.

458. SHAPIRO, E. Y., Alternation and the Computational Complexity of Logic Programs, *Proceedings of the First International Logic Programming Conference*, M. VAN CANEGHEM, ed., Marseille, France, September 14-17, 1982, 154-163. Also available as Technical Report from Yale University, and The Journal of Logic Programming, Vol 1, No 1, June 1984.

459. SHAPIRO, E. Y., *Algorithmic Program Debugging*, MIT Press, 1983. Ph.D. thesis,Yale University,May 1982.

460. SHAPIRO, S. C. and MCKAY, D. P., Inference with Recursive Rules, *Proceedings of NCAI*, 1980.

461. SHEPERDSON, J. C., Negation As Failure: A Comparison of Clark's Completed Data Base and Reiter's Closed World Assumption, *The Journal Of Logic Programming 1*, 1 (June 1984), 51-79.

462. SHORTLIFFE, E. H., ERIKSSON, L. and JOHANSSON, A. L., Computer-Based Synthesis of Logic Programs, *Proceedings of the Fifth International Symposium on Programming*, M. DEZANI-CIANCAGLINE and U. MONTANARI, eds., 1982.

463. SHOSTAK, R. E. and OTHERS, Proceedings of the 7th International Conference on Automated Deduction, *Lecture notes in computer science 170*, Berlin, 1984.

464.   SICKEL, S., A Search Technique for Clause Interconnectivity Graphs, *IEEE Trans. Comput.* *25*, 8 (August 1976), 823-834.

465.   SICKEL, S., Invertibility of Logic Programs, *Proceedings of the 4th Workshop on Automated Deduction*, 1979.

466.   SIEGEL, P. and BOSSU, G., La Saturation au Secours de la Non-Monotonie, These de 3ieme Cycle, Groupe d'Intelligence Artificielle, Universite d'Aix-Marseille II, 1981.

467.   SIEKMANN, J., Unification of Commutative Terms, in *Symbolic and Algebraic Computation*, E. W. NG, (ed.), Springer-Verlag, 1979.

468.   SIEKMANN, J. and SZABO, P., Universal Unification and a Classification of Equational Theories, in *Lecture Notes in Computer Science - 138*, W. WALHSTER, (ed.), Springer Verlag, 1982, 102-141.

469.   SIEKMANN, J. and WRIGHTSON, G., *Automation of Reasoning. Part 1: Classical Papers on Computational Logic 1957-1966*, Springer-Verlag, Berlin, 1983. Editors.

470.   SIEKMANN, J. and WRIGHTSON, G., *Automation of Reasoning. Part 2: Classical Papers on Computational Logic 1967-1970*, Springer-Verlag, Berlin, 1983. Editors.

471.   SINTZOFF, M., Bounded-Horizon Success-Complete Restriction of Inference Programs, *Proceedings of the Second International Logic Programming Conference*, S. A. TARNLUND, ed., Uppsala University, Uppsala, Sweden, July 2-6, 1984, 139-150.

472.   SPYRATOS, N., The Partition Model: A Deductive Data Base Model, Technical Report No. 286, Institut National de Recherche en Informatique et en Automatique, April, 1984.

473. SRINIVASAN, C. V., CK-LOG: A Calculus for Knowledge Processing in Logic, Technical Report DCS-TR-153, Department of Computer Science, Rutgers University, 1985.

474. STABLER, E. P. and ELCOCK, E. W., Knowledge Representation in an Efficient Deductive Inference System, *Proceedings of Workshop on Logic Programming*, Algarve, Portugal, 1983.

475. STEELS, L., Descriptions as Constraints in Object-Oriented Representation, *Proceedings of the International Joint Conference on Artificial Intelligence*, Karlsruhe, Germany, 1983.

476. STEPANKOVA, O. and STEPANEK, P., Transformations of Logic Programs, *The Journal of Logic Programming 1*, 4 (December, 1984).

477. STERLING, L., Implementing Problem-Solving Strategies Using the Meta-level, *Proceedings of the Jerusalem Conference In Information Technology*, Jerusalem, Israel, 1984. Also available from Edinburgh as Research Paper 185.

478. STICKEL, M. E., Specification and Derivation of Logic Programs, in *Theoretical Foundations of Computer Science*, M. BROY and G. SCHMIDT, (eds.), Reidel Publishing Company, Boston, 1982.

479. STICKEL, M. E., A Unification Algorithm for Associative-Commutative Functions, *Journal of the ACM 28*, 3 (1981), 423-434.

480. STICKEL, M. E., A Prolog Technology Theorem Prover, *Proceedings of the International IEEE Conference on Logic Programming*, Atlantic City, 1984.

481. SUBRAHMANYAM, P. A. and YOU, J. H., FUNLOG: A
Computational Model Integrating Logic Programming and
Functional Programming, Technical Report UTEC-83-040,
Department of Computer Science, University of Utah. Also in,
D. DeGroot, G. Lindstrom, Functional Programming and Logic
Programming, June 1985, Prentice Hall.

482. SUBRAHMANYAM, P. A. and YOU, J. H., On Embedding Function
in Logic, *Information Processing Letters 19*, (1984), 41-46.

483. SYKORA, O., An Optimal Algorithm for Renaming a Set of
Clauses into the Horn Set, *Computer and Artificial Intelligence
4*, 1 (1985), 37-43.

484. SZEREDI, J., Mixed Language Programming: A Method for
Producing Efficient Prolog Programs, *SZKI Collection of Logic
Programming Papers*, 1982.

485. TAKEUTI, G., *Proof Theory*, Studies in Logic and the
Foundations of Mathematics, Volume 81, North-Holland, 1975.

486. TAMAKI, H., Semantics of a Logic Programming Language with
a Reducibility Predicate, *Proceedings of the International IEEE
Conference on Logic Programming*, Atlantic City, 1984.

487. TAMAKI, H. and SATO, T., Prolog Transformation Through
Meta-shifting, *New Generation Computing 1*, 1 (1983).

488. TAMAKI, H. and SATO, T., Unfold/Fold Transformation of Logic
Programs, *Proceedings of the Second International Logic
Programming Conference*, S. A. TARNLUND, ed., Uppsala
University, Uppsala, Sweden, July 2-6, 1984, 127-138.

489. TARNLUND, S. A., An Interpreter for the Programming
Language Predicate Logic, *Proceedings Fourth International
Joint Conference on Artificial Intelligence*, Tblisi, 1975.

490. TARNLUND, S. A., Logic Information Processing, Technical Report TRITA-IBADS-1034, University of Stockholm, 1975.

491. TARNLUND, S. A., A Logical Basis for Data Bases, Technical Report TRITA-IBABB-1029, Computer Science Department, Royal Institute of Technology, University of Stockholm, 1976.

492. TARNLUND, S. A., Programming as a Deductive Method, Technical Report TRITA-IBABB-1031, Computer Science Department, Royal Institute of Technology, University of Stockholm, 1976.

493. TARNLUND, S. A., Horn Clause Computability, *BIT 17*, 2 (1977), 215-226.

494. TARNLUND, S. A., An Axiomatic Data Base Theory, Technical Report, Computer Science Department, Royal Institute of Technology, University of Stockholm, 1978.

495. TARNLUND, S. A., A Programming Language Based on a Natural Deduction System, Technical Report, Computer Science Department, Uppsala University, 1981.

496. TAZI, S., Elimination de la Recursion Gauche et Analyse Ascendante et Descendante en Prolog, Technical Report, Department of Computer Science, INRIA, Toulouse, France, 1984. In French.

497. TOGASHI, A. and NOGUCHI, S., A Program Transformation From Equational Programs Into Logic Programs, *International Conference On Fifth Generation Computer Systems*, November 1984.

498. TOWNSEND, H. R. A., Determinism Rules O.K.: Another Notation for Prolog, *AISB Quarterly 44*, (Summer, 1982), 12-14.

499. TRUM, P., Logik as Spezifikationsprache, Diplomarbeit, Universitat Kaiserslautern, 1980.

500. TRUM, P. and WINTERSTEIN, G., Description and Practical Comparison of Unification Algorithms, Technical Report, University of Kaiserslautern, Germany, 1978.

501. TURNER, S. J., W-Grammars for Logic Programming, Technical Report W-113, Computer Science Department, University of Exeter, 1983.

502. TURNER, S. J., W-Grammars for Logic Programming, in *Implementations of Prolog*, J. A. CAMPBELL, (ed.), Ellis Horwood, 1984.

503. ULLMAN, J. D. and VAN GELDER, A., Testing Applicability of Top Down Capture Rules, Draft Paper, Stanford University, 1985.

504. VERE, S., Induction of Concepts in the Predicate Calculus, *Proceedings of the International Joint Conference on Artificial Intelligence*, 1975.

505. VERE, S., Relational Production Systems, *Artificial Intelligence 8*, 1 (1977).

506. VITTER, J. S. and SIMONS, R. A., Parallel Algorithms for Unification and other Complete Problems in P, in *Proc ACM-84*, October 1984, 75-84.

507. VODA, P. J., A View of Programming Languages as Symbiosis of Meaning and Control, Technical Report 84-9, Department of Computer Science, University of British Columbia, Canada, 1984. New Generation Computing, Vol 3, No 1, 1984.

508. WARREN, D. H. D., Applied Logic - Its Use and Implementation as Programming Tool, Ph.D. thesis, University of Edinburgh, U.K., 1977. Reprinted as Technical Note 290, 1983, Artificial Intelligence Center, SRI International, Menlo Park, California.

509. WINTERSTEIN, G., Pradikatenlogik-Programme mit Evaluierbare Functionen, Technical Report, Doctoral Dissertation, University of Kaiserslautern, Germany, 1978.

510. WINTERSTEIN, G., DAUSMAN, M. and PERSCH, G., Deriving Different Unification Algorithms from a Specification in Logic, in *Workshop on Logic Programming*, S. TARNLUND, (ed.), Debrecen, Hungary, July 1980.

511. WISE, M. J., A Set Theoretic Interpretation for Logic, DCS Report No 8306, University of New South Wales, July, 1983.

512. WOLFRAM, D. A., MAHER, M. J. and LASSEZ, J. L., A Unified Treatment of Resolution Strategies for Logic Programs, *Proceedings of the 2nd International Logic Programming Conference*, Sweden, July 2-6, 1984. Also Technical Report 83/12, Dept. of Computer Science, University of Melbourne, 36pp.

513. WOS,, L., OVERBEEK,, R. A., BOYLE., J. and LUSK,, E. L., *Automated reasoning: introduction and applications* , Englewood Cliffs, NJ, Prentice-Hall,, 1984..

514. WRIGHT, D. J., Prolog as a Relationally Complete Database Query Language Which Can Handle Least Fixed Point Operators, Technical Report, University of Kentucky, 1981.

515. WRIGHTSON, G., Semantic Tableaux, Unification and Links, Technical Report, CSD-ANZARP-84-001, May, 1984.

516. YAMASAKI, S. and YOSHIDA, M., The Satisfiability Problem for a Class Consisting of Horn Sentences and Some Non-Horn Sentences in Propositional Logic, *Information and Control 59*, 1-3 (1983), 1-12. Erratum in Information and Control, Vol.61, 1984, page 174.

517. YAMASAKI, S., YOSHIDA, M., DOSHITA, S. and HIRATA, M., A New Combination for Input and Unit Deductions for Horn Sentences, *Information Processing Letters 18*, (1984), 209-213.

CHAPTER 3

Unification - Theory and Practice

518. ABRAMSON, H., Unification-Based Conditional Binding Constructs, *Proceedings of the First International Logic Programming Conference*, Marseille, France, September, 1982.

519. ABRAMSON, H., A Prological Definition of HASL a Purely Functional Language with Unification Based Conditional Binding Expressions, *New Generation Computing 2*, 1 (1984).

520. ANDERSON, R. and BLEDSOE, W. W., A Linear Format for Resolution with Merging and a New Technique For Establishing Completeness, *Journal of the ACM 30*, (1983), 525-534.

521. BANDES, R. G., Constraining-Unification and the Programming Language Unicorn, *POPL*, Salt Lake City, Utah, January, 1984.

522. BAXTER, L. D., An Efficient Unification Algorithm, Technical Report CS-73-23, Applied Analysis and Computer Science Department, University of Waterloo, 1973.

523. BAXTER, L. D., A Practical Linear Algorithm, Technical Report CS-76-13, Applied Analysis and Computer Science Department, University of Waterloo, 1976.

524. BERGER-SABBATEL, G., DANG, W., IANESELLI, J. C. and NGUYEN, G. T., Unification for a Prolog Data Base Machine, *Proceedings of the Second International Logic Programming Conference*, S. TARNLUND, ed., Uppsala University, Uppsala, Sweden, July 2-6, 1984, 207-218.

525. CHANG, C. L. and LEE, R., *Symbolic Logic and Mechanical Theorem Proving*, Academic Press, New York, 1973.

526. CHEN, T. Y., LASSEZ, J. L. and PORT, G. S., Maximal Unifiable Subsets and Minimal Non-unifiable Subsets, Report 84/16, Department of Computer Science, University of Melbourne, 1984.

527. CORBIN, J. and BIDOIT, M., A Rehabilitation of Robinson's Unification Algorithm, in *Information Processing 1983*, R. E. MASON, (ed.), Elsevier, 1983, 627-636.

528. COX, P. T., On Determining the Clauses of Non Unifiability, Technical Report, Department of Computer Science, Auckland University, 1982.

529. DIGRICOLI, V. J., Resolution by Unification and Equality, *Proceedings of the 4th Workshop on Automated Deduction*, Austin, Texas, 1979, 43-52.

530. DILGER, W. and JANSON, A., Unification Graphs for Intelligent Backtracking in Deduction Symbols, *Proceedings of GWAI 83*, Dassel, Germany, 1983. Informatik-Fachbericht series.

531. DILGER, W. and MULLER, J. P., PUNIFY: An AI-Machine for Unification, in *Proceedings of the 6th European Conference on Artificial Intelligence*, T. O'SHEA, (ed.), Elsevier Publishing Company, Pisa, Italy, 1984.

532. DWORK, C., KANELLAKIS, P. C. and MITCHELL, J. C., On The Sequential Nature Of Unification, *The Journal Of Logic Programming 1*, 1 (June 1984), 35-50.

533. EDER, E., Properties of Substitutions and Unifications, *Proceedings of GWAI 83*, Dassel, Germany, 1983. Informatik-Fachbericht series.

534. ERIKSSON, L., Synthesis Of A Unification Algorithm In a Logic Programming Calculus, *The Journal Of Logic Programming 1*, 1 (June 1984), 3-18. Also available as UPMAIL Technical Report 22B.

535. FAGES, F., Note sur l'Unification des Tremes de Premier Ordre Finis et Infinis, Technical Report, Institut National de Recherche en Informatique et en Automatique, France, 1984.

536. FAGES, F., Associative-Commutative Unification, Technical Report No. 287, Institut National de Recherche en Informatique et en Automatique, 1984.

537. FAY, M. J., First-order unification in an equational theory, M.S. Thesis, Information Sciences Board, University of California at Santa Cruz, May 1978.

538. FAY, M. J., First-order unification in an equational theory, *Proceedings of the Fourth Workshop on Automated Deduction*, February 1979, 161-167.

539. FISHMAN, D. H. and MINKER, J., Pi-Representation: A Clause Representation for Parallel Search, *Artificial Intelligence 6*, (1975), 103-127.

540. FRIBOURG, L., Oriented Equational Clauses as a Programming Language, *The Journal Of Logic Programming 1*, 2 (August 1984), 165-178.

541. GOGUEN, J. A. and MESEGUER, J., Equality, Types, Modules and Generics for Logic Programming, *Proceedings of the Second International Logic Programming Conference*, S. TARNLUND, ed., Uppsala University, Uppsala, Sweden, July 2-6, 1984, 115-126. Also as Technical Report, SRI, Stanford.

542. HARIDI, S. and SAHLIN, D., Efficient Implementation of Unification of Cyclic Structures, in *Implementations of Prolog*, J. A. CAMPBELL, (ed.), Ellis Horwood, 1984.

543. HUET, G., Algebraic Aspects of Unification, *Proceedings of Workshop on Automated Theorem Proving*, Oberwolfach, Germany, 1976.

544. ITAI, A. and MAKOWSKY, J. A., Unification as a Complexity Measure for Logic Programming, Technical Report 301, Technion - Israel Institute of Technology, November 1983.

545. JAFFAR, J., Efficient Unification Over Infinite Terms, *New Generation Computing 2*, 3 (January 1984). Also, Technical Report, Monash University, Clayton, Victoria, Australia.

546. KAHN, K. M., Uniform: A Language Based Upon Unification Which Unifies Much of LISP, Prolog and Act 1, *Proceedings of the Seventh International Joint Conference on Artificial Intelligence*, Vancouver, Canada, 1981.

547. KAPUR, D., KRISHNAMOORTY, M. S. and NARENDRAN, P., A New Linear Algorithm for Unification, Technical Report, General Electric, Schenectady, New York, 1982.

548. KAY, M., Unification in Grammar, *Proceedings of an International Workshop on Natural Language Understanding and Logic Programming*, University of Rennes, September, 1985.

549. KOMOROWSKI, H. J. and MALUSZYNSKI, J., Unification-Free Execution of Logic Programs, *Proceedings of the 2nd IEEE International Symposium on Logic Programming*, Boston, USA, July, 1985.

550. LASSEZ, J. L. and MAHER, M. J., *The Semantics of Logic Programs*, Oxford University Press, . In Preparation.

551. LASSEZ, J. L. and MAHER, M. J., Antiunification, Technical Report 84-5, Department of Computer Science, University of Melbourne, Australia, 1984.

552. LEVY, J., A Unification Algorithm For Concurrent Prolog, *Proceedings of the Second International Logic Programming Conference*, S. TARNLUND, ed., Uppsala University, Uppsala, Sweden, July 2-6, 1984, 331-342. Also available as a Technical Report from the Weizmann Institute of Science, Rechovot, Israel.

553. MAHER, M. J., Semantics of Logic Programs, PhD Thesis, University of Melbourne, Department of Computer Science, 1985.

554. MALUSZINSKI, J. and FULLSON, J. F., A Notion of Grammatical Unification Applicable to Logic Programming Languages, Technical Report, University of Denmark, 1981.

555. MANNA, Z. and WALDINGER, R., Deductive Synthesis of the Unification Algorithm, Tech. Note 246, SRI International, July 1981.

556. MARTELLI, A. and MONTANARI, U., Unification in Linear Time and Space, Technical Report B76-16, University of Pisa, Italy, 1976.

557. MARTELLI, A. and MONTANARI, U., An Efficient Unification Algorithm, *ACM Transactions on Programming Languages & Systems 4*, 2 (1982), 258-282.

558. MARTELLI, A. and ROSSI, G., Efficient Unification With Infinite Terms In Logic Programming, *International Conference On Fifth Generation Computer Systems*, November 1984.

559. McCUME, W. W., An Inference Mechanism For Resolution-style Theorem Provers, Master's Thesis, Northwestern University, 1981.

560. MILLS, P., A Systolic Unification Algorithm for VLSI, *International Conference On Fifth Generation Computer Systems*, November 1984.

561. MOROKHOVETS, M. K., A Modified Unification Procedure, *Cybernetics 20 20*, 1 (1984), 147-152 .

562. MORRIS, J. B., E-resolution: Extension of Resolution to Include the Equality Relation, *Proceedings of the International Joint Conference on Artificial Intelligence*, Washington, D.C., May 7-9, 1969, 287-294.

563. MUKAI, K., A Unification Algorithm for Infinite Trees, *Proceedings of the International Joint Conference on Artificial Intelligence*, Karlsruhe, Germany, 1983.

564. NAISH, L. and LASSEZ, J. L., Most Specific Logic Programs, Technical Report 84/9, 1984.

565. PATERSON, M. S. and WEGMAN, M. N., Linear Unification, *Proceedings of the 8th ACM Symposium on the Theory of Computing*, 1978. Also in Computer and System Sciences, Vol 16, 1978.

566. PEREIRA, F. C. N., A Structure-Sharing Representation for Unification-Based Grammar Formalisms, *Proceedings of the 23rd Annual Meeting of the Association for Computational Linguistics*, American Association for Computational Linguistics, July, 1985.

567. RAULEFS, P., SIEKMANN, J., SZABO, P. and UNVERICHT, E., A Short Survey on the State of the Art in Matching and Unification Problems, *AISB Quarterly 32*, (December, 1978), 17-21.

568. ROBINSON, G. and WOS, L., Paramodulation and Theorem Proving in First Order Theories with Equality, *Machine Intelligence 4*, (1969), 135-150, American Elsevier.

569. ROBINSON, J. A., Automatic Deduction with Hyper-resolution, *International Journal of Computer Mathematics 1*, (1965), 227-234.

570. ROBINSON, J. A., A review of automatic theorem proving, *Proc. of the Symposia in Applied Mathematics 19*, (1969), 1-18, American Mathematical Society.

571. ROBINSON, J. A., Computational Logic: the Unification Computation, *Machine intelligence 6*, (1971), 63-72.

572. ROBINSON, J. A., Fast Unification, *Proceedings of Workshop on Automated Theorem Proving*, Oberwolfach, Germany, 1976.

573. ROBINSON, J. A., Fundamentals of Machine-Oriented Deductive Logic, in *Introductory Readings in Expert Systems*, D. MICHIE, (ed.), Gordon and Breach, New York, 1982, 81-92.

574. SATO, M. and SAKURAI, T., Qute: A Functional Language Based On Unification, *International Conference On Fifth Generation Computer Systems*, November 1984.

575. SATO, M. and SAKURAI, T., QUTE: A Functional Language Based on Unification, in *Logic Programming: Relations, Functions, and Equations*, D. D. G. LINDSTROM, (ed.), Prentice-Hall, Inc., Inglewood Cliffs, 1985.

576. SIEKMANN, J., Unification of Commutative Terms, in *Symbolic and Algebraic Computation*, E. W. NG, (ed.), Springer-Verlag, 1979.

577. SIEKMANN, J. and SZABO, P., Universal Unification and a Classification of Equational Theories, in *Lecture Notes in Computer Science - 138*, W. WALHSTER, (ed.), Springer Verlag, 1982, 102-141.

578. SMOLKA, G., Fresh: A Higher-Order Language with Unification and Multiple Results, in *Logic Programming: Relations, Functions, and Equations*, D. D. G. LINDSTROM, (ed.), Prentice-Hall, Inc., Inglewood Cliffs, 1985.

579. STICKEL, M. E., A Unification Algorithm for Associative-Commutative Functions, *Journal of the ACM 28*, 3 (1981), 423-434.

580. TAMAKI, H., A Distributed Unification Scheme for Systolic Logic Programs, *Proceedings of the 1985 International Conference on Parallel Processing*, St. Charles, Illinois, USA, August, 1985.

581. TRUM, P. and WINTERSTEIN, G., Description and Practical Comparison of Unification Algorithms, Technical Report, University of Kaiserslautern, Germany, 1978.

582. VITTER, J. S. and SIMONS, R. A., Parallel Algorithms for Unification and other Complete Problems in P, in *Proc ACM-84*, October 1984, 75-84.

583. WINTERSTEIN, G., Pradikatenlogik-Programme mit Evaluierbare Functionen, Technical Report, Doctoral Dissertation, University of Kaiserslautern, Germany, 1978.

584. WINTERSTEIN, G., DAUSMAN, M. and PERSCH, G., Deriving Different Unification Algorithms from a Specification in Logic, in *Workshop on Logic Programming*, S. TARNLUND, (ed.), Debrecen, Hungary, July 1980.

585. WOLFRAM, D. A., MAHER, M. J. and LASSEZ, J. L., A Unified Treatment of Resolution Strategies for Logic Programs, *Proceedings of the 2nd International Logic Programming Conference*, Sweden, July 2-6, 1984. Also Technical Report 83/12, Dept. of Computer Science, University of Melbourne, 36pp.

586. WOO, N., A Hardware Unification Unit: Design and Analysis, *Proceedings of the 12th International Symposium on Computer Architecture*, Boston, June, 1985.

587. WRIGHTSON, G., Semantic Tableaux, Unification and Links, Technical Report, CSD-ANZARP-84-001, May, 1984.

588. YASUURA, H., On Parallel Computational Complexity Of Unification, *International Conference On Fifth Generation Computer Systems*, November 1984. Also, Technical Report TR-0027, ICOT - Institute for New Generation Computer Technology, 1983.

CHAPTER 4

Semantics of Prolog and
Logic Programming in General

589. ALLISON, L., An Executable Prolog Semantics, *Algol Bulletin 50*, (December, 1983).

590. ASIRELLI, P., Some Aspects of the Static Semantics of Logic Programs with Monadic Functions, *Proceedings of 2nd Workshop on Logic Programming*, Algarve, Portugal, 1983, 485-505.

591. BALOGH, K., On a Logical Method Serving the Proof of the Semantic Features of Programs, Technical Report, Department of Computer Science, Eotvos Lorand University, Budapest, 1979. In Hungarian.

592. BELLIA, M., DEGANO, P. and LEVI, G., The Call by Name Semantics of a Clause Language with Functions, in *Logic Programming*, K. L. CLARK and S. TARNLUND, (eds.), Academic Press, New York, 1982, 281-298. A.P.I.C. Studies in Data Processing No. 16.

593. BLAIR, H. A., The Recursion-Theoretic Complexity of the Semantics of Predicate Logic as a Programming Language, Technical Report, Iowa University, 1982. Also Appeared in Information and Control, 54, 25-47, 1982.

594. BROWN, F. M., A Semantic Theory for Logic Programming, DAI Report 51, Department of Artificial Intelligence, University of Edinburgh, 1978.

595. DEGANO, P. and DIOMEDI, S., A First-Order Semantics of a Connective Suitable to Express Concurrency, *Proceedings of Workshop on Logic Programming*, Algarve, Portugal, 1983.

596. DERANSART, P., An Operational Algebraic Semantics of Prolog Programs, *Proceedings of Workshop on Logic Programming*, Algarve, Portugal, 1983.

597. DERANSART, P., An Operational Semantics of Prolog Programs, Technical Report, Institut National de Recherche en Informatique et en Automatique, France, 1984.

598. VAN EMDEN, M. H. and KOWALSKI, R. A., The Semantics of Predicate Logic as a Programming Language, *Journal of the ACM 23*, 4 (1976), 733-742.

599. VAN EMDEN, M. H. and NAIT-ABDALLAH, M. A., Top-Down Semantics of Fair Computations of Logic Programs, Technical Report CS-84-27, Department of Computer Science, University of Waterloo, Canada.

600. FAGES, F., Note Sur L'unification Des Termes De Premier Ordre Finis Et Infinis, *Actes du Seminaire Programmation En Logique*, M. DINCBAS, ed., March, 1983.

601. FALASCHI, M., LEVI, G. and PALAMIDESSI, C., On the Fixed Point Semantic of Horn Clauses with Infinite Terms, *Proceedings of 2nd Workshop on Logic Programming*, Algarve, Portugal, 1983, 474-484.

602. FALASCHI, M., LEVI, G. and PALAMIDESSI, C., A Synchronization Logic: Axiomatics and Formal Semantics of Generalized Horn Clauses, *Proceedings Janos Bolyai Mathematical Society, Colloquim on Algebra, Combinatorics and Logic in Computer Science*, Gyor, Hungary, 1983.

603. FALASCHI, M., LEVI, G. and PALAMIDESSI, C., Synchronization in Logic Programming: Formal Semantics of Extended Horn Clauses, *Proceedings of Colloqium on Algebra, Combinatorics and Logic in Computer Science*, Hungary, 1983.

604. GOGUEN, J. A. and MESEGUER, J., Equality, Types, Modules and Generics for Logic Programming, *Proceedings of the Second International Logic Programming Conference*, S. TARNLUND, ed., Uppsala University, Uppsala, Sweden, July 2-6, 1984, 115-126. Also as Technical Report, SRI, Stanford.

605. HEUSCHEN, L. J., Semantic Resolution For Horn Sets, *IEEE Transactions On Computers 25*, 8 (1976).

606. JAFFAR, J., LASSEZ, J. L. and MAHER, M. J., A Theory of Complete Logic Programs With Equality, Technical Report, Monash University, Clayton, Victoria, Australia, May, 1984. Also FGCS Conference Proceedings, 1984.

607. JAFFAR, J., LASSEZ, J. L. and MAHER, M. J., A Logical Foundation For Prolog II, Technical Report, Monash University, Clayton, Victoria, Australia, September, 1984.

608. JONES, N. D. and MYCROFT, A., Stepwise Development of Operational and Denotational Semantics for Prolog, *Proceedings of the International IEEE Conference on Logic Programming*, Atlantic City, 1984.

609. KAHN, G., The Semantics of a simple language for parallel programming, *Information Processing*, 74.

610. LASSEZ, J. L. and MAHER, M. J., *The Semantics of Logic Programs*, Oxford University Press, . In Preparation.

611. LASSEZ, J. L. and MAHER, M. J., Chaotic Semantics of Programming Logic, Technical Report, University of Melbourne, Department of Computer Science, Australia, 1982.

612. LASSEZ, J. L. and MAHER, M. J., The denotational semantics of Horn Clauses as a Production System, in *Proceedings of National Conference on Artificial Intelligence (AAAI-83)*, Washington D.C., August 1983, 229-231.

613. LASSEZ, J. L. and MAHER, M. J., Optimal Fixedpoints of Logic Programs, in *Proc. 3rd Inter. Conf. on the Foundations of Software Technology and Theoretical Computer Science*, Bangalore, India, December 1983.

614. LASSEZ, J. L. and MAHER, M. J., Closures and Fairness in the Semantics of Programming Logic, *Theoretical Computer Science 29*, (1984), 167-184. Also as Technical Report 83/3, Department of Computer Science, University of Melbourne.

615. LEVI, G. and PALAMIDESSI, C., The Declarative Semantics of Logical Read-only Variables, *Proceedings of the 2nd IEEE International Symposium on Logic Programming*, Boston, USA, July, 1985.

616. LLOYD, J. W. and TOPOR, R. W., Making Prolog More Expressive, Technical Report 84/8, Department Of Computer Science, University Of Melbourne, 1984. To appear in the Journal of Logic Programming, 1984.

617. MAHR, B. and MAKOWSKY, J. A., An Axiomatic Approach to Semantics of Specification Languages, *Proceedings, 6th GI Conference on Theoretical Computer Science, Dortmund, Springer-Verlag Lecture Notes in Computer Science 145*, (1983).

618. MAHR, B. and MAKOWSKY, J. A., Characterizing Specification Languages which Admit Initial Semantics, *Theoretical Computer Science 31*, (1984.), 49-60.

619. MAKOWSKY, J. A., Why Horn Formulas Matter in Computer Science: Initial Structures and Generic Examples, Technical Report, Department of Computer Science, Technion, Haifa, Israel, 1985.

620. MARQUE-PUCHEU, G., Relational Set of Trees and the Algebraic Semantics of Logic Programming, *Acta Informatica 20*, (1983), 249-260.

621. MCCORD, M. C., Semantic Interpretation for the Epistle System, *Proceedings of the Second International Logic Programming Conference*, S. A. TARNLUND, ed., Uppsala University, Uppsala, Sweden, July 2-6, 1984, 65-76.

622. MINKER, J. and PERLIS, D., On the Semantics of Circumscription, Technical Report, University Of Maryland, 1983.

623. PALMER, M. S., Where to connect? - Solving Problems in Semantics, Working Paper 22, Department of Artificial Intelligence, University of Edinburgh, July, 1977.

624. PEREIRA, L. M. and MONTEIRO, L. F., The Semantics of Parallelism and Coroutining in Logic Programming, *Colloquium on Mathematical Logic in Programming*, Hungary, 1978. Published by North-Holland in 1981.

625. REDDY, U., Narrowing as the Operational Semantics of Functional Languages, *Proceedings of the 2nd IEEE International Symposium on Logic Programming*, Boston, USA, July, 1985.

626. SATO, M., Negation and Semantics of Prolog Programs, *Proceedings of the First International Logic Programming Conference*, Marseille, France, September, 1982.

627. SINTZOFF, M., Bounded-Horizon Success-Complete Restriction of Inference Programs, *Proceedings of the Second International Logic Programming Conference*, S. A. TARNLUND, ed., Uppsala University, Uppsala, Sweden, July 2-6, 1984, 139-150.

628.   SKUCE, D., Formal Semantics of KNOWLOG, Technical Report
       TR-83-15, Department of Computer Science, University of
       Ottawa, Canada, 1983.

629.   TAMAKI, H., Semantics of a Logic Programming Language with
       a Reducibility Predicate, *Proceedings of the International IEEE
       Conference on Logic Programming*, Atlantic City, 1984.

630.   TARLECKI, A., Abstract Algebraic Institutions which Strongly
       Admit Initial Semantics, CSR-165-84, University of Edinburgh,
       Computer Science Department, 1984.

631.   VODA, P. J., A View of Programming Languages as Symbiosis
       of Meaning and Control, Technical Report 84-9, Department of
       Computer Science, University of British Columbia, Canada,
       1984. New Generation Computing, Vol 3, No 1, 1984.

632.   WOLFRAM, D. A., MAHER, M. J. and LASSEZ, J. L., A Unified
       Treatment of Resolution Strategies for Logic Programs,
       *Proceedings of the 2nd International Logic Programming
       Conference*, Sweden, July 2-6, 1984. Also Technical Report
       83/12, Dept. of Computer Science, University of Melbourne,
       36pp.

633.   WRIGHTSON, G., Semantic Tableaux, Unification and Links,
       Technical Report, CSD-ANZARP-84-001, May, 1984.

CHAPTER 5

Implementation Issues of
Logic Programming Languages

634. AISO, H., Fifth Generation Computer Architecture, in *Fifth Generation Computer Systems*, T. MOTO-OKA, (ed.), North-Holland, New York, 1981. Proceedings of the First International Conference on Fifth Generation Computer Systems.

635. AKUTAGAWA, T., DASAI, T., OGINO, T., AKITA, K. and TAMURA, T., Enhanced Prolog for Industrial Applications, Publication PB84-218197, National Technical Information Service, Springfield, Virginia, 1984. (In Japanese).

636. AMAMIYA, M. and OTHERS, New Architecture for Knowledge Base Mechanisms, in *Fifth Generation Computer Systems*, T. MOTO-OKA, (ed.), North-Holland, New York, 1981. Proceedings of the First International Conference on Fifth Generation Computer Systems.

637. BALLIEU, G., A Virtual Machine to Implement Prolog, *Proceedings of Workshop on Logic Programming*, Algarve, Portugal, 1983.

638. BALOGH, K., FUTO, I., SZEREDI, P. and LABADI, K., On the Implementation Methods and the Theoretical Foundations of the Prolog Language, SZKI Technical Report, SZKI Institute, Budapest, Hungary, 1979. In Hungarian.

639. BARBERYE, G., JOUBERT, T. and MARTIN, M., Les Nouvelles Possibilites de Prolo-Pascal/Multics, *CNET* , Paris, France, 1984.

640. BATTANI, G. and FUENMAYOR, M. E., Optimizing Prolog Programs Containing Static Calls to Databases, Technical Report, Computer Science Department, Simon Bolivar University, Venezuela, 1983.

641. BATTANI, G. and MELONI, H., Interpreteur du Langage de Programmation Prolog, Technical Report, Groupe d'Intelligence Artificielle, Universite d'Aix-Marseille II, Marseille, France, 1973.

642. BEKKERS, Y., CANET, B., RIDOUX, O. and UNGARO, L., A Short Note On Garbage Collection In Prolog Interpreters, *Logic Programming Newsletter*, Winter, 1983/1984.

643. BEKKERS, Y., CANET, B., RIDOUX, O. and UNGARO, L., Presentation Simplifiee d'une Machine de gestion de Memoire pour les Interpreteurs Prolog, Technical Report 280, Laboratoires INRIA, Rocquencourt, France, 1984.

644. BEKKERS, Y., CANET, B., RIDOUX, O. and UNGARO, L., Specification d'une Machine de Gestion de Memoire pour les Interpreteurs de Langages Logiques, Technical Report 283, Laboratoires INRIA, Rocquencourt, France, 1984.

645. BEKKERS, Y., CANET, B., RIDOUX, O. and UNGARO, L., A Memory Management Machine For Prolog Interpreters, *Proceedings of the Second International Logic Programming Conference*, S. TARNLUND, ed., Uppsala University, Uppsala, Sweden, July 2-6, 1984, 343-354.

646. BEKKERS, Y., CANET, B. and UNGARO, L., Problemes de Gestion de Memoire dans les Interpreteurs Prolog, Technical Report, INRIA-IRISA, Rennes, 1982. Also in Actes du Seminaire Programmation En Logique, 1982.

647. BELLIA, M., DAMERI, E., DEGANO, P., LEVI, G. and MARTELLI, M., A Formal Model for Lazy Implementations of a Prolog compatible Functional Language, in *Issues in Prolog Implementations*, J. A. CAMPBELL, (ed.), Ellis Horwood, 1984.

648. BELLIA, M., DEGANO, P., LEVI, G., DAMERI, E. and MARTELLI, A., A Formal Model for Demand-Driven Implementations of Rewriting Systems and its Application to Prolog Processes, Technical Report 81-3, University of Pisa, Italy, 1983.

649. BELLIA, M., LEVI, G. and MARTELLI, M., On Compiling Prolog Programs on Demand-Driven Architectures, *Proceedings of the 2nd Workshop on Logic Programming*, Algarve, Portugal, 1983, 518-535.

650. BENDL, J. and OTHERS, A User's Documentation of the MProlog System, NIM IGUSZI Technical Report, SZKI Institute, Budapest, Hungary, 1979. In Hungarian.

651. BENDL, J., KOSA, M. and SZEREDI, P., A Rough Description of the MProlog compiler for IBM-like Architectures, NIM IGUSZI Technical Report, SZKI Institute, Budapest, Hungary, 1980. In Hungarian.

652. BENDL, J., KOVES, P. and SZEREDI, P., The MProlog system, in *Proceedings of the Logic Programming Workshop*, S. TARNLUND, (ed.), 1980, 201-209.

653. BENDL, J., VARGA, K., KOSA, M. and BALOGH, K., The Specification of an Interpreter of a Modular prolog, NIM IGUSZI Technical Report, SZAMKI, Hungary, 1978. In Hungarian.

654. BERGER-SABBATEL, G., IANESELLI, J. C. and NGUYEN, G. T., A Prolog Database Machine, *Proceedings of the Third International Workshop on Database Machines*, Munchen, Germany, September, 1983.

655. BOIZUMAULT, P., Sur La Transformation De L'appel Terminal En Iteration Dans Un Interprete Prolog, *Actes du Seminaire Programmation En Logique*, M. DINCBAS, ed., March, 1983.

656. BORGWARDT, P., Parallel Prolog Using Stack Segments on Shared-Memory Multi Processors, *Proceedings of the International IEEE Conference on Logic Programming*, Atlantic City, 1984.

657. BOWEN, D. L., BYRD, L. and CLOCKSIN, W. F., A Portable Prolog Compiler, *Workshop on Logic Programming*, Algarve, Portugal, 1983.

658. BROUGH, D. R. and WALKER, A., Some Practical Properties of Logic Programming Interpreters, *Proceedings of the 1984 Conference on Fifth Generation Computer Systems*, Tokyo, Japan, November, 1984.

659. BRUYNOOGHE, M., An Interpreter for Predicate Logic Programs : Part 1, Report CW 10, Applied Mathematics and Programming Division, Katholieke Universiteit, Leuven, Belgium, October, 1976.

660. BRUYNOOGHE, M., The Memory Management of Prolog Implementations, in *Workshop on Logic Programming*, S. TARNLUND, (ed.), Debrecen, Hungary, July 1980. Also in Logic Programming, Clark and Tarnlund, Academic Press, 1982.

661. BRUYNOOGHE, M., Prolog-C Implementation, Internal Report, Applied Mathematics and Programming Division, Katholieke Universiteit, Leuven, Belgium, 1981.

662. BRUYNOOGHE, M., A Note on Garbage Collection in Prolog Interpreters, *Proceedings of the First International Logic Programming Conference*, M. VAN CANEGHEM, ed., Marseille, France, September 14-17, 1982, 52-55.

663. BRUYNOOGHE, M., Some Reflections on Implementation Issues of Prolog, *Proceedings of Workshop on Logic Programming*, Algarve, Portugal, 1983.

664. BRUYNOOGHE, M., Implementatie van Prolog, Internal Report, Katholieke Universiteit Leuven, Belgium, 1983. (In Dutch).

665. BRUYNOOGHE, M., Garbage Collection in Prolog Interpreters, in *Implementations of Prolog*, J. A. CAMPBELL, (ed.), Ellis Horwood, 1984.

666. BUNDY, A., BYRD, L. and RAE, R., Implementation of a Machine Independent Prolog, *Workshop on Logic Programming*, Long Beach, Los Angeles, September 1981.

667. BYRD, L., The New Prolog Interpreter, DAI Report, Department of Artificial Intelligence, University of Edinburgh, 1979.

668. BYRD, L., User's Guide to the EMAS Prolog, Occasional Paper 26, Edinburgh University, U.K., 1981.

669. BYRD, L., PEREIRA, F. C. N. and WARREN, D. H. D., A Guide to Version 3 of DEC-10 Prolog, Occasional Paper 19, Department of Artificial Intelligence, University of Edinburgh, Scotland, July, 1980.

670. J. A. CAMPBELL, ed., *Implementation Issues of Prolog Systems*, Ellis Horwood, 1984. (Available from Halstead Press, 605 Third Avenue, NY, NY 10158).

671. VAN CANEGHEM, M., Compilation D'un Sous-Prolog, *Actes du Seminaire Programmation En Logique*, M. DINCBAS, ed., March, 1983.

672. VAN CANEGHEM, M., Compilation d'un Sous-Prolog, Technical Report, Faculte de Sciences de Luminy, Marseille, France, 1984.

673. CAREY, M., DEWITT, D. and GRAEFE, G., Mechanisms for Concurrency Control and Recovery in Prolog - A Proposal, *Proceedings of the First International Workshop on Expert Database Systems*, Kiawah Island, South Carolina, October 24-27, 1984.

674. CARLSSON, M., (Re)Implementing Prolog in LISP or YAQ - Yet Another QLISP, Technical Report, Computer Science Department, Uppsala University, 1982.

675. CARLSSON, M., On Implementing Prolog in Functional Programming, *Proceedings of the International IEEE Conference on Logic Programming*, Atlantic City, 1984. Also UPMAIL Technical Report 5B, Uppsala University.

676. CARLSSON, M., LM-Prolog: The Language and Its Implementation, UPMAIL Technical Report 30, Uppsala University, 1984.

677. CARLSSON, M., A Microcoded Unifier for Lisp Machine Prolog, *Proceedings of the 2nd IEEE International Symposium on Logic Programming*, Boston, USA, July, 1985.

678. CHAKRAVARTHY, U. S., KASIF, S., KOHLI, M., MINKER, J. and CAO, D., Logic Programming on ZMOB: A Highly Parallel Machine, *Proceedings og the 1982 International Conference in Parallel processing*, New York, 1982, 347-349.

679. CHANG, J. H. and DESPAIN, A. M., Semi-Intelligent Backtracking of Prolog Based on Static Data Dependency Analysis, *Proceedings of the IEEE Spring CompCon Conference*, San Francisco, February, 1985.

680. CHENG, M. H. M., Design and Implementation of the Waterloo Prolog Environment, Technical Report CS-84-47, Department of Computer Science, University of Waterloo, Ontario, Canada, 1984.

681. CHENG, M. H. M. and GOEBEL, R. G., Waterloo Prolog Implementation Manual, Technical Report, Department of Computer Science, University of Waterloo, Ontario, Canada, 1985.

682. CIEPIELEWSKI, A., Towards a Computer Architecture for the OR-Parallel Execution of Logic Progams, Ph.D. Thesis, Royal Institute of Technology, Stockholm, Sweden, 1984.

683. CIEPIELEWSKI, A. and HARIDI, S., Storage Models for OR-Parallel Execution of Logic Progams, Technical Report TRITA-CS-8301, Royal Institute of Technology, Stockholm, Sweden, 1983.

684. CIEPIELEWSKI, A. and HARIDI, S., Control of Activities in the OR-Parallel Token Machine, *Proceedings of the International IEEE Conference on Logic Programming*, Atlantic City, 1984, 49-57.

685. CLARK, K. L., ENNALS, J. R. and MCCABE, F. G., A Micro-Prolog Primer, Technical Report, Logic Programming Associates, London, 1981.

686. CLARK, K. L. and MCCABE, F. G., The Control Facilities of IC-Prolog, in *Expert Systems in the Microelectronic Age*, D. MICHIE, (ed.), University of Edinburgh, Scotland, 1979, 153-167.

687. CLARK, K. L. and MCCABE, F. G., IC-Prolog - Language Features, in *Workshop on Logic Programming*, S. TARNLUND, (ed.), Debrecen, Hungary, July 1980. Also in Logic Programming, Clark and Tarnlund, Academic Press, 1982.

688. CLARK, K. L. and MCCABE, F. G., IC-Prolog Aspects of its implementation, in *Logic Programming*, K. L. CLARK and S. TARNLUND, (eds.), Academic Press, 1982.

689. CLARK, K. L., MCCABE, F. G. and ENNALS, J. R., ZX Spectrum Micro-Prolog Primer, Sinclair Research, Logic Programming Group, Imperial College, 1983.

690. CLOCKSIN, W. F., Design and Implementation of a Sequential Prolog Machine, *New Generation Computing 3*, 1 (1985).

691. CLOCKSIN, W. F. and MELLISH, C. S., *The UNIX Prolog System Software Report 5 (Second Edition)*, Department of Artificial Intelligence, University of Edinburg, September 1980.

692. COLMERAUER, A. and OTHERS, Etude et Realization d'un Systeme Prolog, Technical Report 77030, Convention de Reserche IRIA-Sesori, 1973.

693. COLMERAUER, A., Infinite Trees and Inequalities in Prolog, *Proceedings of the Prolog Programming Environments Workshop*, Linkoping University, Sweden, 1982.

694. COLMERAUER, A., Prolog-II Manuel de Reference et Modele Theorique, Groupe Intelligence Artificelle, Univerisite d'Aix-Marseille II, 1982.

695. COLMERAUER, A., Prolog and Infinite Trees, in *Logic Programming*, K. L. CLARK and S. A. TARNLUND, (eds.), Academic Press, New York, 1982. A.P.I.C. Studies in Data Processing No. 16.

696. COLMERAUER, A., KANOUI, H. and VAN CANEGHEM, M., Last Steps Towards an Ultimate Prolog, *Proceedings of the Seventh International Joint Conference on Artificial Intelligence*, Vancouver, 1977.

697. COX, P. T., Finding Backtrack Points for Intelligent Backtracking, in *Implementations of Prolog*, J. A. CAMPBELL, (ed.), Ellis Horwood, 1984.

698. Cox, P. T. and Pietrzykowski, T., Deduction plans: A Basis for Intelligent Backtracking, *IEEE Transactions on Pattern Analysis and Machine Intelligence PAMI-3*, 1 (1981), 52-65. Also available as a Technical Report from Auckland University, 1981.

699. Damas, A., *Information about EMAS Prolog*, Department of Computer Science, University of Edinburgh, 1979.

700. Dasai, T., Mukai, K., Suzuki, K., Igusa, H. and Sato, H., Kanji Prolog Programming System , Publication PB84-218197), National Technical Information Service, Springfield, Virginia, 1984. (In Japanese).

701. Despain, A. M. and Patt, Y. N., The Berkeley Prolog Machine, *Proceedings of the IEEE Spring CompCon Conference*, San Francisco, February, 1985.

702. Doyle, J., What Should Artificial Intelligence Want from the Super Computers ?, *Artificial Intelligence Magazine 4*, 4 (1983).

703. Emanuelson, P., From Abstract Model to Efficient Compilation of Patterns, Technical Report, Department of Computer Science, Linkoping University, 1982.

704. Van Emden, M. H., An Algorithm for Interpreting Prolog Programs, Technical Report CS-81-28, Department of Computer Science, University of Waterloo,Canada, 1981. Also appeared in Implementation Issues of Prolog Systems, by John Campbell, Ellis Horwood, 1984.

705. Van Emden, M. H., An Interpreting Algorithm for Prolog Programs, *Proceedings of the First International Logic Programming Conference*, M. Van Caneghem, ed., Marseille, France, September 14-17, 1982, 56-64.

706. FAGIN, B., Issues in Caching Prolog Goals, Technical Report UCB/CSD 84/204, Computer Science Division, University of California, Berkeley, November 1984.

707. FERGUSON, R. J., An Implementation of Prolog in C, M.S. Thesis, University of Waterloo, 1978.

708. FILGUEIRAS, M., Un Interpreteur de Prolog, Technical Report, Groupe Intelligence Artificielle, University Aix-Marseille, France, 1982.

709. FILGUEIRAS, M., On the Implementation of Control in Logic Programming Languages, Technical Report, Departamento de Informatica, Universidade Nova de Lisboa, 1982.

710. FILGUEIRAS, M., A Prolog Interpreter Working with Infinite Terms, Technical Report, Departamento de Informatica, Universidade Nova de Lisboa, 1982. Also in Implementations of Prolog (J.A. Campbell ed) Ellis Horwood.

711. FOGELHOLM, R., Exeter Prolog: An Experimental Prolog System Written in LISP, Technical Report M-103, Department of Computer Science, Exeter University, 1982.

712. FOGELHOLM, R., Exeter Prolog: Some Thoughts on Prolog Design by a LISP User, in *Implementations of Prolog*, J. A. CAMPBELL, (ed.), Ellis Horwood, 1984.

713. FORBUS, K., Implementation Issues in Common Sense Reasoning Programs, *Proceedings of the Prolog Programming Environments Workshop*, Linkoping University, Sweden, 1982.

714. FRIBOURG, L., SLOG: A Logic Programming Language Interpreter Based on Clausal Superposition and Rewriting, *Proceedings of the 2nd IEEE International Symposium on Logic Programming*, Boston, USA, July, 1985.

715. FURUKAWA, K., MITTA, K. and MATSUMOTO, Y., A Back-Up Parallel Interpreter for Prolog Programs, in *Logic Programming and Its Applications*, M. VAN CANEGHEM and D. H. D. WARREN, (eds.), Ablex Publishing Company, 1984.

716. FURUKAWA, K., NITTA, K. and MATSUMOTO, Y., Prolog Interpreter Based on Concurrent Programming, in *Proc. of the First International Logic Programming Conference*, M. VAN CANEGHEM, (ed.), ADDP-GIA, Facult'e des Sciences de Luminy, Marseille, France, September 14-17, 1982, 38-44.

717. GABBAY, D., What Is Negation In A System And When Is Failure A Negation, Doc 84/10, Department of Computing, Imperial College, 1984.

718. GABBAY, D. and SERGOT, M. J., Negation As Inconsistency, Doc 84/7, Department of Computing, Imperial College, 1984.

719. GABRIEL, J. R., LINDHOLM, T. G., LUSK, E. L. and OVERBEEK, R. A., A Short Note on Achieveable LIPS Rates Using the Warren Abstract Prolog Machine, Technical Report MCS-TM-36, Mathematics and Computer Science Division, Argonne National Laboratories, 1984.

720. GALLIER, J. and RAATZ, S., Graph-Based Logic Programming Interpreters, *Proceedings of the 2nd IEEE International Symposium on Logic Programming*, Boston, USA, July, 1985.

721. GARRETA, H., Prolog II VAX Installation and Utilisation guide, Technical Report, Department of Computer Science, University of Marseille, March, 1983.

722. LE GLOAN, A., Implantation de Prolog, Technical Report, Department of Computer Science, Universite de Montreal, Canada, 1974.

723. GREGORY, S., Towards the Compilation of Annotated Logic Programs, Report CCD 80/16, Imperial College, London, 1980.

724. HABATA, S. and NAKZAKI, Y., On Garbage Collection Processing for Prolog Machines, Technical Memorandum TM-0015, ICOT - Institute for New Generation Computer Technology, Tokyo, Japan, 1983. In Japanese.

725. HANSSON, A., HARIDI, S. and TARNLUND, S. A., Some Aspects of a Logic Machine Prototype, in *Workshop on Logic Programming*, S. A. TARNLUND, (ed.), Debrecen, Hungary, July 1980.

726. HARIDI, S. and SAHLIN, D., An Abstract Machine for LPL0, Technical Report TRITA-CS-8302, Royal Institute of Technology, Stockholm, Sweden, 1983.

727. HARIDI, S. and SAHLIN, D., Efficient Implementation of Unification of Cyclic Structures, in *Implementations of Prolog*, J. A. CAMPBELL, (ed.), Ellis Horwood, 1984.

728. HSU, L. S., A Direct Execution Prolog System, *Proceedings of the 1985 ACM Sigsmall Symposium on Small Systems*, Danvers, Massachusetss, May, 1985.

729. HUDAK, P. and BLOSS, A., Avoiding Copying in Functional and Logic Programming Languages, *Symposium on the Principles of Programming Languages*, Los Angeles, 1985.

730. ITO, N., ONAI, R., MASUDA, K. and SHIMIZU, H., Prolog Machine Based on the Data Flow Mechanism, Technical Memorandum TM-0007, ICOT - Institute for New Generation Computer Technology, Tokyo, Japan, 1983.

731. JURKIEWICS, Z., System Prolog na Maszynie CDC/Cyber 72, in *Zastosowanie Maszyn Matematycznych do Badani Nad Jezykiem Naturalnym III*, L. BOLC, (ed.), Wydawnicta Uniwersytetu Warsawkiego, 1980, 273-323. In Polish.

732. KACSUK, P., A Highly Parallel Prolog Interpreter Based on The Generalized Data Flow Model, *Proceedings of the Second International Logic Programming Conference*, S. TARNLUND, ed., Uppsala University, Uppsala, Sweden, July 2-6, 1984, 195-206.

733. KAHN, K. M., Unique Features of Lisp Machine Prolog, *Proceedings of the Prolog Programming Environments Workshop*, Linkoping University, Sweden, 1982.

734. KAHN, K. M., A Pure Prolog Written in Pure Lisp, *Logic Programming Newsletter*, Winter 1983/1984.

735. KAHN, K. M. and CARLSSON, M., The Compilation of Prolog Programs without the Use of a Prolog Compiler, UPMAIL Technical Report 27, Uppsala University, 1984.

736. KAHN, K. M. and CARLSSON, M., How To Implement Prolog On a Lisp Machine, in *Issues In Prolog Implementations*, J. CAMPBELL, (ed.), 1984.

737. KANOUI, H., L'environment De Prolog III, *Actes du Seminaire Programmation En Logique*, M. DINCBAS and M. FEUERSTEIN, eds., February, 1982.

738. KLAHR, P., Planning Techniques for Rule Selection in Deductive Question-answering, in *Pattern Directed Inference Systems*, D. A. WATERMAN and R. HAYES-ROTH, (eds.), Academic Press, 1978, 223-229.

739. KLUZNIAK, F., IIUW-Prolog, *Logic Programming Newsletter*, Spring, 1981.

740. KLUZNIAK, F., Prolog for SM-4, Technical Report, Department of Computer Science, Warsaw University, Poland, 1983.

741. KLUZNIAK, F., The Marseille Interpreter: A Personal Perspective, in *Implementations of Prolog*, J. A. CAMPBELL, (ed.), Ellis Horwood, 1984.

742. KLUZNIAK, F., MATWIN, S. and SZPAKOWICZ, S., Opis Systemu Prolog, Technical Report, Maszynopis Powielony, Warsaw University, Poland, 1979.

743. KLUZNIAK, F. and SZPAKOWICZ, S., Prolog: A Panacea?, in *Implementations of Prolog*, J. A. CAMPBELL, (ed.), Ellis Horwood, 1984.

744. KOMOROWSKI, H. J., A Specification of an Abstract Prolog Machine and its Application to Partial Evaluation, Technical Report, Informatics Lab, Linkopping University, Sweden, 1981.

745. KOMOROWSKI, H. J., Partial Evaluation as a Means for Inferencing Data Structures in an Applicative Language: a Theory and Implementation in the Case of Prolog, *Conference Record of the Ninth Annual ACM Symposium on Principles of Programming Languages*, 1982, 255-268.

746. KOVES, P., A Preliminary User's Manual of Debugging and Trace Subsystem of MProlog Real Multi-Variable Analalytic Functions of Great Complexity, Technical Report SOFTTECH D32, SZAMKI, Hungary, 1979. In Hungarian.

747. KOVES, P., The MProlog Programming Environment: Today and Tomorrow, *Proceedings of the Prolog Programming Environments Workshop*, Linkoping University, Sweden, 1982.

748. LAZINSKI, M., The Prolog Compiler for a CDC 6000 Computer, M.Sc. Thesis, Instytut Informatyki Uniwersytetu Warsaskiego, Warsaw University, 1981. In Polish.

749. LINDSTROM, G. and PANANGDEN, P., Stream-Based Execution of Logic Programming, *Proceedings of the International IEEE Conference on Logic Programming*, Atlantic City, 1984.

750. LLOYD, J. W., Implementing Clause Indexing in Deductive Database Systems, Technical Report 81/4, Department of Computer Science, University of Melbourne, Melbourne, Australia, 1981.

751. LLOYD, J. W. and RAMAMOHANARAO, K., Partial Match Retrieval for Dynamic Files, *BIT 22*, (1983), 150-168.

752. LOWRY, A., TAYLOR, S. and STOLFO, S. J., LPS Algorithms: A Detailed Examination, Technical Report CUCS-112-84, Department of Computer Science, Columbia University, 1984.

753. LOWRY, A., TAYLOR, S. and STOLFO, S. J., LPS Algorithms: A Critical Analysis, Technical Report CUCS-113-84, Columbia University, Department of Computer Science, 1984.

754. LUSK, E. L., MCCUME, W. W. and OVERBEEK, R. A., Logic Machine Architecture: Kernel Functions, in *Lecture Notes in Computer Science 138: 6th Conference on Automated Deduction*, D. W. LOVELAND, (ed.), Springer-Verlag, New York, 1982.

755. LUSK, E. L. and OVERBEEK, R. A., Research Topics: Multiprocessing Algorithms for Computational Logic, Technical Report MCS-TM-31, Mathematical and Computer Science Division, Argonne National Laboratories, 1984.

756. LUSK, E. and OVERBEEK, R. A., Comment Atteindre le Milliard d'Inferences par Seconde, *Intelligence Artificielle et Productique 3*, (November, 1984), 5-7. (in French).

757. MANUEL, T., Artificial Intelligence LISP and Prolog Machines are Proliferating, *Electronics*, November 3, 1983, 132-137.

758. MARTIN, M., Les Nouvelles Possibilites De Prolog/Pascal-Multics, *Actes du Seminaire Programmation En Logique*, M. DINCBAS, ed., March, 1983.

759. MARTIN, M. and JOUBERT, T., Interpreteur De Prolog En Pascal sous Multics, *Actes du Seminaire Programmation En Logique*, M. DINCBAS and M. FEUERSTEIN, eds., February, 1982.

760. MATSUMOTO, Y., NITTA, K. and FURUKAWA, K., Prolog Interpreter and its Parallel Extension, Technical Report, ICOT, Japan, 1982.

761. MATWIN, S. and PIETRZYKOWSKI, T., Exponential improvement of exhaustive backtracking: data structure and implementation, *Proceedings of the 6th Conference on Automated Deduction*, 1982, 240-259.

762. MCCABE, F. G., Tiny Prolog, in *Workshop on Logic Programming*, S. A. TARNLUND, (ed.), Debrecen, Hungary, July 1980.

763. MCCABE, F. G., Abstract Prolog Machine: A Specification, Technical Report, Computer Science Department, Imperial College, London, 1983.

764. MELLISH, C. S., An Alternative to Structure-Sharing in the Implementation of a Prolog interpreter, *Workshop on Logic Programming*, Debrecen, Hungary, 1980. Also in Logic Programming, Clark and Tarnlund, Academic Press, 1982.

765. MELLISH, C. S. and CROSS, M., The UNIX Prolog System, Software Report 5, Department of Artificial Intelligence, University of Edinburgh, 1979.

766. MOORE, J. S., Computational Logic: Structure Sharing and Proof of Program Properties - Parts I and II, Working Paper 67, Department of Artificial Intelligence, University of Edinburgh, 1973.

767. MORRIS, P. H., A Dataflow Interpreter for Logic Programs, in *Workshop on Logic Programming*, S. A. TARNLUND, (ed.), Debrecen, Hungary, July 1980.

768. MOSS, C. D., The comparison of several Prolog systems, *Proceedings of the Logic Programming Workshop*, Debrecen, Hungary, July 14-16, 1980, 198-200.

769. MOSS, C. D., A Comparison of Several Prolog Systems, in *Workshop on Logic Programming*, S. A. TARNLUND, (ed.), Debrecen, Hungary, July 1980.

770. MURAKAMI, K., KAKUTA, T., MIYAZAKI, N., SHIBAYAMA, S. and YOKOTA, H., A Relational Database Machine: First Step to Knowledge Base Machine, Technical Report TR-012, ICOT - Institute for New Generation Computer Technology, Tokyo, Japan, 1983. Also in ACM SIGARCH Newsletter, Vol. 11(3), 1983, pp. 423-425.

771. NAISH, L., Negation and Control in PROLOG, Ph.D. Thesis, Department of Computer Science, University of Melbourne, 1985.

772. NAISH, L., MU-Prolog 3.2db Reference Manual, Internal Memorandum, Department of Computer Science, University of Melbourne, 1985.

773. NAISH, L. and THOM, J. A., The MU-Prolog Deductive Database, Technical Report 83-10, Department of Computer Science, University of Melbourne,Australia, 1983.

774. NAKAGAWA, H., And Parallel Prolog with Divided Assertion Set, *Proceedings of the International IEEE Conference on Logic Programming*, Atlantic City, 1984, 22-28.

775. NAKAMURA, K., Associative Evaluation of Prolog Programs, in *Implementations of Prolog*, J. A. CAMPBELL, (ed.), Ellis Horwood, 1984.

776. NAKASHIMA, H., Prolog/KR User's Manual, Technical Report METR-82-4, Department of Computer Science, University of Tokyo, Japan, 1981.

777. NAKAZAKI, R. and OTHERS, Design of a High-Speed Prolog Machine, *Proceedings of the 12th International Symposium on Computer Architecture*, Boston, June, 1985.

778. NG, P., *An implementation of Waterloo UNIX Prolog*, University of Waterloo, Computer Science Department, 1982. in preparation.

779. NILSSON, J. F., On The Compilation Of Domain-Based Prolog, *Information Processing 83*, R. E. A. MASON, ed., 1983.

780. NILSSON, M., FOOLOG - A Small and Efficient Prolog Interpreter, Technical Report 20, UPMAIL, Computing Science Department, Uppsala University, Sweden, 1983.

781. NILSSON, M., The Importance of Declarative Determinism in Prolog Implementations, UPMAIL Technical Report, Uppsala University, 1983.

782. NILSSON, M., Declarative Determinism in Prolog Implementations, UPMAIL Technical Report 26, Uppsala University, 1984.

783. NILSSON, M., The World's Shortest Prolog Interpreter?, in *Implementations of Prolog*, J. A. CAMPBELL, (ed.), Ellis Horwood, 1984.

784. NISHIKAWA, H., YOKOTA, M., YAMAMOTO, A., TAKI, K. and UCHIDA, S., The Personal Inference Machine (PSI): Its Design Philosophy and Machine Architecture, Technical Report TR-013, ICOT - Institute for New Generation Computer Technology, Tokyo, Japan, 1983. Also in Proceedings of the Logic Programming Workshop, 1983, Algarve, Portugal.

785. OLIVARES, J., Cooperation entre une Machine Prolog et une Base de Donnees Generalisees, Research Report DEA, Laboratoires IMAG, France, 1983.

786. PALMER, M., MCKAY, D. P., NORTON, L. M., HIRSCHMAN, L. and FREEMAN, M. W., Selective Depth-First Search in Prolog, *Proceedings of the First IEEE Conference on Artificial Intelligence Applications*, Denver, Colorado, December, 1984.

787. PERCEBOIS, C. and LARTIGUE, A., Deux Outils Complementaires Pour La Recuperation De La Memoire Dans Les Interpretes Prolog, *Actes du Seminaire Programmation En Logique*, M. DINCBAS, ed., March, 1983.

788. PERCEBOIS, C. and LARTIGUE, A., Deux Outils Complementaires Pour la Recuperation de la Memoire dans les Interpretes Prolog, Technical Report, Universite Paul Sabatier, Toulouse, France, 1984.

789. PERCEBOIS, C. and SANSONNET, J. P., A LISP Machine to Implement Prolog, *Proceedings of the First International Logic Programming Conference*, Marseille, France, 1981.

790. PEREIRA, L. M., A Prolog Demand Driven Computation Interpreter, *Logic Programming Newsletter*, 1982, 6-7. Issue of Winter 82/83.

791. PEREIRA, L. M. and PORTO, A., Intelligent Backtracking and Sidetracking in Horn Clause Programs: The Implementation, Research Report, Departemento de Informatica, Universidade Nova de Lisboa, Portugal, 1979.

792. PEREIRA, L. M. and PORTO, A., Selective backtracking for logic programs, *5th Conference on Automated Deduction*, Les Arcs, France, 1980, 306-317.

793. PEREIRA, L. M. and PORTO, A., An Interpreter of Logic Programs Using Selective Backtracking, Research Report CIUNL No. 9/80, Departemento de Informatica, Universidade Nova de Lisboa, Portugal, 1980. Also in the Proceedings of the Workshop on Logic Programming Debrecen, Hungary July 1980.

794. PEREIRA, L. M. and PORTO, A., A Prolog Implementation of a Large System on a Small Machine, *Proceedings of the First International Logic Programming Conference,* M. VAN CANEGHEM, ed., Marseille, France, 1982.

795. PEREIRA, L. M. and PORTO, A., Selective Backtracking, in *Logic Programming,* K. L. CLARK and S. TARNLUND, (eds.), Academic Press, 1982.

796. PIETRZYKOWSKI, T. and MATWIN, S., Exponential improvement of exhaustive backtracking: a strategy for plan based deduction, *PROC of the 6th CONF on Automated Deduction,* 1982, 223-239.

707. PITTOMBILS, E. and BRUYNOOGHE, M., A Real Time Garbage Collector for Prolog, *Proceedings of the 2nd IEEE International Symposium on Logic Programming,* Boston, USA, July, 1985.

798. POLLARD, G. H., Parallel Execution of Horn Clause Programs, Technical Report, Computer Science Department, Imperial College, London, 1983. Ph.D. Dissertation.

799. RAMAMOHANARAO, K. and LLOYD, J. W., Dynamic Hashing Schemes, *Computer Journal 25,* (1982), 478-485.

800. RAMAMOHANARAO, K., LLOYD, J. W. and THOM, J. A., Partial Match Retrieval using Hash and Descriptors, *ACM Transactions on Database Systems 8,* (1983).

801. ROBERTS, G. M., An Implementation of Prolog, Master's thesis, Dept of Computer Science, University of Waterloo, Canada, 1977.

802. ROUSSEL, P., Prolog: Manuel de Reference et d'Utilisation, Technical Report, Groupe d'Intelligence Artificielle Marseille-Luminy, September, 1975.

803. VAN ROY, P., A Prolog Compiler for the PLM, Technical
      Report UCB/CSD 84/203, Computer Science Division,
      University of California, Berkeley, November 1984.

804. SAMMUT, R. A. and SAMMUT, C. A., The Implementation of
      UNSW-Prolog, *The Australian Computer Journal 15*, 2 (May
      1983).

805. SAWAMURA, J. and TAKESHIMA, T., Recursive Unsolvability of
      Determinacy, Solvable Cases of Determinacy, and Their
      Applications to Prolog Optimization, *Proceedings of the 2nd
      IEEE International Symposium on Logic Programming*, Boston,
      USA, July, 1985.

806. SLOMAN, M., KRAMER, J., MAGEE, J. and SAASAT, S., Towards
      the Compilation of Annotated Logic Programs, Report CCD
      80/15, Imperial College, London, 1980.

807. SMITH, B., Logic Programming on the FFP machine,
      *Proceedings of the International IEEE Conference on Logic
      Programming*, Atlantic City, 1984.

808. SMITH, D. E. and GENESERETH, M. R., Ordering Conjunctive
      Queries, *Artificial Intelligence 26*, (1985), 171-215.

809. SPIVEY, J. M., University of York Portable Prolog System -
      Release 1, Technical Report, Computer Science Department,
      York University, 1982.

810. STOLFO, S. J., Knowledge Engineering: Theory and Practice,
      *IEEE 1983 Proceedings of Trends and Applications in Artificial
      Intelligence*, 1983.

811. SZPAKOWICZ, S. and SZAFRAN, K., The Programmer's Guide to
      IIUW Prolog, Technical Report, Department of Computer
      Science, Warsaw University, 1981. In Polish.

812. TAMURA, N. and KANEDA, Y., Implementing Prolog on a Multiprocessor Machine, *Proceedings of the International IEEE Conference on Logic Programming*, Atlantic City, 1984.

813. TARNLUND, S. A., An Interpreter for the Programming Language Predicate Logic, *Proceedings Fourth International Joint Conference on Artificial Intelligence*, Tblisi, 1975.

814. TAYLOR, S., LOWRY, A., STOLFO, S. J. and MAQUIRE, G., Logic Programming Using Parallel Associative Operations, *Proceedings of the International IEEE Conference on Logic Programming*, Atlantic City, 1984. Also Technical Report, Department of Computer Science, Columbia University, 1982.

815. TAYLOR, S., MAGUIRE, G., LOWRY, A. and STOLFO, S. J., Analyzing Prolog Programs, Technical Report CUCS-117-84, Department of Computer Science, Columbia University, 1984.

816. TAYLOR, S., MAIO, C., STOLFO, S. J. and SHAW, D. E., Prolog on the DADO Machine: A Parallel System for High-Speed Computing, Technical Report, Department of Computer Science, Columbia University, 1983. Also 3rd Annual Phoenix Conference On Computers and Communication,IEEE, March 1984.

817. TAYLOR, S., TZOAR, D. and STOLFO, S. J., Unification in a Parallel Environment, Technical Report CUCS-97-84, Department of Computer Science, Columbia University, 1984.

818. TICK, E., An Overlapped Prolog Processor, Technical Report 308, SRI International, 1983.

819. TICK, E. and WARREN, D. H. D., Towards a Pipelined Prolog Processor, *Proceedings of the International IEEE Conference on Logic Programming*, Atlantic City, 1984.

820. UCHIDA, S., YOKOTA, M., YAMAMOTO, A., TAKI, K. and NISHIKAWA, H., Outline of the Personal Sequential Inference Machine, Technical Memorandum TM-0005, ICOT - Institute for New Generation Computer Technology, Tokyo, Japan, 1983.

821. ULLMAN, J. D., Implementation of Logical Query Languages for Databases, Technical Report STAN-CS-84-1000, Stanford University, 1984.

822. ULLMAN, J. D. and VAN GELDER, A., Testing Applicability of Top Down Capture Rules, Draft Paper, Stanford University, 1985.

823. VENKEN, R., A Debugging System for Prolog, Internal Report, Belgian Institute of Management, Everberg, Belgium, 1984.

824. VENKEN, R., A Prolog Meta-Interpreter For Partial Evaluation And Its Application To Source-to-Source Transformation and Query Optimisation, *Sixth European Conference On Artificial Intelligence*, Pisa, September, 1984.

825. WARREN, D. H. D., Applied Logic - Its Use and Implementation as Programming Tool, Ph.D. thesis, University of Edinburgh, U.K., 1977. Reprinted as Technical Note 290, 1983, Artificial Intelligence Center, SRI International, Menlo Park, California.

826. WARREN, D. H. D., Implementing Prolog - Compiling Predicate Logic Programs., Research Reports 39 & 40, Dept of Artificial Intelligence, University of Edinburgh, 1977.

827. WARREN, D. H. D., How Should Clauses in a Logic Data Base be Indexed, *Proceedings of Workshop on Logic and Databases*, Toulouse, France, 1977.

828. WARREN, D. H. D., Prolog on the DECsystem-10, in *Expert Systems in the Microelectronic Age*, D. MICHIE, (ed.), University of Edinburgh, Scotland, 1979, 153-167.

829. WARREN, D. H. D., An Improved Prolog Implementation which Optimises Tail Recursion, *Workshop on Logic Programming*, Debrecen, Hungary, July 1980. Also available as Technical Report from University of Edinburgh.

830. WARREN, D. H. D., An Abstract Prolog Instruction Set, Technical Report 309, SRI International, 1983.

831. WARREN, D. H. D., PEREIRA, L. M. and PEREIRA, F. C. N., Prolog: The Language and its Implementation Compared with LISP, *Proceedings of the Symposium on Artificial Intelligence and Programming Languages. SIGPLAN/SIGART Notices 12*, 8 (August 1977), 109-115.

832. WARREN, D. S., The Run-Time Environment for a Prolog Compiler, Technical Report TR-82-052, Department of Computer Science, SUNY at Stony Brook, 1983.

833. WARREN, D. S., Efficient Prolog Memory Management for Flexible Control Strategies, *Proceedings of the International IEEE Conference on Logic Programming*, Atlantic City, 1984.

834. WARREN, D. S., The Runtime Environment For A Prolog Compiler Using A Copy Algorithm, Manuscript, Computer Science Department, SUNY at Stony Brook, March, 1984. Revision of TR 83/052.

835. WARREN, D. S., AHAMED, M., DEBRAY, S. and KALE, L. V., Executing Distributed Prolog Programs on a Broadcast Network, Technical Report TR-82-054, Department of Computer Science, SUNY at Stony Brook, 1983. Also in Proceedings of the International IEEE Logic Programming Conference, 1984.

836. WEINER, J. L., The Logical Record Keeper: Prolog on the IBM, *Byte 9*, 9 (1984), 125-131.

837. WISE, M. J. and POWERS, D. M. W., Indexing Prolog Clauses via Superimposed Code Words and Field Encoded Words, *Proceedings of the International IEEE Conference on Logic Programming*, Atlantic City, January, 1984, 203-210.

838. WOO, N., A Hardware Unification Unit: Design and Analysis, *Proceedings of the 12th International Symposium on Computer Architecture*, Boston, June, 1985.

839. YASUURA, H., On Parallel Computational Complexity Of Unification, *International Conference On Fifth Generation Computer Systems*, November 1984. Also, Technical Report TR-0027, ICOT - Institute for New Generation Computer Technology, 1983.

840. YOKOTA, H. and OTHERS, How Can we Combine A Relational Database and a Prolog-Based Inference Mechanism ?, Technical Report TR-031, ICOT - Institute for New Generation Computer Technology, Tokyo, Japan, 1983. In Japanese.

841. YOKOTA, M., YAMAMOTO, A., TAKI, K., NISHIKAWA, H. and UCHIDA, S., The Design and Implementation of the Personal Inference machine: PSI, *New Generation Computing 2*, (1983), Springer Verlag.

CHAPTER 6

Programming Concepts
in Logic Programming

842. AIELLO, L., ATTARDI, G. and PRINI, G., Towards a More Declarative Programming Style, in *Formal Description of Programming Concepts*, J. NEUHOLD, (ed.), North-Holland, New-York, 1978.

843. ALBERT, P., Prolog and Objects, *Proceedings of the Fifth International Workshop on Expert Systems and Their Applications*, Avignon, France, May, 1985.

844. BALOGH, K., Logic Based Program Design, *Proceedings of the First National Conference of the von Neumann Computer Science Society*, Szeged, Hungary, 1979, 36-45. In Hungarian.

845. BERGMAN, M. and DERANSART, P., Abstract Data Types And Rewriting Systems: Application To The Programming Of Algebraic Abstract Data Types In Prolog, *CAAP'81 Trees In Algebra And Programming, 6th Colloqium*, March 1981. Also Lecture Notes in Computer Science no. 112.

846. BOWEN, K. A. and KOWALSKI, R. A., Amalgamating Language and Metalanguage in Logic Programming, in *Logic Programming*, K. L. CLARK and S. TARNLUND, (eds.), Academic Press, New York, 1982, 153-173. A.P.I.C. Studies in Data Processing No. 16 (Also available as Technical Report from Syracuse University).

847. BROUGH, D. R., Loop Trapping in Logic Programs, Technical Report 79-9, Computer Science Department, Imperial College, London, 1979.

848. BRUYNOOGHE, M., Adding Redundancy to Obtain more Reliable and more Readable Prolog Programs, *Proceedings of the First International Logic Programming Conference*, Marseille, France, September, 1982.

849. BUNDY, A. and WELHAM, B., Utility Procedures In Prolog, Occasional Paper 009, Edinburgh University, U.K., 1977.

850. BURSTALL, R. M., Programming with Modules as Typed Functional Programming, *Proceedings of the 1984 Conference on Fifth Generation Computer Systems*, Tokyo, Japan, November, 1984.

851. BYRD, L., Prolog Debugging Facilities, Working Paper, Department of Artificial Intelligence, University of Edinburgh, 1980.

852. BYRD, L., Understanding the Control Flow of Prolog Programs, in *Workshop on Logic Programming*, S. TARNLUND, (ed.), Debrecen, Hungary, July 1980.

853. CARLSSON, M., Constraints for Problem Solving, *Logic Programming Newsletter*, Universidade Nova de Lisboa, Winter 1984.

854. CHABRIER, J., Presentation et Utilisation du Language Prolog, Technical Report (Thesis), Groupe d'Intelligence Artificielle, University de Nancy, France, 1982.

855. CHANG, J. and DESPAIN, A. M., Semi-Intelligent Backtracking of Prolog Based on a Static Data Dependency Analysis, *Proceedings of the 2nd IEEE International Symposium on Logic Programming*, Boston, USA, July, 1985.

856. CHIKAYAMA, T., Unique Features of ESP, *International Conference On Fifth Generation Computer Systems*, November 1984.

857. CHOMICKI, J. and H.MINSKY, N., Towards a Programming Environment for Large Prolog Programs, *Proceedings of the 2nd IEEE International Symposium on Logic Programming*, Boston, USA, July, 1985.

858. CIEPIELEWSKI, A. and HARIDI, S., Execution of Bagof on the Or-Parallel Token Machine, *International Conference On Fifth Generation Computer Systems*, November 1984.

859. CLARK, K. L., The Practice of Logic Programming, in *Infotech State of the Art Report Series 9 No 8*, E. H. BOND, (ed.), Pergamon Infotech Limited, Maidenhead, Bershire, England, 1981, 205-218. Issue on Machine Intelligence.

860. CLARK, K. L., Predicate Logic as a Computational Formalism, Research Report, Imperial College, London, 1983.

861. CLARK, K. L., McKEEMAN, W. M. and SICKEL, S., Logic Program Specification of Numerical Integration, Technical Report 82-3, Computer Science Department, Imperial College, London, 1983.

862. K. L. CLARK and S. A. TARNLUND, eds., *Logic Programming*, Academic Press, 1982. A.P.I.C. Studies in Data Processing No. 16.

863. CLOCKSIN, W. F. and MELLISH, C. S., *Programming in Prolog*, Springer Verlag (2nd Edition), New York, 1984.

864. COELHO, H., Prolog: A Programming Tool for Logical Domain Modelling, *Proceedings of the IFIP/IIASA Working Conference on Processes and Tools for Decision Support*, July, 1982. Also Published in Processes and Tools for Decision Support, H.G. Sol (Editor) by North-Holland, 1982.

865. COELHO, H., COTTA, J. C. and PEREIRA, L. M., How To Solve it with Prolog, Technical Report, Laboratorio Nacional de Engenharia Civil, Lisbon, Portugal, 1980. Collection of examples.

866. COHEN, S., Multi-Version Structures In Prolog, *International Conference On Fifth Generation Computer Systems*, November 1984. Also University of California, Berkeley, Computer Science Division, Technical Report UCB/CSD 84/178.

867. COLMERAUER, A., Prolog without Magic, *Proceedings of the International Joint Conference on Artificial Intelligence*, 1981.

868. COLMERAUER, A., Prolog in 10 Figures, *Proceedings of the International Joint Conference on Artificial Intelligence*, Karlsruhe, Germany, 1983. Also, CNET Working Conference on Logic Programming, Lannion, France, March 1983.

869. COLMERAUER, A., KANOUI, H. and VAN CANEGHEM, M., Prolog, Bases Theoriques et Developpements Actuels, *Techniques et Science Informatiques 2*, 4 (1983).

870. CONERY, J. S., MORRIS, P. H. and KIBLER, D. F., Efficient Logic Programs: A Research Proposal, Technical Report 166, Computer Science Department, University of California, Irvine, 1981.

871. COVINGTON, M. A., Eliminating Unwanted Loops in Prolog, *Sigplan Notices 20*, 1 (January 1985).

872. CREELMAN, P., Improving Prolog Programs, *SIGART Newsletter*, July, 1984.

873. CUNNINGHAM, R. J. and ZAPPACOSTA-AMBOLDI, S., Software Tools for First Order Logic, Technical Report 82-19, Computer Science Department, Imperial College, London, 1982.

874. DAHL, V., Logic Programming as a Representation of Knowledge, *Computer 16*, 10 (October 1983).

875. DARVAS, F., FUTO, I. and CHOLNOKY, E., Practical Applications of an AI Language: Prolog, *Proceeding of the Second Hungarian Computer Science Conference*, Budapest, Hungary, , 388-399. In Hungarian.

876. DAVID, G., Problem Solving = Knowledge + Strategy, *Proceedings of the International Conference on Artificial Intelligence and Information Control Systems of Robots*, 1980.

877. DODSON, D. C. and TECTOR, A. L., LOGAL: Algorithmic Control Structures for Prolog, *Proceedings of the International Joint Conference on Artificial Intelligence*, Karlsruhe, Germany, 1983.

878. DOMOLKI, B. and SZEREDI, P., Prolog in Practice, *Information Processing*, R. E. A. MASON, ed., 1983, 627-636.

879. DONZ, P., FOLL: Une Extension au Langage Prolog, Technical Report, CRISS, Universite des Sciences Sociales, Grenoble, November, 1983.

880. EGGERT, P. R. and SCHORRE, D. V., Logic Enhancement: A Method for Extending Logic Programming Languages, *Proceedings 1982 ACM Symposium on LISP and Functional Programming*, Pittsburgh, PA, 1982, 74-80.

881. EIMERMACHER, M., Eine Progammierumgebung fur Prolog, KIT Report 6, Fachbereich Informatik, Technische Universitat Berlin, 1983.

882. ELCOCK, E. W., Logic and Programming Methodologies, *Workshop on Logic Programming*, Long Beach, Los Angeles, September 1981.

883. ELCOCK, E. W., How Complete are Knowledge-Representation Systems?, *Computer 16*, 10 (October 1983).

884. VAN EMDEN, M. H., McDermott on Prolog: A Rejoinder, *SIGART Newsletter*, 1980.

885. VAN EMDEN, M. H., Warren's Doctrine on the Slash, *Logic Programming Newsletter 4*, (January 1983).

886. ENNALS, J. R., Logic as a Computer Language for Children - Term Two, Technical Report, Imperial College, London, 1981.

887. ENNALS, J. R., Logic as a Computer Language for Children: A One Year Course, Technical Report 81-6, Imperial College, London, 1981.

888. ENNALS, J. R., Children Programs in Prolog, Technical Report 81-8, Computer Science Department, Imperial College, London, 1981.

889. ENNALS, J. R., Prolog can Link Diverse Subjects with Logic and Fun, *Practical Computing*, March 1981.

890. ENNALS, J. R., Teaching Logic as a Computer Language in Schools, *Proceedings of the First International Logic Programming Conference*, M. VAN CANEGHEM, ed., Marseille, France, September 14-17, 1982, 99-104. Also Published in New Horizons in Educational Computing, M. Yazdani (ed), Ellis Horwood, 1984.

891. ENNALS, J. R., *Beginning Micro-Prolog*, Ellis Horwood and Heinemann, Chichester, England, 1983.

892. ENNALS, J. R. and BRIGGS, J. H., Micro-Prolog Across The Curriculum: Collected Papers 1982-84, Doc 84/17, Department of Computing, Imperial College, 1984.

893. ENNALS, J. R., BRIGGS, J. H. and BROUGH, D. R., What The Naive User Wants From Prolog, in *Issues in Prolog Implementation*, J. CAMPBELL, (ed.), Ellis Horwood, 1984.

894. FARKAS, Z., SZEREDI, J. and SANTANE-TOTH, E., LDM - A Program Specification Support System, *Proceedings of the First International Logic Programming Conference*, Marseille, France, September 14-17, 1982.

895. FERGUSON, R. J., Prolog: A Step Towards the Ultimate Computer Language, *Byte*, November 1981, 384-399.

896. FRANCEZ, N., GOLDENBERG, S., PINTER, R., TIOMKIN, M. and TZUR, S., An Environment for Logic Programming, *Proceedings of the ACM Sigplan on Language Issues in Programming Environments*, Seattle, Washington, June 25-28, 1985.

897. FURUKAWA, K., NAKAJIMA, R. and YONEZAWA, A., Modularization and Abstraction in Logic Programming, *New Generation Computing 1*, 2 (1983), Springer Verlag. Also available as Technical Report TR-022 from ICOT - Institute for New Generation Computer Technology Tokyo, Japan.

898. GALLAIRE, H. and LASSERRE, C., A Control Metalanguage for Logic Programming, *Workshop on Logic Programming*, Debrecen, Hungary, 1980, 123-132. Also in Logic Programming, Clark and Tarnlund, Academic Press, 1982.

899. GANZINGER, H. and HANUS, M., Modular Logic Programming of Compilers, *Proceedings of the 2nd IEEE International Symposium on Logic Programming*, Boston, USA, July, 1985.

900. GERGELY, T. and SZOTS, M., Cuttable Formulas for Logic Programming, *Proceedings of the International IEEE Conference on Logic Programming*, Atlantic City, 1984.

901. GLASGOW, J. I., JENKINS, M. A. and MCCROSKY, C. D., User-Defined Parallel Control Strategies, *Proceedings of the 2nd IEEE International Symposium on Logic Programming*, Boston, USA, July, 1985.

902. GOTO, S., DURAL: An Extended Prolog Language, *Lecture Notes in Computer Science*, 1981. Springer Verlag.

903. GOTO, S., DURAL: A Modal Extension of Prolog Language:, *Proceedings of the Prolog Conference*, Tukuba, Japan, 1982. In Japanese.

904. GREENWOOD, S., A Menu-Driven Shell for Use with Any Prolog Program, *Logic Programming Newsletter*, Universidade Nova de Lisboa, Winter 1984.

905. GUIZOL, J. and MELONI, H., Prolog Modulaire, Technical Report, Groupe d'Intelligence Artificielle, Universite d'Aix-Marseille II Marseille, France, 1976.

906. GUTIERREZ, C., Prolog Compared with LISP, *ACM Symposium on LISP and Functional Programming*, 1982.

907. HANSSON, A. and TARNLUND, S. A., Program Transformation by a Function that Maps Simple Lists into D-Lists, in *Workshop on Logic Programming*, S. A. TARNLUND, (ed.), Debrecen, Hungary, July 1980.

908. HANSSON, A. and TARNLUND, S. A., Program Transformation by Data Structure Mapping, in *Logic Programming*, K. L. CLARK and S. A. TARNLUND, (eds.), Academic Press, New York, 1982. A.P.I.C. Studies in Data Processing No. 16.

909. HAWLEY, R., Turtledove,Hurtle and Prolog, *AISB Easter Conference on Artificial Intelligence and Education*, University of Exeter,U.K., April 1983.

910. HECK, N. and AVENHAUS, J., Automatic Implementation Of Abstract Data Types Specified By The Logic Programming Language, *International Conference On Fifth Generation Computer Systems*, November 1984.

911. HOGGER, C. J., Derivation of Logic Programs, Technical Report, University of London, 1979. Ph.D. Dissertation.

912. HOGGER, C. J., Derivation of Logic Programs, *Journal of the ACM 28*, 2 (April 1981), 372-392.

913. HSIANG, J. and SRIVAS, M., A Prolog Environment for Developing and Reasoning about Data Types, Technical Report 84/074, State University of New York, Stony Brook, 1984.

914. INCE, D. C., Module Interconnection Languages and Prolog, *ACM SIGPLAN Notices 19*, 8 (August, 1984).

915. JONES, S., Structured Programming Techniques in Prolog, in *Workshop on Logic Programming*, S. A. TARNLUND, (ed.), Debrecen, Hungary, July 1980.

916. KAHN, K. M., Experiences in Transporting Concurrent Prolog and the Bagel Simulator to LM-PROLOG - Part I of a Report of a Visit to ICOT November 1983, *Draft Paper*, 1984.

917. KAHN, K. M., Partial Evaluation, Programming Methodology, and Artificial Intelligence, *The AI Magazine 5*, 1 (Spring 1984).

918. KAPOSI, A. A. and MARKUSZ, Z. S., Primlog: A Case of Augmented Prolog Programming, *Proceedings of Informatica 79*, Bled, Yougouslavia, 1979.

919. KLUZNIAK, F., Remarks On Coroutine in Prolog, IInf UW Report nr.105, University of Warsaw, 1981.

920. KLUZNIAK, F., Prolog For Programmers, Technical Report IInf UW 104, Department of Computer Science, University of Warsaw, 1981.

921. KLUZNIAK, F. and SZPAKOWICZ, S., A Note on Teaching Prolog, in *Workshop on Logic Programming*, S. TARNLUND, (ed.), Debrecen, Hungary, July 1980.

922. KLUZNIAK, F. and SZPAKOWICZ, S., *Prolog for Programmers*, Academic Press, 1985.

923. KOMOROWSKI, H. J. and OMORI, S., Logic Programming Engineering Shell, *Proceedings of the ACM Sigplan on Language Issues in Programming Environments*, Seattle, Washington, June 25-28, 1985.

924. KOVES, P., The MProlog Programming Environment: Today and Tomorrow, *Proceedings of the Prolog Programming Environments Workshop*, Linkoping University, Sweden, 1982.

925. KOVES, P. and SZEREDI, P., A Programming Support Environment for Prolog Program Development, *Proceedings Logic Programming Workshop*, Long Beach, CA, September 1981.

926. KOWALSKI, R. A., *Logic for Problem Solving*, Elsevier North-Holland, New-York, 1979.

927. KOWALSKI, R. A., Prolog as a Logic Programming Language, Technical Report 81-26, Computer Science Department, Imperial College, London, 1981. Presented at the AICA Congress, Pavia, Italy, 1981.

928. KOWALSKI, R. A., Logic as a Computer Language for Children, Technical Report 82-23, Computer Science Department, Imperial College, London, 1982. Also Published in New Horizons in Educational Computing, M. Yazdani (ed), Ellis Horwood, 1984.

929. KOWALSKI, R. A., Logic as a Computer Language, in *Logic Programming*, K. L. CLARK and S. TARNLUND, (eds.), Academic Press, New York, 1982. A.P.I.C. Studies in Data Processing No. 16 (Also available as Technical Report from Imperial College, London).

930. KOWALSKI, R. A., Logic Programming, *Proceedings of the IFIP-83 Congress*, Amsterdam, 1983, 133-145.

931. KOWALSKI, R. A., AI and Software Engineering, *Datamation*, November, 1984.

932. KOWALSKI, R. A. and SERGOT, M. J., Micro-Prolog For Problem Solving, in *Micro-Prolog: Programming In Logic*, K. L. CLARK and S. A. TARNLUND, (eds.), Prentice Hall, 1984.

933. KURUKAWA, T., Logic Programming: What Does It Bring To Software Engineering ?, *Proceedings of the First International Logic Programming Conference*, Marseille, France, September, 1982.

934. LEE, R. M., Applications Software and Organizational Change: Issues in the Representation of Knowledge, *Information Systems 8*, 3 (1983), 187-194.

935. LENGAUER, C., A Short Note on Predicative Programming: Global and Local Chaos, Technical Report 84-06, Department of Computer Science, University of Texas, Austin, 1984.

936. LICHTMAN, B. M., Features of Very High Level Programming with Prolog, Technical Report, M.S. Thesis, Department of Computing and Control, Imperial College, London, 1975.

937. LLOYD, J. W. and TOPOR, R. W., Making Prolog More Expressive, Technical Report 84/8, Department Of Computer Science, University Of Melbourne, 1984. To appear in the Journal of Logic Programming, 1984.

938. MAIBAUM, T. S. and VELOSO, P. A. S., A Logical Theory of Data Types Motivated by Programming, Technical Report 81-28, Computer Science Department, Imperial College, London, 1981.

939. MANNA, Z. and WALDINGER, R., A deductive approach to program synthesis, *ACM TOPLAS 2*, 1 (January 1980), 92-121.

940. MANNA, Z. and WALDINGER, R., Special Relations in Program-synthetic Deduction, *Logic and Computation Proceedings of a Conference 1*, J. N. CROSSLEY and J. JAFFAR, eds., (1983).

941. MARKUSZ, Z. S. and KAPOSI, A. A., A Design Methodology in Prolog Programming, *Proceedings of the First International Logic Programming Conference*, Marseille, France, 1981.

942. MCCABE, F. G. and GREGORY, S., Getting Started with IC-Prolog, Technical Report 81-29, Computer Science Department, Imperial College, London, 1981.

943. MCDERMOTT, D. V., The Prolog Phenomenon, *SIGART Newsletter*, July 1980, 16-20.

944. MELLISH, C. S., Automatic Generation of Mode Declarations in Prolog Programs, *Workshop on Logic Programming*, Long Beach, Los Angeles, September 1981.

945. MELONI, H., Prolog - Mise en Route de l'Interpreteur et Exercices, Technical Report, Groupe d'Intelligence Artificielle, Universite d'Aix-Marseille II Marseille, France, 1976.

946. MIZOGUCHI, F., A Software Environment for Developing Knowledge-Based Systems, in *Computer Science and Technologies: 1982*, T. KITAGAWA, (ed.), Elsevier North-Holland, New-York, 1982, 334-349.

947. Moss, C., Declarative Input/Output in Prolog, Technical
     Report, Department of Computer Science, University of
     Pennsylvania, 1984.

948. MYCROFT, A. and O'KEEFE, R. A., A Polymorphic Type
     System for Prolog, *Proceedings of Logic Programming
     Workshop*, Universidade Nova de Lisboa, Portugal, 1983. Also
     Research Paper 211, Department of Artificial Intelligence,
     University of Edinburgh.

949. NAISH, L., An Introduction to MU-Prolog, Technical Report 82-
     2, Department of Computer Science, University of Melbourne,
     1982. Revised in 1983.

950. NAISH, L., Automatic Generation of Control for Logic
     Programs, Technical Report 83-6, Department of Computer
     Science, University of Melbourne, 1983.

951. NAISH, L., All Solutions Predicate In Prolog, Technical Report
     84/4, Department of Computer Science, University of
     Melbourne, 1984.

952. NAISH, L., Prolog Control Rules, Technical Report 84/13,
     Department of Computer Science, University of Melbourne,
     1984. Also in International Joint Conference on Artificial
     Intelligence 1985.

953. NAISH, L., Automating Control for Logic Programs, *The
     Journal of Logic Programming (To appear)*, 1985.

954. NAKASHIMA, H., UEDA, K. and TOMURA, S., What Is A Variable
     In Prolog?, *International Conference On Fifth Generation
     Computer Systems*, November 1984.

955. O'KEEFE, R. A., A Smooth Applicative Merge Sort, DAI
     Research Paper No. 182, Department of Artificial Intelligence,
     University of Edinburgh, 1982.

956. O'KEEFE, R. A., Programming Meta-logical Operations in Prolog, Working Paper 142, Department of Artificial Intelligence, University of Edinburgh, June, 1983.

957. O'KEEFE, R. A., Updatable Arrays in Prolog, Working Paper 150, Department of Artificial Intelligence, University of Edinburgh, August, 1983.

958. O'KEEFE, R. A., Classification: A Worked Exercise in Prolog, Working Paper 150, Department of Artificial Intelligence, University of Edinburgh, August, 1983.

959. O'KEEFE, R. A., Concept Formation With Numeric Attributes, Working Paper 154, Department of Artificial Intelligence, University of Edinburgh, August, 1983.

960. O'KEEFE, R. A., Reading Sentences In Prolog, Working Paper 159, Department of Artificial Intelligence, University of Edinburgh, January, 1984.

961. O'KEEFE, R. A., On the Treatment of Cuts in Prolog Source-Level Tools, *Proceedings of the 2nd IEEE International Symposium on Logic Programming*, Boston, USA, July, 1985.

962. ONAI, R., MASUDA, K. and ASOU, M., Static Analyzer of Sequential Prolog Program, Technical Report TR-032, ICOT - Institute for New Generation Computer Technology, Tokyo, Japan, 1983. In Japanese.

963. PEREIRA, F. C. N., Can Drawing Be Liberated from the von Neumann Style, *Proceedings of 1983 ACM Database Week*, 1983.

964. PEREIRA, L. M., Rational Debugging of Logic Programs, Technical Report, Department of Computer Science, Universidade Nova de Lisboa, Lisbon, Portugal, 1984.

965. PEREIRA, L. M. and PORTO, A., All Solutions, *Logic Programming Newsletter No. 2*, 1981. Autumn.

966. PEREIRA, L. M. and PORTO, A., A Prolog Implementation of a Large System on a Small Machine, *Proceedings of the First International Logic Programming Conference*, M. VAN CANEGHEM, ed., Marseille, France, 1982.

967. PEREIRA, L. M. and PORTO, A., Selective Backtracking, in *Logic Programming*, K. L. CLARK and S. TARNLUND, (eds.), Academic Press, New York, 1982. Also available as Technical Report from University of Lisbon and was also published in Lecture Notes in Computer Science no 87, Springer Verlag,1981.

968. PORTO, A., Two-Level Prolog, *International Conference On Fifth Generation Computer Systems*, November 1984.

969. POWERS, D. M. W., Playing Mastermind more Logically Or Writing Prolog more Efficiently, *SIGART*, July, 1984, 15-18.

970. POWERS, D. M. W., Prolog - Not just another programming language, *Electronics Today International (Australia)*, R. HARRISON, ed., July 1984, 73-76.

971. POWERS, D. M. W., Prolog - Goto considered impossible, *Electronics Today International (Australia)*, R. HARRISON, ed., August 1984, 127-130.

972. POWERS, D. M. W., Prolog - The wood for the trees, *Electronics Today International (Australia)*, R. HARRISON, ed., September 1984, 132-136.

973. POWERS, D. M. W. and MCMAHON, G. B., A Compendium of interesting Prolog programmes, DCS Report 8313, University of New South Wales, December 1983 .

974. ROBINSON, J. A., Problems and Trends for the Future of Logic Programming, in *Introductory Readings in Expert Systems*, D. MICHIE, (ed.), Gordon and Breach, New York, 1982, 81-92.

975. ROBINSON, J. A., Logic Programming: Past, Present and Future, *New Generation Computing 2*, (1983), Springer Verlag. Also available as ICOT Technical Report TR-015.

976. SCHNUPP, P., Prolog as Spezifikations- und Modelierungswerkzeug, in *Requirements Engineering - Arbeitstagung der GI*, G. H. D. KRONIG, (ed.), Springer-Verlag, Informatik-Fackberichte 74, Berlin, 1983, 173-182.

977. SCHULTZ, J. W., The Use Of First-order Predicate Calculus As A Logic Programming System, M.Sc Thesis, Department Of Computer Science, University Of Melbourne, 1984.

978. SEBELIK, J. and STEFANEK, P., Graphs as Data in Prolog Programs, *Proceedings of the First International Logic Programming Conference*, Marseille, France, 1981.

979. SHAPIRO, E. Y., Methodology of Prolog Programming, *Proceedings of Workshop on Logic Programming*, Algarve, Portugal, 1983.

980. SHMUELI, O., TSUR, S. and ZFIRAH, H., Rule Support in Prolog, *Proceedings of the First International Workshop on Expert Database Systems*, Kiawah Island, South Carolina, October 24-·27, 1984.

981. SHOHAM, Y. and MCDERMOTT, D. V., Knowledge Inversion, *Proceedings of the Conference of the American Association for Artificial Intelligence*, Austin, Texas, 1984, 295-299. AAAI-84.

⌐82. SHOHAM, Y. and MCDERMOTT, D. V., Directed Relations And The Inversion Of Prolog Programs, *International Conference On Fifth Generation Computer Systems*, November 1984.

983. SICKEL, S. and MCKEEMAN, W. M., Hoare's FIND Revisited, in *Workshop on Logic Programming*, S. A. TARNLUND, (ed.), Debrecen, Hungary, July 1980.

984. SMOLKA, G., Making Control and Data Flow of Logic Programs More Explicit, *Proceedings of the 1984 ACM Symposium on LISP and Functional Programming*, Austin, Texas, August, 1984.

985. SZENES, K., An Application of A Parallel Systems Planning Language In Decision Support - Production Scheduling, in *Advances In Production Management Systems*, IFIP WG 5.7 Working Conference on Advances in Production Management Systems-APMS 82, G. DOUMEINGTS and W. A. CARTER, (eds.), North Holland Publishing Company, 1982.

986. SZEREDI, J., Mixed Language Programming: A Method for Producing Efficient Prolog Programs, *Proceedings Logic Programming Workshop*, Long Beach, CA, September 1981. Also available from SZKI as Collection Of Logic Programming Papers.

987. SZEREDI, J., Module Concepts for Prolog, *Proceedings of the Prolog Programming Environments Workshop*, Linkoping University, Sweden, 1982.

988. SZEREDI, J., BALOGH, K., SANTANE-TOTH, E. and FARKAS, Z., LDM - A Logic Based Software Development Method, in *Workshop on Logic Programming*, S. A. TARNLUND, (ed.), Debrecen, Hungary, July 1980.

989. SZOTS, M., A Comparison of Two Logic Programming Languages: A Case Study, *Proceedings of the Second International Logic Programming Conference*, S. A. TARNLUND, ed., Uppsala University, Uppsala, Sweden, July 2-6, 1984, 41-52.

990. SZPAKOWICZ, S. and SWIDZINSKI, M., A Case-Study in Prolog Programming - Railway Guide, *Informatyka XIV*, 12 (1979). In Polish.

991. TARNLUND, S. A., Programming as a Deductive Method, Technical Report TRITA-IBABB-1031, Computer Science Department, Royal Institute of Technology, University of Stockholm, 1976.

992. UEDA, K. and CHIKAYAMA, T., Efficient Stream/Array Processing In Logic Programming Language, *International Conference On Fifth Generation Computer Systems*, November 1984.

993. UMRIGAR, Z. D. and PITCHUMANI, V., An Experiment in Programming with Full First-Order Logic, *Proceedings of the 2nd IEEE International Symposium on Logic Programming*, Boston, USA, July, 1985.

994. VATAJA, P. and UKKONEN, E., Finding Temporary Terms In Prolog Programs, *International Conference On Fifth Generation Computer Systems*, November 1984.

995. VENKEN, R., A Debugging System for Prolog, Internal Report, Belgian Institute of Management, Everberg, Belgium, 1984.

996. VODA, P. J. and YU, B., RF-Maple: A Logic Programming Language with Functions, Types and Concurrency, *International Conference On Fifth Generation Computer Systems*, November 1984.

997. WARREN, D. H. D., A View of the Fifth Generation and its Impact, Research Report, SRI International, Menlo Park, 1982. Also in Artificial Intelligence Magazine, Fall 1982.

998. WARREN, D. H. D., Higher-Order Extensions to Prolog: Are They Needed ?, *Machine Intelligence*, 1982.

999. WELHAM, R., Solving Problems in Prolog, *Computer Age*, August, 1980.

1000. YOKOMORI, T., A Note On The Set Abstraction In Logic Programming Language, *International Conference On Fifth Generation Computer Systems*, November 1984.

1001. ZANIOLO, C., Object-Oriented Programming in Prolog, Technical Report TR-83-04, Bell Laboratories, Holmdel, 1983. Also in Proceedings of the International IEEE Logic Programming Conference, 1984.

CHAPTER 7

Alternatives to Prolog as a Logic Programming Language

1002. ABRAMSON, H., A Prological Definition of HASL a Purely Functional Language with Unification Based Conditional Binding Expressions, *New Generation Computing 2*, 1 (1984).

1003. ALLEN, J. F., FRISCH, A. M. and GUILIANO, M., The HORNE Reasoning System, Technical Report TR-126, Computer Science Department, University of Rochester, 1984.

1004. ALPS, R. A. and NEVELN, R. C., A predicate logic based on indefinite description and two notions of identity, *Notre Dame Journal of Formal Logic 22*, 3 (1981), 251-263.

1005. ATTARDI, G. and SIMI, M., Consistency and Completeness of OMEGA, a Logic for Knowledge Representation, *Proceedings of the Seventh International Joint Conference on Artificial Intelligence*, Vancouver, Canada, 1981.

1006. BALDWIN, J. F. and ZHOU, S. Q., A fuzzy relational inference language, *Fuzzy Sets and Systems 14*, 2 (1984), 155-174.

1007. BANDES, R. G., Constraining-Unification and the Programming Language Unicorn, *POPL*, Salt Lake City, Utah, January, 1984.

1008. BARBUTI, R., BELLIA, M., LEVI, G. and MARTELLI, M., On the Integration of Logic Programming and Functional Programming, *Proceedings of the International IEEE Conference on Logic Programming*, Atlantic City, 1984.

1009. BARBUTI, R., BELLIA, M., LEVI, G. and MARTELLI, M., LEAF: a language which integrates logic, equations and functions, in *Functional Programming and Logic Programming*, D. DEGROOT and G. LINDSTROM, (eds.), Prentice Hall, June 1985.

1010. BELLIA, M., DEGANO, P. and LEVI, G., A Functional plus Predicate Logic Programming Language, *Workshop on Logic Programming*, Debrecen, Hungary, July 1980.

1011. BLACK, F., A Deductive Question-answering System, in *Semantic Information Processing*, M. MINSKY, (ed.), MIT Press, Cambridge, 1968.

1012. BOLEY, H., Artificial Intelligence Language and Machines, Technical Report IFI-HH-B-94-82, University of Hamburg, Germany, 1982. Also published in Technology and Science of Informatics,2(3), June, 1983.

1013. BOLEY, H., FIT - Prolog: A Functional/Relational Language Comparison, Technical Report SEKI-83-14, University of Kaiserslautern, Germany, 1983.

1014. BORGAULT, S., DINCBAS, M. and FEUERSTEIN, D., LISLOG: L'an II, *Actes du Seminaire Programmation En Logique*, M. DINCBAS, ed., March, 1983.

1015. BOURGAULT, S., DINCBAS, M. and FEUERSTEIN, D., LISLOG 1.1, Note Technique NT-LAA-SLC-89, CNET, Lannion, France, 1982.

1016. BOURGAULT, S., DINCBAS, M., FEUERSTEIN, D. and PAPE, J. P. L., LISLOG: L'an II, *CNET*, Lannion, France, 1984.

1017. BOURGAULT, S., DINCBAS, M. and LE PAPE, J. P., LISLOG: Programmation En Prolog En Environnement Lisp, *4eme Congres Reconnaissance Des Formes Et Intelligence Artificielle*, January, 1984.

1018. BOWEN, K. A., Programming with Full First-Order Logic, *Presented at Workshop on Logic Programming for Intelligent Systems*, Long Beach, California, 1982. Published in Machine Intelligence 10, 1982, 421-440.

1019. BRODA, K. and GREGORY, S., Parlog for Discrete Event Simulation, *Proceedings of the Second International Logic Programming Conference*, S. TARNLUND, ed., Uppsala University, Uppsala, Sweden, July 2-6, 1984, 301-312.

1020. BURSTALL, R. M., MACQUEEN, D. B. and SOMMELLA, D. T., HOPE: An Experimental Applicative Language, *Proceedings of the LISP Conference*, University of Stanford, 1980.

1021. CARLSSON, M., (Re)Implementing Prolog in LISP or YAQ - Yet Another QLISP, Technical Report, Computer Science Department, Uppsala University, 1982.

1022. CARLSSON, M., LM-Prolog: The Language and Its Implementation, UPMAIL Technical Report 30, Uppsala University, 1984.

1023. CARLSSON, M. and KAHN, K. M., LM-Prolog User Manual, UPMAIL Technical Report 24, Computer Science Department, Uppsala University, 1983.

1024. CARRE, F. and SALLE, P., Acteurs Et Programmation En Logique, *Actes du Seminaire Programmation En Logique*, M. DINCBAS, ed., March, 1983.

1025. CARTWRIGHT, R. and MCCARTHY, J., First Order Programming Logic, in *6th POPL*, 1979, 68-80.

1026. CHESTER, D., Using HCPRVR, Technical Report, Department of Computer Science, University of Texas, Austin, 1980.

1027. CHESTER, D. L., HCPRVR: A Logic Program Interpreter in LISP, *Proceedings of the First Annual National Conference on Artificial Intelligence*, 1980.

1028. CHIKAYAMA, T., ESP - Extended Self-Contained Prolog as a Preliminary Kernel Language of Fifth Generation Computers, *New Generation Computing 1*, (1983), Springer Verlag.

1029. CHIKAYAMA, T., ESP as Preliminary Kernel Language of Fifth Generation Computers, Technical Report TR-005, ICOT - Institute for New Generation Computer Technology, Tokyo, Japan, 1983.

1030. CHIKAYAMA, T., ESP reference manual, ICOT TR-044, February, 1984.

1031. CHIKAYAMA, T., Unique Features of ESP, *International Conference On Fifth Generation Computer Systems*, November 1984.

1032. CLARK, K. L. and GREGORY, S., Notes On Systems Programming In PARLOG, *International Conference On Fifth Generation Computer Systems*, November 1984.

1033. COHEN, S., The APPLOG Language: Prolog vs. LISP -- If you Can't Fight them Join them, Technical Report UCB/CSD 84/179, Computer Science Division, University of California, Berkeley,, May 1984.

1034. COX, P. T., Advanced Programming Aids in PROGRAPH, *Proceedings of the 1985 ACM Sigsmall Symposium on Small Systems*, Danvers, Massachusetss, May, 1985.

1035. COX, P. T., Compiling the Graphical Functional Language PROGRAPH, *Proceedings of the 1985 ACM Sigsmall Symposium on Small Systems*, Danvers, Massachusetss, May, 1985.

1036. Cox, P. T. and PIERTRZYKOWSKI, T., Surface Deduction: a uniform mechanism for logic programming, Technical Report 8405, School of Computer Science, Technical University of Nova Scotia, October 1984.

1037. DARLINGTON, J. and BURSTALL, R. M., A transformational system for developing recursive programs, *JACM 29*, 1982.

1038. DEBENHAM, J. K. and MCGRATH, G. M., LOFE: A Language for Virtual Relational Databases, *The Australian Computer Journal 15*, 3 (1983), 2-9.

1039. *Functional Programming and Logic Programming*, D. DEGROOT and G. LINDSTROM, (eds.), Prentice Hall, June 1985.

1040. DERSHOWITZ, N. and JOSEPHSON, N. A., Logic Programming by Completion, *Proceedings of the Second International Logic Programming Conference*, S. A. TARNLUND, ed., Uppsala University, Uppsala, Sweden, July 2-6, 1984, 313-320.

1041. DINCBAS, M. and LE PAPE, J. P., Nouvelle Implementation De Metalog, *Actes du Seminaire Programmation En Logique*, M. DINCBAS, ed., March, 1983.

1042. DINCBAS, M. and LE PAPE, J. P., Metacontrol of Logic Programs in METALOG, *International Conference On Fifth Generation Computer Systems*, November 1984.

1043. ELCOCK, E. W. and OTHERS, ABSET: a Programming Language Based on Sets, in *Machine Intelligence 6*, D. MICHIE, (ed.), 1971.

1044. FOSTER, A. and ELCOCK, E. W., Absys1: An Incremental Compiler for Assertions: An Introduction, in *Machine Intelligence 4*, B. MELTZER and D. MITCHIE, (eds.), Edinburgh University Press, 1969.

1045. FRISCH, A. M., ALLEN, J. F. and GUILIANO, M., An Overview of the HORNE Logic Programming System, Technical Report, Computer Science Department, University of Rochester, 1982.

1046. FURBACH, U. and HOLLDOBLER, S., The Combination of Functional and Logic Programming Languages, Technical Report 84-09, Hochschule des Bundeswehr, Munchen, 1984.

1047. GABBAY, D. M. and REYLE, U., N-Prolog: An Extension of Prolog with Hypothetical Implications.I., *The Journal of Logic Programming 1*, 4 (December, 1984).

1048. GABBAY, D. and REYLE, U., New-Prolog! An Extension Of PROLOG With Causal Implications, Doc Report 84/2, Department of Computing, Imperial College, 1984.

1049. GALLIER, J. H., HORNLOG: A First-Order Theorem Prover for Negations of Horn Clauses Based on Graph-Rewriting, Technical Report, Department of Computer Science, University of Pennsylvania, 1984.

1050. GERGELY, T. and SZOTS, M., Some Features of A New Logic Programming Language, *Workshop and Conference on Applied AI and Knowledge-Based Expert Systems*, Stockholm, November, 1984.

1051. GIBSON, J., POP-11 : An AI Programming Language, in *New Horizons in Educational Programming*, M. YAZDANI, (ed.), Ellis Horwood, 1984.

1052. GLASGOW, J. I., Logic Programming in NIAL, Technical Report 84-158, Department of Computer Science, Queen's University, 1984.

1053. GOTO, S., DURAL: An Extended Prolog Language, *Lecture Notes in Computer Science*, 1981. Springer Verlag.

1054. GOTO, S., DURAL: A Modal Extension of Prolog Language:, *Proceedings of the Prolog Conference*, Tukuba, Japan, 1982. In Japanese.

1055. GREEN, C. C., Theorem proving by resolution as a basis for question-answering systems, in *Machine Intelligence*, vol. 4, B. MELTZER and D. MICHIE, (eds.), American Elsevier, New York, 1969, 183-205.

1056. GREUSSAY, P., Un Mariage Heureux Entre LISP et Prolog: Le Systeme LOVLISP, *Actes du Seminaire Programmation En Logique*, M. DINCBAS, ed., March, 1983.

1057. GREUSSAY, P., LOVLISP: Une Extension de VLISP vers Prolog, Technical Report, Universite de Paris 8, France, 1984.

1058. HANSSON, A., HARIDI, S. and TARNLUND, S. A., Language Features of LPL, A Logic Programming Language, Technical Report RITA-CS-8103, Department of Telecommunication and Computer Systems, The Royal Institute of Technology, Stockholm, August, 1981.

1059. HANSSON, A. and TARNLUND, S. A., A Natural Programming Calculus, *Proceedings Sixth Joint Conference on Artificial Intelligence*, 1979.

1060. HANSSON, A. and TARNLUND, S. A., Program Transformation by a Function that Maps Simple Lists into D-Lists, in *Workshop on Logic Programming*, S. A. TARNLUND, (ed.), Debrecen, Hungary, July 1980.

1061. HARDY, S., A New Software Environment for List Processing and Logic Programming, in *Artificial Intelligence: Tools, Techniques and Applications*, T. O'SHEA and A. M. EISENSTADT, (eds.), Harper and Row, New York, 1984.

1062. HARDY, S. and SLOMAN, A., POPLOG: A Multi-User, Multi-Language Program Development Environment, Technical Report, Computer Science Department, University of Sussex, 1982.

1063. HOARE, C. A. R. and ROSCOE, A. W., Programs As Executable Predicates, *International Conference On Fifth Generation Computer Systems*, November 1984.

1064. HORSTER, P. J., Complete Reduction Systems, *Proceedings of GWAI 83*, Dassel, Germany, 1983. Informatik-Fachbericht series.

1065. HUAI-MIN, S. and LI-GUO, W., A Model Theory of Programming Logic, *Internal Note, Beijing Institute of Aeronautics and Astronautics*, Beijing, China, 1983.

1066. KAHN, K. M., Uniform: A Language Based Upon Unification Which Unifies Much of LISP, Prolog and Act 1, *Proceedings of the Seventh International Joint Conference on Artificial Intelligence*, Vancouver, Canada, 1981.

1067. KAHN, K. M., The Implementation of Uniform: A Knowledge-Representation and Programming Language Based upon Equivalence of Descriptions, UPMAIL Technical Report 9, Uppsala University, 1982.

1068. KELLOG, C., Logic Programming in DADM, Technical Report, System Development Corporation, Santa Monica, 1981.

1069. KOMOROWSKI, H. J., The QLOG Interactive Environment, Technical Report LITH-MAR-R-79-19, Informatics Lab, Linkopping University, Sweden, 1979.

1070. KOMOROWSKI, H. J., QLOG - The Software for Prolog and Logic Programming, in *Workshop on Logic Programming*, S. TARNLUND, (ed.), Debrecen, Hungary, July 1980.

1071. KOMOROWSKI, H. J., Embedding Prolog in LISP: an example of a LISP craft technique, LITH-MATH-R-1981-2, Linkoping University, Informatics Laboratory, Linkoping, Sweden, March, 1981.

1072. KOMOROWSKI, H. J., QLOG - The Programming Environment for Prolog in LISP, in *Logic Programming*, K. L. CLARK and S. A. TARNLUND, (eds.), Academic Press, New York, 1982. A.P.I.C. Studies in Data Processing No. 16.

1073. KONAGAYA, A. and UNEMURA, M., Knowledge Information Processing Language: Shapeup, Technical Report, NEC Corporation, Japan, 1983.

1074. KORNFELD, W. A., Equality for Prolog, *Proceedings of the International Joint Conference on Artificial Intelligence*, Karlsruhe, Germany, 1983.

1075. KOWLASKI, R., A Proof Procedure using Connection Graphs, *Journal of the ACM 22*, 4 (October 1975).

1076. KUNIFUJI, S. and OTHERS, Conceptual Specification of the Fifth Generation Kernel Language Version 1 (preliminary draft), ICOT Technical Memorandum, 1983.

1077. LAPALME, G. and CHAPLEAU, S., Logicon: An Integration of Prolog into Icon, Technical Report 516, Departement d'Informatique et de Recherche Operationnelle., Universite de Montreal. , 1984.

1078. LUSK, E. L. and OVERBEEK, R. A., Experiments With Resolution-based Theorem-proving Algorithms, *Computers and Mathematics with Applications 8*, 3 (1982), 141-152.

1079. LUSK, E. L. and OVERBEEK, R. A., An LMA-based Theorem Prover, ANL-82-75, Argonne National Laboratory, December, 1982.

1080. LUSK, E. L. and OVERBEEK, R. A., A Portable Environment for Research in Automated Reasoning, in *Proceedings of the 7th International Conference on Automated Deduction*, R. SHOSTAK, (ed.), Springer-Verlag, 1984, 43-52.

1081. MAIBAUM, T. S. and SADLER, M. R., Logical Specification And Implementation, *Fourth Conference On The Foundations Of Software Technology And Theoretical Computer Science*, December, 1984.

1082. MALACHI, Y., MANNA, Z. and WALDINGER, R., TABLOG: The Deductive-Tableau Programming Language, *ACM Symposium on Lisp and Functional Programming*, 1984.

1083. McCABE, F. G., Lambda Prolog, *Proceedings of the Logic Programming Workshop*, Algarve, Portugal, 1983.

1084. McCORD, M. C., LP: A Prolog Interpreter written in LISP, Technical Report TR-85-82, University of Kentucky, 1982.

1085. McROBBIE, M. A., MEYER, R. K. and THISTLEWAITE, P. B., Computer-aided Investigations into the Decision Problem For Relevant Logics: The Search for a Free Associative Connective, Department of Philosophy Preprint 4/82, University of Melbourne, December 1982. Also appeared in the Proceedings of the 6th Australian Computer Science Conference.

1086. MELLISH, C. S. and HARDY, S., Integrating Prolog into the POPLOG Environment, *Proceedings of the International Joint Conference on Artificial Intelligence*, Karlsruhe, Germany, 1983.

1087. MERRET, T. H., The Relational Algebra as a Typed Language for Logic Programming, *Proceedings of the First International Workshop on Expert Database Systems*, Kiawah Island, South Carolina, October 24-27, 1984. Also Technical Report, Department of Computer Science, McGill University, Canada, 1984.

1088. MINKER, J., A Set-Oriented Predicate Logic Programming Language, Technical Report, Computer Science Department, University of Maryland, 1975. Also Published in Proceedings Logic Programming Workshop, Debrecen, 1981.

1089. MINKER, J., Set Operations and Inferences over Relational Databases, Technical Report 427, Computer Science Department, University of Maryland, 1975.

1090. MURRAY, N. V., Completely Non-Clausal Theorem Proving, *Artificial Intelligence 18*, (1982), 67-85.

1091. MYCROFT, A., Logic Programs and Many-Valued Logic, *Proceedings of Symposium on Theoretical Aspects of Computer Science*, Paris, 1984.

1092. NAISH, L., Negation and Control in PROLOG, Ph.D. Thesis, Department of Computer Science, University of Melbourne, 1985.

1093. NAKAMURA, K., Associative Concurrent Evaluation of Logic Programs, *Proceedings of the Second International Logic Programming Conference*, S. TARNLUND, ed., Uppsala University, Uppsala, Sweden, July 2-6, 1984, 321-330.

1094. NAKASHIMA, H., Prolog/KR User's Manual, Technical Report METR-82-4, Department of Computer Science, University of Tokyo, Japan, 1981.

1095. NAKASHIMA, H., Prolog K/R - Language Features, *Proceedings of the First International Logic Programming Conference*, Marseille, France, September, 1982.

1096. NAKASHIMA, H., A Knowledge Representation System: Prolog/KR, Doctoral Dissertation, University of Tokyo, 1983.

1097. NAKASHIMA, H., Knowledge Representation in Prolog/KR, *Proceedings of the International IEEE Conference on Logic Programming*, Atlantic City, 1984.

1098. NAKASHIMA, H. and SUZUKI, N., Data Abstraction in Prolog/KR, *New Generation Computing 1*, (1983), Springer Verlag.

1099. NARAIN, S., *MYCIN: The Expert System and Its Implementation in LOGLISP*, Department of Computer Science, Syracuse University, 1981.

1100. NARAIN, S., MYCIN in a Logic Programming Environment, *Proceedings of COMPCON 84*, Spring 1984.

1101. NEWTON, M. O., A Combined Logical and Functional Programming Language, Technical Report 85-5172, California Institute of Technology, Los Angeles, California, 1985.

1102. OVERBEEK, R. A., A New Class of Automated Theorem-proving Algorithms, Ph.D Thesis, Penn. State Univ, 1971.

1103. OVERBEEK, R. A., A New Class of Automated Theorem-proving Algorithms, *Journal of the ACM 21*, (1974), 191-200.

1104. OVERBEEK, R. A., An Implementation of Hyper-resolution, *Computers and Mathematics with Applications 1*, (1975), 201-214.

1105. PEREIRA, L. M. and NASR, R., DELTA-Prolog: A Distributed Logic Programming Language, *International Conference On Fifth Generation Computer Systems*, November 1984.

1106. PIETRZYKOWSKI, T., PROGRAPH As Environment For Prolog DB applications, *Proceedings of The Logic Programming Workshop'83*, 1983.

1107. PORTO, A., EPILOG: A Language for Extended Programming in Logic, *Proceedings of the First International Logic Programming Conference*, M. VAN CANEGHEM, ed., Marseille, France, September 14-17, 1982, 31-37.

1108. PORTO, A., Controlo Sequencial de Programas em Logica, Ph.D. Dissertation, Department of Computer Science, Universidade Nova de Lisboa, Lisbon, Portugal, 1984. In Portuguese.

1109. PORTO, A., EPILOG: A Language for Extended Programming in Logic, in *Implementations of Prolog*, J. A. CAMPBELL, (ed.), Ellis Horwood, 1984.

1110. RADENSKI, A., Functional Programming in the Style of Logic Programming, *C.R. Academic Bulgarian Science 37*, 6 (1984), 741-744.

1111. REDDY, U. S., Transformation of Logic Programs into Functional Programs, *Proceedings of the International IEEE Conference on Logic Programming*, Atlantic City, 1984.

1112. REDDY, U. S., On the Relationship between Logic and Functional Languages, in *Functional and Logic Programming*, D. DEGROOT and G. LINDSTROM, (eds.), Prentice-Hall, 1985.

1113. ROBINSON, J. A. and SIBERT, E. E., Logic Programming in Lisp, Technical Report 8-80, School of Computer and Information Science, Syracuse University, Syracuse, New York, December, 1980.. Also, Technical Report RADC-TR-80-379, January 1981, Rome Air Development Center.

1114. ROBINSON, J. A. and SIBERT, E. E., LOGLISP: An Alternative to Prolog, *Machine Intelligence*, 1982.

1115. ROBINSON, J. A. and SIBERT, E. E., LOGLISP: Motivation, Design and Implementation, in *Logic Programming*, K. L. CLARK and S. A. TARNLUND, (eds.), Academic Press, New York, 1982. Also A.P.I.C. Studies in Data Processing No. 16.

1116. SANDEWALL, E., PCF-2, A First-Order Calculus for Expressing Conceptual Information, Technical Report, Computer Science Department, Uppsala University, 1972.

1117. SATO, M. and SAKURAI, T., Qute: A Prolog/LISP Type Language for Logic Programming, *Proceedings of the International Joint Conference on Artificial Intelligence*, Karlsruhe, Germany, 1983. Also Technical Report TR-016, ICOT - Institute for New Generation Computer.

1118. SATO, M. and SAKURAI, T., Qute: A Functional Language Based On Unification, *International Conference On Fifth Generation Computer Systems*, November 1984.

1119. SCHOPPERS, M. J., Logic-programming production systems with Metalog, *Software Practice and Experience 13*, (1983).

1120. SCHOPPERS, M. J. and HARANDI, M. T., Metalog: a language for knowledge representation and manipulation, *Conference on Artificial Intelligence*, Rochester, Michigan, April, 1983.

1121. SCHORRE, V. and STEIN, J., The Interactive Theorem Prover (ITP) User's Manual, Technical Report, System Development Corp, Santa Monica, CA, 1980.

1122. SCHRAG, R. C., Notes of the Conversion of LOGLISP from Rutgers/UCI-LISP to INTERLISP, Technical Report RADC-TM-83-1, Rome Air Development Center, January 1983.

1123. SCHRAG, R. C., LogLisp Sequential Forms with Resolution Semantics, Technical Report, Rome Air Development Center, Griffis Air Force Base, New York, 1984.

1124. SCHRAG, R. C., LISP Implementation Baseline Investigation, Technical Report, Rome Air Development Center, Griffis Air Force Base, New York, 1984.

1125. SCHRAG, R. C., Compilation and Environment Optimizations for LogLisp, Technical Report, Rome Air Development Center, Griffis Air Force Base, New York, 1984.

1126. SHAPIRO, S. C., Representing and Locating Deduction Rules in a Semantic Network, *SIGART Newsletter*, June 1977.

1127. SHAPIRO, S. C., The SNePS Semantic Network Processing System, in *Associative Networks*, N. V. FINDLER, (ed.), Academic Press, 1979, 179-203.

1128. SHAPIRO, S. C., MCKAY, D. P., MARTINS, J. and MOGADO, E., SNePSLOG: A Higher Order Logic Programming Language, Technical Report No. 8, Computer Science Department, SUNY at Buffalo, Amherst, NY, 1981.

1129. SIMMONS, R. F., Rule Based Computations on English, in *Pattern-Directed Inference Systems*, D. A. WATERMAN and F. HAYES-ROTH, (eds.), Academic Press, New York, 1978.

1130. SIMMONS, R. F., A Narrative Schema in Procedural Logic, in *Logic Programming*, K. L. CLARK and S. A. TARNLUND, (eds.), Academic Press, New York, 1982. A.P.I.C. Studies in Data Processing No. 16.

1131. SIMMONS, R. F., *Computations from the English*, Prentice-Hall, Englewood Cliffs, 1983.

1132. SLOMAN, A., HARDY, S. and GIBSON, J., POPLOG: A Multi-Language Program Development Environment, *Information Technology: Research and Development 2*, (1983), 109-122.

1133. SMITH, B., Logic Programming on the FFP machine, *Proceedings of the International IEEE Conference on Logic Programming*, Atlantic City, 1984.

1134. SRIVASTAVA, A., OXLEY, D. and SRIVASTAVA, A., An(other) Integration of Logic and Functional Programming, *Proceedings of the 2nd IEEE International Symposium on Logic Programming*, Boston, USA, July, 1985.

1135. SUBRAHMANYAM, P. A. and YOU, J. H., FUNLOG: A Computational Model Integrating Logic Programming and Functional Programming, Technical Report UTEC-83-040, Department of Computer Science, University of Utah. Also in, D. DeGroot, G. Lindstrom, Functional Programming and Logic Programming, June 1985, Prentice Hall.

1136. SUBRAHMANYAM, P. A. and YOU, J. H., Conceptual Basis and Evaluation Strategies for Integrating Functional and Logic Programming, *Proceedings of the International IEEE Conference on Logic Programming*, Atlantic City, 1984.

1137. SZOTS, M., A Comparison of Two Logic Programming Languages: A Case Study, *Proceedings of the Second International Logic Programming Conference*, S. A. TARNLUND, ed., Uppsala University, Uppsala, Sweden, July 2-6, 1984, 41-52.

1138. TANCIG, P. and BOJADZIEV, D., SOVA - An Integrated Question-Answering System Based on ATN (for Syntax) and Prolog (for Semantics) in a LISP Environment, in *Workshop on Logic Programming*, S. A. TARNLUND, (ed.), Debrecen, Hungary, July 1980.

1139. VODA, P. J., R-Maple: A Concurrent Programming Language Based on Predicate Logic. Part I: Syntax and Computation, Technical Report TR-83-9, Department of Computer Science, University of British Columbia, Canada, 1983.

1140. VODA, P. J. and YU, B., RF-Maple: A Logic Programming Language with Functions, Types and Concurrency, *International Conference On Fifth Generation Computer Systems*, November 1984.

1141. WALLACE, R. S., PiL (Prolog in Lisp), Technical Report TR-1284, University of Maryland, Computer Science Technical Report Series, 1983.

1142. WEYRAUCH, R. W., Proglomena to a Theory of Mechanized Formal Reasoning, *Artificial Intelligence 13*, (1980).

1143. WILSON, W. W., Beyond Prolog: Software Specification by Grammar, *ACM SIGPLAN Notices 17*, 9 (September 1982), 34-43.

1144. WISE, M. J., A Parallel Prolog: The Construction of a Data Driven Model, *Conference on LISP and Functional Programming*, August, 1982, 55-66.

1145. WISE, M. J., EPILOG = Prolog + Data Flow: Arguments for Combining Prolog with a Data Driven Mechanism, *ACM SIGPLAN Notices 17*, 12 (December, 1982), 80-86.

1146. WISE, M. J., EPILOG: Re-interpreting and Extending Prolog for a Multiprocessor Environment, in *Issues in Prolog Implementation*, J. A. CAMPBELL, (ed.), Ellis Horwood (U.K.), 1984.

1147. WOS,, L., OVERBEEK,, R. A., BOYLE., J. and LUSK,, E. L., *Automated reasoning: introduction and applications* , Englewood Cliffs, NJ, Prentice-Hall,, 1984..

1148. YOKOTA, M. and OTHERS, A Microprogrammed Interpreter Of The Personal Inference Machine, *International Conference On Fifth Generation Computer Systems*, November 1984.

1149. ZANON, G., PROLISP, CERT, 1984.

CHAPTER 8

Papers Related to Fifth
Generation Computer Systems

1150. AIDA, H., TANAKA, H. and MOTO-OKA, T., A Prolog Extension for Handling Negative Knowledge, *New Generation Computing 1*, (1983), Springer Verlag.

1151. AMAMIYA, M. and OTHERS, New Architecture for Knowledge Base Mechanisms, in *Fifth Generation Computer Systems*, T. MOTO-OKA, (ed.), North-Holland, New York, 1981. Proceedings of the First International Conference on Fifth Generation Computer Systems.

1152. BRANDIN, D. H., The Challenge of the Fifth Generation, *Communications of the ACM 25*, 8 (August 1982).

1153. BRECHT, H., Prolog, Taal Voor Vijfde Generatie Systemen, *Personal Computer & Software*, July 1983. In Dutch.

1154. CHIKAYAMA, T., ESP - Extended Self-Contained Prolog as a Preliminary Kernel Language of Fifth Generation Computers, *New Generation Computing 1*, (1983), Springer Verlag.

1155. CHIKAYAMA, T., ESP as Preliminary Kernel Language of Fifth Generation Computers, Technical Report TR-005, ICOT - Institute for New Generation Computer Technology, Tokyo, Japan, 1983.

1156. CHIKAYAMA, T., ESP reference manual, ICOT TR-044, February, 1984.

1157. CHIKAYAMA, T., Unique Features of ESP, *International Conference On Fifth Generation Computer Systems*, November 1984.

1158. CHIKAYAMA, T., YOKOTA, M. and HATTORI, T., Fifth Generation Kernel Language: Version 0, *Proceedings of the Logic Programming Conference*, 1983.

1159. CLARK, K. L. and GREGORY, S., PARLOG: Parallel Programming in Logic, DoC Report 84/4, Department of Computing, Imperial College, 1984.

1160. VAN EMDEN, M. H., Towards a Western Fifth Generation Computer System Project, Technical Report CS-84-14, Department of Computer Science, University of Waterloo, Canada, 1984.

1161. FEIGENBAUM, E. A., Innovation and Symbol Manipulation in the Fifth Generation Computer Systems, in *Fifth Generation Computer Systems*, T. MOTO-OKA, (ed.), North-Holland, New York, 1981. Proceedings of the First International Conference on Fifth Generation Computer Systems.

1162. FEIGENBAUM, E. A. and MCCORDUCK, P., *The Fifth Generation*, Addison-Wesley, Reading, Massachusetts, 1983.

1163. FUCHI, K., Aiming for Knowledge Information Processing Systems, in *Fifth Generation Computer Systems*, T. MOTO-OKA, (ed.), North-Holland, New York, 1981. Proceedings of the First International Conference on Fifth Generation Computer Systems.

1164. FUCHI, K., The Direction the FGCS Project Will Take, *New Generation Computing 1*, 1 (1983), 3-9.

1165. FURUKAWA, K. and OTHERS, Problem Solving and Inference Mechanisms, in *Fifth Generation Computer Systems*, T. MOTO-OKA, (ed.), North-Holland, New York, 1981. Proceedings of the First International Conference on Fifth Generation Computer Systems.

1166. FURUKAWA, K. and FUCHI, K., Knowledge Engineering and the Fifth Generation Computers, *IEEE Database Engineering 6*, 4 (December 1983).

1167. FURUKAWA, K., KUNIFUJI, S., TAKEUCHI, A. and UEDA, K., The Conceptual Specification of the Kernel Language Version 1, *Draft Paper*, 1984.

1168. FURUKAWA, K., NAKAJIMA, R. and YONEZAWA, A., Modularization and Abstraction in Logic Programming, *New Generation Computing 1*, 2 (1983), Springer Verlag. Also available as Technical Report TR-022 from ICOT - Institute for New Generation Computer Technology Tokyo, Japan.

1169. FURUKAWA, K., TAKEUCHI, A. and KUNIFUJI, S., Mandala: Knowledge Programming and System in the Logic-type Language, ICOT TR-043, February, 1984.

1170. FURUKAWA, K., TAKEUCHI, A., YASUKAWA, H. and KUNIFUJI, S., Mandala: A Logic Based Knowledge Programming System, *International Conference On Fifth Generation Computer Systems*, November 1984.

1171. GOTO, S., TANAKA, H. and MOTO-OKA, T., Highly Parallel Inference Engine PIE - Goal Rewriting Model and Machine Architecture, *New Generation Computing 2*, 1 (1984).

1172. HATTORI, T. and YOKOI, T., Basic Constructs Of The SIM Operating System, *New Generation Computing 1*, 1 (1983).

1173. HERTZBERGER, L. O., The Architecture Of Fifth Generation Inference Computers, *Future Generation Computer Systems 1*, 1 (July, 1984).

1174. KARATSU, H., What is Required of the Fifth Generation Computer - Social Needs and Impact, in *Fifth Generation Computer Systems*, T. MOTO-OKA, (ed.), North-Holland, New York, 1981. Proceedings of the First International Conference on Fifth Generation Computer Systems.

1175. KITSUREGAWA, M., TANAKA, H. and MOTO-OKA, T., Application Of Hash To Data Base Machine And Its Architecture, *New Generation Computing 1*, 1 (1983).

1176. KOHOUTEK, H., Quality Issues In New Generation Computing, *International Conference On Fifth Generation Computer Systems*, November 1984.

1177. KOWALSKI, R. A., Logic Programming for the Fifth Generation, *International Conference of Fifth Generation Systems*, 1982.

1178. KOWALSKI, R. A., Software Engineering and Artificial Intelligence in New Generation Computing, *Future Generation Computer Systems 1*, 1 (June, 1984).

1179. KUNIFUJI, S. and OTHERS, Conceptual Specification of the Fifth Generation Kernel Language Version 1 (preliminary draft), ICOT Technical Memorandum, 1983.

1180. KUNIFUJI, S., ASOU, M., TAKEUCHI, A., MIYACHI, T., KITAKAMI, H., YOKOTA, H., YASAKUWA, H. and FURUKAWA, K., Amalgamation of Object Knowledge and Meta Knowledge by Prolog and Its Applications, *Knowledge Engineering and Artificial Intelligence Working Group of the Information Processing Society of Japan*, June, 1983. preprint 30-1, TR-009.

1181. KUNIFUJI, S., TAKEUCHI, A., FURUKAWA, K., UEDA, K. and KURUKAWA, T., A Logic Programming Language for Knowledge Utilization and Realization, *Proceedings of the Prolog Conference*, Tukuba, Japan, 1982. In Japanese.

1182. KURUKAWA, T., TSUJI, J., TOJO, S., IIMA, Y., NAKASAWA, O. and ENOMOTO, H., Dialogue Management In The Personal Sequential Inference Machine (PSI), ICOT Technical Report TR-046, 1984.

1183. LASSEZ, J. L. and MAHER, M. J., Begriffschrift - a Fifth Generation Language, Internal Note, Dept. of Computer Science, University of Melbourne, 1983.

1184. LEHMAN, M. M., The Role of Systems and Software Technology in the Fifth Generation, Technical Report, Computer Science Department, Imperial College, London, 1983.

1185. MOTO-OKA, T. and OTHERS, Challenge for Knowledge Information Processing Systems, in *Fifth Generation Computer Systems*, T. MOTO-OKA, (ed.), North-Holland, New York, 1981. Proceedings of the First International Conference on Fifth Generation Computer Systems.

1186. MOTO-OKA, T., Overview to the fifth generation computer system project, *ACM SIGARCH Newsletter 11*, 3 (1983), 417-422.

1187. MOTO-OKA, T. and FUCHI, K., The Architectures In The Fifth Generation Computers, *Information Processing 83*, R. E. A. MASON, ed., 1983.

1188. MOTO-OKA, T. and STONE, H. S., Fifth-Generation Computer Systems: A Japanese Project, *Computer 17*, 3 (March 1984), 6-13.

1189. ONAI, R., SHIMIZU, H., ITO, N. and MASUDA, K., The proposal of Prolog machine based on reduction machine, First Research Laboratory, ICOT Research Center, Tokyo, Japan, 1982.

1190. RIET, R. P. V., Knowledge Bases: De Databanken van de Toekomst, *Informatie 25*, 5 (1983), 16-23. In Dutch.

1191. SHAPIRO, E. Y., Japan's Fifth Generation Computers Project - A Trip Report, Research Report CS83-07, Department of Applied Mathematics, The Weizmann Institute of Science, Rehovot, Israel, 1983.

1192. TRELEAVEN, P. C., *Proceedings of the Fifth Generation: the dawn of the second computer age*, SPL International, London, England, July 7-9, 1982.

1193. TRELEAVEN, P. C., The New Generation of Computer Architecture, *ACM SIGARCH Newsletter 11*, 3 (1983), 402-409.

1194. TRELEAVEN, P. C. and BROWNBRIDGE, D. R., Data-Driven and Demand-Driven Computer Architecture, *ACM Computing Surveys 14*, 1 (March 1982).

1195. TRELEAVEN, P. C. and LIMA, I. G., Japan's fifth-generation computer systems, *IEEE Computer 15*, 8 (1982), 79-88.

1196. WARREN, D. H. D., A View of the Fifth Generation and its Impact, Research Report, SRI International, Menlo Park, 1982. Also in Artificial Intelligence Magazine, Fall 1982.

1197. YOKOI, T., A Perspective on the Japanese FGCS Project, Technical Memorandum TM-0026, ICOT - Institute for New Generation Computer Technology, Tokyo, Japan, 1983.

CHAPTER 9

Hardware Architectures
for Logic Programming

1198. AISO, H., Fifth Generation Computer Architecture, in *Fifth Generation Computer Systems*, T. MOTO-OKA, (ed.), North-Holland, New York, 1981. Proceedings of the First International Conference on Fifth Generation Computer Systems.

1199. AMAMIYA, M. and OTHERS, New Architecture for Knowledge Base Mechanisms, in *Fifth Generation Computer Systems*, T. MOTO-OKA, (ed.), North-Holland, New York, 1981. Proceedings of the First International Conference on Fifth Generation Computer Systems.

1200. BELLIA, M., DEGANO, P., LEVI, G., DAMERI, E. and MARTELLI, A., A Formal Model for Demand-Driven Implementations of Rewriting Systems and its Application to Prolog Processes, Technical Report 81-3, University of Pisa, Italy, 1983.

1201. BELLIA, M., LEVI, G. and MARTELLI, M., On Compiling Prolog Programs on Demand-Driven Architectures, *Proceedings of the 2nd Workshop on Logic Programming*, Algarve, Portugal, 1983, 518-535.

1202. BIC, L., Execution of Logic Programs On A Dataflow Architecture, *Proceedings of the 11th Annual International Symposium on Computer Architecture*, Ann Arbor, Michigan, June 5-7, 1984. Published as SIGARCH Newsletter, Vol 12, Issue 3.

1203. BIC, L., A Data-driven Model for Parallel Interpretation of Logic Programs, *International Conference On Fifth Generation Computer Systems*, November 1984.

1204. CHAKRAVARTHY, U. S., KASIF, S., KOHLI, M., MINKER, J. and CAO, D., Logic Programming on ZMOB: A Highly Parallel Machine, *Proceedings og the 1982 International Conference in Parallel processing*, New York, 1982, 347-349.

1205. CIEPIELEWSKI, A., Towards a Computer Architecture for the OR-Parallel Execution of Logic Progams, Ph.D. Thesis, Royal Institute of Technology, Stockholm, Sweden, 1984.

1206. CIEPIELEWSKI, A. and HARIDI, S., Storage Models for OR-Parallel Execution of Logic Progams, Technical Report TRITA-CS-8301, Royal Institute of Technology, Stockholm, Sweden, 1983.

1207. CIEPIELEWSKI, A. and HARIDI, S., Execution of Bagof on the Or-Parallel Token Machine, *International Conference On Fifth Generation Computer Systems*, November 1984.

1208. CRAMMOND, J. A. and MILLER, C. D. F., An Architecture of Parallel Logic Languages, *Proceedings of the Second International Logic Programming Conference*, S. TARNLUND, ed., Uppsala University, Uppsala, Sweden, July 2-6, 1984, 183-194.

1209. DARLINGTON, J. and REEVE, M., ALICE: A Multi-Processor Reduction Machine for the Parallel Evaluation of Applicative Languages, *Proceedings of the Conference on Functional Programming Languages and Computer Architecture*, Portsmouth, New Hampshire, October 1981, 65-75.

1210. DIEL, H., Concurrent Data Access Architecture, *International Conference On Fifth Generation Computer Systems*, November 1984.

1211. DOBRY, T. P., PRATT, Y. N. and DESPAIN, A. M., Design Decisions Influencing the Microarchitecture for a Prolog Machine, *Proceedings of the 17th Microprogramming Conference*, 1985, 217-231.

1212. DOBRY, T., DESPAIN, A. M. and PRATT, Y. N., Performance Studies of a Prolog Machine Architecture, *Proceedings of the 12th International Symposium on Computer Architecture*, Boston, June, 1985.

1213. DOYLE, J., What Should Artificial Intelligence Want from the Super Computers ?, *Artificial Intelligence Magazine 4*, 4 (1983).

1214. FIAT, A., SHAMIR, A. and SHAPIRO, E. Y., Polymorphic arrays: an architecture for a programmable systolic machine, Weizmann Institute of Technical Report CS84-20, 1984.

1215. FUSAOKA, A., SEKI, H. and TAKAHASHI, K., Description and Reasoning of VLSI Circuit in Temporal Logic, *New Generation Computing 2*, 1 (1984).

1216. GOTO, S., TANAKA, H. and MOTO-OKA, T., Highly Parallel Inference Engine PIE - Goal Rewriting Model and Machine Architecture, *New Generation Computing 2*, 1 (1984).

1217. HANSSON, A., HARIDI, S. and TARNLUND, S. A., Some Aspects of a Logic Machine Prototype, in *Workshop on Logic Programming*, S. A. TARNLUND, (ed.), Debrecen, Hungary, July 1980.

1218. HERTZBERGER, L. O., The Architecture Of Fifth Generation Inference Computers, *Future Generation Computer Systems 1*, 1 (July, 1984).

1219. ITO, N., ONAI, R., MASUDA, K. and SHIMIZU, H., Prolog Machine Based on the Data Flow Mechanism, Technical Memorandum TM-0007, ICOT - Institute for New Generation Computer Technology, Tokyo, Japan, 1983.

1220. KACSUK, P., A Highly Parallel Prolog Interpreter Based on The Generalized Data Flow Model, *Proceedings of the Second International Logic Programming Conference*, S. TARNLUND, ed., Uppsala University, Uppsala, Sweden, July 2-6, 1984, 195-206.

1221. KALE, L. V. and WARREN, D. S., A Class of Architectures For A Prolog Machine, *Proceedings of the Second International Logic Programming Conference*, S. TARNLUND, ed., Uppsala University, Uppsala, Sweden, July 2-6, 1984, 159-170.

1222. KIM, J. I., MAENG, S. R. and CHO, J. W., A Relational Data Flow Data Base Machine Based on Hierarchical Ring Network, *International Conference On Fifth Generation Computer Systems*, November 1984.

1223. LINDSTROM, G. and PANANGDEN, P., Stream-Based Execution of Logic Programming, *Proceedings of the International IEEE Conference on Logic Programming*, Atlantic City, 1984.

1224. LIOUPIS, D., REDUCE: A Dynamically Reconfigurable General Purpose Parallel Computer, Doc 84/12, Department of Computing, Imperial College, 1984.

1225. LOWRY, A. and TAYLOR, S., LPS Algorithms, *International Conference On Fifth Generation Computer Systems*, November 1984.

1226. LUSK, E. L., McCUME, W. W. and OVERBEEK, R. A., Logic Machine Architecture: Kernel Functions, in *Lecture Notes in Computer Science 138: 6th Conference on Automated Deduction*, D. W. LOVELAND, (ed.), Springer-Verlag, New York, 1982.

1227. LUSK, E. L. and OVERBEEK, R. A., Logic Machine Architecture Inference Mechanisms - Layer 2 User Reference Manual, ANL-82-84, Argonne National Laboratory, December, 1982.

1228. MAY, D. and SHEPHERD, R., The Transputer Implementation of OCCAM, *International Conference On Fifth Generation Computer Systems*, November 1984.

1229. McCABE, F. G., Abstract Prolog Machine: A Specification, Technical Report, Computer Science Department, Imperial College, London, 1983.

1230. MILLS, P., A Systolic Unification Algorithm for VLSI, *International Conference On Fifth Generation Computer Systems*, November 1984.

1231. MIRANKER, D., Performance Estimates For The DADO Machine: A Comparison of TREAT & RETE, *International Conference On Fifth Generation Computer Systems*, November 1984.

1232. MORI, H., MITSUMOTO, K., FUJITA, M. and GOTO, S., Knowledge-Based VLSI Routing System-WIREX-, *International Conference On Fifth Generation Computer Systems*, November 1984, 383-388.

1233. MOTO-OKA, T. and FUCHI, K., The Architectures In The Fifth Generation Computers, *Information Processing 83*, R. E. A. MASON, ed., 1983.

1234. MOTO-OKA, T., TANAKA, H., AIDA, H., HIRATA, K. and MARAYUMA, T., The Architecture Of A Parallel Inference Engine-PIE, *International Conference On Fifth Generation Computer Systems*, November 1984.

1235. MURAKAMI, K., KAKUTA, T., MIYAZAKI, N., SHIBAYAMA, S. and YOKOTA, H., A Relational Database Machine: First Step to Knowledge Base Machine, Technical Report TR-012, ICOT - Institute for New Generation Computer Technology, Tokyo, Japan, 1983. Also in ACM SIGARCH Newsletter, Vol. 11(3), 1983, pp. 423-425.

1236. NISHIKAWA, H., YOKOTA, M., YAMAMOTO, A., TAKI, K. and UCHIDA, S., The Personal Inference Machine (PSI): Its Design Philosophy and Machine Architecture, Technical Report TR-013, ICOT - Institute for New Generation Computer Technology, Tokyo, Japan, 1983. Also in Proceedings of the Logic Programming Workshop, 1983, Algarve, Portugal.

1237. ONAI, R., SHIMIZU, H., ITO, N. and MASUDA, K., The proposal of Prolog machine based on reduction machine, First Research Laboratory, ICOT Research Center, Tokyo, Japan, 1982.

1238. PERCEBOIS, C. and SANSONNET, J. P., A LISP Machine to Implement Prolog, Proceedings of the First International Logic Programming Conference, Marseille, France, 1981.

1239. PEREIRA, L. M. and NASR, R., DELTA-Prolog: A Distributed Logic Programming Language, International Conference On Fifth Generation Computer Systems, November 1984.

1240. POLLARD, G. H., Parallel Execution of Horn Clause Programs, Technical Report, Computer Science Department, Imperial College, London, 1983. Ph.D. Dissertation.

1241. SAKAI, H. and OTHERS, Design And Implementation Of The Relational Data Base Engine, International Conference On Fifth Generation Computer Systems, November 1984.

1242. SHAPIRO, E. Y., Let's Build A Programmable Systolic Machine, International Conference On Fifth Generation Computer Systems, November 1984.

1243. SHIBAYAMA, S. and OTHERS, Query Processing Flow On RDBM Delta's Functionally-distributed Architecture, International Conference On Fifth Generation Computer Systems, November 1984.

1244. SHIBAYAMA, S., KAKUTA, T., MIYAZAKI, N., YOKOTA, H. and MURAKAMI, K., On RDBM Delta's Relational Algebra Processing Algorithm, Technical Memorandum TM-0023, ICOT - Institute for New Generation Computer Technology, Tokyo, Japan, 1983.

1245. SHIBAYAMA, S., MIYAZAKI, N., KAKUTA, T. and YOKOTA, H., A Relational Database Machine DELTA, Technical Memorandum TM-0002, ICOT - Institute for New Generation Computer Technology, Tokyo, Japan, 1982.

1246. SMITH, B., Logic Programming on the FFP machine, *Proceedings of the International IEEE Conference on Logic Programming*, Atlantic City, 1984.

1247. STOLFO, S. J., MIRANKER, D. and SHAW, D. E., Architecture and Applications of DADO, A Large Parallel Computer for Artificial Intelligence, *Proceedings of the 8th International Joint Conference on Artificial Intelligence*, Karlsruhe, Gemany, August 1983, 850-854.

1248. STOLFO, S. J. and SHAW, D. E., DADO: A Tree Structured Machine Architecture for Production Systems, *Proceedings of the National Conference on Artificial Intelligence, International Joint Conference on Artificial Intelligence 1*, (August 1982).

1249. SUZUKI, N., KUBOTA, K. and AOKI, T., Sword32: A Byte Emulating Microprocessor for Object-Oriented Languages, *International Conference On Fifth Generation Computer Systems*, November 1984.

1250. TAKI, K., NISHIKAWA, H., YAMAMOTO, A., YOKOTA, M. and UCHIDA, S., Hardware Design And Implementation Of The Personal Sequential Inference Machine (PSI), *International Conference On Fifth Generation Computer Systems*, November 1984.

1251. TAMURA, N. and KANEDA, Y., Implementing Prolog on a Multiprocessor Machine, *Proceedings of the International IEEE Conference on Logic Programming*, Atlantic City, 1984.

1252. TAMURA, N., KANEDA, Y., WADA, K., MAEKAWA, S. and MATSUDA, H., Sequential Prolog Machine PEK, *International Conference On Fifth Generation Computer Systems*, November 1984.

1253. TANAKA, Y., MPDC: Massive Parallel Architecture for Very Large Data Bases, *International Conference On Fifth Generation Computer Systems*, November 1984.

1254. TAYLOR, S., MAIO, C., STOLFO, S. J. and SHAW, D. E., Prolog on the DADO Machine: A Parallel System for High-Speed Computing, Technical Report, Department of Computer Science, Columbia University, 1983. Also 3rd Annual Phoenix Conference On Computers and Communication,IEEE, March 1984.

1255. TICK, E., An Overlapped Prolog Processor, Technical Report 308, SRI International, 1983.

1256. TICK, E., Towards a Multiple Pipeline Prolog Processor, *International Workshop on High-Level Computer Architecture*, 1984.

1257. TICK, E., Sequential Prolog machine: image and host architectures, *Proceedings of the 17th Microprogramming Conference*, 1985, 204-216.

1258. TICK, E. and WARREN, D. H. D., Towards a Pipelined Prolog Processor, *Proceedings of the International IEEE Conference on Logic Programming*, Atlantic City, 1984.

1259. TRELEAVEN, P. C., *Proceedings of the Fifth Generation: the dawn of the second computer age*, SPL International, London, England, July 7-9, 1982.

1260. TRELEAVEN, P. C., The New Generation of Computer Architecture, *ACM SIGARCH Newsletter 11*, 3 (1983), 402-409.

1261. TRELEAVEN, P. C. and BROWNBRIDGE, D. R., Data-Driven and Demand-Driven Computer Architecture, *ACM Computing Surveys 14*, 1 (March 1982).

1262. TRELEAVEN, P. C. and LIMA, I. G., Japan's fifth-generation computer systems, *IEEE Computer 15*, 8 (1982), 79-88.

1263. UCHIDA, S. and OTHERS, New Architectures for Inference Mechanisms, in *Fifth Generation Computer Systems*, T. MOTO-OKA, (ed.), North-Holland, New York, 1981.

1264. UCHIDA, S., Inference Machine: From Sequential to Parallel, Technical Report TR-011, ICOT - Institute for New Generation Computer Technology, Tokyo, Japan, 1983. Also Published in the proceedings of the 10th International Symposium on Computer Architecture, June 1983, pp. 410-416.

1265. UCHIDA, S., YOKOTA, M., YAMAMOTO, A., TAKI, K. and NISHIKAWA, H., Outline of the Personal Sequential Inference Machine, Technical Memorandum TM-0005, ICOT - Institute for New Generation Computer Technology, Tokyo, Japan, 1983.

1266. WARREN, D. H. D., An Abstract Prolog Instruction Set, Technical Report 309, SRI International, 1983.

1267. YAMAGUCHI, Y., HERATH, J., TODA, K. and YUBA, T., EM-3: A Lisp-based Data-driven Machine, *International Conference On Fifth Generation Computer Systems*, November 1984.

CHAPTER 10

Parallelism and Logic Programming

1268. AIDA, H. and MOTO-OKA, T., Performance Measurement of the Parallel Logic Programming System PARALOG, *Proceedings of the Prolog Programming Environments Workshop*, Linkoping University, Sweden, 1982.

1269. ASOU, M. and ONAI, R., Xp's: An Extended Or-Parallel Prolog System, Technical Report TR-023, ICOT - Institute for New Generation Computer Technology, Tokyo, Japan, 1983. In Japanese.

1270. BIC, L., A Data-driven Model for Parallel Interpretation of Logic Programs, *International Conference On Fifth Generation Computer Systems*, November 1984.

1271. BONKOWSKI, B., DIDUR, P., MALCOLM, M. A., STAFFORD, G. and YOUNG, T., Programming in Waterloo Port, Technical Report, Department of Computer Science, University of Waterloo, Ontario, Canada, 1984.

1272. BORGWARDT, P., Parallel Prolog Using Stack Segments on Shared-Memory Multi Processors, *Proceedings of the International IEEE Conference on Logic Programming*, Atlantic City, 1984.

1273. BOSCO, P. G., GIANDONATO, G. and GIOVANETTI, E., A Prolog System For The Verification of Concurrent Processes Against Temporal Logic Specifications, *Proceedings of the Second International Logic Programming Conference*, S. TARNLUND, ed., Uppsala University, Uppsala, Sweden, July 2-6, 1984, 219-230.

1274. BOWEN, K. A., Concurrent Execution of Logic, *Proceedings of the First International Logic Programming Conference*, M. VAN CANEGHEM, ed., Marseille, France, September 14-17, 1982, 26-30.

1275. BRODA, K. and GREGORY, S., Parlog for Discrete Event Simulation, *Proceedings of the Second International Logic Programming Conference*, S. TARNLUND, ed., Uppsala University, Uppsala, Sweden, July 2-6, 1984, 301-312.

1276. BRUYNOOGHE, M. and CLARK, K. L., Parallel Programming in Predicate Logic, Technical Report, Departement Toegepaste Wiskunde en Programmatie, Katholieke Universiteit Leuven, Belgium, 1979.

1277. CIEPIELEWSKI, A., Towards a Computer Architecture for the OR-Parallel Execution of Logic Progams, Ph.D. Thesis, Royal Institute of Technology, Stockholm, Sweden, 1984.

1278. CIEPIELEWSKI, A. and HARIDI, S., Formal Models for OR-Parallel Execution of Logic Progams, CSALAB Working Paper 821121, Royal Institute of Technology, Stockholm, Sweden, 1982. Also Published in the Proceedings of IFIP 83, North-Holland.

1279. CIEPIELEWSKI, A. and HARIDI, S., Storage Models for OR-Parallel Execution of Logic Progams, Technical Report TRITA-CS-8301, Royal Institute of Technology, Stockholm, Sweden, 1983.

1280. CIEPIELEWSKI, A. and HARIDI, S., Control of Activities in the OR-Parallel Token Machine, *Proceedings of the International IEEE Conference on Logic Programming*, Atlantic City, 1984, 49-57.

1281. CLARK, K. L. and GREGORY, S., A Relational Language for Parallel Programming, *Proceedings of the ACM Conference of Functional Programming Languages and Computer Architectures,* October 1981, 171-178. Also available as a Technical Report from Imperial College, London.

1282. CLARK, K. L. and GREGORY, S., PARLOG: A Parallel Logic Programming Language, Technical Report TR-83-5, Imperial College, London, 1983.

1283. CLARK, K. L. and GREGORY, S., PARLOG: Parallel Programming in Logic, DoC Report 84/4, Department of Computing, Imperial College, 1984.

1284. CLARK, K. L. and GREGORY, S., Notes On Systems Programming In PARLOG, *International Conference On Fifth Generation Computer Systems,* November 1984.

1285. CONERY, J. S., The AND/OR Process Model for Parallel Interpretation of Logic Programs, Technical Report 204, Computer Science Department, University of California, Irvine, 1983. Ph.D. Dissertation.

1286. CONERY, J. S. and KIBLER, D. F., A Relational Dataflow System, Technical Report 48, Department of Computer Science, University of California, Irvine, May, 1980.

1287. CONERY, J. S. and KIBLER, D. F., Parallel Interpretation of Logic Programs, *Proceedings of the 1981 ACM Conference on Functional Programming Languages and Computer Architectures,* 1981.

1288. CONERY, J. S. and KIBLER, D. F., Parallel Query Processing in Logic Databases, *Proceedings of the International Joint Conference on Artificial Intelligence,* Karlsruhe, Germany, 1983.

1289. CONERY, J. S. and KIBLER, D. F., AND Parallelism in Logic Programs, *Proceedings of the International Joint Conference on Artificial Intelligence*, Karlsruhe, Germany, 1983.

1290. CONERY, J. S. and KIBLER, D. F., AND Parallellism and Nondeterminism in Logic Programs, *New Generation Computing 3*, 1 (1985).

1291. CRAMMOND, J. A. and MILLER, C. D. F., An Architecture of Parallel Logic Languages, *Proceedings of the Second International Logic Programming Conference*, S. TARNLUND, ed., Uppsala University, Uppsala, Sweden, July 2-6, 1984, 183-194.

1292. DARLINGTON, J. and REEVE, M., ALICE: A Multi-Processor Reduction Machine for the Parallel Evaluation of Applicative Languages, *Proceedings of the Conference on Functional Programming Languages and Computer Architecture*, Portsmouth, New Hampshire, October 1981, 65-75.

1293. DAUSMAN, M., PERSCH, G. and WINTERSTEIN, G., Concurrent Logic, *Proceedings of the Fourth Workshop On Artificial Intelligence*, Bad Honef, Germany, 1979.

1294. DAUSMAN, M., PERSCH, G. and WINTERSTEIN, G., A New Method for Describing Concurrent Problems Based on Logic, Interne Berichte No 10, Universitat Karlsruhe, 1980.

1295. DEGANO, P. and DIOMEDI, S., A First-Order Semantics of a Connective Suitable to Express Concurrency, *Proceedings of Workshop on Logic Programming*, Algarve, Portugal, 1983.

1296. DEGROOT, D., Logic programming and parallel processing, *T.J. Watson Research Center*, September, 1983.

1297. DEGROOT, D., Restricted And-Parallelism, *International Conference On Fifth Generation Computer Systems*, November 1984.

1298. DEGROOT, D., Alternative Graph Expressions for Restricted AND-Parallism, *Proceedings of the IEEE Spring CompCon Conference*, San Francisco, February, 1985.

1299. DIDUR, P., MALCOLM, M. A. and McWEENY, P. A., Waterloo Port User's Guide, Technical Report, Department of Computer Science, University of Waterloo, Ontario, Canada, 1984.

1300. DOMAN, A., An Applicative Language for Highly Parallel Programming, SZKI Technical Report, Budapest, 1981.

1301. EDELMAN, S. and SHAPIRO, E. Y., Quadtrees in Concurrent Prolog, Technical Report CS84-19, Computer Science Department, Weizman Institute, Israel, 1984.

1302. EISINGER, N., KASIF, S. and MINKER, J., Logic Programming: A Parallel Approach, *Proceedings of the First International Logic Programming Conference*, Marseille, France, September, 1982. Also available as a Technical Report 1128 from the University of Maryland.

1303. VAN EMDEN, M. H. and GOEBEL, R. G., Waterloo UNIX Prolog Tutorial Version 1.2, Technical Report, Department of Computer Science, University of Waterloo, Ontario, Canada, 1984.

1304. VAN EMDEN, M. H. and LUCENA, G. J., Predicate Logic as a Language for Parallel Programming, Technical Report CS-77-15, Department of Computer Science, University of Waterloo, Canada, 1980. Also in Logic Programming, Clark and Tarnlund, Academic Press, 1982.

1305. FALASCHI, M., LEVI, G. and PALAMIDESSI, C., Synchronization in Logic Programming: Formal Semantics of Extended Horn Clauses, *Proceedings of Colloqium on Algebra, Combinatorics and Logic in Computer Science*, Hungary, 1983.

1306. FISHMAN, D. H. and MINKER, J., Pi-Representation: A Clause Representation for Parallel Search, *Artificial Intelligence 6*, (1975), 103-127.

1307. FURUKAWA, K., MITTA, K. and MATSUMOTO, Y., A Back-Up Parallel Interpreter for Prolog Programs, in *Logic Programming and Its Applications*, M. VAN CANEGHEM and D. H. D. WARREN, (eds.), Ablex Publishing Company, 1984.

1308. FURUKAWA, K., NITTA, K. and MATSUMOTO, Y., Prolog Interpreter Based on Concurrent Programming, in *Proc. of the First International Logic Programming Conference*, M. VAN CANEGHEM, (ed.), ADDP-GIA, Facult'e des Sciences de Luminy, Marseille, France, September 14-17, 1982, 38-44.

1309. FURUKAWA, K., TAKEUCHI, A. and KUNIFUJI, S., Mandala: A Knowledge Programming Language based on Concurrent Prolog, ICOT Technical Memorandum TM-0028 (in Japanese) ICOT Technical Report TR-029 (in English), 1983.

1310. FUTO, I. and GERGELY, T., Planning Activity Of Cooperative I-Actors, *IPAC International Symposium on AI*, Leningrad, USSR, October, 1983.

1311. FUTO, I. and GERGELY, T., A Logic Simulation Language For Modeling Cooperative Problem Solving System, *AFCNET Information Congress, Hardware and Software Components and Architecture for the 5th Generation*, Paris, France, March, 1985.

1312. GELERNTER, D., A Note on Systems Programming in Concurrent Prolog, Technical Report, Yale University, 1983. Also in Proceedings of the International IEEE Logic Programming Conference, 1984.

1313. GREGORY, S., Getting Started with PARLOG, Manual DOC 83/28, Department of Computing, Imperial College, London, 1983. Also Technical Memorandum, ICOT, Tokyo, 1983.

1314. HARIDI, S. and CIEPIELEWSKI, A., An Or-Parallel Token Machine, Technical Report TRITA-CS-83-8303, Royal Institute of Technology, Stockholm, Sweden, 1983. Also Published in Proceedings Logic Programming Workshop, 1983, Algarve, Portugal.

1315. HARIDI, S. and CIEPIELEWSKI, A., A Formal Model for Or-Parallel Execution of Logic Programs, in *Information Processing*, R. E. A. MASON, (ed.), Elsevier Science Publishers B.V., 1983. Also available as CSALAB Working Paper 821121, the Royal Institute of Technology, Stockholm, Sweden.

1316. HARIDI, S. and SAHLIN, D., An Abstract Machine for LPL0, Technical Report TRITA-CS-8302, Royal Institute of Technology, Stockholm, Sweden, 1983.

1317. HELLERSTEIN, L. and SHAPIRO, E. Y., Algorithmic Programming in Concurrent Prolog: the MAXFLOW experience, Technical Report TR CS83-12, Department of Applied Mathematics, The Weizmann Institute of Science, 1983. Also in Proceedings of the International IEEE Logic Programming Conference, 1984.

1318. HOGGER, C. J., Concurrent Logic Programming, in *Logic Programming*, K. L. CLARK and S. TARNLUND, (eds.), Academic Press, 1982.

1319. ITO, N., MASUDA, K. and SIMIZU, H., Nondeterministic Control Mechanism in Dataflow Prolog Machines, Technical Memorandum TM-0014, ICOT - Institute for New Generation Computer Technology, Tokyo, Japan, 1983. In Japanese.

1320. ITO, N., SHIMIZU, H., KISHI, M., KUNO, E. and ROKUSAWA, K., Data-Flow Based Execution Mechanisms of Parallel and Concurrent Prolog, *New Generation Computing 3*, 1 (1985).

1321. KACSUK, P., A Highly Parallel Prolog Interpreter Based on The Generalized Data Flow Model, *Proceedings of the Second International Logic Programming Conference*, S. TARNLUND, ed., Uppsala University, Uppsala, Sweden, July 2-6, 1984, 195-206.

1322. KAHN, G., The Semantics of a simple language for parallel programming, *Information Processing*, 74.

1323. KAHN, G. and MACQUEEN, D., Coroutines and Networks of Parallel Process, *Information Processing*, 77.

1324. KASIF, S., KOHLI, M. and MINKER, J., PRISM: A Parallel Inference System for Problem Solving, *Proceedings of the International Joint Conference on Artificial Intelligence*, Karlsruhe, Germany, 1983. Also in Proceedings of Logic Programming Workshop, Portugal, 1983.

1325. KHABAZA, T., A Process-Oriented AND/OR Parallel Execution Scheme for Horn Clause Programs, Technical Report, Cognitive Studies Department, University of Sussex, 1984.

1326. KHABAZA, T., Negation as Failure and Parallellism, *Proceedings of the International IEEE Conference on Logic Programming*, Atlantic City, 1984.

1327. KIRAKAWA, H., Chart Parsing in Concurrent Prolog, Technical Report TR-008, ICOT - Institute for New Generation Computer Technology, Tokyo, Japan, 1983.

1328. KIRAKAWA, H., ONAI, R. and FURUKAWA, K., Implementing an OR-Parallel Optimizing System (POPS) in Concurrent Prolog, Technical Report TR-020, ICOT - Institute for New Generation Computer Technology, Tokyo, Japan, 1983.

1329. KUSALIK, A. J., Bounded-Wait Merge in Shapiro's Concurrent Prolog, Technical Report, Department of Computer Science, University of British Columbia, 1984.

1330. KUSALIK, A. J., Serialization of Process Reduction in Concurrent Prolog, *New Generation Computing 2*, 3 (1984).

1331. LEE, R. K. S., Concurrent Prolog in a Multi-Process Environment, Technical Report CS-84-46, Department of Computer Science, University of Waterloo, Ontario, Canada, 1984.

1332. LEE, R. and GOEBEL, R., Concurrent Prolog in a Multi-Process Environment, *Proceedings of the 2nd IEEE International Symposium on Logic Programming*, Boston, USA, July, 1985.

1333. LINDSTROM, G., Or-Parallelism on Applicative Architectures, *Proceedings of the Second International Logic Programming Conference*, S. TARNLUND, ed., Uppsala University, Uppsala, Sweden, July 2-6, 1984, 159-170.

1334. LOWRY, A. and TAYLOR, S., LPS Algorithms, *International Conference On Fifth Generation Computer Systems*, November 1984.

1335. MALUSZYNSKI, J. and DEMBINSKI, P., AND-Parallelism with Intelligent Backtracking for Annotated Logic Programs, *Proceedings of the 2nd IEEE International Symposium on Logic Programming*, Boston, USA, July, 1985.

1336. MATSUMOTO, Y., NITTA, K. and FURUKAWA, K., Prolog Interpreter and its Parallel Extension, Technical Report, ICOT, Japan, 1982.

1337. MIEROWSKY, C., Design and Implementation of Flat Concurrent Prolog, Technical Report CS84-21, Computer Science Department, Weizman Institute, Israel, 1984.

1338. MIYAZAKI, T., TAKEUCHI, A. and CHIKAYAMA, T., A Sequential Implementation of Concurrent Prolog Based on the Shallow Binding Scheme, *Proceedings of the 2nd IEEE International Symposium on Logic Programming*, Boston, USA, July, 1985.

1339. MONTEIRO, L. F., Distributed Logic: A Logical System for Specifying Cocurrency, Technical Report CIUNL-5-81, Department of Computer Science, Universidade Nova de Lisboa, 1981.

1340. MONTEIRO, L. F., An Extension to Horn Clause Logic Allowing the Definition of Concurrent Processes, in *Lecture Notes in Computer Science 108: International Colloquim on the Formalization of Programming Concepts*, Springer-Verlag, New York, 1981. Also available as Technical Report CIUNL-11/80 from Universidade Nova de Lisboa.

1341. MONTEIRO, L. F., A Logical Formalism for Specifying Concurrency, Technical Report CIUNL-5/81, Universidade Nova de Lisboa, 1981.

1342. MONTEIRO, L. F., A Small Interpreter for Distributed Logic, *Logic Programming Newsletter 3*, (1982).

1343. MONTEIRO, L. F., A New Presentation of Distributed Logic, Technical Report CIUNL-7/82, Universidade Nova de Lisboa, 1982.

1344. MONTEIRO, L. F., A Small Interpreter for Distributed Logic, Technical Report, Universidade Nova de Lisboa, 1982. Also in Logic Programming Newsletter, Vol 3, 1982.

1345. MONTEIRO, L. F., A Horn Clause-Like Logic For Specifying Concurrency, *Proceedings of the First International Logic Programming Conference*, M. VAN CANEGHEM, ed., Marseille, France, September 14-17, 1982, 1-8.

1346. MONTEIRO, L. F., Uma Logica Para Processos Distribuidos, Ph.D. Dissertation, Department of Computer Science, University of Lisbon, 1983.

1347. MONTEIRO, L. F., A Proposal for Distributed Programming in Logic, in *Implementations of Prolog*, J. A. CAMPBELL, (ed.), Ellis Horwood, 1984.

1348. MOTO-OKA, T., TANAKA, H., AIDA, H., HIRATA, K. and MARAYUMA, T., The Architecture Of A Parallel Inference Engine-PIE, *International Conference On Fifth Generation Computer Systems*, November 1984.

1349. MULLER, J. P., PARALOG: A Parallel Logic Programming System, *Sixth European Conference On Artificial Intelligence*, Pisa, September, 1984.

1350. NAKAGAWA, H., And Parallel Prolog with Divided Assertion Set, *Proceedings of the International IEEE Conference on Logic Programming*, Atlantic City, 1984, 22-28.

1351. NAKAMURA, K., Associative Concurrent Evaluation of Logic Programs, *Proceedings of the Second International Logic Programming Conference*, S. TARNLUND, ed., Uppsala University, Uppsala, Sweden, July 2-6, 1984, 321-330.

1352. OVERBEEK, R. A. and LUSK, E. L., Implementation of Logic Programming on HEP, in *Parallel MIMD Computation: HEP Supercomputer and Its Applications*, J. S. KOWALIK, (ed.), MIT Press, 1985.

1353. PEREIRA, L. M. and MONTEIRO, L. F., The Semantics of Parallelism and Coroutining in Logic Programming, *Colloquium on Mathematical Logic in Programming*, Hungary, 1978. Published by North-Holland in 1981.

1354. POLLACK, J. and WALTZ, D., Parallel Interpretation of Natural Language, *International Conference On Fifth Generation Computer Systems*, November 1984.

1355. POLLARD, G. H., Parallel Execution of Horn Clause Programs, Technical Report, Computer Science Department, Imperial College, London, 1983. Ph.D. Dissertation.

1356. PORTO, A., EPILOG: A Language for Extended Programming in Logic, *Proceedings of the First International Logic Programming Conference*, M. VAN CANEGHEM, ed., Marseille, France, September 14-17, 1982, 31-37.

1357. PORTO, A., EPILOG: A Language for Extended Programming in Logic, in *Implementations of Prolog*, J. A. CAMPBELL, (ed.), Ellis Horwood, 1984.

1358. SHAFRIR, A. and SHAPIRO, E. Y., Distributed Programming in Concurrent Prolog, Technical Report, Department of Applied Mathematics, The Weizmann Institute of Science, 1984.

1359. SHAPIRO, E. Y., A Subset of Concurrent Prolog and Its Interpreter, Technical Report TR-003, ICOT - Institute for New Generation Computer Technology, Tokyo, Japan, January, 1983.

1360. SHAPIRO, E. Y., Lecture Notes on the Bagel: A Systolic Concurrent Prolog Machine, TM-0031, ICOT - Institute for New Generation Computer Technology, Tokyo, Japan, November 1983.

1361. SHAPIRO, E. Y., Lecture Notes on the Bagel: A Systolic Concurrent Prolog Machine, Technical Report CS84-10, Computer Science Department, Weizman Institute, Israel, 1984.

1362. SHAPIRO, E. Y., Concurrent Prolog as a Multiprocessor's Kernel Language, *POPL*, Salt Lake City, Utah, January, 1984.

1363. SHAPIRO, E. Y., Systems Programming in Concurrent Prolog, *POPL*, Salt Lake City, Utah, January, 1984.

1364. SHAPIRO, E. Y. and MIEROWSKY, C., Fair, Biased, and Self-Balancing Merge Operators: Their Specification and Implementation in Concurrent Prolog, Technical Report, Department of Applied Mathematics, The Weizmann Institute of Science, 1983. Also in Proceedings of the International IEEE Logic Programming Conference, Atlantic City, New Jersey, February 6-9, 1984, pp. 83-91.

1365. SHAPIRO, E. Y. and TAKEUCHI, A., Object Oriented Programming in Concurrent Prolog, *New Generation Computing 1*, (1983), Springer Verlag. Also ICOT Technical Report.

1366. SUZUKI, N., Experience with Specification and Verification of Complex Computer Hardware Using Concurrent Prolog, in *Logic Programming and it Applications*, D. H. D. WARREN and M. CANEGHEM, (eds.), Lawrence Erlbaum Press, 1984.

1367. SUZUKI, N., Concurrent Prolog as an Efficient VLSI Design Language, *IEEE Computer 18*, 2 (February, 1985).

1368. SZENES, K., FUTO, I. and SZEREDI, J., A Comparison of the Traditional and a New-principle Way Of Parallel Systems, Description, Simulation and Planning, *CL & CL*, 1985. Computer and Automation Institute, Hungarian Institute, Hungarian Academy of Sciences. (To appear).

1369. TAKEUCHI, A. and FURUKAWA, K., Interprocess Communication in Concurrent Prolog, Technical Report TR-006, ICOT - Institute for New Generation Computer Technology, Tokyo, Japan, 1983.

1370. TAM, C. M., The Design of a Distributed Interpreter for Concurrent Prolog, Technical Report 84-21, Department of Computer Science, University of British Columbia, Canada, 1984.

1371. TANAKA, Y., MPDC: Massive Parallel Architecture for Very Large Data Bases, *International Conference On Fifth Generation Computer Systems*, November 1984.

1372. TAYLOR, S., LOWRY, A., STOLFO, S. J. and MAQUIRE, G., Logic Programming Using Parallel Associative Operations, *Proceedings of the International IEEE Conference on Logic Programming*, Atlantic City, 1984. Also Technical Report, Department of Computer Science, Columbia University, 1982.

1373. TAYLOR, S., MAIO, C., STOLFO, S. J. and SHAW, D. E., Prolog on the DADO Machine: A Parallel System for High-Speed Computing, Technical Report, Department of Computer Science, Columbia University, 1983. Also 3rd Annual Phoenix Conference On Computers and Communication,IEEE, March 1984.

1374. UCHIDA, S., Inference Machine: From Sequential to Parallel, Technical Report TR-011, ICOT - Institute for New Generation Computer Technology, Tokyo, Japan, 1983. Also Published in the proceedings of the 10th International Symposium on Computer Architecture, June 1983, pp. 410-416.

1375. UEDA, K., TAKEUCHI, A., KUNIFUJI, S. and FURUKAWA, K., String Manipulation in Concurrent Prolog, Technical Report TR-036, ICOT - Institute for New Generation Computer Technology, Tokyo, Japan, 1983. In Japanese.

1376. UMEYAMA, S. and TAMURA, N., Parallel Execution of Logic Programs, *Proceedings of the 10th Symposium on Computer Architecture*, Stockholm, 1983.

1377. VITTER, J. S. and SIMONS, R. A., Parallel Algorithms for Unification and other Complete Problems in P, in *Proc ACM-84*, October 1984, 75-84.

1378. VODA, P. J., R-Maple: A Concurrent Programming Language Based on Predicate Logic. Part I: Syntax and Computation, Technical Report TR-83-9, Department of Computer Science, University of British Columbia, Canada, 1983.

1379. WARREN, D. H. D., Coroutining Facilities for Prolog, Implemented in PROLOG, DAI Research Paper, Department of Artificial Intelligence, University of Edinburgh, 1979.

1380. WISE, M. J., A Parallel Prolog: The Construction of a Data Driven Model, *Conference on LISP and Functional Programming*, August, 1982, 55-66.

1381. WISE, M. J., EPILOG = Prolog + Data Flow: Arguments for Combining Prolog with a Data Driven Mechanism, *ACM SIGPLAN Notices 17*, 12 (December, 1982), 80-86.

1382. WISE, M. J., EPILOG: Re-interpreting and Extending Prolog for a Multiprocessor Environment, in *Issues in Prolog Implementation*, J. A. CAMPBELL, (ed.), Ellis Horwood (U.K.), 1984.

1383. WISE, M. J., Concurrent Prolog on a Multiprocessor: A critique of Concurrent Prolog and Comparison with EPILOG, Department of Computer Science Report 8403, January, 1984.

1384. YASUHARA, H. and NITADORI, K., ORBIT: a parallel computing model of Prolog, *New Generation Computing 2*, 3 (1984), 277-288.

CHAPTER 11

Concurrent Prolog

1385. BONKOWSKI, B., DIDUR, P., MALCOLM, M. A., STAFFORD, G. and YOUNG, T., Programming in Waterloo Port, Technical Report, Department of Computer Science, University of Waterloo, Ontario, Canada, 1984.

1386. CLEARY, J. G., Implementation of Concurrent Prolog using Message Passing, *Draft Paper*, Alberta, Canada, 1984.

1387. DIDUR, P., MALCOLM, M. A. and MCWEENY, P. A., Waterloo Port User's Guide, Technical Report, Department of Computer Science, University of Waterloo, Ontario, Canada, 1984.

1388. EDELMAN, S. and SHAPIRO, E., Quadtrees in Concurrent Prolog, *Proceedings of the 1985 International Conference on Parallel Processing*, St. Charles, Illinois, USA, August, 1985.

1389. EDELMAN, S. and SHAPIRO, E. Y., Quadtrees in Concurrent Prolog, Technical Report CS84-19, Computer Science Department, Weizman Institute, Israel, 1984.

1390. VAN EMDEN, M. H. and GOEBEL, R. G., Waterloo UNIX Prolog Tutorial Version 1.2, Technical Report, Department of Computer Science, University of Waterloo, Ontario, Canada, 1984.

1391. FIAT, A., SHAMIR, A. and SHAPIRO, E. Y., Polymorphic arrays: an architecture for a programmable systolic machine, Weizmann Institute of Technical Report CS84-20, 1984.

1392. FURUKAWA, K., TAKEUCHI, A. and KUNIFUJI, S., Mandala: A Knowledge Programming Language based on Concurrent Prolog, ICOT Technical Memorandum TM-0028 (in Japanese) ICOT Technical Report TR-029 (in English), 1983.

1393. GELERNTER, D., A Note on Systems Programming in Concurrent Prolog, Technical Report, Yale University, 1983. Also in Proceedings of the International IEEE Logic Programming Conference, 1984.

1394. HELLERSTEIN, L., A Concurrent Prolog Based Region Finding Algorithm, Honors Thesis, Computer Science Department, Harvard University, May 1984.

1395. HELLERSTEIN, L. and SHAPIRO, E. Y., Algorithmic Programming in Concurrent Prolog: the MAXFLOW experience, Technical Report TR CS83-12, Department of Applied Mathematics, The Weizmann Institute of Science, 1983. Also in Proceedings of the International IEEE Logic Programming Conference, 1984.

1396. HIRAKAWA, H., CHIKAYAMA, T. and FURUKAWA, K., Eager and Lazy Enumerations in Concurrent Prolog, *Proceedings of the Second International Logic Programming Conference*, S. A. TARNLUND, ed., Uppsala University, Uppsala, Sweden, July 2-6, 1984, 89-100. Also available as ICOT TM-0036 Technical Report, 1984.

1397. ITO, N., SHIMIZU, H., KISHI, M., KUNO, E. and ROKUSAWA, K., Data-Flow Based Execution Mechanisms of Parallel and Concurrent Prolog, *New Generation Computing 3*, 1 (1985).

1398. KAHN, K. M., Experiences in Transporting Concurrent Prolog and the Bagel Simulator to LM-PROLOG - Part I of a Report of a Visit to ICOT November 1983, *Draft Paper*, 1984.

1399. KIRAKAWA, H., Chart Parsing in Concurrent Prolog, Technical Report TR-008, ICOT - Institute for New Generation Computer Technology, Tokyo, Japan, 1983.

1400. KIRAKAWA, H., ONAI, R. and FURUKAWA, K., Implementing an OR-Parallel Optimizing System (POPS) in Concurrent Prolog, Technical Report TR-020, ICOT - Institute for New Generation Computer Technology, Tokyo, Japan, 1983.

1401. KUSALIK, A. J., Bounded-Wait Merge in Shapiro's Concurrent Prolog, Technical Report, Department of Computer Science, University of British Columbia, 1984.

1402. KUSALIK, A. J., Serialization of Process Reduction in Concurrent Prolog, *New Generation Computing 2*, 3 (1984).

1403. LEE, R. K. S., Concurrent Prolog in a Multi-Process Environment, Technical Report CS-84-46, Department of Computer Science, University of Waterloo, Ontario, Canada, 1984.

1404. LEE, R. and GOEBEL, R., Concurrent Prolog in a Multi-Process Environment, *Proceedings of the 2nd IEEE International Symposium on Logic Programming*, Boston, USA, July, 1985.

1405. LEVI, G. and PALAMIDESSI, C., The Declarative Semantics of Logical Read-only Variables, *Proceedings of the 2nd IEEE International Symposium on Logic Programming*, Boston, USA, July, 1985.

1406. LEVY, J., A Unification Algorithm For Concurrent Prolog, *Proceedings of the Second International Logic Programming Conference*, S. TARNLUND, ed., Uppsala University, Uppsala, Sweden, July 2-6, 1984, 331-342. Also available as a Technical Report from the Weizmann Institute of Science, Rechovot, Israel.

1407. MIEROWSKY, C., Design and Implementation of Flat Concurrent Prolog, Technical Report CS84-21, Computer Science Department, Weizman Institute, Israel, 1984.

1408. MIYAZAKI, T., TAKEUCHI, A. and CHIKAYAMA, T., A Sequential Implementation of Concurrent Prolog Based on the Shallow Binding Scheme, *Proceedings of the 2nd IEEE International Symposium on Logic Programming*, Boston, USA, July, 1985.

1409. SARASWAT, V., Problems with Concurrent Prolog, Technical Report, Department of Computer Science, Carnegie Mellon University, 1985.

1410. SHAFRIR, A. and SHAPIRO, E. Y., Distributed Programming in Concurrent Prolog, Technical Report, Department of Applied Mathematics, The Weizmann Institute of Science, 1984.

1411. SHAPIRO, E. Y., A Subset of Concurrent Prolog and Its Interpreter, Technical Report TR-003, ICOT - Institute for New Generation Computer Technology, Tokyo, Japan, January, 1983.

1412. SHAPIRO, E. Y., Lecture Notes on the Bagel: A Systolic Concurrent Prolog Machine, TM-0031, ICOT - Institute for New Generation Computer Technology, Tokyo, Japan, November 1983.

1413. SHAPIRO, E. Y., Lecture Notes on the Bagel: A Systolic Concurrent Prolog Machine, Technical Report CS84-10, Computer Science Department, Weizman Institute, Israel, 1984.

1414. SHAPIRO, E. Y., Concurrent Prolog as a Multiprocessor's Kernel Language, *POPL*, Salt Lake City, Utah, January, 1984.

1415. SHAPIRO, E. Y., Systems Programming in Concurrent Prolog, *POPL*, Salt Lake City, Utah, January, 1984.

1416. SHAPIRO, E. Y. and MIEROWSKY, C., Fair, Biased, and Self-Balancing Merge Operators: Their Specification and Implementation in Concurrent Prolog, Technical Report, Department of Applied Mathematics, The Weizmann Institute of Science, 1983. Also in Proceedings of the International IEEE Logic Programming Conference, Atlantic City, New Jersey, February 6-9, 1984, pp. 83-91.

1417. SHAPIRO, E. Y. and TAKEUCHI, A., Object Oriented Programming in Concurrent Prolog, *New Generation Computing 1*, (1983), Springer Verlag. Also ICOT Technical Report.

1418. SUZUKI, N., Experience with Specification and Verification of Complex Computer Hardware Using Concurrent Prolog, in *Logic Programming and it Applications*, D. H. D. WARREN and M. CANEGHEM, (eds.), Lawrence Erlbaum Press, 1984.

1419. SUZUKI, N., Concurrent Prolog as an Efficient VLSI Design Language, *IEEE Computer 18*, 2 (February, 1985).

1420. TAKEUCHI, A. and FURUKAWA, K., Interprocess Communication in Concurrent Prolog, Technical Report TR-006, ICOT - Institute for New Generation Computer Technology, Tokyo, Japan, 1983.

1421. TAM, C. M., The Design of a Distributed Interpreter for Concurrent Prolog, Technical Report 84-21, Department of Computer Science, University of British Columbia, Canada, 1984.

1422. WISE, M. J., Concurrent Prolog on a Multiprocessor: A critique of Concurrent Prolog and Comparison with EPILOG, Department of Computer Science Report 8403, January, 1984.

CHAPTER 12

Functional Programming and Equality: their Relationship with Logic Programming

1423. BARBUTI, R., BELLIA, M., LEVI, G. and MARTELLI, M., On the Integration of Logic Programming and Functional Programming, *Proceedings of the International IEEE Conference on Logic Programming*, Atlantic City, 1984.

1424. BARBUTI, R., BELLIA, M., LEVI, G. and MARTELLI, M., LEAF: a language which integrates logic, equations and functions, in *Functional Programming and Logic Programming*, D. DEGROOT and G. LINDSTROM, (eds.), Prentice Hall, June 1985.

1425. BELLIA, M., DEGANO, P. and LEVI, G., A Functional plus Predicate Logic Programming Language, *Workshop on Logic Programming*, Debrecen, Hungary, July 1980.

1426. BELLIA, M., DEGANO, P. and LEVI, G., The Call by Name Semantics of a Clause Language with Functions, in *Logic Programming*, K. L. CLARK and S. TARNLUND, (eds.), Academic Press, New York, 1982, 281-298. A.P.I.C. Studies in Data Processing No. 16.

1427. BURSTALL, R. M., Programming with Modules as Typed Functional Programming, *Proceedings of the 1984 Conference on Fifth Generation Computer Systems*, Tokyo, Japan, November, 1984.

1428. CARLSSON, M., (Re)Implementing Prolog in LISP or YAQ - Yet Another QLISP, Technical Report, Computer Science Department, Uppsala University, 1982.

1429. CARLSSON, M., On Implementing Prolog in Functional Programming, *Proceedings of the International IEEE Conference on Logic Programming*, Atlantic City, 1984. Also UPMAIL Technical Report 5B, Uppsala University.

1430. COHEN, S., The APPLOG language , in *Functional Programming and Logic Programming*, D. DEGROOT and G. LINDSTROM, (eds.), Prentice Hall, June 1985.

1431. COX, P. T., Advanced Programming Aids in PROGRAPH, *Proceedings of the 1985 ACM Sigsmall Symposium on Small Systems*, Danvers, Massachusetss, May, 1985.

1432. COX, P. T., Compiling the Graphical Functional Language PROGRAPH, *Proceedings of the 1985 ACM Sigsmall Symposium on Small Systems*, Danvers, Massachusetss, May, 1985.

1433. DARLINGTON, J. and BURSTALL, R. M., A transformational system for developing recursive programs, *JACM 29*, 1982.

1434. DARLINGTON, J. and REEVE, M., ALICE: A Multi-Processor Reduction Machine for the Parallel Evaluation of Applicative Languages, *Proceedings of the Conference on Functional Programming Languages and Computer Architecture*, Portsmouth, New Hampshire, October 1981, 65-75.

1435. *Functional Programming and Logic Programming*, D. DEGROOT and G. LINDSTROM, (eds.), Prentice Hall, June 1985.

1436. DIGRICOLI, V. J., Resolution by Unification and Equality, *Proceedings of the 4th Workshop on Automated Deduction*, Austin, Texas, 1979, 43-52.

1437. FRIBOURG, L., Oriented Equational Clauses as a Programming Language, *The Journal Of Logic Programming 1*, 2 (August 1984), 165-178.

1438. GOGUEN, J. A. and MESEGUER, J., Equality, Types, Modules and Generics for Logic Programming, *Proceedings of the Second International Logic Programming Conference,* S. TARNLUND, ed., Uppsala University, Uppsala, Sweden, July 2-6, 1984, 115-126. Also as Technical Report, SRI, Stanford.

1439. GREUSSAY, P., LOVLISP: Une Extension de VLISP vers Prolog, Technical Report, Universite de Paris 8, France, 1984.

1440. GUTIERREZ, C., Prolog Compared with LISP, *ACM Symposium on LISP and Functional Programming*, 1982.

1441. HUDAK, P. and BLOSS, A., Avoiding Copying in Functional and Logic Programming Languages, *Symposium on the Principles of Programming Languages*, Los Angeles, 1985.

1442. JAFFAR, J., LASSEZ, J. L. and MAHER, M. J., A Theory of Complete Logic Programs With Equality, Technical Report , Monash University, Clayton, Victoria, Australia, May, 1984. Also FGCS Conference Proceedings, 1984.

1443. JAFFAR, J., LASSEZ, J. L. and MAHER, M. J., A Logic Programming Language Scheme, in *Functional Programming and Logic Programming*, D. DEGROOT and G. LINDSTROM, (eds.), Prentice Hall, June 1985.

1444. KOMOROWSKI, H. J., Embedding Prolog in LISP: an example of a LISP craft technique, LITH-MATH-R-1981-2, Linkoping University, Informatics Laboratory, Linkoping, Sweden, March, 1981.

1445. KORNFELD, W. A., Equality for Prolog, *Proceedings of the International Joint Conference on Artificial Intelligence*, Karlsruhe, Germany, 1983.

1446. KOWALSKI, R. A., The Case For Using Equality Axioms In Automatic Demonstration, in *Anthology Of Automated Theorem-Proving Papers, Vol. 1*, Springer Verlag, 1982. Symposium On Automatic Demonstration.

1447. LINDSTROM, G., Functional Programming and the Logical Variable, *Symposium on the Principles of Programming Languages*, Los Angeles, 1985.

1448. MAHER, M. J., Semantics of Logic Programs, PhD Thesis, University of Melbourne, Department of Computer Science, 1985.

1449. MALACHI, Y., MANNA, Z. and WALDINGER, R., TABLOG: The Deductive-Tableau Programming Language, *ACM Symposium on Lisp and Functional Programming*, 1984.

1450. MORRIS, J. B., E-resolution: Extension of Resolution to Include the Equality Relation, *Proceedings of the International Joint Conference on Artificial Intelligence*, Washington, D.C., May 7-9, 1969, 287-294.

1451. O'KEEFE, R. A., Prolog Compared with LISP ?, *ACM Sigplan Notices*, August 1983. Also available as a Research Paper from Artificial Intelligence Department, University of Edinburgh.

1452. REDDY, U. S., Transformation of Logic Programs into Functional Programs, *Proceedings of the International IEEE Conference on Logic Programming*, Atlantic City, 1984.

1453. REDDY, U. S., On the Relationship between Logic and Functional Languages, in *Functional and Logic Programming*, D. DEGROOT and G. LINDSTROM, (eds.), Prentice-Hall, 1985.

1454. REITER, R., Equality and Domain Closure for first order databases, *Journal of the ACM 27*, 2 (April 1980), 235-249.

1455. ROBINSON, G. and WOS, L., Paramodulation and Theorem Proving in First Order Theories with Equality, *Machine Intelligence 4*, (1969), 135-150, American Elsevier.

1456. SATO, M. and SAKURAI, T., Qute: A Prolog/LISP Type Language for Logic Programming, *Proceedings of the International Joint Conference on Artificial Intelligence*, Karlsruhe, Germany, 1983. Also Technical Report TR-016, ICOT - Institute for New Generation Computer.

1457. SATO, M. and SAKURAI, T., Qute: A Functional Language Based On Unification, *International Conference On Fifth Generation Computer Systems*, November 1984.

1458. SMOLKA, G., Fresh: A Higher-Order Language with Unification and Multiple Results, in *Logic Programming: Relations, Functions, and Equations*, D. D. G. LINDSTROM, (ed.), Prentice-Hall, Inc., Inglewood Cliffs, 1985.

1459. SRIVASTAVA, A., OXLEY, D. and SRIVASTAVA, A., An(other) Integration of Logic and Functional Programming, *Proceedings of the 2nd IEEE International Symposium on Logic Programming*, Boston, USA, July, 1985.

1460. SUBRAHMANYAM, P. A. and YOU, J. H., FUNLOG: A Computational Model Integrating Logic Programming and Functional Programming, Technical Report UTEC-83-040, Department of Computer Science, University of Utah. Also in, D. DeGroot, G. Lindstrom, Functional Programming and Logic Programming, June 1985, Prentice Hall.

1461. SUBRAHMANYAM, P. A. and YOU, J. H., On Embedding Function in Logic, *Information Processing Letters 19*, (1984), 41-46.

1462. TORII, K., SUGIYAMA, Y. and MORISAWA, Y., Functional Programming and Logic Programming for Telegram Analysis Problem, *Proceedings of the Seventh IEEE International Conference on Software Engineering*, 1984.

1463. VODA, P. J. and YU, B., RF-Maple: A Logic Programming Language with Functions, Types and Concurrency, *International Conference On Fifth Generation Computer Systems*, November 1984.

1464. WINTERSTEIN, G., Pradikatenlogik-Programme mit Evaluierbare Functionen, Technical Report, Doctoral Dissertation, University of Kaiserslautern, Germany, 1978.

CHAPTER 13

Other Application Areas
of Logic Programming

1465. ABRAMSON, H., A Prological Definition of HASL, *Proceedings of Workshop on Logic Programming*, Algarve, Portugal, 1983.

1466. ALLEN, J. F. and LUCKHAM, D., An Interactive Theorem-proving Program, in *Machine Intelligence*, vol. 5, B. MELTZER and D. MICHIE, (eds.), American Elsevier, New York, 1970, 321-336.

1467. ANDERSON, S. O., NEVES, J. C. and WILLIAMS, M. H., Extended Integrity Constraints in Query-By-Example, Technical Report, Heriot-Watt University, Edinburg, 1982.

1468. APONTE, M. V., FERNANDEZ, J. A. and ROUSSEL, P., Editing First-Order Proofs: Programmed Rules Versus Derived Rules, *Proceedings of the International IEEE Conference on Logic Programming*, Atlantic City, 1984.

1469. AZEMA, P., JUANOLE, G. and SANCHIS, E., Specification and Verification of Distributed Systems using Prolog Interpreted Petri Nets, *Proceedings of the Seventh IEEE International Conference on Software Engineering*, 1984.

1470. BACKHOUSE, R. C., NEVES, J. C., WILLIAMS, M. H. and ANDERSON, S. O., A Prolog Implementation of Query-By-Example, Technical Report, Heriot-Watt University, Edinburg, 1982. Also in Proceedings of the Seventh International Symposium on Computing, Germany.

1471. BALL, D., PrologO: Turtle Graphics in Micro-Prolog on the Research Machines 380Z, Technical Report, Department of Computer Science, Unversity of Leicester, 1982.

1472. BALOGH, K. and OTHERS, The Application of the Prolog Language to the Design of Software and Hardware Objects, NIM IGUSZI and SZKI Technical Report, SZKI Institute, Budapest, Hungary, 1978. In Hungarian.

1473. BALOGH, K., On a Logical Method Serving the Proof of the Semantic Features of Programs, Technical Report, Department of Computer Science, Eotvos Lorand University, Budapest, 1979. In Hungarian.

1474. BALOGH, K., FUTO, I. and LABADI, K., The Documentation of a Prolog Program Verification System, Technical Report NIM IGUSZI, Eotvos Lorand University, Budapest, 1977. In Hungarian.

1475. BALOGH, K., FUTO, I. and LABADI, K., On an Interactive Program Verifier for Prolog Programs, *Proceedings of a Colloqium on Mathematical Logic in Programming*, 1978.

1476. BALOGH, K. and LABADI, K., Software Applications for the Mathematical Logic, *Proceedings of the Conference on Programming Systems*, Szeged, Hungary, 1975, 26-44. In Hungarian.

1477. BALZER, R. M., Imprecise Program Specification, Technical Report RR-75-36, Information Sciences Institute, Marina Del Rey, 1975.

1478. BANDES, R. G., Algebraic Specification and Prolog, Technical Report TR-82-12-02, Department of Computer Science, University of Washington, Seattle, 1982.

1479. BARROW, H. G., Proving the Correctness of Digital Hardware Designs, *Proceedings of the National Conference on Artificial Intelligence*, Washington D.C., August, 1983. AAAI-83.

1480. BARROW, H. G., VERIFY: A Program for Proving Correctness of Digital Hardware Designs, in *Qualitative Reasoning about Physical Systems*, D. G. BOBROW, (ed.), MIT Press, 1985.

1481. BARTHES, J. P., VAYSSADE, M. and MIACZYNSKA, M., Property Driven Data Bases, International Joint Conference on Artificial Intelligence, Tokyo, Japan, 1979.

1482. BATTANI, G. and MELONI, H., Un Bel Example de Prolog en Analyse et Synthese, Technical Report, Groupe d'Intelligence Artificielle, Universite d'Aix-Marseille II, Marseille, France, 1974.

1483. BAXTER, L. D., Prolog Comments, *ACM Sigart Newsletter 73*, (October 1980), 18.

1484. BAXTER, L. D., A Prolog Program Illustrating a Verify and Choose Method, Technical Report, Computer Science Department, York University, 1981.

1485. BECKER, J. M., AQ-Prolog User's Guide and Program Description, Technical Report, Department of Computer Science, University of Illinois, December 1983.

1486. BELLIA, M., DEGANO, P., LEVI, G., DAMERI, E. and MARTELLI, A., From Term Rewriting Systems to Distributed Program Specifications, Technical Report, University of Pisa, Italy, 1982.

1487. BELOVARI, G., Progress in Prolog-Based Robot Problem Solving, Technical Report, Department of Computer Science, University of Uppsala, Sweden, 1984.

1488. BELOVARI, G. and CAMPBELL, J. A., Generating Contours of Integration: An Application of Prolog in Symbolic Computing, in *Lecture Notes in Computer Science 87: 5th Conference on Automated Deduction*, W. BIBEL and R. A. KOWALSKI, (eds.), Springer-Verlag, Berlin, Germany, 1980, 14-23.

1489. BENDL, J., LUGOSI, G. and MARKUSZ, Z. S., An Interactive System for Checking Air Pollution, *Informacio-Elektronika XIV*, 1 (1979), 55-58. In Hungarian.

1490. BERGER-SABBATEL, G., Logique Conceptuelle, Technical Report, Groupe d'Intelligence Artificielle, Marseille, France, 1979.

1491. BERGMAN, M., Resolution par la Demonstration Automatique de Quelques Problemes en Integration Symbolique sur Calculateur, Technical Report, Groupe d'Intelligence Artificielle, Universite d'Aix-Marseille II, Marseille, France, 1973. Thesis.

1492. BERGMAN, M. and DERANSART, P., Abstract Data Types And Rewriting Systems: Application To The Programming Of Algebraic Abstract Data Types In Prolog, *CAAP'81 Trees In Algebra And Programming, 6th Colloqium*, March 1981. Also Lecture Notes in Computer Science no. 112.

1493. BERGMAN, M. and KANOUI, H., Application of Mechanical Theorem Proving to Symbolic Calculus, *In Third International Symposium on Advanced Computing Methods in Theoretical Physics C.N.R.S.*, 1973. Also available as Technical Report from the University of Marseille.

1494. BERGMAN, M. and KANOUI, H., Sycophante: Systeme de Calcul Formel et d'Interrogation Symbolique sur l'Ordinateur, Technical Report, Groupe d'Intelligence Artificielle, Universite d'Aix-Marseille II, Marseille, France, October 1975.

1495. BESNARD, P., QUINIOU, R. and QUINTON, P., A Theorem-Prover for a Decidable Subset of Default Logic, in *Proceedings of National Conference on Artificial Intelligence*, Washington D.C., August 1983. AAAI-83.

1496. BIJL, A., Dumb Drawing Systems and Knowledge Engineering, Technical Report TR-81-08, EdCaad Department, University of Edinburgh, 1981. Also in Proceedings of CAD-82.

1497. BORNING, A., A Powerful Matcher for Algebraic Equation Solving, Working Paper 67, Department of Artificial Intelligence, University of Edinburgh, Scotland, May, 1980.

1498. BORNING, A. and BUNDY, A., Using Matching in Algebraic Equation Solving, *Proceedings of the International Conference on Artificial Intelligence 1981*, 1981, 466-471. Also available from The University of Edinburgh as DAI Research Paper No. 158.

1499. BOSCO, P. G., GIANDONATO, G. and GIOVANETTI, E., A Prolog System For The Verification of Concurrent Processes Against Temporal Logic Specifications, *Proceedings of the Second International Logic Programming Conference*, S. TARNLUND, ed., Uppsala University, Uppsala, Sweden, July 2-6, 1984, 219-230.

1500. BOUCHON, P. and VIDAL, J., An Intelligent Router for VLSI Design, Technical Report CSD 840058, Department of Computer Science, University of California, Los Angeles, 1984.

1501. BOURGAULT, S. and DINCBAS, M., Using Artificial Intelligence Techniques In The Design Of Software For Digital Switching Systems, *Proceedings of the 11th International Switching Symposium*, Florence, Italy, May, 1984.

1502. BRATKO, I., Knowledge-Based Problem-Solving in AL3, in *Intelligent Systems: Practice and Experience - Machine Intelligence 10*, J. E. HAYES, D. MICHIE and Y. H. PAO, (eds.), 1982, 73-100.

1503. BRAZDIL, P., A Model for Error Detection and Correction, DAI Research Report 47, Department of Artificial Intelligence, University of Edinburgh, 1981. Ph.D. Dissertation.

1504. BRAZDIL, P., Symbolic Derivations of Chess Patterns, *Proceedings of the European Conference on Artificial Intelligence 1982*, Orsay, France, 1982.

1505. BRAZDIL, P., Use Of Metalogical Primitives In Communication, *Sixth European Conference On Artificial Intelligence*, Pisa, September, 1984.

1506. BRIGGS, J. H., Teaching Mathematics with Prolog, Technical Report, Department of Computer Science, Imperial College, London, 1982.

1507. BRIGGS, J. H., Applying Logic Programming Techniques To History Teaching, Technical Report, Department of Computing, Imperial College, 1984.

1508. BRIGGS, J. H., Designing And Implementing A Child-oriented Interface to Micro-Prolog, Technical Report, Department of Computing, Imperial College, 1984.

1509. BRIGGS, J. H., FRENCH, P. and STEELE, B. D., Logic Programming For Expert Systems: A Two Day Course, The Logic Training Partnership, Imperial College, London, 1984.

1510. BRUYNOOGHE, M., An Interface between Prolog and Cyber-EDMS, *Proceedings of Workshop on Logic and Databases*, Toulouse, France, 1977.

1511. BRUYNOOGHE, M. and VENKEN, R., Prolog as a language for Prototyping of Information Systems, in *Approaches To Prototyping*, R. BUDDE, (ed.), Springer-Verlag, Berlin, 1984.

1512. BUNDY, A., Will It Reach the Top? Predictions in the Mechanics World, *Artificial Intelligence 10*, (1978), 129-146. Also in Cognitive Science, 1, 1977, 193-215, and DAI Research Report 31,Department of Artificial Intelligencea, University of Edinburgh.

1513. BUNDY, A., Mathematical Reasoning Course Notes, DAI Report I Department of Artificial Intelligence, University of Edinburgh, 1979.

1514. BUNDY, A., Meta-Level Inference and Consciousness, DAI Research Paper No 187, Department of Artificial Intelligence, University of Edinburgh, 1983.

1515. BUNDY, A., The Impress Proof Plan Revisited, Working Paper 138, Department of Artificial Intelligence, University of Edinburgh, April, 1983.

1516. BUNDY, A., Proof Analysis: A Technique For Concept Formation, Research Paper 198, Department of Artificial Intelligence, University of Edinburgh, September, 1983.

1517. BUNDY, A., BYRD, L., LUGER, G., MELLISH, C. S. and PALMER, M. S., Solving Mechanics Problems Using Meta-Level Inference, in *Expert Systems in the Microelectronic Age*, D. MICHIE, (ed.), University of Edinburgh, Scotland, 1979, 153-167. Also in Proceedings International Joint Conference on Artificial Intelligence-79 and available as a Edinburgh Research Report.

1518. BUNDY, A., BYRD, L. and MELLISH, C. S., Special Purpose, but Domain Independent Inference Mechanisms, *Proceedings of European Conference on Artificial Intelligence*, 1982. Also available from Edinburgh as DAI Research Paper No. 179.

1519. BUNDY, A., LUGER, G., MELLISH, C. S. and PALMER, M. S., Knowledge about Knowledge: Making Decisions in Mechanics Problem Solving, *Proceedings of AISB-78*, University of Edinburgh, 1978, 71-82.

1520. BUNDY, A. and SILVER, B., Homogenization: Preparing Equations for Change of Unknown, *Proceedings of International Joint Conference on Artificial Intelligence-81*, R. SCHANK, ed., 1981. Longer version available from Edinburgh as DAI Research Paper No. 159.

1521. BUNDY, A. and SILVER, B., A Critical Survey of Rule Learning Programs, *Proceedings of the European Conference on Artificial Intelligence*, 1982.

1522. BUNDY, A. and STERLING, L., Meta-Level Inference in Algebra, Research Paper 164, Department of Artificial Intelligence, University of Edinburgh, Scotland, September, 1981. Presented at the Workshop on Logic Programming for Intelligent Systems, Long Beach, California, 1981.

1523. BUNDY, A. and WELHAM, B., Using Meta-Level Inference for Selective Application of Multiple Rewrite Rules in Algebraic Manipulation, *Artificial Intelligence 16*, 2 (1981), 189-212. Also in Lecture Notes in Computer Science No. 87 by Springer-Verlag.

1524. M. VAN CANEGHEM, ed., *Proceedings of the First International Logic Programming Conference*, Marseille, France, September, 1982.

1525. M. VAN CANEGHEM and D. H. D. WARREN, eds., *Logic Programming and Its Applications*, Ablex Publishing Company, 1984.

1526. CARRE, M. F. and SALLE, P., Acteurs et Programmation en Logique, Technical Report, Ecole Nationale Superieure d'Electronique et d'Informatique, Toulouse, France, 1984.

1527. CARROLL, J. M. and WU, O., Using Prolog to Assess Security Risks in Data Processing Systems Programs, *Logic Programming Newsletter*, December, 1982.

1528. CHANG, C. L. and WALKER, A., PROSQL: A Prolog Programming Interface with SQL/DS, Technical Report RJ 4314, IBM Watson Research Center, 1984.

1529. CHOURAQUI, E., Construction of Data Structures for Representing Real World Knowledge, *Proceedings of the IFIP*, 1979.

1530. CLARK, K. L. and DARLINGTON, J., Algorithmic Classification Through Synthesis, *The Computer Journal 23*, 1 (1980).

1531. CLARK, K. L. and VAN EMDEN, M. H., Consequence Verification of Flowcharts, Technical Report 79-8, Computer Science Department, Imperial College, London, 1979. Also in IEEE Transactions on Software Engineering, Vol SE-7, No 1, 1981.

1532. CLARK, K. L., McKEEMAN, W. M. and SICKEL, S., Logic Program Specification of Numerical Integration, Technical Report 82-3, Computer Science Department, Imperial College, London, 1983.

1533. K. L. CLARK and S. A. TARNLUND, eds., *Logic Programming*, Academic Press, 1982. A.P.I.C. Studies in Data Processing No. 16.

1534. CLARK, M. J. N., HAYES, P. J., MARKS, J. O., PETTITT, P. and REEDER, M. W., Representation of Legislation & Aids for its Interpretation, *International Conference On Fifth Generation Computer Systems*, November 1984.

1535. CLOCKSIN, W. F., Real-Time Functional Queue Operations Using the Logical Variable, *Information Processing Letters 17*, (1983), 173-175.

1536. COELHO, H., TUGA user's manual, DI Report, Laboratoria Nacional De Engenharia Civil, Lisbon, Portugal, 1979.

1537. COELHO, H., How to Solve it with Prolog, DI Report - Third Edition, Laboratoria Nacional De Engenharia Civil, Lisbon, Portugal, 1979.

1538. COELHO, H., Logic Programming at Work: The Case of a Civil Engineering Environment, in *Artificial Intelligence and Information-Control Systems of Robots*, I. PLANDER, (ed.), Elsevier, 1984.

1539. COELHO, H., COTTA, J. C. and PEREIRA, L. M., How To Solve it with Prolog, Technical Report, Laboratorio Nacional de Engenharia Civil, Lisbon, Portugal, 1980. Collection of examples.

1540. COELHO, H. and PEREIRA, L. M., GEOM: A Prolog Geometry Theorem Prover, Technical Report Memo 525, Laboratorio Nacional de Engenharia Civil, Lisbon, Portugal, 1979.

1541. CORY, H. T., HAMMOND, P., KOWALSKI, R. A., KRIWACZEK, F. R., SADRI, F. and SERGOT, M. J., The British Nationality Act As A Logic Program, Department of Computing, Imperial College, 1984.

1542. DAHL, V. and ABRAMSON, H., On Gapping Grammars, *Proceedings of the Second International Logic Programming Conference*, S. A. TARNLUND, ed., Uppsala University, Uppsala, Sweden, July 2-6, 1984, 77-88.

1543. DARVAS, F., A Program for the Automatic Filtering of Drug Interactions, *Proceedings of the Colloquim on the Application of Computing in Medecine and Biology*, Szegded, Hungary, 1976. In Hungarian.

1544. DARVAS, F., Computer Analysis of the Relationship between the Biological Effect and the Chemical Structure, *Kemai Kozlemenyek*, 1978, 97-116. In Hungarian.

1545. DARVAS, F. and OTHERS, A Prolog-Based Drug Design System, *Proceedings of the Conference on Programming Systems*, Szeged, Hungary, 1978. In Hungarian.

1546. DARVAS, F. and OTHERS, A Logic Based Chemical Information System, *Proceedings of the First National Conference of the von Neumann Computer Science Society*, Szeged, Hungary, 1979, 92-96. In Hungarian.

1547. DARVAS, F., Logic Programming in Chemical Information Handling and Drug Design, in *Workshop on Logic Programming*, S. A. TARNLUND, (ed.), Debrecen, Hungary, July 1980.

1548. DARVAS, F., BEIN, K. and GABANYI, Z., A Logic-Based Expert System for Model Building in Regression Analysis, *Proceedings of Workshop on Logic Programming*, Algarve, Portugal, 1983.

1549. DARVAS, F., FUTO, I. and CHOLNOKY, E., Practical Applications of an AI Language: Prolog, *Proceeding of the Second Hungarian Computer Science Conference*, Budapest, Hungary, , 388-399. In Hungarian.

1550. DARVAS, F., FUTO, I. and SZEREDI, P., A Logic Based Program System for Predicting Drug Interactions, *International Journal of Biomedical Computing 9*, 4 (1977).

1551. DARVAS, F., FUTO, I. and SZEREDI, P., Some Applications of Theorem Proving Based Machine Intelligence in Qsar, *Proceedings of a Sumposium on Chemical-Biological Activity*, 1978, 251-256.

1552. DARVAS, F., FUTO, I. and SZEREDI, P., Expected Interactions of Spirololactions: Predictions by Computer, *Proceedings of the Conference on Pathogenesis of Hyperaldosteronism*, Hungary, 1979, 219-220. In Hungarian.

1553. DARVAS, F., LOPATA, A. and MATRAI, G., A Specific QSAR Model for Peptides, in *Quantitative Structure Activity Analysis*, F. DARVAS, (ed.), Akademiai Kiado, Budapest, Hungary, 1980, 265-278.

1554. DAVIS, R. E., Generating Correct Programs from Logic Specifications, Technical Report TR-05-001, Computer Science Department, University of California, Santa Cruz, 1979.

1555. DAVIS, R. E., Runnable Specification as a Design Tool, *Workshop on Logic Programming*, Debrecen, Hungary, July 1980.

1556. DEAN, J. and MICHOL, J., Computer Assisted Learning In History: BOGBOD, A Detective Exercise Written In Prolog, *AISB Easter Conference on Artificial Intelligence and Education*, 1983.

1557. DEBENHAM, J. K. and McGRATH, G. M., The Description in Logic of a Large Commercial Database: A Methodology Put to the Test, *Australian Computer Science Communications 5*, (1982), 12-21.

1558. DELIYANNI, A. and KOWALSKI, R. A., Logic and Semantic Networks, *Communications of the ACM 22*, 3 (March 1979), 184-192.

1559. DEMOLOMBE, R., Assigning Meaning to Ill-Defined Queries Expressed in Predicate Calculus Language, *Proceedings of the Workshop on Logic and Databases*, Toulouse, France, 1977.

1560. DERBY, H., Using Logic Programming for Compiling APL, Technical Report 84-5134, California Institute of Technology, Los Angeles, California, 1984.

1561. DOMOLKI, B. and SZEREDI, P., Prolog in Practice, *Information Processing*, R. E. A. MASON, ed., 1983, 627-636.

1562. DROSTEN, K. and EHRICH, H. D., Translating Algebraic Specifications to Prolog Programs, Technical Report 84-08 84-08, Department of Computer Science, Technical University of Braunschweig, 1984.

1563. DWIGGINGS, D., Prolog as a System Design Tool, *Proceedings of the 16th Annual Hawaii International Conference on System Sciences*, 1983.

1564. DWIGGINGS, D. and SILVA, G., A Knowledge-Based Automated Message Understanding Methodology for an Advanced Indications Systems, Technical Report R79-006, Operating Systems Division, Logicon, Woodland Hills, Ca, 1979.

1565. EDER, G., A System for Cautious Planning, Working Paper 27, Department of Artificial Intelligence, University of Edinburgh, 1976.

1566. EDGAR, G. A., A Compiler Written in Prolog, *Dr. Dobbs Journal*, May, 1985.

1567. EDMAN, A. and TARNLUND, S. A., Mechanization of an Oracle in a Debugging System, *Proceedings of the International Joint Conference on Artificial Intelligence*, Karlsruhe, Germany, 1983.

1568. EGGERT, P. R. and CHOW, K. P., Logic Programming Graphics and Infinite Terms, TR 83-02, Department of Computer Science, University of California, Santa Barbara, June 1983.

1569. EGGERT, P. R. and SCHORRE, D. V., Logic Enhancement: A Method for Extending Logic Programming Languages, *Proceedings 1982 ACM Symposium on LISP and Functional Programming*, Pittsburgh, PA, 1982, 74-80.

1570. EHRLICH, S. M. and GABRIEL, J. R., Cutsets with Required Arcs: A Prolog-Based Approach, Technical Report ANL-MCS-TM-11, Argonne National Laboratory, Illinois, 1983.

1571. EHRLICH, S. M., GABRIEL, J. R., GONEN, A. and KUCHNIR, L., Graph Theoretic Approaches to Diagnostics: Applications of Logic Programming and Cutset Theory to Aspects of Reactor and Circuit Analysis, Technical Report ANL-84-74, Mathematical and Computer Science Division, Argonne National Laboratories, January, 1985.

1572. EMDE, W., HABEL, C. U. and ROLLINGER, C. R., The Discovery of the Equator or Concept Driven Learning, *Proceedings of the International Joint Conference on Artificial Intelligence*, Karlsruhe, Germany, 1983, 455-458.

1573. VAN EMDEN, M. H., Relational Programming Illustrated by a Program for the Game of Mastermind, Technical Report CS-78-48, Department of Computer Science, University of Waterloo,Canada, 1978.

1574. VAN EMDEN, M. H., Chess-Endgame Advice: A Case Study in Computer Utilization of Knowledge, Technical Report CS-80-05, Department of Computer Science, University of Waterloo,Canada, 1980. Published in the Proceedings of the Infotech State-of-the-Art Conference on Expert Systems, London 1980.

1575. VAN EMDEN, M. H., A Runnable Specification of AVL-Tree Insertion, Technical Report CS-81-14, Department of Computer Science, University of Waterloo,Canada, 1981.

1576. VAN EMDEN, M. H. and GOEBEL, R. G., Prolog Programming Environments, *Logic Programming Group Bulletin*, December, 1983, 1-2.

1577. VAN EMDEN, M. H. and MAIBAUM, T. S., Equations Compared with Clauses for Specification of Abstract Data Types, Technical Report, Department of Computer Science, University of Waterloo,Canada, 1979. Also appeared in Advances in Database Theory, H. Gallaire, J. Minker, and J.M. Nicolas (eds), Plenum Press, 1981..

1578. ENNALS, J. R., Teaching Logic as a Computer Language in Schools, *Proceedings of the First International Logic Programming Conference*, M. VAN CANEGHEM, ed., Marseille, France, September 14-17, 1982, 99-104. Also Published in New Horizons in Educational Computing, M. Yazdani (ed), Ellis Horwood, 1984.

1579. ENNALS, J. R., Revolution in Education, *Practical Computing*, December, 1982, 137-138.

1580. ENNALS, J. R., BRIGGS, J. H. and WEIR, D., Logic Across the Curriculum, *AISB Easter Conference on Artificial Intelligence and Education*, University of Exeter , U.K., April 1983.

1581. ERIKSSON, L. and JOHANSSON, A. L., Natded, A Derivation Editor, Technical Report, Computer Science Department, Uppsala University, 1982.

1582. ERIKSSON, L. and JOHANSSON, A. L., Computer-based Synthesis of Logic Programs, in *Lecture Notes in Computer Science 137, International Symp On Programming, 5th colloquium*, April 1982.

1583. ERIKSSON, L., JOHANSSON, A. L. and TARNLUND, S. A., Toward a Derivation Editor, *Proceedings of the First International Logic Programming Conference*, Marseille, France, September, 1982.

1584. ERIKSSON, L. and RAYNER, M., Incorporating Mutable Arrays in Logic Programming, *Proceedings of the Second International Logic Programming Conference*, S. A. TARNLUND, ed., Uppsala University, Uppsala, Sweden, July 2-6, 1984, 101-114.

1585. FARKAS, Z., FILEMAN, J., MARKUS, A. and MARKUSZ, Z. S., Fixture Design by Prolog, Technical Report, University of Budapest, 1981.

1586. FEIGENBAUM, E. A., Innovation and Symbol Manipulation in the Fifth Generation Computer Systems, in *Fifth Generation Computer Systems*, T. MOTO-OKA, (ed.), North-Holland, New York, 1981. Proceedings of the First International Conference on Fifth Generation Computer Systems.

1587. FERRAND, G., Error Diagnosis in Logic Programming, An Adaptation of E.Y. Shapiro's Method, Technical Report 375, INRIA, Le Chesnay, France, 1985.

1588. FEUER, A., Building Libraries in Prolog, *Proceedings of the International Joint Conference on Artificial Intelligence*, Karlsruhe, Germany, 1983.

1589. FREY, W., REYLE, U. and ROHRER, C., Automatic Construction of a Knowledge Base by Analysing Texts in Natural Language, *Proceedings of the International Joint Conference on Artificial Intelligence*, Karlsruhe, Germany, 1983, 727-729.

1590. FUJITA, M., TANAKA, H. and MOTO-OKA, T., Verification with Prolog and Temporal Logic, *Proceedings of the Sixth Conference on Computer Hardware Description Languages*, 1983.

1591. FUJITA, M., TANAKA, H. and MOTO-OKA, T., Temporal Logic Based Hardware and its Verification with Prolog, *New Generation Computing 1*, 2 (1983), Springer Verlag.

1592. FUJITA, M., TANAKA, H. and MOTO-OKA, T., Specifying Hardware In Temporal Logic & Efficient Synthesis Of State-diagrams Using Prolog, *International Conference On Fifth Generation Computer Systems*, November 1984.

1593. FURUKAWA, K. and OTHERS, Problem Solving and Inference Mechanisms, in *Fifth Generation Computer Systems*, T. MOTO-OKA, (ed.), North-Holland, New York, 1981. Proceedings of the First International Conference on Fifth Generation Computer Systems.

1594. FURUKAWA, K. and FUCHI, K., Knowledge Engineering and the Fifth Generation Computers, *IEEE Database Engineering 6*, 4 (December 1983).

1595. FURUKAWA, K., TAKEUCHI, A., YASUKAWA, H. and KUNIFUJI, S., Mandala: A Logic Based Knowledge Programming System, *International Conference On Fifth Generation Computer Systems*, November 1984.

1596. FUTO, I., Intelligent and Programmable Backtracking Possibilities for the Communicating Possibilities of TS-Prolog, Technical Report, Institute for the Coordination of Computer Techniques, Budapest, Hungary, 1983. In Hungarian.

1597. FUTO, I., Goal Oriented Discrete/Continuous Simulation and Problem Solving in TS-Prolog, Technical Report, Institut for Coordination of Computer Techniques, Budapest, Hungary, 1984.

1598. FUTO, I., Combined Discrete/Continuous Modeling and Problem Solving, *SCS MultiConference on AI, Graphics and Simulation*, San Diego, California, January, 1985.

1599. FUTO, I., DARVAS, F. and CHOLNOKY, E., Practical Applications of an Artificial Intelligence Language Prolog, *Proceedings of the Second Hungarian Computer Science Conference*, Budapest, 1977.

1600. FUTO, I., DARVAS, F. and SZEREDI, J., The Application of Prolog to the Development of QA and DBM Systems, in *Logic and Databases*, H. GALLAIRE and J. MINKER, (eds.), Plenum Press, 1978.

1601. FUTO, I. and GERGELY, T., System Simulation on Prolog Basis, *Logic Programming Newsletter 4*, (1982).

1602. FUTO, I. and GERGELY, T., A Logical Approach to Simulation, *Proceedings of the International Conference on Model Realism*, Bad Honef, Germany, April, 1982.

1603. FUTO, I. and GERGELY, T., A Logical Approach to Simulation, in *Adequate Simulation of Systems*, M. WEDDE, (ed.), Springer-Verlag, 1983, 25-46.

1604. FUTO, I. and GERGELY, T., Planning Activity Of Cooperative I-Actors, *IPAC International Symposium on AI*, Leningrad, USSR, October, 1983.

1605. FUTO, I. and GERGELY, T., A Logic Simulation Language For Modeling Cooperative Problem Solving System, *AFCNET Information Congress, Hardware and Software Components and Architecture for the 5th Generation*, Paris, France, March, 1985.

1606. FUTO, I. and SZEREDI, J., A Discrete Simulation System Based on Artificial Intelligence Methods, in *Discrete Simulation and Related Fields*, A. JAVOR, (ed.), North-Holland, 1982.

1607. FUTO, I. and SZEREDI, J., Meta Control of process Synchronisation in T-Prolog, *Logic Programming Newsletter*, December, 1982.

1608. FUTO, I. and SZEREDI, J., System Simulation and Co-Operative Problem Solvng on a Prolog Basis, in *Implementations of Prolog*, J. A. CAMPBELL, (ed.), Ellis Horwood, 1984.

1609. FUTO, I., SZEREDI, J., BARATH, E. and SZALO, P., Using T-Prolog for a Long-Range Regional Planning Problem, in *Workshop on Logic Programming*, S. TARNLUND, (ed.), Debrecen, Hungary, July 1980.

1610. FUTO, I., SZEREDI, J. and SZENES, K., A Modelling Tool Based on Mathematical Logic: T-Prolog, *Acta Cybernetica 5*, 3 (1981), 68-74. In Hungarian.

1611. FUTO, I., SZEREDI, J. and SZENES, K., A Modelling Tool Based on Mathematical Logic - T-Prolog, *Acta Cybernetica*, 1985. Universitas Szegediensis de Attila Jozsef Nominata Forum Centrale Publicationum Cyberneticarum Hungaricarum, Hungary. (To Appear).

1612. GABRIEL, J. R., Algorithms for Automated Diagnosis of Faults in Physical Plants, Technical Report ANL-83-70, Argonne National Laboratory, Illinois, 1983.

1613. GABRIEL, J. R. and ROBERTS, P. R., A Signal Flow Model for Sequential Logic Built from Combinatorial Logic Elements and Its Implementation in Prolog, Technical Report ANL-84-89, Mathematics and Computer Science Division, Argonne National Laboratories, September, 1984.

1614. GARRETT, R., Glog: A Prolog Semi-Compiler for Non-Procedural Software Tools, M.S. Thesis, Department of Computer Science, Florida Atlantic University, Boca Raton, 1984.

1615. GIRAUD, C., Logique et Conception Assistee par Ordinateur, These de Troisieme Cycle, University d'Aix-Marseille, France, 1980.

1616. GIRAUD, C., The Presque Half-Plane: Towards a General Representation Scheme, Technical Report TR-83-04, EdCaad Department, University of Edinburgh, 1983.

1617. GOEBEL, R. G., *Using Hilbert terms to embed descriptions in Prolog*, Syracuse University, Logic Programming Workshop, April 8-10, 1981.

1618. GOEBEL, R. G., Intelligent UNIX Shell project, *Logic Programming Group Bulletin*, December 1983, 5-5.

1619. GONZALEZ, J. C., WILLIAMS, M. H. and AITCHISON, I. E., Evaluation of the Effectiveness of Prolog for a CAD Application, *Comp. Graphics and Applications?*, Mar. 1984, 67-75.

1620. GOTO, S. and OTHERS, *Proceedings of the RIMS Symposia on Software Science and Engineering*, Springer Verlag, 1983. Lecture Notes in Computer Science - 147.

1621. GRAU, B., Stalking "Coherence" In The Topical Jungle, *International Conference On Fifth Generation Computer Systems*, November 1984.

1622. GRAY, P. M. D. and MOFFAT, D. S., Manipulating Descriptions of Programs for Database Access, *Proceedings of the International Joint Conference on Artificial Intelligence*, Karlsruhe, Germany, 1983, 21-24.

1623. GREGORY, S., NEELY, R. and RINGWOOD, G., Prolog for Specification, Verification and Simulation., *7TH International Symposium On Computer Hardware Description Languages And Their Applications* , Tokyo, August 1985.

1624. HAGERT, G. and HANSSON, A., Logic Modelling of Cognitive Reasoning, UPMAIL Technical Report 21, Uppsala University, 1983.

1625. HAGERT, G. and HANSSON, A., Reasoning Models within a Logical Famework, UPMAIL Technical Report 25, Uppsala University, 1984.

1626. HAGERT, G. and TARNLUND, S. A., Deductive Modelling of Cognitive Processes: A First Example, *Working Papers of the Cognitive Seminar no. 5*, 1979.

1627. HAGERT, G. and TARNLUND, S. A., Deductive Modelling of Human Cognition, *Proceedings of the International Joint Conference on Artificial Intelligence*, Vancouver, Canada, 1981. Also Technical Report, Computer Science Department, Uppsala University.

1628. HAGINO, T., HONDA, M., KOGA, A., NAKAJIMA, R., SHIBAYAMA, E. and YUASA, T., Iota on Dec System 20 - KWIC Example, Technical Report 419, Department of Computer Science, University of Kyoto, December 1982.

1629. HAMMOND, P., A Listing of a Prolog Program Describing Entitlement to Supplementary Benefit, Technical Report, Department of Computer Science, Imperial College, London, June 1983.

1630. HECK, N. and AVENHAUS, J., Automatic Implementation Of Abstract Data Types Specified By The Logic Programming Language, *International Conference On Fifth Generation Computer Systems*, November 1984.

1631. HOGGER, C. J., Logic Programming and Program Verification: Advances and Application, in *Infotech State of the Art Report Series 10 No 2*, P. J. L. WALLIS, (ed.), Pergamon Infotech Limited, Maidenhead, Bershire , England, 1982. Issue on Programming Technology.

1632. HORSTMANN, P. W., Digital Logic Simulation in prolog, Technical Report, Department of Computer Science, University of Waterloo, February 1983.

1633. ISHII, A., Handling of Bit Tables in Prolog, Technical Memorandum TM-0013, ICOT - Institute for New Generation Computer Technology, Tokyo, Japan, 1983. In Japanese.

1634. JARKE, M., External Semantic Query Simplification: A Graph-Theoretic Approach and Its Implementation in Prolog, Technical Report CRIS 75, Graduate School of Business, New York University, 1984.

1635. JARKE, M., CLIFFORD, J. and VASSILIOU, Y., An Optimizing Prolog Front-End to a Relational Query System, *Proceedings of the ACM SIGMOD Conference*, Boston, 1984. Also Technical Report CRIS 65, Graduate School of Business, New York University.

1636. JARKE, M. and SIVASANKARAN, T., Formula Management Stategies in an Actuarial Consulting System, Technical Report CRIS-69, Graduate School of Management, New York University, 1984.

1637. JENKINS, L. E., Compiling High-Level Chip Descriptions into an Intermediate Representation, DAI Research Paper No 117, Department of Artificial Intelligence, University of Edinburgh, 1983.

1638. JOHANSSON, A. L., Using Symmetry For The Derivation of Logic Programs, *Proceedings of the Second International Logic Programming Conference*, S. A. TARNLUND, ed., Uppsala University, Uppsala, Sweden, July 2-6, 1984, 243-252.

1639. JULIEN, S., Graphics in Micro-Prolog, Technical Report 82-17, Computer Science Department, Imperial College, London, 1982.

1640. KAHN, K. M., Intermission - Actors in Prolog, in *Workshop on Logic Programming*, S. TARNLUND, (ed.), Debrecen, Hungary, July 1980. Also in Logic Programming, Clark and Tarnlund, Academic Press, 1982.

1641. KAHN, K. M., A Partial Evaluator of Lisp Programs Written in Prolog, *Proceedings of the First International Logic Programming Conference*, M. VAN CANEGHEM, ed., Marseille, France, September 14-17, 1982, 19-25.

1642. KAHN, K. M., A Pure Prolog Written in Pure Lisp, *Logic Programming Newsletter*, Winter 1983/1984.

1643. KAHN, K. M., Experiences in Transporting Concurrent Prolog and the Bagel Simulator to LM-PROLOG - Part I of a Report of a Visit to ICOT November 1983, *Draft Paper*, 1984.

1644. KAHN, K. M., Partial Evaluation, Programming Methodology, and Artificial Intelligence, *The AI Magazine 5*, 1 (Spring 1984).

1645. KAHN, K. M. and CARLSSON, M., How To Implement Prolog On a Lisp Machine, in *Issues In Prolog Implementations*, J. CAMPBELL, (ed.), 1984.

1646. KANOUI, H., Application de la Demonstration Automatique aux Manipulations Algebriques et a l'Integration Formelle sur Ordinateur, Technical Report, Groupe d'Intelligence Artificielle, Universite d'Aix-Marseille II Marseille, France, 1973.

1647. KAPOSI, A. A. and MARKUSZ, Z. S., Introduction of a Complexity Measure for Control of Design Errors in Logic Based Programs, *Proceedings of CAD-80, Held in Brighton*, Brighton, England, 1980.

1648. KASIF, S., A Note on Translating Flowchart and Recursive Schemas to Prolog Schemas, Technical Report TR-1273, Department of Computer Science, University of Maryland, 1983.

1649. KITAGAWA, T., *Computer Science and Technologies*, North-Holland, 1982.

1650. KLUZNIAK, F., SPOQUEL: A Simple Prolog-Oriented Query Language, Technical Report, Department of Computer Science, Warsaw University, Poland, 1983.

1651. KOFALUSI, V., A Prolog Program for Generating the First n Formal Deratives of Given, Real Multi-Variable Analalytic Functions of Great Complexity, in *Technical Report SOFTTECH D42*, SZAMKI, Hungary, 1979. In Hungarian.

1652. KOFALUSI, V. and BARTHA, F., On a Possible Application and Extension of Prolog: Applications Based on State Space Sets, in *Technical Report SOFTTECH D42*, SZAMKI, Hungary, 1979. In Hungarian.

1653. KOGAN, D. and FREILING, M., SIDUR-Structure Formalism For Knowledge Information Processing, *International Conference On Fifth Generation Computer Systems*, November 1984.

1654. KOMOROWSKI, H. J., Interactive and Incremental Programming Environments: Experience, Foundations, and Future, Technical Report TR-09-83, Department of Computer Science, Harvard University, 1983.

1655. KOMOROWSKI, H. J., Rapid Software Development in a Database Framework - A Case Study, *Proceedings of the IEEE International Conference on Data Engineering*, Los Angeles, 1984.

1656. KOWALSKI, R. A., Logic for Data Description, in *Logic and Databases*, H. GALLAIRE and J. MINKER, (eds.), Plenum Press, 1978, 77-103.

1657. KOWALSKI, R. A., *Logic for Problem Solving*, Elsevier North-Holland, New-York, 1979.

1658. KOWALSKI, R. A., Logic Programming, *Proceedings of the IFIP-83 Congress*, Amsterdam, 1983, 133-145.

1659. KOWALSKI, R. A., AI and Software Engineering, *Datamation*, November, 1984.

1660. KRIWACZEK, F. R., Some Applications of Prolog to Decision Support Systems, Technical Report, Department of Computer Science, Imperial College, London, 1982.

1661. KRIWACZEK, F. R., A Critical Path Analysis Program, in *Micro-Prolog: Programming In Logic*, K. L. CLARK and S. A. TARNLUND, (eds.), Prentice Hall, 1984.

1662. KUKICH, K., Knowledge-Based Report Generation: A Technique for Automatically Generating Natural Language Reports from Databases, *Proceedings of the ACM SIGIR Conference on Research and Development in Information Retrieval*, Bethesda, June, 1983, 307-344.

1663. KUNIFUJI, S., TAKEUCHI, A., FURUKAWA, K., UEDA, K. and KURUKAWA, T., A Logic Programming Language for Knowledge Utilization and Realization, *Proceedings of the Prolog Conference*, Tukuba, Japan, 1982. In Japanese.

1664. KUSALIK, A. J., The File System of a Logical Operating System, Technical Report 84-21, Department of Computer Science, University of British Columbia, Canada, 1984.

1665. LASSEZ, C., Problem Solving with the Computer: Logo versus Prolog, *Proc. of ACS Computers in Education Conference*, Sydney, 1984.

1666. LEIBRANDT, U. and SCHNUPP, P., R. BUDDE, ed., *An Evaluation of Prolog as a Prototyping System*, Springer-Verlag, Berlin, 1984.

1667. LIEBERMAN, H., Programming Descriptive Analogies By Example, *Internal Paper, AI Laboratory, MIT*, December 1983.

1668. LITTLEFORD, A., A Mycin-Like Expert System in Prolog, *Proceedings of the Second International Logic Programming Conference*, S. TARNLUND, ed., Uppsala University, Uppsala, Sweden, July 2-6, 1984, 289-300.

1669. LOGRIPPO, L. and SKUCE, D., File Structures, Program Structures and Attributes Grammars, *IEEE Transactions on Software Engineering 9*, 3 (May 1983).

1670. LUGER, G., Mathematical Model Building in the Solution of Mechanics Problems: Human Protocols and the Mecho Trace, *Cognitive Science 5*, (1981), 55-77.

1671. MANGIR, T. and CHEN-ELLIS, G., Rule Based Generation of Test Structures for VLSI, Technical Report CSD-840059, Department of Computer Science, University of California, Los Angeles, 1984.

1672. MANGIR, T. and SOETERMAN, B., Control Structures in a Prolog-Based Production System, Technical Report CSD-840054, Department of Computer Science, University of California, Los Angeles, 1984.

1673. MARKUS, A. and MOLNAR, E., Logic Programming in the Modelling of Machine Ports, *Proceedings of Compcontrol 81*, Varna, Bulgaria, 1981.

1674. MARKUS, A., MOLNAR, E. and SZELKE, E., Logic Programming in the Design of Production Control Systems, *Proceedings of Compcontrol 81*, Varna, Bulgaria, 1981.

1675. MARKUSZ, Z. S., How to Design Variants of Flats Using the Programming Language Prolog based on Mathematical Logic, *Proceedings IFIP 77*, 1977, 885-889. North Holland.

1676. MARKUSZ, Z. S., The Application of the Programming Language Prolog for Panel House Design, *Informacio-Elektronika XII*, 3 (1977), 124-230. In Hungarian.

1677. MARKUSZ, Z. S., Logic Based Programming Method and Its Applications for Architectural Design Problems, Ph.D. Dissertation, Eotvos Lorand University, Budapest, Hungary, 1980. In Hungarian.

1678. MARKUSZ, Z. S., Applications of Prolog in Designing Many-Storied Dwelling Houses, in *Workshop on Logic Programming*, S. A. TARNLUND, (ed.), Debrecen, Hungary, July 1980.

1679. MARKUSZ, Z. S., Design in Logic, Working Paper Ap-13, SZTAKI, Budapest, Hungary, 1981. In Hungarian.

1680. MARKUSZ, Z. S., Knowledge Representation of Design in Many-Sorted Logic, *Proceedings Seventh International Joint Conference on Artificial Intelligence*, August 1981.

1681. MARKUSZ, Z. S., Design in Logic, *Computer-Aided design 14*, 6 (1982), 335-343.

1682. MARKUSZ, Z. S. and KAPOSI, A. A., A Design Methodology in Prolog Programming, *Proceedings of the First International Logic Programming Conference*, Marseille, France, 1981.

1683. MARUYAMA, F. and FUJITA, M., Hardware Verification, *IEEE Computer 18*, 2 (February, 1985).

1684. MARUYAMA, F. and YONEZAWA, A., A Prolog-Based Natural Language Front-End System, *New Generation Computing 2*, 1 (1984).

1685. MASUDA, K., ITO, N. and SHIMIZU, H., Simulating Evaluation of Dataflow Prolog Machines, Technical Memorandum TM-0020, ICOT - Institute for New Generation Computer Technology, Tokyo, Japan, 1983. In Japanese.

1686. MATOS, A., A Prolog Implementation of the Knuth-Rendix Reduction System, Technical Report, Universidade do Porto, Portugal, 1982.

1687. MATRAI, G., The Application of Prolog for Search of Similar Substructures of Enzyme Sequences, MTA SBZK Technical Report, Budapest, Hungary, 1979. In Hungarian.

1688. MELLISH, C. S., An Approach to the GUS Travel Agent Problem Using Prolog, Working Paper 19, Department of Artificial Intelligence, University of Edinburgh, 1977.

1689. MELLISH, C. S., Automatic Generation of Mode Declarations in Prolog Programs, *Workshop on Logic Programming*, Long Beach, Los Angeles, September 1981.

1690. MIZOGUCHI, F., A Software Environment for Developing Knowledge-Based Systems, in *Computer Science and Technologies: 1982*, T. KITAGAWA, (ed.), Elsevier North-Holland, New-York, 1982, 334-349.

1691. MIZOGUCHI, F., KATAYAMA, Y. and OWADA, H., LOOKS: Knowledge Representation System For Designing Expert System In The Framework of Logic Programming, *International Conference On Fifth Generation Computer Systems*, November 1984.

1692. MONTGOMERY, C. A. and RUSPINI, E. H., The Active Information System: A Data-Driven System for the Analysis of Imprecise Data, Workshop on Logic Programming, Long Beach, Los Angeles, September 1981. Also in VLDB 1981.

1693. MORRIS, P. H., Transporting Values via Relative Assertions, *Logic Programming Newsletter*, March 1981.

1694. MOSS, C. D., A Formal Definition of ASPLE Using Predicate Logic, Report 80-81, Imperial College, London, 1980.

1695. MOSS, C. D., The Formal Description of Programming Languages Using Predicate Logic, Technical Report, Imperial College, London, 1981. P.H. Dissertation.

1696. MOSS, C. D., How to Define a Language Using Prolog, *Proceedings of the 1982 ACM Conference on LISP and Functional Programming*, Pittsburgh, 1982, 67-73.

1697. MOTODA, H., YAMADA, N. and YOSHIDA, K., A Knowledge Based System For Plant Diagnosis, *International Conference On Fifth Generation Computer Systems*, November 1984.

1698. MOZETIC, I., BRATKO, I. and NAVRAO, L., An Experiment in Automatic Synthesis of Expert Knowledge through Qualitative Modelling, *Proceedings of Workshop on Logic Programming*, Algarve, Portugal, 1983.

1699. MYCROFT, A. and O'KEEFE, R. A., A Polymorphic Type System for Prolog, *Proceedings of Logic Programming Workshop*, Universidade Nova de Lisboa, Portugal, 1983. Also Research Paper 211, Department of Artificial Intelligence, University of Edinburgh.

1700. NARAIN, S., A Technique for Doing Lazy Evaluation in Logic, *Proceedings of the 2nd IEEE International Symposium on Logic Programming*, Boston, USA, July, 1985.

1701. NICHOL, J. and DEAN, J., Pupils, Computers and History Teaching, in *New Horizons in Educational Programming*, M. YAZDANI, (ed.), Ellis Horwood, 1984.

1702. NICOLAS, J. M. and GALLAIRE, H., Databases: Theory Versus Interpretation, in *Logic and Databases*, H. GALLAIRE and J. MINKER, (eds.), Plenum Press, 1978.

1703. NILSSON, M., A Logical Model of Knowledge, *Proceedings of the International Joint Conference on Artificial Intelligence*, Karlsruhe, Germany, 1983, 374-376.

1704. NILSSON, M., A Logical Model of Knowledge and Belief, UPMAIL Technical Report 28, Uppsala University, 1984.

1705. NILSSON, M., Prolog As A Tool For Optimizing PROLOG Unifiers, *Proceedings of the Second International Logic Programming Conference*, S. TARNLUND, ed., Uppsala University, Uppsala, Sweden, July 2-6, 1984, 13-22.

1706. NOELKE, U. and SAVORY, S., Prolog-Systeme im Vergleich, *Angewandte Informatik*, 1984, 108-112.

1707. NORTON, L. M., Automated Analysis of Instructional Text, *Artificial Intelligence 20*, 3 (May, 1983), 307-344.

1708. O'KEEFE, R. A., A Smooth Applicative Merge Sort, DAI Research Paper No. 182, Department of Artificial Intelligence, University of Edinburgh, 1982.

1709. O'KEEFE, R. A., Automated Statistical Analysis, DAI Research Paper No 104, Department of Artificial Intelligence, University of Edinburgh, 1982.

1710. O'SHEA, T. and EISENSTADT, M., *Artificial Intelligence: Tools, Techniques and Applications*, Harper and Row, New York, 1984. Editors.

1711. OHSUGA, S., Knowledge-Based Systems as a New Interactive Computer System of the Next Generation, in *Computer Science and Technologies: 1982*, T. KITAGAWA, (ed.), Elsevier North-Holland, New-York, 1982, 227-249.

1712. PAKALNS, J. L., AHA, A UNIX Consultant, Technical Report-Master's Thesis, Department of Computer Science, University of Waterloo, 1983.

1713. PALMER, M. S., Inference-Driven Semantic Analysis, in *Proceedings of National Conference on Artificial Intelligence AAAI-83*, Washington D.C., August 1983.

1714. PEREIRA, F. C. N., SeeLog: A Prolog Graphics Interface, Technical Report, EdCaad, University of Edinburgh, 1982.

1715. PIQUE, J. F., Drawing Trees and their Equations in Prolog, *Proceedings of the Second International Logic Programming Conference*, S. A. TARNLUND, ed., Uppsala University, Uppsala, Sweden, July 2-6, 1984, 23-34.

1716. PLAISTED, D. A., An Efficient Bug Location Algorithm, *Proceedings of the Second International Logic Programming Conference*, S. A. TARNLUND, ed., Uppsala University, Uppsala, Sweden, July 2-6, 1984, 151-158.

1717. POLLIT, A. S., End User Touch Searching for Cancer Therapy Literature - A Rule Based Approach, *Proceedings of the ACM SIGIR Conference on Research and Development in Information Retrieval*, Bethesda, June, 1983, 136-145.

1718. PORTO, A., A Prolog Program for the S-P Problem, *Logic Programming Newsletter*, March 1981.

1719. POWERS, D. M. W., Robot Intelligence, Departmental Report 8304, Department of Computer Science, EECS, University of New South Wales, Sydney, NSW, Australia, March 1983. Also in Electronics Today International (Australia) December 1983.

1720. POWERS, D. M. W., Playing Mastermind more Logically Or Writing Prolog more Efficiently, *SIGART*, July, 1984, 15-18.

1721. POWERS, D. M. W. and MCMAHON, G. B., A Compendium of interesting Prolog programmes, DCS Report 8313, University of New South Wales, December 1983 .

1722. RICH, C., Knowledge Representation Languages and Predicate Calculus: How to Have Your Cake and Eating it Too, *Proceedings of the National Conference on Artificial Intelligence*, Carnegie-Mellon University, August 1982. AAAI-82.

1723. RIDD, S., An Investigation of Prolog as an Aid to French Teaching and Language Translation, Technical Report, Department of Computer Science, Imperial College, London, 1982.

1724. RIET, R. P. V., Knowledge Bases: De Databanken van de Toekomst, *Informatie 25*, 5 (1983), 16-23. In Dutch.

1725. ROACH, J. W., A Prolog Simulation of Migration Decision-Making in a Less Developed Country, *Proceedings of the First International Logic Programming Conference*, Marseille, France, 1981.

1726. ROY, S. and HILL, D. D., Prolog in CMOS Circuit Design, *Proceedings of the IEEE Spring CompCon Conference*, San Francisco, February, 1985.

1727. SAFRA, M. and SHAPIRO, E. Y., A Rational Design For Prolog Systems, *Draft Paper*, Rechovot, Israel, 1984.

1728. SAGIV, Y. and SAINT-DIZIER, P., Modelling Human-Computer Interactions in a Friendly Interface, *Proceedings of Workshop on Logic Programming*, Algarve, Portugal, 1983.

1729. SANDEWALL, E., A Programming Tool for Management of a Predicate-Calculus Oriented Data Base, *Proceedings of the Second International Joint Conference on Artificial Intelligence*, London, 1971.

1730. SANTANE-TOTH, E. and SZEREDI, P., Prolog Applications in Hungary, in *Logic Programming*, K. L. CLARK and S. TARNLUND, (eds.), Academic Press, New York, 1982. A.P.I.C. Studies in Data Processing No. 16.

1731. DE SARAM, H., Prolog for Children and Teachers, *AISB Easter Conference on Artificial Intelligence and Education*, University of Exeter,U.K., April 1983.

1732. SCHNUPP, P., Prolog as Spezifikations- und Modelierungswerkzeug, in *Requirements Engineering - Arbeitstagung der GI*, G. H. D. KRONIG, (ed.), Springer-Verlag, Informatik-Fackberichte 74, Berlin, 1983, 173-182.

1733. SCHNUPP, P. and SYLLA, K. H., Objectorientierte Organisation von Wissenbasen oder die Klasse prolog in einer Software-Entwicklungsumgebung, in *Objectorientierte Software- und Hardwarearchitecturen - Tagung II/1983 des German Chapter of the ACM*, H. S. H. WEDEKIND, (ed.), Berlin, May 1983.

1734. SEBELIK, J. and STEFANEK, P., Horn Clause Programs for Recursive Functions, in *Logic Programming*, K. L. C. S. TARNLUND, (ed.), Academic Press, New York, 1982. A.P.I.C. Studies in Data Processing No. 16.

1735. SEIDEL, R., A New method for Solving Constraint Satisfaction Problems, *Proceedings of the Seventh International Conference on Artificial Intelligence*, Vancouver, August, 1981, 338-342.

1736. SERGOT, M. J., Prospects for Representing the Law as Logic Programs, in *Logic Programming*, K. L. CLARK and S. TARNLUND, (eds.), Academic Press, New York, 1982. A.P.I.C. Studies in Data Processing No. 16.

1737. SERGOT, M. J., A Query-The-User Facility for Logic Programs, in *Integrated Interactive Computer Systems*, P. DEGANO and E. SANDWELL, (eds.), North-Holland, 1983. Also available as Technical Report 82-18 from Imperial College, London - Also Published in New Horizons in Educational Computing, M. Yazdani (ed), Ellis Horwood, 1984.

1738. SHAPIRO, E. Y., *Algorithmic Program Debugging*, MIT Press, 1983. Ph.D. thesis,Yale University,May 1982.

1739. SHAPIRO, E. Y., Playing Mastermind Logically, *ACM SigArt Newsletter 85*, (July, 1983), 28-29.

1740. SHIDU, D. P., Logic and Protocol Verification, Technical Report, SDC - Burroughs, 1983.

1741. SHIDU, D. P., Logic Programming and Validation of Key Distribution Protocols, Technical Report, SDC - Burroughs, 1983.

1742. SHIDU, D. P., Protocol Verification via Executable Logic Specification, *Proceedings of the Third International Workshop on Protocol Specification, Testing and Verification*, Switserland, June, 1983.

1743. SHOHAM, Y., FAME: A Prolog Program that Solves Problems in Combinatorics, *Proceedings of the Second International Logic Programming Conference*, S. A. TARNLUND, ed., Uppsala University, Uppsala, Sweden, July 2-6, 1984, 277-288.

1744. SILVER, B., Learning Algebraic Methods from Examples - A Progress Report, DAI Research Paper No 129, Department of Artificial Intelligence, University of Edinburgh, 1982.

1745. SILVER, B., An Algebra Learning Program - Thesis Proposal, DAI Working Paper No 111, Department of Artificial Intelligence, University of Edinburgh, 1982.

1746. SILVER, B., The Application of Homogenization to Simultaneous Equations, *6th Conference on Automated Deduction*, D. W. LOVELAND, ed., 1982, 132-143. Also Lecture Notes in Computer Science No. 138, and, DAI Research Paper No 166, Department of Artificial Intelligence, University of Edinburgh.

1747. SILVER, B. and BUNDY, A., Homogenization : Preparing Equations for Change of Unknown, DAI Research Paper No 159, Department of Artificial Intelligence, University of Edinburgh, 1981.

1748. SKUCE, D., Towards Communicating Qualitative Knowledge between Scientists and Machines, Ph.D. Dissertation, Department of Computer Science, McGill University , Montreal, 1977.

1749. SKUCE, D., An Approach to Defining and Communicating the Conceptual Structure of Data, Technical Report TR-79-05, Department of Computer Science, University of Ottawa, Canada, 1979.

1750. SKUCE, D., Module Development Based on Program Transformation and Automatic Generation of the Input-Output Relation, *Proceedings of the First International Logic Programming Conference*, M. VAN CANEGHEM, ed., Marseille, France, September 1982.

1751. SMITH, P. and STERLING, L., Of Integration by Man and Machine, *SIGSAM Bulletin 17*, 3&4 (1983), 21-24. Also available from Edinburgh as Rsearch Paper 210.

1752. SPACEK, L., A Portable Prolog Tracing Package, Technical Report, University of Sussex, England, 1982.

1753. STEPANKOVA, O., A Decision Method for Process Logic, in *Workshop on Logic Programming*, S. A. TARNLUND, (ed.), Debrecen, Hungary, July 1980.

1754. STEPANKOVA, O. and STEPANEK, P., Computation Trees and Transformation of Logic Programs, *Proceedings of the Second International Logic Programming Conference*, S. A. TARNLUND, ed., Uppsala University, Uppsala, Sweden, July 2-6, 1984, 53-64.

1755. STERLING, L., IMPRESS - Meta-Level Concepts in Theorem Proving, DAI Research Paper No 119, Department of Artificial Intelligence, University of Edinburgh, 1983.

1756. STERLING, L. and BUNDY, A., Meta-Level Inference and Program Verification, in *Lecture Notes in Computer Science 138: 6th Conference on Automated Deduction*, D. W. LOVELAND, (ed.), Springer-Verlag, 1982, 144-150. Also available from Edinburgh as DAI Research Paper no. 168.

1757. STERLING, L., BUNDY, A., BYRD, L., O'KEEFE, R. A. and
SILVER, B., Solving Symbolic Equations with PRESS, in *Lecture
Notes in Computer Science 144 : Computer Algebra*, J.
CALMET, (ed.), Springer-Verlag, New York, 1982, 109-116.
Longer version available from Edinburgh as Research Paper
171.

1758. SUN, H. and WANG, L., A Model Theory of Logic Programming
Methodology, *Proceedings of the Second International Logic
Programming Conference*, S. A. TARNLUND, ed., Uppsala
University, Uppsala, Sweden, July 2-6, 1984, 253-263.

1759. SUWA, M. and OTHERS, Knowledge Base Mechanisms, in *Fifth
Generation Computer Systems*, T. MOTO-OKA, (ed.), North-
Holland, New York, 1981. Proceedings of the First
International Conference on Fifth Generation Computer
Systems.

1760. SUZUKI, N., Concurrent Prolog as an Efficient VLSI Design
Language, *IEEE Computer 18*, 2 (February, 1985).

1761. SWINSON, P. S. G., Prescriptive and Descriptive Programming,
Technical Report TR-80-11, EdCaad Department, University of
Edinburgh, 1980. Also Published in the Proceedings of the
Logic Programming Conference of 1981, held in Debrecen,
Hungary.

1762. SWINSON, P. S. G., Logic Programming - A Computing Tool for
the Architect of the Future, *Computer-Aided Design 14*, 2
(March 1982).

1763. SWINSON, P. S. G., Prolog: A Prelude to a New Generation of
CAAD, Technical Report TR-83-01, EdCaad Department,
University of Edinburgh, 1983.

1764. SWINSON, P. S. G., PEREIRA, F. C. N. and BIJL, A., A Fact Dependency System for the Logic Programmer, *Computer-Aided Design*, July, 1983. Also available as EdCaad Technical Report 82-03, University of Edinburgh.

1765. SZENES, K., FUTO, I. and SZEREDI, J., A Comparison of the Traditional and a New-principle Way Of Parallel Systems, Description, Simulation and Planning, *CL & CL*, 1985. Computer and Automation Institute, Hungarian Institute, Hungarian Academy of Sciences. (To appear).

1766. SZEREDI, J., On the Application of Mathematical Logic in Computer Techniques, Ph.D. Dissertation, Hungary. In Hungarian.

1767. SZPAKOWICZ, S., Papers in Logic Programming, Report nr. 104, Warsaw University, Poland, 1982.

1768. SZUBA, T., Automatic Program Synthesis Systems for N.C. Machine Tools Based on PC-Prolog, *Angewandte Informatik*, 1984, 171-243.

1769. TAGAKI, S., YOKOI, T., UCHIDA, S., KUROKAWA, T., HATTORI, T., CHIKAYAMA, T., SAKAI, K. and TSUJI, J., Overall Design Of Simpos, *Proceedings of the Second International Logic Programming Conference*, S. A. TARNLUND, ed., Uppsala University, Uppsala, Sweden, July 2-6, 1984, 1-12.

1770. TAMAKI, H. and SATO, T., A Transformation System for Logic Programs which Preserves Equivalence, Technical Report TR-018, ICOT - Institute for New Generation Computer Technology, Tokyo, Japan, 1983.

1771. TANAKA, H. and OTHERS, Intelligent Man-Machine Interface, in *Fifth Generation Computer Systems*, T. MOTO-OKA, (ed.), North-Holland, New York, 1981. Proceedings of the First International Conference on Fifth Generation Computer Systems.

1772. S. A. TARNLUND, ed., *Proceedings of the 1980 Logic Programming Workshop, Debrecen, Hungary,* Department of Computer Science, University of Stockholm, Sweden., 1981.

1773. TODD, S., Automatic Constraint Maintenance and Updating Defined Relations, in *Information Processing,* B. GILCHRIST, (ed.), IFIP, North-Holland, 1977, 145-148.

1774. TOKORO, M., ISHIKAWA, Y., MARUICHI, T. and KAWAMURA, M., An Object Oriented Approach To Knowledge Systems, *International Conference On Fifth Generation Computer Systems,* November 1984.

1775. TORII, K., SUGIYAMA, Y. and MORISAWA, Y., Functional Programming and Logic Programming for Telegram Analysis Problem, *Proceedings of the Seventh IEEE International Conference on Software Engineering,* 1984.

1776. UEHARA, K. and OTHERS, Steps Toward An Actor-oriented Integrated Parser, *International Conference On Fifth Generation Computer Systems,* November 1984.

1777. UEHARA, T. and KAWATO, N., Logic Circuit Synthesis Using Prolog, *New Generation Computing 1,* 2 (1983), Springer Verlag.

1778. VASSEY, P., AVL-Tree Insertion Re-Visited, *Logic Programming Newsletter,* July, 1982.

1779. WALKER, A., SYLLOG: An Approach to Prolog for Nonprogrammers, Technical Report RJ 3950, IBM Watson Research Center, 1983.

1780. WALLEN, L. A., Using Proof Plans to Control Deduction, Research Paper 185, Department of Artificial Intelligence, University of Edinburgh, February, 1983.

1781. WALLEN, L. A., Towards the Provision of a Natural Mechanism for Expressing Domain-Specific Global Strategies in General Purpose Theorem-Provers, Research Paper 202, Department of Artificial Intelligence, University of Edinburgh, September, 1983.

1782. WARREN, D. H. D., WARPLAN: A System for Generating Plans, DCL Memo 76, Department of Artificial Intelligence, University of Edinburgh Scotland, 1974.

1783. WARREN, D. H. D., Generating Conditional Plans and Program, *Proceedings of the AISB Summer Conference*, Edinburgh, Scotland, July, 1976.

1784. WARREN, D. H. D., Applied Logic - Its Use and Implementation as Programming Tool, Ph.D. thesis, University of Edinburgh, U.K., 1977. Reprinted as Technical Note 290, 1983, Artificial Intelligence Center, SRI International, Menlo Park, California.

1785. WARREN, D. H. D., Logic for Compiler Writing, *Software Practice and Experience 10*, 1 (1980), 97-125. Also available as DAI Research Paper 44 from Department of Artificial Intelligence, University of Edinburgh.

1786. WARREN, D. H. D., Perpetual Processes - An Unexploited Prolog Technique, *Proceedings of the Prolog Programming Environments Workshop*, Linkoping University, Sweden, 1982.

1787. WEIR, D., Teaching Logic Programming: An Interactive Approach, Technical Report, Department of Computer Science, Imperial College, London, 1982.

1788. WEIR, D., Teaching Logic Programming, M.Sc. Thesis, Imperial College, London, 1982.

1789. WELHAM, R., Solving Algebraic Equations: An Artificial Intelligence Approach, *Computer Age*, September, 1980.

1790. WILSON, W. G. and JOHN, C. C., Semantic Code Analysis, *Proceedings of the International Joint Conference on Artificial Intelligence*, Karlsruhe, Germany, 1983.

1791. WISSKIRCHEN, P., NIEHUIS, S. and VICTOR, F., Ein Rechnergestutzter Burosimulator auf der Basis von Petri-Netzen und Prolog, *Angewandte Informatik*, 1984, 181-188.

1792. WOEHL, K., Automatic Classification Of Office Documents By Coupling Relational Databases And Prolog Expert Systems, *Proceedings of the Tenth Conference On Very Large Data Bases*, Singapore, August, 1984.

1793. WOS, L., Achievements in Automated Reasoning, *SIAM News*, July, 1984, 4-5.

1794. WOS, L., Automated Reasoning Programs: How They Work, *SIAM News*, September, 1984, 4-5.

1795. WOS, L., Automated Reasoning, *American Mathematical Monthly 92*, (February, 1985), 85-92.

1796. YAZDANI, M., *Intelligent Educational Computing*, Ellis Horwood, 1983.

1797. YAZDANI, M., *New Horizons in Educational Programming*, Ellis Horwood, 1984. Editor.

1798. YAZDANI, M., Towards a Micro-Prolog World for Children, *Proceedings of the 2nd Commodores in Education Conference*, Chichester, 1984.

1799. YOKOI, T. and OTHERS, Logic Programming and a Dedicated High-Performance Personal Computer, in *Fifth Generation Computer Systems*, T. MOTO-OKA, (ed.), North-Holland, New York, 1981. Proceedings of the First International Conference on Fifth Generation Computer Systems.

1800. ZARRI, G. P., Intelligent Information Retrieval: An Interesting Application Area For The New Generation Computer Systems, *International Conference On Fifth Generation Computer Systems*, November 1984.

1801. ZAUMEN, W. T., Computer Assisted Circuit Evaluation in Prolog for VLSI, *Proceedings of ACM/SIGMOD Conference on Modelling of Data*, 1983.

CHAPTER 14

Application of Logic Programming to Expert Systems

1802. ALBERT, P., Prolog and Objects, *Proceedings of the Fifth International Workshop on Expert Systems and Their Applications*, Avignon, France, May, 1985.

1803. ATTARDI, G. and SIMI, M., Consistency and Completeness of OMEGA, a Logic for Knowledge Representation, *Proceedings of the Seventh International Joint Conference on Artificial Intelligence*, Vancouver, Canada, 1981.

1804. BAINBRIDGE, S. and SKUCE, D., Knowledge Acquisition and Representation Using Logic, Set Theory and Natural Language Structures, *Proceedings of the Third National Conference of the Canadian Society for Computational Studies of Intelligence*, 1980.

1805. BALDWIN, J. F. and PILSWORTH, B. W., An Inferential Fuzzy Logic Knowledge Base, Technical Report, Department of Engineering and Mathematics, University of Bristol, U.K., 1982. Presented at the Workshop on Logic Programming Long Beach, Los Angeles September 1981.

1806. BOSC, P., COURANT, M., ROBIN, S. and TRILLING, L., Havane: Un Systeme de Mise en Relation Automatique de Petites Annonces, Rapport de Recherce 223, INRIA Rennes, 1983.

1807. BOSSU, G. and SIEGEL, P., Non Monotonic Reasoning and Databases, *Proceedings of Workshop on Logical Bases for Databases*, Toulouse, France, 1982.

1808. BRIGGS, J. H., FRENCH, P. and STEELE, B. D., Logic Programming For Expert Systems: A Two Day Course, The Logic Training Partnership, Imperial College, London, 1984.

1809. BROUGH, D. R. and PARFITT, N., An Expert System For The Ageing Of A Domestic Animal, *CAA84*, Birmingham, 1984.

1810. BUNDY, A., Incidence Calculus: A Mechanism For Probabilistic Reasoning, *International Conference On Fifth Generation Computer Systems*, November 1984.

1811. BUNDY, A. and BYRD, L., Using The Methods of Fibres in Mecho To Calculate Radii Gyration, in *Mental Models*, A. STEVENS and D. GENTNER, (eds.), Erlbaum, 1983. Also available as Research Paper 152, Department of Artificial Intelligence, University of Edinburgh.

1812. BUNDY, A., BYRD, L., LUGER, G., MELLISH, C. S., MILNE, R. and PALMER, M. S., Mecho: A Program to Solve Mechanics Problems, Working Paper 50, Department of Artificial Intelligence, University of Edinburgh, 1979.

1813. BUNDY, A., LUGER, G., STONE, M. and WELHAM, B., Mecho: Year One, Working Paper 22, Department of Artificial Intelligence, University of Edinburgh, 1977. Also in Proceedings of AISB-76.

1814. BYRD, L. and BORNING, A., Extending Mecho to Solve Statistics Problems, *Proceedings of AISB-80*, S. HARDY, ed., Amsterdam, Holland, 1980. Also available from University of Edinburgh as Department of Artificial Intelligence Research Paper No 137.

1815. CHANG, C. L., An Experience of Building an Expert System with Prolog, Technical Report RJ 3925, IBM Watson Research Center, 1983.

1816. CHIN, M. Y., Computer Interrogation System CISP, M.Sc. Thesis, Imperial College, London, 1981.

1817. CLARK, K. L. and McCABE, F. G., Prolog: A Language for Implementing Expert Systems, *Machine Intelligence*, 1982.

1818. CLIFFORD, J., JARKE, M. and VASSILIOU, Y., How Does an Expert System Gets Its Data, Technical Report CRI-50-GBA-82-26-CR, University of New York, 1982.

1819. CLIFFORD, J., JARKE, M. and VASSILIOU, Y., A Short Introduction to Expert Systems, *IEEE Database Engineering 6*, 4 (December 1983).

1820. COTTON, J., BYRD, L. and BUNDY, A., How Can Algebra Steps be Learned by Students with only Arithmetic Skills, Working Paper, Department of Artificial Intelligence, University of Edinburgh, 1981.

1821. DAHL, V., Logic Programming for Constructive Expert Database Systems, *Proceedings of the First International Workshop on Expert Database Systems*, Kiawah Island, South Carolina, October 24-27, 1984.

1822. DARRONNAT, Y., Programmation Logique d'Un Modele de Donnees de Conception, Technical Report, Department of Computer Science, Universite Claude Bernard, Lyon, France, 1983.

1823. DARVAS, F., BEIN, K. and GABANYI, Z., A Logic-Based Expert System for Model Building in Regression Analysis, *Proceedings of Workshop on Logic Programming*, Algarve, Portugal, 1983.

1824. DARVAS, F., FUTO, I. and SZEREDI, P., A Logic Based Program System for Predicting Drug Interactions, *International Journal of Biomedical Computing 9*, 4 (1977).

1825. DAVID, J. M., ERNST, C. and WEBER, Y., Utilisation des Systemes Expert en Maintenance: Une Approche Micro-Informatique, Technical Report, Department of Computer Science, Universite de Nancy, France, 1984. In French.

1826. DEBENHAM, J. K., Knowledge Base Design, *Australian Computer Journal 17*, 1 (February 1985).

1827. DEKEYSER, L., KREKELS, B., WILLEMS, Y. D. and WILLEMS, J. L., A Prolog Meta-Interpreter as Medical Expert System Shell, *M.I.M. News*, July, 1984.

1828. DEKEYSER, L., KREKELS, B., WILLEMS, Y. D. and WILLEMS, J. L., YAPES: Yet Another Prolog-based Expert System Shell, *Sixth European Conference On Artificial Intelligence*, Pisa, September, 1984.

1829. DEUTSCH, T., FUTO, I. and TAMAS, G., Design of Drug Administration by Artificial Intelligence Based Computer Simulation, SZKI, 1985.

1830. DIAS, V. and PEREIRA, L. M., A Survey of Knowledge Based Systems in Prolog, *Logic Programming Newsletter*, Universidade Nova de Lisboa, Winter 1984.

1831. DINCBAS, M., Etude d'un Systeme Expert pour la CAD - Presentation de Peace, Technical Report 3-3122-DERI, CERT, France, 1979.

1832. DINCBAS, M., Le Systeme de Resolution de Problemes METALOG, Technical Report, CERT, France, 1980.

1833. DINCBAS, M., A Knowledge-Based Expert System for Automatic Analysis and Synthesis in CAD, *Proceedings IFIP 80*, 1980, 705-710. AFIPS Press.

1834. DINCBAS, M., The METALOG Problem-Solving System: An Informal Presentation, in *Workshop on Logic Programming*, S. A. TARNLUND, (ed.), Debrecen, Hungary, July 1980, 80-91.

1835. DINCBAS, M., Systemes Expert - Application a l'Electronique et Expression du Controle d'un Systeme Expert, *Presented at the Journees d'Etude Systemes Experts*, AFCET-ADI, 1981.

1836. DINCBAS, M., L'ecole Nationale Superieure De L'Aeronautique Et De L'espace, Doctoral Dissertation, January, 1983.

1837. DWORKIS, C., Experiments in Elementary Rule-Based Reasoning, Internal Report, Operating Systems Division, Logicon, Inc, August, 1981.

1838. ENOMOTO, H., YONEZAKI, N., SAEKI, M. and KUNIFUJI, S., Paradigms of Knowledge Based Software System and Its Service Image, Technical Report TR-030, ICOT - Institute for New Generation Computer Technology, Tokyo, Japan, 1983. Also in 3th Seminar on Software Engineering, Florence, Italy, 1983.

1839. FIESCHI, M., JOUBERT, M., FIESCHI, D. and ROUX, M., SPHINX: An Interactive System for Medical Diagnosis, in *Fuzzy Information and Decision Processes*, M. GUPTA and E. SANCHEZ, (eds.), North-Holland, 1982.

1840. FREEMAN, M. W., HIRSCHMAN, L., MCKAY, D. P., MILLER, F. and SIDHU, D., Logic Programming Applied to Knowledge Based Systems, Modeling and Simulation, *Proceedings of the Conference on Artificial Intelligence*, Rochester, 1983.

1841. FREEMAN, M. W., HIRSCHMAN, L., MCKAY, D. P. and PALMER, M., KNET: A Logic-Based Associative Network Framework for Expert System, Technical Report, Research and Development Division, SDC, 1983.

1842. FURTADO, A. L. and MOURA, C. M. O., Expert Helpers to Data-Based Information Systems, *Proceedings of the First International Workshop on Expert Database Systems*, Kiawah Island, South Carolina, October 24-27, 1984.

1843. FUTO, I., Combined Discrete/Continuous Modeling and Problem Solving, *SCS MultiConference on AI, Graphics and Simulation*, San Diego, California, January, 1985.

1844. FUTO, I. and GERGELY, T., A Logic Simulation Language For Modeling Cooperative Problem Solving System, *AFCNET Information Congress, Hardware and Software Components and Architecture for the 5th Generation*, Paris, France, March, 1985.

1845. GABBAY, D., Theoretical Foundations For Non-Monotonic Reasoning In Expert Systems, Doc 84/11, Department of Computing, Imperial College, 1984.

1846. GOEBEL, R. G., DLOG: A Logic-Based Data Model for the Machine Representation of Knowledge, Technical Report, Department of Computer Science, University of Waterloo,Canada, 1983. A Summary was published in SigArt 87, January 1984.

1847. GOLSHANI, F., Tools for Expert Database Systems, *Proceedings of the First International Workshop on Expert Database Systems*, Kiawah Island, South Carolina, October 24-27, 1984.

1848. GRUMBACH, A., Knowledge Acquisition in Logic Programming, *Proceedings of the First International Logic Programming Conference*, Marseille, France, September, 1982.

1849. GUPTA, N. K. and SEVIORA, R. E., An Expert System Approach to Real Time Debugging, *Proceedings of the First IEEE Conference on Artificial Intelligence Applications*, Denver, Colorado, December, 1984.

1850. HAGERT, G. and TARNLUND, S. A., Deductive Modelling of Human Cognition, *Proceedings of the International Joint Conference on Artificial Intelligence*, Vancouver, Canada, 1981. Also Technical Report, Computer Science Department, Uppsala University.

1851. HAMMOND, P., Logic Programming for Expert Systems, Master's Thesis, Imperial College, London, 1980. Available as Technical Report DOC 82/4.

1852. HAMMOND, P., APES (A Prolog Expert System Shell): A User Manual, Doc Report 82/9, Department of Computing, Imperial College, 1982.

1853. HAMMOND, P., Prolog Representation of Social Security Benefit Regulations, Technical Report, Imperial College, London, 1982.

1854. HAMMOND, P., Appendix to Prolog: A Language for Implementing Expert Systems, *Machine Intelligence 10*, (1982).

1855. HAMMOND, P., Representation of DHSS Regulations as a Logic Program, Technical Report TR-82-26, Imperial College, London, 1982. Also in Proceedings BCS Expert Systems 83.

1856. HAMMOND, P., APES: A User Manual, Technical Report TR-82-9, Imperial College, London, 1983.

1857. HAMMOND, P., APES: A Detailed Description, Technical Report TR-82-10, Imperial College, London, 1983.

1858. HAMMOND, P., Micro-Prolog For Expert Systems, in *Micro-Prolog: Programming in Logic*, K. L. CLARK and F. G. MCCABE, (eds.), Prentice Hall, 1984.

1859. HAMMOND, P. and ALVEY, P., A Comparison of EMYCIN and APES (a Prolog Expert System Shell for Representing a Medical Knowledge Base), Technical Report 82/28, Computer Science Department, Imperial College, London, 1982.

1860. HAMMOND, P. and HOWARTH, R., A Rule-Based Approach to Geological Knowledge, Technical Report, 82/27, Computer Science Department, Imperial College, London, 1982.

1861. HAMMOND, P. and SERGOT, M. J., A Prolog Based Expert System Shell, *Proceedings BCS Expert Systems*, Cambridge, 1983.

1862. HAMMOND, P. and SERGOT, M. J., Logic For Representing Data And Expertise, in *Database Design Update*, G. J. BAKER and S. HOLLOWAY, (eds.), 1984. The British Computer Society's Database Specialist Group.

1863. HELM, R. A., LASSEZ, C. and MARRIOT, K. G., Prolog For Expert Systems: An Evaluation, Technical Report 85/3, University of Melbourne, 1985.

1864. HUSTLER, A., Programming Law in Logic, Technical Report CS-82-13, Department of Computer Science, University of Waterloo, May 1982.

1865. JARKE, M. and VASSILIOU, Y., Coupling Expert Systems with Database Management Systems, in *Artificial Intelligence Applications for Business*, W. REITMAN, (ed.), Ablex Publishing Company, 1984.

1866. JOUBERT, M., FIESCHI, M. and ROUX, M., Aide a la Decision en Medecine: Les Bases Logiques du Systeme Sphinx, *Proceedings of the First International Logic Programming Conference*, Marseille, France, September, 1982.

1867. KANAI, N. and ISHIZUKA, M., Prolog-ELF Incorporating Fuzzy Logic, *Report of the Technical Group on Knowledge Engineering and Artificial Intelligence of the Information Processing Society of Japan 84*, 4 (1984). (In Japanese).

1868. KITAKAMI, H. and OTHERS, A Method of Realizing a Knowledge Assimilation Mechanism, Technical Report TR-010, ICOT - Institute for New Generation Computer Technology, Tokyo, Japan, 1983. In Japanese.

1869. KITAKAMI, H., MIYACHI, T., KUNIFUJI, S. and FURUKAWA, K., A Methodology for Implementation of a Knowledge Acquisition System, Technical Memorandum TM-0024, ICOT - Institute for New Generation Computer Technology, Tokyo, Japan, 1983. Also in Proceedings of the International IEEE Logic Programming Conference, 1984.

1870. KOMOROWSKI, H. J., QLOG - The Software for Prolog and Logic Programming, in *Workshop on Logic Programming*, S. TARNLUND, (ed.), Debrecen, Hungary, July 1980.

1871. KOWALSKI, R. A., Logic For Expert Systems, *Proceedings BCS Expert Systems*, Cambridge, 1983.

1872. KOWALSKI, R. A., Software Engineering and Artificial Intelligence in New Generation Computing, *Future Generation Computer Systems 1*, 1 (June, 1984).

1873. KUNIFUJI, S., MIYACHI, T., KITAKAMI, H. and FURUKAWA, K., Knowledge Acquisition and Meta Inference, Technical Memorandum TM-0016, ICOT - Institute for New Generation Computer Technology, Tokyo, Japan, 1983. In Japanese.

1874. KUNIFUJI, S., MIYACHI, T., KITAKAMI, H. and FURUKAWA, K., A Method of Realizing a Knowledge Acquisition System, Technical Memorandum TM-0017, ICOT - Institute for New Generation Computer Technology, Tokyo, Japan, 1983. In Japanese.

1875. LAVRAC, N., BRATKO, I., MOZETIC, I., CERCEK, B., GRAD, A. and HORVAT, M., KARDIO-E: An Expert System for Electrocardiographic Diagnosis of Cardiac Arrhythmias, *Expert Systems 2*, 1 (January, 1985).

1876. LEE, N. S. and ROACH, J. W., GUESS-1: A General Purpose Expert System Shell, Technical Report Tr-85-3, Department of Computer Science, Virginia Polytechnic Institute and State University, Blackburg, Virginia,USA, 1985.

1877. LEE, R. M., CANDID: A Logical Calculus for Describing Financial Contracts, Technical Report WP-80-06-02, Wharton School, University of Pennsylvania in Philadelphia, 1980.

1878. LEE, R. M., CANDID Description of Commercial and Financial Concepts: A Formal Semantics Approach to Knowledge Representation, Technical Report WP-81-162, International Institute for Applied Systems Analysis, Laxenburg, Austria, 1981.

1879. LITTLEFORD, A., A Mycin-Like Expert System in Prolog, *Proceedings of the Second International Logic Programming Conference*, S. TARNLUND, ed., Uppsala University, Uppsala, Sweden, July 2-6, 1984, 289-300.

1880. LYALL, A., HAMMOND, P., BROUGH, D. R. and GLOVER, D., BIOLOG - A DNA Sequence Analysis System in Prolog, *Nucleic Acids Research 12*, 1 (1984).

1881. MARUYAMA, F., HAYASHI, K., UEHARA, T., MANO, T., KAKUDA, T. and KAWATO, N., Prolog-based Expert System for Logic Design, *International Conference On Fifth Generation Computer Systems*, November 1984.

1882. MICHOGUCHI, F., MIWA, K. and HONMA, Y., An Approach to Prolog-Based Expert Systems, *Proceedings of the Logic Programming Conference*, Tokyo, March 1983.

1883. MINKER, J., Issues in Developing Expert Systems, *Proceedings of Workshop on Logic Programming*, Algarve, Portugal, 1983.

1884. MISSIKOFF, M. and WIEDERHOLD, G., Towards a Unified Approach to Expert and Database Systems, *Proceedings of the First International Workshop on Expert Database Systems*, Kiawah Island, South Carolina, October 24-27, 1984.

1885. MIYACHI, T., KITAKAMI, H., KUNIFUJI, S. and FURUKAWA, K., A Knowledge Assimilation Method for Logic Databases, Technical Report TR-0025, ICOT - Institute for New Generation Computer Technology, Tokyo, Japan, 1983.

1886. MIZOGUCHI, F., A Software Environment for Developing Knowledge-Based Systems, in *Computer Science and Technologies: 1982*, T. KITAGAWA, (ed.), Elsevier North-Holland, New-York, 1982, 334-349.

1887. MIZOGUCHI, F., Prolog Based Expert Systems, *New Generation Computing 1*, (1983), Springer Verlag.

1888. MIZOGUCHI, F., KATAYAMA, Y. and OWADA, H., LOOKS: Knowledge Representation System For Designing Expert System In The Framework of Logic Programming, *International Conference On Fifth Generation Computer Systems*, November 1984.

1889. MORRIS, P. H., Relational Production Systems and Logic Programs, *Proceedings of the First International Logic Programming Conference*, Marseille, France, September, 1982.

1890. MOTODA, H., YAMADA, N. and YOSHIDA, K., A Knowledge Based System For Plant Diagnosis, *International Conference On Fifth Generation Computer Systems*, November 1984.

1891. MOZETIC, I., BRATKO, I. and NAVRAO, L., An Experiment in Automatic Synthesis of Expert Knowledge through Qualitative Modelling, *Proceedings of Workshop on Logic Programming*, Algarve, Portugal, 1983.

1892. NARAIN, S., *MYCIN: The Expert System and Its Implementation in LOGLISP*, Department of Computer Science, Syracuse University, 1981.

1893. NARAIN, S., MYCIN in a Logic Programming Environment, *Proceedings of COMPCON 84*, Spring 1984.

1894. O'KEEFE, R. A., Concept Formation from Very Large Training Sets, *Proceedings of the International Joint Conference on Artificial Intelligence*, Karlsruhe, Germany, 1983.

1895. OLIVEIRA, E., Developing Expert System Builders in Logic Programs, *Proceedings of Workshop on Logic Programming*, Algarve, Portugal, 1983. Also New Generation Computing, Vol 2, pp 187-194, 1984.

1896. OLIVEIRA, E., Engenharia do Conhecimento: Sistemas Periciais e Prolog, Ph.D. Dissertation, Department of Computer Science, Universidade Nova de Lisboa, Lisbon, Portugal, 1984. In Portuguese.

1897. OLIVEIRA, E., Developing Expert Systems Builders in Logic Programming, *New Generation Computing 2*, (1984), 187-194, Ohmsha and Springer-Verlag.

1898. PARCY, J. P., Un Systeme Expert en Diagnostique sur Reacteurs a Neutrons Rapides, Technical Report, Groupe d'Intelligence Artificielle, Marseille, France, 1982.

1899. PARSAYE, K., EDD, An Expert System for Database Design, Internal Report, Hewlett Packard Laboratories, 1982.

1900. PARSAYE, K., Database Management, Knowledge Base Management and Expert System Development in Prolog, *Proceedings of Workshop on Logic Programming*, Algarve, Portugal, 1983.

1901. PASZTORNE-VARGA, K., A Solution to a CAD Problem in Prolog, *Presented at Workshop on Logic Programming for Intelligent Systems*, Long Beach, California, 1982.

1902. PEREIRA, L. M., SABATIER, P. and DE OLIVEIRA, E., ORBI, An Expert System for Environmental Resource Evaluation Through Natural Language, *Proceedings of the First International Logic Programming Conference*, M. VAN CANEGHEM, ed., Marseille, France, September 1982.

1903. POE, M., Control Of Heuristic Search In A Prolog-based Microcode Synthesis Expert, *International Conference On Fifth Generation Computer Systems*, November 1984.

1904. POLLIT, A. S., A Front-End System: An Expert System as an Online Search Intermediary, *Aslib Proceedings 36*, 5 (May, 1984), 229-234.

1905. POOLE, D. L., The Theory of CES: A Complete Expert System, Ph.D. Dissertation, Department of Computer Science, University of Waterloo, Canada, 1982.

1906. POOLE, D. L., A Computational Logic of Default Reasoning, Technical Report, Department of Computer Science, University of Waterloo, Canada, 19824.

1907. REITMAN, W., *Artificial Intelligence Applications for Business*, Ablex Publishing Company, 1984. Editor.

1908. ROACH, J. W., VIRKAR, R. S., WEAVER, M. J. and DRAKER, C. R., POMME: A Computer-Based Consultation System for Apple Orchard Management Using Prolog, *Expert Systems 2*, 2 (April, 1985).

1909. ROBINSON, J. A., Fundamentals of Machine-Oriented Deductive Logic, in *Introductory Readings in Expert Systems*, D. MICHIE, (ed.), Gordon and Breach, New York, 1982, 81-92.

1910. SAKAI, K. and MIYACHI, T., Incorporating Naive Negation into Prolog, Technical Report TR-0028, ICOT - Institute for New Generation Computer Technology, Tokyo, Japan, 1983.

1911. SAMMUT, C. A., Concept Development for Expert System Knowledge Bases, *Australian Computer Journal 17*, 1 (February 1985).

1912. SCHLOBOHM, D., Tax Advisor: A Prolog Program Analyzing Tax Issues, *Dr. Dobbs Journal*, March, 1985, 64-92.

1913. SERGOT, M. J., Programming Law: LEGOL as a Logic Programming Language, Technical Report, Imperial College, London, 1980.

1914. SERGOT, M. J., Prospects for Representing the Law as Logic Programs, in *Logic Programming*, K. L. CLARK and S. TARNLUND, (eds.), Academic Press, New York, 1982. A.P.I.C. Studies in Data Processing No. 16.

1915. SHAPIRO, E. Y., Logic Programs With Uncertainties: A Tool for Implementing Rule-Based Systems, *Proceedings of the International Joint Conference on Artificial Intelligence*, Karlsruhe, Germany, 1983.

1916. SHARPE, W. P., Logic Programming for the Law, in *Research and Development of Expert Systems*, M. A. BRAMER, (ed.), Cambridge University Press, Cambridge, United Kingdom, 1984.

1917. SHMUELI, O., TSUR, S. and ZFIRAH, H., Rule Support in Prolog, *Proceedings of the First International Workshop on Expert Database Systems*, Kiawah Island, South Carolina, October 24-27, 1984.

1918. SKUCE, D., Expressing Qualitative Biomedical Knowledge Exactly Using the Language LESK, *International Journal of Computing in Biology and Medecine 15*, 1 (1982), 57-69.

1919. SKUCE, D., LESK: A Language Synthesizing Natural Language, Computer Language and Logic, *Proceedings Annual Conference on Computational Linguistics COLING-82*, Prague, July 1982.

1920. SKUCE, D., LESK Tutorial, Technical Report TR-83-12, Department of Computer Science, University of Ottawa, Canada, 1983.

1921. SKUCE, D., Expressing Academic Regulations in LESK, Technical Report TR-83-13, Department of Computer Science, University of Ottawa, Canada, 1983.

1922. SKUCE, D., Expressing UNIX Knowledge in LESK, Technical Report TR-83-14, Department of Computer Science, University of Ottawa, Canada, 1983.

1923. SKUCE, D., Formal Semantics of KNOWLOG, Technical Report TR-83-15, Department of Computer Science, University of Ottawa, Canada, 1983.

1924. SKUCE, D., KNOWLOG: A Prolog Extension for Implementing Expert Knowledge Systems, Technical Report TR-83-05, Department of Computer Science, University of Ottawa, Canada, 1983.

1925. SPACEK, L., Controlling Prolog and Expert Systems, Technical Report, University of Sussex, England, 1980.

1926. SPACEK, L., Production Systems and Prolog, Technical Report, University of Sussex, England, 1981.

1927. SPACEK, L., *The production systems and Prolog (A framework for the techniques of Artificial Intelligence)*, University of Essex, Cognitive Studies Centre, October, 1981.

1928. STEELE, B. D., EXPERT - The Implementation of Data-Independent Expert Systems with Quasi-Natural Language Information Input, M.Sc. Thesis, Imperial College, London, 1981.

1929. STERLING, L., Expert System = Knowledge + Meta-Interpreter, Technical Report CS84-17, Computer Science Department, Weizman Institute, Israel, 1984.

1930. SUGIYAMA, K., KAMEDA, M., AKIYAMA, K. and MAKINOUCHI, A., A Knowledge Representation System in Prolog, Technical Report TR-0024, ICOT - Institute for New Generation Computer Technology, Tokyo, Japan, 1983.

1931. VALTORTA, M., *The Graduate Course Advisor*, Computer Science Department, Duke University, 1983. M.S. Thesis.

1932. VALTORTA, M., Knowledge Refinement in Rule Bases for Expert Systems: An Application Driven Approach, *Proceedings of the First International Workshop on Expert Database Systems*, Kiawah Island, South Carolina, October 24-27, 1984.

1933. VASSILIOU, Y., CLIFFORD, J. and JARKE, M., Access to Specific Declarative Knowledge by Expert Systems: The Impact of Logic Programming, Technical Report, School of Business, University of New York, 1983.

1934. VASSILIOU, Y., JARKE, M. and CLIFFORD, J., Expert Systems for Business Applications, *IEEE Database Engineering 6*, 4 (December 1983).

1935. WALKER, A., SYLLOG: A Knowledge-Based Data Management System From Knowledge, 034-3481, Department of Computer Science, New York University, 1981.

1936. WALKER, A., Automatic Generation of Explanations of Results From Knowledge Bases, RJ-3481, IBM T.J. Watson Research Center, 1982.

1937. WALKER, A., Data Bases, Expert Systems, and Prolog, RJ-3870, IBM Research Center San Jose, 1982.

1938. WALKER, A., Prolog/Ex1, An Inference Engine Which Explains Both Yes and No Answers, RJ-3771, IBM San Jose, 1983. Also in Proceedings International Joint Conference on Artificial Intelligence-83.

1939. WALKER, A. and PORTO, A., A Knowledge-Based Garden Store Assistant, *Proceedings of Workshop on Logic Programming*, Algarve, Portugal, 1983.

1940. WOEHL, K., Automatic Classification Of Office Documents By Coupling Relational Databases And Prolog Expert Systems, *Proceedings of the Tenth Conference On Very Large Data Bases*, Singapore, August, 1984.

1941. YOKOTA, H., KATUTA, T., MIYAZAKI, N., SHIBAYAMA, S. and MURAKAMI, K., An Investigation for Building Knowledge Base Machines, Technical Memorandum TM-0019, ICOT - Institute for New Generation Computer Technology, Tokyo, Japan, 1983. In Japanese.

CHAPTER 15

Databases - Relationship with Logic Programming

1942. ACHARYA, S. and BUCKLEY, G., Transaction Restarts in Prolog Database Systems, *Proceedings of the 1985 ACM Sigmod Conference*, Austin, Texas, May, 1985.

1943. ADIBA, M. and NGUYEN, G. T., Logic Programming for a Generalized Data Management System, Research Report TIGRE No 12, Laboratoires IMAG, France, January, 1984.

1944. ADIBA, M. and NGUYEN, G. T., Handling Constraints and Meta-Data on a Generalized Data Management System, *Proceedings of the First International Workshop on Expert Database Systems*, Kiawah Island, South Carolina, October 24-27, 1984.

1945. ANDERSON, S. O., NEVES, J. C. and WILLIAMS, M. H., Extended Integrity Constraints in Query-By-Example, Technical Report, Heriot-Watt University, Edinburg, 1982.

1946. BACKHOUSE, R. C., NEVES, J. C., WILLIAMS, M. H. and ANDERSON, S. O., A Prolog Implementation of Query-By-Example, Technical Report, Heriot-Watt University, Edinburg, 1982. Also in Proceedings of the Seventh International Symposium on Computing, Germany.

1947. BALDWIN, J. F. and PILSWORTH, B. W., An Inferential Fuzzy Logic Knowledge Base, Technical Report, Department of Engineering and Mathematics, University of Bristol, U.K., 1982. Presented at the Workshop on Logic Programming Long Beach, Los Angeles September 1981.

1948. BANCILHON, F. and RICHARD, P., Managing Texts and Facts in a Mixed Database Environment, in *New Applications of Databases*, G. GARDARIN and E. GELENBE, (eds.), Academic Press, 1984.

1949. BANNING, R. W., A Prolog-Based Framework for Model Management, *Proceedings of the First International Workshop on Expert Database Systems*, Kiawah Island, South Carolina, October 24-27, 1984.

1950. BARTHES, J. P., VAYSSADE, M. and MIACZYNSKA, M., Property Driven Data Bases, International Joint Conference on Artificial Intelligence, Tokyo, Japan, 1979.

1951. BERGER-SABBATEL, G., COEUR, A., TOAN, N. G. and WINNIGER, P., La Machine Bases de Donnees Opale, Technical Report, Laboratoire IMAG, Saint-Martin-d'Heres, France, 1984.

1952. BERGER-SABBATEL, G., DANG, W., IANESELLI, J. C. and NGUYEN, G. T., Unification for a Prolog Data Base Machine, *Proceedings of the Second International Logic Programming Conference*, S. TARNLUND, ed., Uppsala University, Uppsala, Sweden, July 2-6, 1984, 207-218.

1953. BERGER-SABBATEL, G., IANESELLI, J. C. and NGUYEN, G. T., A Prolog Database Machine, *Proceedings of the Third International Workshop on Database Machines*, Munchen, Germany, September, 1983.

1954. BERGER-SABBATEL, G. and NGUYEN, G. T., La Machine Base De Donnees OPALE, *Actes du Seminaire Programmation En Logique*, M. DINCBAS, ed., March, 1983.

1955. VAN EMDE BOAS-LUBSEN, H., VAN EMDE BOAS, P. and DOEDENS, C. F. J., Extending A Relational Database with Logic Programming Facilities, TR 13.195, IBM INS-Development Center, Uithoorn, The Netherlands, October 1984.

1956. BOWEN, K. A., Logic Programming and Relational Databases, in *Workshop on Logic Programming*, S. TARNLUND, (ed.), Debrecen, Hungary, July 1980.

1957. BRODIE, M. and JARKE, M., On Integrating Logic Programming and Databases, *Proceedings of the First International Workshop on Expert Database Systems*, Kiawah Island, South Carolina, October 24-27, 1984.

1958. BRUYNOOGHE, M., An Interface between Prolog and Cyber-EDMS, *Proceedings of Workshop on Logic and Databases*, Toulouse, France, 1977.

1959. VAN CANEGHEM, M., Systeme d'Analyse et de Synthese Morphologique en Francais pour l'Exploitation de Banques de Donnees (Vol 1,2), Technical Report, Groupe d'Intelligence Artificielle, Universite d'Aix-Marseille II Marseille, France, 1977.

1960. CHAKRAVARTHY, U. S., FISHMAN, D. H. and MINKER, J., Semantic Query Optimization in Expert Systems and Database Systems, *Proceedings of the First International Workshop on Expert Database Systems*, Kiawah Island, South Carolina, October 24-27, 1984.

1961. CHAKRAVARTHY, U. S., MINKER, J. and TRAN, D., Interfacing Predicate Logic Languages and Relational Databases, Technical Report, University of Maryland, College Park, 1982. Also in Proceedings of the First International Logic Programming Conference Marseille, France, 91-98..

1962. CHANDRA, A. and HAREL, D., Horn Clause Queries and Generalizations, *Proceedings of Symposium on Principles of Database Systems*, 1982.

1963. CHANG, C. L. and WALKER, A., PROSQL: A Prolog Programming Interface with SQL/DS, Technical Report RJ 4314, IBM Watson Research Center, 1984.

1964. CHOMICKI, L. and GRUNDZINSKI, T., A Database Support System for Prolog, *Proceedings of Workshop on Logic Programming*, Algarve, Portugal, 1983.

1965. COELHO, H., On a Conversational Interface between Users and a Database, DI Report, Laboratoria Nacional De Engenharia Civil, Lisbon, Portugal, 1976.

1966. COELHO, H., Natural Language and Databases, DI Report, Laboratoria Nacional De Engenharia Civil, Lisbon, Portugal, 1977.

1967. COELHO, H., Database Interrogation by Means of Natural Language, *Proceedings the First International Workshop on Natural Language Communication with Computers*, Warsaw, Poland, September, 1980. Held in Warsaw, Poland.

1968. COELHO, H., Prolog for Databases, *Computer and Artificial Intelligence 2*, 1 (February, 1983), 35-46.

1969. CONERY, J. S. and KIBLER, D. F., Parallel Query Processing in Logic Databases, *Proceedings of the International Joint Conference on Artificial Intelligence*, Karlsruhe, Germany, 1983.

1970. DAHL, V., Logical Design of Deductive Natural Language Consultable Data Bases, *Proceedings Fifth International Conference on Very Large Data Bases*, Rio De Janeiro, Brazil, 1979.

1971. DAHL, V., Towards Constructive Data Bases, Workshop on Logic Programming, Long Beach, Los Angeles, September 1981.

1972. DAHL, V., On Database Systems Development Through Logic, *ACM Transactions on Database Systems 7*, 1 (March 1982), 102-123.

1973. DAHL, V., Logic Programming for Constructive Expert Database Systems, *Proceedings of the First International Workshop on Expert Database Systems*, Kiawah Island, South Carolina, October 24-27, 1984.

1974. DEBENHAM, J. K. and MCGRATH, G. M., The Description in Logic of a Large Commercial Database: A Methodology Put to the Test, *Australian Computer Science Communications 5*, (1982), 12-21.

1975. DEBENHAM, J. K. and MCGRATH, G. M., LOFE: A Language for Virtual Relational Databases, *The Australian Computer Journal 15*, 3 (1983), 2-9.

1976. DEMOLOMBE, R., Assigning Meaning to Ill-Defined Queries Expressed in Predicate Calculus Language, *Proceedings of the Workshop on Logic and Databases*, Toulouse, France, 1977.

1977. DEMOLOMBE, R., Interface Entre Prolog Et Un SGBD, *Actes du Seminaire Programmation En Logique*, M. DINCBAS, ed., March, 1983.

1978. DEMOLOMBE, R., Interface entre Prolog et un SGBD, Technical Report, ONERA-CERT, Toulouse, France, 1984.

1979. DIEL, H., Concurrent Data Access Architecture, *International Conference On Fifth Generation Computer Systems*, November 1984.

1980. ELCOCK, E. W., STABLER, E. P., WYATT, D. and YOUNG, A., *Database Management in Prolog*, Department of Computer Science, University of Western Ontario, 1984.

1981. VAN EMDEN, M. H., Deductive Information Retrieval On Virtual Relational Databases, Technical Report CS-76-42, Department of Computer Science, University of Waterloo,Canada, 1976.

1982. VAN EMDEN, M. H., Logic Programs for Querying Relational Databases, Technical Report, Department of Computer Science, University of Waterloo,Canada, 1976.

1983. FAGIN, R., Horn Clauses And Data Base Dependencies, *Proceedings Of The 12th Annual ACM-SIGACT Symposium On The Theory Of Computing,* , 123-134.

1984. FAGIN, R., Functional Dependencies in a Relational Database and Propositional Logic, *IBM Journal of Research and Development 21,* 6 (November 1977), 534-544.

1985. FAGIN, R., Horn Clauses and Database Dependencies, *Journal of the ACM 29,* 4 (October 1982), 952-985.

1986. FISHMAN, D. H. and NAQVI, S. A., An Intelligent Database System: AIDS, *Proceedings of Workshop on Logical Bases for Databases,* Toulouse, France, 1982.

1987. FRANK, A., Extending a Network Database with Prolog, *Proceedings of the First International Workshop on Expert Database Systems,* Kiawah Island, South Carolina, October 24-27, 1984.

1988. FUHLROTT, O., Prolog als Databank- und Programmiersprache, Technical Report, University of Hamburg, Germany, 1982.

1989. FURTADO, A. L. and MOURA, C. M. O., Expert Helpers to Data-Based Information Systems, *Proceedings of the First International Workshop on Expert Database Systems,* Kiawah Island, South Carolina, October 24-27, 1984.

1990. FURUKAWA, K., A Deductive Question-answering System On Relational Databases, *Proceedings 5th International Joint Conference on Artificial Intelligence Conference*, Cambridge, August 1977, 59-66.

1991. FURUKAWA, K., An Intelligent Access to Relational Databases, in *Computer Science and Technologies: 1982*, T. KITAGAWA, (ed.), Elsevier North-Holland, New-York, 1982, 334-349.

1992. FUTO, I., DARVAS, F. and SZEREDI, J., The Application of Prolog to the Development of QA and DBM Systems, in *Logic and Databases*, H. GALLAIRE and J. MINKER, (eds.), Plenum Press, 1978.

1993. GALLAIRE, H., Impacts of Logic on Data Bases, *Proceedings Seventh International Conference on Very Large Data Bases*, Cannes, France, 1981.

1994. GALLAIRE, H., Logic Databases versus Deductive Databases, *Proceedings of Workshop on Logic Programming*, Algarve, Portugal, 1983.

1995. GALLAIRE, H., Prolog et Bases De Donnees, *Actes du Seminaire Programmation En Logique*, M. DINCBAS, ed., March, 1983.

1996. GALLAIRE, H. and MINKER, J., *Logic and Databases*, Plenum Press, 1978. Editors.

1997. GALLAIRE, H., MINKER, J. and NICOLAS, J. M., An Overview and Introduction to Logic and Databases, in *Logic and Databases*, H. GALLAIRE and J. MINKER, (eds.), Plenum Press, New York, 1978, 123-134.

1998. GALLAIRE, H., MINKER, J. and NICOLAS, J. M., *Advances in Database Theory*, Plenum Press, 1981. Editors.

1999. GALLAIRE, H., MINKER, J. and NICOLAS, J. M., Logic and Databases: A Deductive Approach, *ACM Computing Surveys 16*, 2 (June 1984).

2000. GARDARIN, G. and GELENBE, E., *New Applications of Databases*, Academic Press, Orlando, Florida, 1984. (Editors).

2001. GRANT, J. and MINKER, J., Optimization in a Deductive Relational System, *Proceedings Workshop on Formal Bases for Data Bases*, Toulouse, France, 1979.

2002. GRANT, J. and MINKER, J., Answering Queries in Indefinite Data Bases and the Null Value Problem, Technical Report, Department of Computer Science, University of Maryland, 1983.

2003. GRANT, J. and MINKER, J., Answering Queries in Indefinite Databases and the Null Value Problem, Technical Report TR-1374, Department of Computer Science, University of Maryland, 1984.

2004. GRAY, P. M. D., *Logic, Algebra and Databases*, Ellis Horwood Series, England, 1984.

2005. GRAY, P. M. D., Efficient Prolog Access to CODASYL and FDM Databases, *Proceedings of the 1985 ACM Sigmod Conference*, Austin, Texas, May, 1985.

2006. HAMMOND, P. and SERGOT, M. J., Logic For Representing Data And Expertise, in *Database Design Update*, G. J. BAKER and S. HOLLOWAY, (eds.), 1984. The British Computer Society's Database Specialist Group.

2007. HAN, J., Planning in Expert DB Systems by Using Rules, *Proceedings of the First International Workshop on Expert Database Systems*, Kiawah Island, South Carolina, October 24-27, 1984.

2008. HENSCHEN, L. J. and NAQVI, S. A., An Improved Filter for Literal Indexing in Resolution Systems, *Proceedings of the 7th International Joint Conference on Artificial Intelligence*, Vancouver, August, 1981, 528-529.

2009. HENSCHEN, L. J. and NAQVI, S. A., Synthesizing Least Fixed Point Queries into Iterative Programs, *Proceedings International Joint Conference on Artificial Intelligence*, Karlsruhe, Germany, 1983.

2010. HENSCHEN, L. J. and NAQVI, S. A., On Compiling Queries in Recursive First-Order Databases, *Journal of the ACM 1*, (January, 1984).

2011. IRANI, K. B. and SHIH, Y., Implementation of Very Large Prolog-Based Knowledge Bases on Data Flow Architectures, *Proceedings of the First IEEE/AAAI Conference on Artificial Intelligence Applications*, Denver, Colorado, December, 1984.

2012. JANANAMING, M., JOHANSSON, A. L. and TARNLUND, S. A., *Predicate Logic: A New Basis For Data Bases*, University Of Stockholm, 1975.

2013. JARKE, M., External Semantic Query Simplification: A Graph-Theoretic Approach and Its Implementation in Prolog, Technical Report CRIS 75, Graduate School of Business, New York University, 1984.

2014. JARKE, M., CLIFFORD, J. and VASSILIOU, Y., An Optimizing Prolog Front-End to a Relational Query System, *Proceedings of the ACM SIGMOD Conference*, Boston, 1984. Also Technical Report CRIS 65, Graduate School of Business, New York University.

2015. JARKE, M. and VASSILIOU, Y., Coupling Expert Systems with Database Management Systems, in *Artificial Intelligence Applications for Business*, W. REITMAN, (ed.), Ablex Publishing Company, 1984.

2016. KELLOG, C., Knowledge Management: A Practical Amalgam of Knowledge and Data Base Technology, *Proceedings of the National Conference on Artificial Intelligence*, Carnegie-Mellon University, August 1982.

2017. KELLOG, C., KLAHR, P. and TRAVIS, L., Deductive Planning and Pathfinding for Relational Data Bases, in *Logic and Databases*, H. GALLAIRE and J. MINKER, (eds.), Plenum Press, 1978.

2018. KELLOG, C. and TRAVIS, L., Reasoning with Data in a Deductively Augmented Data Base Management System, in *Advances in Database Theory*, H. GALLAIRE, J. MINKER and J. M. NICOLAS, (eds.), Plenum Press, 1981.

2019. KITSUREGAWA, M., TANAKA, H. and MOTO-OKA, T., Application Of Hash To Data Base Machine And Its Architecture, *New Generation Computing 1*, 1 (1983).

2020. KLUZNIAK, F., SPOQUEL: A Simple Prolog-Oriented Query Language, Technical Report, Department of Computer Science, Warsaw University, Poland, 1983.

2021. KOMOROWSKI, H. J., Rapid Software Development in a Database Framework - A Case Study, *Proceedings of the IEEE International Conference on Data Engineering*, Los Angeles, 1984.

2022. KOULOUMDJIAN, J., Couplage entre FOLL-Prolog et les Systemes de Gestion de Bases de Donnees, *Journees d'Etude*, Universite des Sciences Sociale de Grenoble, France, January, 1984.

2023. KOWALSKI, R. A., Logic as a Database Language, *Workshop on Logic Programming*, Long Beach, Los Angeles, September 1981. Also available as Technical Report from Imperial College, London; and in Proceedings of Advanced Seminar on Theoretical Issues in Data Bases, Cetraro, Italy..

2024. KUNIFUJI, S. and YOKOTA, H., Prolog and Relational Databases for Fifth Generation Computer, *Proceedings of Workshop on Logical Bases for Databases*, Toulouse, France, 1982. Also available as Report TR-002 from ICOT.

2025. KUPER, G. M., ULLMAN, J. D. and VARDI, M. Y., On the Equivalence of Logical Databases, Technical Report RJ-4203, IBM Watson Research Center, 1984.

2026. KUPER, G. M. and VARDI, M. Y., A New Approach to Database Logic, Technical Report RJ-4202, IBM Watson Research Center, 1984.

2027. KUPER, G. M. and VARDI, M. Y., On the Expressive Power of the Logical Data Model, *Proceedings of the 1985 ACM Sigmod Conference*, Austin, Texas, May, 1985.

2028. LLOYD, J. W., An Introduction To Deductive Data Base Systems, Technical Report, Department of Computer Science, University of Melbourne,Australia, 1982. Also in the Australian Computer Journal, 15, 2, 1983.

2029. LOZINSKI, E. L., Deduction in Relational Databases Directed by Problem Specific Data, *Proceedings of the First International Workshop on Expert Database Systems*, Kiawah Island, South Carolina, October 24-27, 1984.

2030. MARQUE-PUCHEU, G., MARTIN-GALLAUSIAUX, J. and JOMIER, G., Interfacing Prolog and Relational Database Management System, in *New Applications of Databases*, G. GARDARIN and E. GELENBE, (eds.), Academic Press, 1984.

2031. MINKER, J., Performing Inferences over Relational Databases, *Proceedings of the 1975 ACM SIGMOD International Conference on Management of Data*, 1975, 79-91. Also available as Technical Report from the University of Maryland.

2032. MINKER, J., Set Operations and Inferences over Relational Databases, Technical Report 427, Computer Science Department, University of Maryland, 1975.

2033. MINKER, J., An Experimental Relational Data Base System Based on Logic, in *Logic and Databases*, H. GALLAIRE and J. MINKER, (eds.), Plenum Press, 1978.

2034. MINKER, J., Search Strategy and Selection Function for an Inferential Relational System, *ACM Transactions on Database Systems 3*, 1 (March, 1978), 1-31.

2035. MINKER, J., Logical Inference as an Aid to Analysis in Large Databases, Technical Report TR-879, Department of Computer Science, University of Maryland, 1980.

2036. MINKER, J., On Indefinite Databases and the Closed World Assumption, *Proceedings of the First International Logic Programming Conference*, Marseille, France, 1981. Also in 6th Conference on Automated Deduction, 1982.

2037. MINKER, J., On Deductive Relational Databases, in *Proceedings of the Fifth International Conference on Collective Phenomena*, Annals of the New York Academy of Sciences, Vol. 10, J. L. LEBOWITZ, (ed.), 1982, 181-280.

2038. MINKER, J., On Theories of Definite and Indefinite Databases, Technical Report TR-1250, Department of Computer Science, University of Maryland, 1983.

2039. MINKER, J. and NICOLAS, J. M., On Recursive Axioms in Deductive Databases, *Information Systems 8*, 1 (January, 1982).

2040. MINKER, J. and ZANON, G., An Extension to Linear Resolution with Selection Function, *Information Processing Letters 14*, 4 (June, 1982), 191-194.

2041. MINSKY, N., ROZENSHTEIN, D. and CHOMICKI, J., Unifying the Use and Evolution of Database Systems: A Case Study in Prolog, Technical Report DCS-TR-68, Department of Computer Science, Rutgers University, 1985.

2042. MISSIKOFF, M. and WIEDERHOLD, G., Towards a Unified Approach to Expert and Database Systems, *Proceedings of the First International Workshop on Expert Database Systems*, Kiawah Island, South Carolina, October 24-27, 1984.

2043. MIYACHI, T., KITAKAMI, H., KUNIFUJI, S. and FURUKAWA, K., A Knowledge Assimilation Method for Logic Databases, Technical Report TR-0025, ICOT - Institute for New Generation Computer Technology, Tokyo, Japan, 1983.

2044. MIYACHI, T., KUNIFUJI, S., KITAKAMI, H., FURUKAWA, K., TAKEUCHI, A. and YOKOTA, H., A Proposed Knowledge Assimilation Method for Logic Databases, Technical Memorandum TM-0004 (In Japanese), ICOT - Institute for New Generation Computer Technology, Tokyo, Japan, 1983. English Version in Proceedings of the International IEEE Logic Programming Conference, 1984.

2045. MURAKAMI, K., KAKUTA, T., MIYAZAKI, N., SHIBAYAMA, S. and YOKOTA, H., A Relational Database Machine: First Step to Knowledge Base Machine, Technical Report TR-012, ICOT - Institute for New Generation Computer Technology, Tokyo, Japan, 1983. Also in ACM SIGARCH Newsletter, Vol. 11(3), 1983, pp. 423-425.

2046. NAISH, L., Negation and Control in PROLOG, Ph.D. Thesis, Department of Computer Science, University of Melbourne, 1985.

2047. NAISH, L., MU-Prolog 3.2db Reference Manual, Internal Memorandum, Department of Computer Science, University of Melbourne, 1985.

2048. NAISH, L. and THOM, J. A., The MU-Prolog Deductive Database, Technical Report 83-10, Department of Computer Science, University of Melbourne,Australia, 1983.

2049. NAQVI, S. A., Prolog and Relational Databases: A Road to Data-Intensive Expert Systems, *Proceedings of the First International Workshop on Expert Database Systems*, Kiawah Island, South Carolina, October 24-27, 1984.

2050. NAQVI, S. A. and HENSCHEN, L. J., Performing Inferences over Recursive Data Bases, *Proceedings NCAI*, 1980.

2051. NEVES, J. C., A Logic Interpreter to Handle Time and Negation in Logic Data Bases Query-By-Example, Technical Report, Universidade do Minho, Braga, Portugal, 1984.

2052. NEVES, J. C., Triggers, Aggregate and Select Operators in a Logic Database Using Query-By-Example, Technical Report, Universidade do Minho, Braga, Portugal, 1984.

2053. NEVES, J. C., Security and Co-Operativeness In A Logic Data Base System, *Sixth European Conference On Artificial Intelligence*, Pisa, September, 1984.

2054. NEVES, J. C. and WILLIAMS, M. H., Towards a Co-Operative Database Management System, *Proceedings of Workshop on Logic Programming*, Algarve, Portugal, 1983.

2055. NEVES, J. C. and WILLIAMS, M. H., A Logical Approach to Security and Integrity in Query-By-Example, Technical Report, Universidade do Minho, Braga, Portugal, 1984.

2056. NEVES, J. C. and WILLIAMS, M. H., An Approach to Co-operativeness in Logic Data Bases, Technical Report, Universidade do Minho, Braga, Portugal, 1984.

2057. NGUYEN, G. T., OLIVARES, J. and WINNIGER, P., Cooperation de Prolog et d'un SGDB Generalise: Principles and Applications, Technical Report 12, Centre de Recherche, Grenoble, INRIA, 1984.

2058. NICOLAS, J. M., A Property of Logical Formulas Corresponding to Integrity Constraints on Database Relations, *Proceedings of the Workshop on Formal Bases for Data Bases*, Toulouse, France, 1979.

2059. NICOLAS, J. M., Logic for Improving Integrity Checking in Relational Databases, *Acta Informatica 18*, 3 (1979).

2060. NICOLAS, J. M., Proceedings of Workshop on Logical Bases for Databases, Technical Report ONERA-CERT, Toulouse, December, 1982. Editor.

2061. NICOLAS, J. M., Bases De Donnees Logiques Et Programmation En Logique, *Actes du Seminaire Programmation En Logique*, M. DINCBAS, ed., March, 1983.

2062. NICOLAS, J. M., Bases de Donnees Logiques, Technical Report, ONERA-CERT, Toulouse, France, 1984.

2063. NICOLAS, J. M. and SYRE, J. C., Natural Question Answering and Automated Deduction in the System SYNTEX, *Proceedings of IFIP*, 1974, 595-599.

2064. NICOLAS, J. M. and YAZDANIAN, K., Integrity Checking in Deductive Databases, in *Logic and Databases*, H. GALLAIRE and J. MINKER, (eds.), Plenum Press Publishing Co., New York, 1978, 325-346.

2065. NICOLAS, J. M. and YAZDANIAN, K., An Outline of BDGEN: a Deductive DBMS, *Proceedings IFIP 83 Congress*, 1983, 711-717. Also Technical Report ONERA-CERT, October 1982.

2066. PARKER, D. S., Logic Programming and Databases, *Proceedings of the First International Workshop on Expert Database Systems*, Kiawah Island, South Carolina, October 24-27, 1984.

2067. PARSAYE, K., Database Management, Knowledge Base Management and Expert System Development in Prolog, *Proceedings of Workshop on Logic Programming*, Algarve, Portugal, 1983.

2068. PARSAYE, K., Logic Programming and Relational Databases, *IEEE Database Engineering 6*, 4 (December 1983).

2069. PEREIRA, L. M. and FILGUEIRAS, M., Relational Databases a la Carte, Research Report, Departemento de Informatica, Universidade Nova de Lisboa, Portugal, 1982. Also in Proceedings of Logic Programming Workshop, Portugal, 1083.

2070. PERICHAUD, L., Consultation en Francais d'une Banque de Donnees sur Fichiers et Mise en Place du Systeme Prolog Necessaire, These du 3ieme Cycle, Groupe Intelligence Artificielle, University Aix-Marseille, France, 1981.

2071. PIETRZYKOWSKI, T., PROGRAPH As Environment For Prolog DB applications, *Proceedings of The Logic Programming Workshop'88*, 1983.

2072. PIQUE, J. F. and SABATIER, P., An Informative, Adaptable and Efficient Natural Language Consultable Database System, *Proceedings of the European Conference on Artificial Intelligence 1982*, Orsay, France, July 1982.

2073. POOLE, D. L., The Logical Definition of Deduction Systems, Technical Report CS-84-12, Department of Computer Science, University of Waterloo, Canada, 1984.

2074. POTTER, W. D., DESIGN-PRO: A Multi-Model Schema Design Tool in Prolog, *Proceedings of the First International Workshop on Expert Database Systems*, Kiawah Island, South Carolina, October 24-27, 1984.

2075. REITER, R., A Sound and Sometimes Complete Query Evaluation Algorithm For Relational Databases with Null Values, *June, 1983*, Canada, .

2076. REITER, R., On Closed World Databases, in *Logic and Databases*, H. GALLAIRE and J. MINKER, (eds.), Plenum Press, 1978, 55-76. Also in Readings in Artificial Intelligence, edited by Webber and Nilsson, published by Tioga, 1981.

2077. REITER, R., Deductive Question-answering on Relational Databases, in *Logic and Databases*, H. GALLAIRE and J. MINKER, (eds.), Plenum Press, 1978, 149-178.

2078. REITER, R., On Structuring a First Order Database, *Proceedings of the 2nd National Conference Canadian Society for Computational Studies of Intelligence*, Toronto, July 1978, 90-99.

2079. REITER, R., On the Integrity of Typed First Order Databases, in *Advances in Data Base Theory*, H. GALLAIRE, J. MINKER and J. M. NICOLAS, (eds.), Plenum Press, 1981.

2080. REITER, R., Towards a Logical Reconstruction of Relational Database Theory, in *Perspectives on Conceptual Modelling*, M. L. BRODIE, J. MYLOPOULOS and J. W. SCHMIDT, (eds.), Springer Verlag, 1983.

2081. ROUSSOPOULOS, N., MARK, L. and CHU, B. T., Update Dependencies in Relational Databases, *Proceedings of the First International Workshop on Expert Database Systems*, Kiawah Island, South Carolina, October 24-27, 1984.

2082. SAGIV, Y. and FAGIN, R., An Equivalence Between Relational Database Dependencies and a Subset of Propositional Logic, Report RJ2500, IBM Research Laboratories, San Jose, March, 1979.

2083. SAGIV, Y. and ULLMAN, J. D., Complexity of a Top-Down Capture Rule, Technical Report STAN-CS-84-1009, Department of Computer Science, Stanford University, July, 1984.

2084. SAKAI, H. and OTHERS, Design And Implementation Of The Relational Data Base Engine, *International Conference On Fifth Generation Computer Systems*, November 1984.

2085. SANDEWALL, E., A Programming Tool for Management of a Predicate-Calculus Oriented Data Base, *Proceedings of the Second International Joint Conference on Artificial Intelligence*, London, 1971.

2086. SCIORE, E. and WARREN, D. S., Towards an Integrated Database Prolog System, Technical Report, Department of Computer Science, State University of New York at Stony Brook, June, 1984.

2087. SCIORE, E. and WARREN, D. S., Towards and Integrated Database-Prolog System, *Proceedings of the First International Workshop on Expert Database Systems*, Kiawah Island, South Carolina, October 24-27, 1984.

2088. SHAPIRO, S. C. and McKAY, D. P., Inference with Recursive Rules, *Proceedings of NCAI*, 1980.

2089. SHIBAYAMA, S. and OTHERS, Query Processing Flow On RDBM Delta's Functionally-distributed Architecture, *International Conference On Fifth Generation Computer Systems*, November 1984.

2090. SHIBAYAMA, S., KAKUTA, T., MIYAZAKI, N., YOKOTA, H. and MURAKAMI, K., On RDBM Delta's Relational Algebra Processing Algorithm, Technical Memorandum TM-0023, ICOT - Institute for New Generation Computer Technology, Tokyo, Japan, 1983.

2091. SHIBAYAMA, S., MIYAZAKI, N., KAKUTA, T. and YOKOTA, H., A Relational Database Machine DELTA, Technical Memorandum TM-0002, ICOT - Institute for New Generation Computer Technology, Tokyo, Japan, 1982.

2092. SILVA, G., MONTGOMERY, C. A. and DWIGGINGS, D., An Application of Automated Language Understanding Techniques to the Generation of Data Base Elements, *Proceedings 17th Annual Meeting of the Association of Computational Linguistics*, UCSD, San Diego, August, 1979.

2093. SMITH, D. E. and GENESERETH, M. R., Ordering Conjunctive Queries, *Artificial Intelligence 26*, (1985), 171-215.

2094. STABLER, E. P., *Database and Theorem prover Designs for Question Answering Systems*, Department of Cognitive Science, University of Western Ontario, 1982.

2095. TANAKA, Y., MPDC: Massive Parallel Architecture for Very Large Data Bases, *International Conference On Fifth Generation Computer Systems*, November 1984.

2096. TARNLUND, S. A., A Logical Basis for Data Bases, Technical Report TRITA-IBABB-1029, Computer Science Department, Royal Institute of Technology, University of Stockholm, 1976.

2097. TARNLUND, S. A., An Axiomatic Data Base Theory, Technical Report, Computer Science Department, Royal Institute of Technology, University of Stockholm, 1978.

2098. THOM, J. A. and THORNE, P. G., Deductive Databases and the Nature of Personal Information , Technical Report 82-11, Department of Computer Science, University of Melbourne, Australia, 1982.

2099. TOPOR, R. W., KEDDIS, T. and WRIGHT, D. W., Deductive Database Tools, Technical Report 84/7, Department Of Computer Science, University Of Melbourne, 1984.

2100. ULLMAN, J. D., Implementation of Logical Query Languages for Databases, Technical Report STAN-CS-84-1000, Stanford University, 1984.

2101. ULLMAN, J. D. and VAN GELDER, A., Testing Applicability of Top Down Capture Rules, Draft Paper, Stanford University, 1985.

2102. VENKEN, R., Een Eenvoudige Relationele Gegevensbank als Uitbreiding van Prolog, Undergraduate Thesis, Departement voor Toegepaste Wiskunde en Programmatie, Katholieke Universiteit Leuven, Belgium, 1981.

2103. VENKEN, R., A Prolog Meta-Interpreter For Partial Evaluation And Its Application To Source-to-Source Transformation and Query Optimisation, *Sixth European Conference On Artificial Intelligence*, Pisa, September, 1984.

2104. WARREN, D. H. D., Efficient Processing of Interactive Relational Database Queries Expressed in Logic, *Proceedings Seventh International Conference on Very Large Data Bases*, Cannes, France, 1981, 272-281.

2105. WARREN, D. S., Database Updates in Pure Prolog, Technical Report 84/073, State University of New York, Stony Brook, 1984.

2106. WARREN, D. S., Data Base Updates In Pure Prolog, *International Conference On Fifth Generation Computer Systems*, November 1984.

2107. WILLIAMS, M. H., NEVES, J. C. and ANDERSON, S. O., Security and Integrity in Logic Data Bases using QB r, *Proceedings of Workshop on Logic Programming*, Algarve, Portugal, 1983.

2108. WISE, M. J. and POWERS, D. M. W., Indexing Prolog Clauses via Superimposed Code Words and Field Encoded Words, *Proceedings of the International IEEE Conference on Logic Programming*, Atlantic City, January, 1984, 203-210.

2109. WOEHL, K., Automatic Classification Of Office Documents By Coupling Relational Databases And Prolog Expert Systems, *Proceedings of the Tenth Conference On Very Large Data Bases*, Singapore, August, 1984.

2110. WRIGHT, D. J., Prolog as a Relationally Complete Database Query Language Which Can Handle Least Fixed Point Operators, Technical Report, University of Kentucky, 1981.

2111. YOKOTA, H., SHIBAYAMA, S., KUNIFUJI, S., MIYAZAKI, N. and MURAKAMI, K., An Enhanced Inference Mechansim for Generating Relational Algebra Queries, Technical Report TR-0026, ICOT - Institute for New Generation Computer Technology, Tokyo, Japan, 1983.

2112. ZANIOLO, C., Prolog: A Database Query Language for All Seasons, *Proceedings of the First International Workshop on Expert Database Systems*, Kiawah Island, South Carolina, October 24-27, 1984.

2113. ZARRI, G. P., Intelligent Information Retrieval: An Interesting Application Area For The New Generation Computer Systems, *International Conference On Fifth Generation Computer Systems*, November 1984.

CHAPTER 16

Grammar Formalisms For
Natural Language Processing

2114. ABRAMSON, H., Definite Clause Translation Grammars, *Proceedings of the International IEEE Conference on Logic Programming*, Atlantic City, 1984.

2115. ABRAMSON, H., Definite Clause Translation Grammars And The Logical Specification Of Data Types As Unambiguous Context Free Grammars, *International Conference On Fifth Generation Computer Systems*, November 1984.

2116. ABRAMSON, H., Definite Clause Translation Grammars and Natural Language Applications, *Proceedings of an International Workshop on Natural Language Understanding and Logic Programming*, University of Rennes, September, 1985.

2117. BATTANI, G. and MELONI, H., Mise en Oeuvre des Constraintes Phonologiques Syntaxiques et Semantiques dans un Systeme de Comphrehension Automatique de la Parole, Technical Report, Groupe d'Intelligence Artificielle, Marseille, France, 1975.

2118. BERWICK, R. and FONG, S., New Approaches to Parsing Conjunctions Using Prolog, *Proceedings of the 23rd Annual Meeting of the Association for Computational Linguistics*, American Association for Computational Linguistics, July, 1985.

2119. BIEN, J. S., Papers In Computational Linguistics I and II, Reports nr. 107 and 110, Warsaw University, Poland, 1982.

2120. BIEN, J. S., Experiments in Parsing Polish, *Proceedings of an International Workshop on Natural Language Understanding and Logic Programming*, University of Rennes, September, 1985.

2121. BIEN, J. S. and LAUS-MACZYNSKA, K., Parsing Free Word Order Languages in Prolog, *Proceedings of the 8th International Conference on Computational Linguistics*, Tokyo, 1980, 346-349.

2122. BOLC, L. and OTHERS, Deductive Question Answering System Dialog, in *Artificial Intelligence and Information-Control Systems of Robots*, I. PLANDER, (ed.), Elsevier, 1984.

2123. BOLC, L. and STRZALKOWSKI, P., Transformation of Medical Texts into a Deductive Data Base, *Proceedings of the 7th ALLC Symposium on Computers in Literary and Linguistic Research*, Pisa, Italy, 1982.

2124. BOLC, L. and STRZALKOWSKI, P., Transformation of Natural Language into Logical Formulas, *Proceedings of the International Conference on Computational Linguistics*, Prague, 1982.

2125. BOSSU, G. and TEMINE, G., Un Systeme Capable de Poser des Questions a un Utilisateur en Vue de la Construction d'une Base de Donnees, Technical Report, Department of Artificial Intelligence, University of Marseille, 1978.

2126. BOYER, M. and LAPALME, G., Generating Sentences from Semantic Networks, *Proceedings of an International Workshop on Natural Language Understanding and Logic Programming*, University of Rennes, September, 1985.

2127. BRAINBRIDGE, A., Montagovian Definite Clause Grammars, *Proceedings of the 2nd Conference of the European Chapter of the Association for Computational Linguistics*, Geneva, Switserland, March, 1985.

2128. VAN CANEGHEM, M., Systeme d'Analyse et de Synthese Morphologique en Francais pour l'Exploitation de Banques de Donnees (Vol 1,2), Technical Report, Groupe d'Intelligence Artificielle, Universite d'Aix-Marseille II Marseille, France, 1977.

2129. DEL CERRO, L. F. and SOULHI, S., Mutual Belief Logic for Processing Definite Reference, *Proceedings of an International Workshop on Natural Language Understanding and Logic Programming*, University of Rennes, September, 1985.

2130. CHESTER, D. L., The Translation of Formal Proofs into English, *Artificial Intelligence 7*, (1976).

2131. CHIN, M. Y., Computer Interrogation System CISP, M.Sc. Thesis, Imperial College, London, 1981.

2132. COELHO, H., On a Conversational Interface between Users and a Database, DI Report, Laboratoria Nacional De Engenharia Civil, Lisbon, Portugal, 1976.

2133. COELHO, H., Natural Language and Databases, DI Report, Laboratoria Nacional De Engenharia Civil, Lisbon, Portugal, 1977.

2134. COELHO, H., TUGA user's manual, DI Report, Laboratoria Nacional De Engenharia Civil, Lisbon, Portugal, 1979.

2135. COELHO, H., Notes on Natural Language Conversations between a Program and its Users, DI Report, Laboratoria Nacional De Engenharia Civil, Lisbon, Portugal, 1979.

2136. COELHO, H., Context and Conversation: A Discussion from a Semantic Point of View, DI Report, Laboratoria Nacional De Engenharia Civil, Lisbon, Portugal, 1979.

2137. COELHO, H., A Program Conversing in Portuguese Providing a Library Service, Ph.D. Thesis, Department of Artificial Intelligence, University of Edinburgh, 1979.

2138. COELHO, H., Database Interrogation by Means of Natural Language, *Proceedings the First International Workshop on Natural Language Communication with Computers*, Warsaw, Poland, September, 1980. Held in Warsaw, Poland.

2139. COELHO, H., Man-Machine Communication in Portuguese: A Friendly Library System, *Information Systems 7*, 2 (1982).

2140. COELHO, H., A Formalism for the Structural Analysis of Dialogues, *Proceedings of the 9th International Conference on Computational Linguistics*, July, 1982.

2141. COLMERAUER, A., Les Systemes-Q ou un Formalisme pour Analyser et Synthetiser des Phrases sur Ordinateur, Internal Publication 43, Departement d'Informatique, Universite de Montreal, Canada, 1970.

2142. COLMERAUER, A., Programmation en Langue Naturelle, Technical Report, Groupe d'Intelligence Artificielle, University d'Aix-Marseille, 1974.

2143. COLMERAUER, A., Les Grammaires de Metamorphose, Technical Report, Groupe d'Intelligence Artificielle, University d'Aix-Marseille, 1975.

2144. COLMERAUER, A., Metamorphosis Grammars, in *Natural Language Communication with Computers*, L. BOLC, (ed.), Springer Verlag, 1978, 133-189. Lecture Notes in Computer Science No. 63.

2145. COLMERAUER, A., Un Sous-Ensemble Interressant du Francais, *RAIRO 13*, 4 (1979).

2146. COLMERAUER, A., An Interesting Subset of Natural Language, in *Logic Programming*, K. L. CLARK and S. TARNLUND, (eds.), Academic Press, 1982. A.P.I.C. Studies in Data Processing No. 16.

2147. COLMERAUER, A., Nothing more than Prolog, *Proceedings of an International Workshop on Natural Language Understanding and·Logic Programming*, University of Rennes, September, 1985.

2148. COLMERAUER, A., DAHL, V. and SAMBUC, R., *Consultation en Francais d'un Catalogue Industriel: Configurateur de la serie d'Ordinateurs SOLAR16*, Rapport Final du Contrat BNIST 291-767, 1972. In French.

2149. COLMERAUER, A., KANOUI, H., PASERO, R. and ROUSSEL, P., Un Systeme de Communication Homme-Machine en Francais, Rapport Technique, Groupe d'Intelligence Artificielle, Univ d'Aix Marseille, Luminy, 1973.

2150. COLMERAUER, A. and PIQUE, J. F., About Natural Logic, Technical Report, Groupe d'Intelligence Artificielle, University d'Aix-Marseille, 1979. Also in Advances in Database Theory (Gallaire, Minker and Nicolas) Vol 1, 343-365, published by Plenum Press 1981.

2151. COTTA, J. C., A Portuguese Question-Answering System for Civil Engineering Legislation - Overview and Experimental Results, *Proceedings the First International Workshop on Natural Language Communication with Computers*, Warsaw, Poland, September, 1980.

2152. COURANT, M. and ROBIN, S., Classified Advertisement Analysis, *Proceedings of an International Workshop on Natural Language Understanding and Logic Programming*, University of Rennes, September, 1985.

2153. COWIE, J. R., Automatic Analysis of Descriptive Texts, *Proceedings of the Conference on Applied Natural Language Processing*, Santa Monica, California, 1983.

2154. DAHL, V., Un Systeme Deductif d'Interrogation de Banques de Donnees en Espagnol, Technical Report, Groupe d'Intelligence Artificielle, Universite d'Aix-Marseille II, 1977.

2155. DAHL, V., Logical Design of Deductive Natural Language Consultable Data Bases, *Proceedings Fifth International Conference on Very Large Data Bases*, Rio De Janeiro, Brazil, 1979.

2156. DAHL, V., Quantification in a Three-Valued Logic for Natural Language Question-Answering Systems, International Joint Conference on Artificial Intelligence, Tokyo, Japan, 1979.

2157. DAHL, V., A Three-Valued Logic for Natural Language Computer Applications, *Proceedings of the 10th International Symposium on Multiple-Valued Logic*, 1980.

2158. DAHL, V., Translating Spanish into Logic Through Logic, *American Journal of Computational Linguistics 7*, 3 (July-September 1981), 149-164.

2159. DAHL, V., Teoria de Lenguajes, Technical Report TR 83-6, Simon Fraser University, 1983.

2160. DAHL, V., Current Trends in Logic Grammars, *Workshop on Logic Programming*, Portugal, 1983. Held in Algarve, Portugal.

2161. DAHL, V., More On Gapping Grammars, *International Conference On Fifth Generation Computer Systems*, November 1984.

2162. DAHL, V. and ABRAMSON, H., On Gapping Grammars, *Proceedings of the Second International Logic Programming Conference*, S. A. TARNLUND, ed., Uppsala University, Uppsala, Sweden, July 2-6, 1984, 77-88.

2163. DAHL, V. and McCORD, M. C., Treating Coordination in Logic Grammars, Internal Report, University of Kentucky, 1983.

2164. DALADIER, A., Programming in Natural Language? At what Cost'?, *Proceedings of an International Workshop on Natural Language Understanding and Logic Programming*, University of Rennes, September, 1985.

2165. DWIGGINGS, D. and SILVA, G., A Knowledge-Based Automated Message Understanding Methodology for an Advanced Indications Systems, Technical Report R79-006, Operating Systems Division, Logicon, Woodland Hills, Ca, 1979.

2166. EIMERMACHER, M., Ein Word Expert Parser in Prolog: Die Semantische Komponente, KIT Report 7, Fachbereich Informatik, Technische Universitat Berlin, 1983.

2167. EIMERMACHER, M., Ein Word Expert Parser in Prolog: Integration von Syntax und Semantik, KIT Report 8, Fachbereich Informatik, Technische Universitat Berlin, 1983.

2168. EIMERMACHER, M., Ein Word Expert Parser in Prolog: Die Lexikalische Komponente, KIT Report 9, Fachbereich Informatik, Technische Universitat Berlin, 1983.

2169. EIMERMACHER, M., Parsing in Prolog - Eine Semantische Komponente, in *Proceedings of the 7th German Workshop on Artificial Intelligence*, B. NEUMANN, (ed.), Springer-Verlag, Dassahel, Germany, 1983, 189-196. Also as, KIT Report 15, Fachbereich Informatik, Technische Universitat Berlin, 1983.

2170. VAN EMDEN, M. H., Relational Equations, Grammars and Programs, Technical Report CS-77-17, Department of Computer Science, University of Waterloo,Canada, 1977. Published in the Proceedings of the Conference on Theoretical Computer Science, University of Waterloo, 1977.

2171. FILGUEIRAS, M., A Kernel for a General Natural Language Interface, *Proceedings of Workshop on Logic Programming*, Algarve, Portugal, 1983.

2172. FILGUEIRAS, M., Compreensao de Linguagem Natural por Computador: Uma Metadologia, Ph.D. Dissertation, Department of Computer Science, Universidade Nova de Lisboa, Lisbon, Portugal, 1984. In Portuguese.

2173. FILGUEIRAS, M., Brief Description of Spiral: A Natural Language Understanding System, *Logic Programming Newsletter*, Universidade Nova de Lisboa, Winter 1984.

2174. FININ, T. W. and PALMER, M. S., Parsing with Logical Variables, *Proceedings of the Conference on Applied Natural Language Processing*, Santa Monica, California, 1983.

2175. FREY, W., Complete NP-Structures and Logic Grammars, *Proceedings of an International Workshop on Natural Language Understanding and Logic Programming*, University of Rennes, September, 1985.

2176. GROSS, M., Lexicon Grammars and Automatic Syntactic Analysis, *Proceedings of an International Workshop on Natural Language Understanding and Logic Programming*, University of Rennes, September, 1985.

2177. GUIZOL, J., Remarques a Propos de la Synthese du Francais, Technical Report, Groupe d'Intelligence Artificielle, Universite d'Aix-Marseille II Marseille, France, 1976.

2178. HADLEY, R., SHADOW: Interpreting English Questions Posed to a Prolog Database, Master's Thesis, Simon Fraser University, Canada, 1983.

2179. HESS, M., About the Role of Control Information in Natural Language Question Answering Systems, *Proceedings of an International Workshop on Natural Language Understanding and Logic Programming*, University of Rennes, September, 1985.

2180. HIRSCHMAN, L. and PUDER, K., Restriction Grammars in Prolog, *Proceedings of the First International Logic Programming Conference*, M. VAN CANEGHEM, ed., Marseille, France, September 14-17, 1982, 85-90.

2181. JOUBERT, M., Un Systeme de Resolution de Problems a Tendance Naturelle Semantiques dans un Systeme de Comphrehension Automatique de la Parole, Technical Report, Groupe d'Intelligence Artificielle, Universite d'Aix-Marseille II Marseille, France, 1974.

2182. KAHN, K. M., A Grammar Kit in Prolog, *AISB Easter Conference on Artificial Intelligence and Education*, University of Exeter,U.K., April 1983. Also Published in New Horizons in Educational Computing, M. Yazdani (ed), Ellis Horwood, 1984.

2183. KAY, M., Unification in Grammar, *Proceedings of an International Workshop on Natural Language Understanding and Logic Programming*, University of Rennes, September, 1985.

2184. KIRAKAWA, H., Chart Parsing in Concurrent Prolog, Technical Report TR-008, ICOT - Institute for New Generation Computer Technology, Tokyo, Japan, 1983.

2185. KISZ, Z., PROSZELY, G. and TOTH, L., Morphological Analysis of Hungarian Texts with Computers, *Computational Linguistics and Computer Languages*, 1980.

2186. KITTREDGE, R., Natural Language Queries for a Linguistic Database Using Prolog, *Proceedings CSCSI/SCEIO Conference*, Victoria, May, 1980.

2187. KITTREDGE, R. and COLMERAUER, A., Tidy French and English Grammars and Their Use, *Proceedings Annual Conference on Computational Linguistics COLING-82*, Prague, July 1982.

2188. KOCH, G., A Prolog Way of Representing Natural Language Fragments, DIKU Rapport nr. 80/16, Datalogisk Institute, Kobenhavns University, 1980.

2189. KUKICH, K., Knowledge-Based Report Generation: A Technique for Automatically Generating Natural Language Reports from Databases, *Proceedings of the ACM SIGIR Conference on Research and Development in Information Retrieval*, Bethesda, June, 1983, 307-344.

2190. LANDSBERGEN, S. P., Syntax and Formal Semantics of English in PHLIQA1, in *Advances in Natural Language Processing*, L. STEELS, (ed.), University of Antwerp (UIA), Belgium, 1976.

2191. LEVINE, S. H., Questioning English with Clausal Logic, Master's Thesis, Department of Computer Science, University of Texas, Austin, 1980.

2192. LOPES, G. P., Implementing Dialogues in a Knowledge Information System, *Proceedings of an International Workshop on Natural Language Understanding and Logic Programming*, University of Rennes, September, 1985.

2193. LOPES, G. P. and VICCARI, R. M., An Intelligent Monitor Interaction In Portugese Language, *Sixth European Conference On Artificial Intelligence*, Pisa, September, 1984.

2194. LUBONSKI, P., Natural Language Interface for a Polish Railway Expert Systems, *Proceedings of an International Workshop on Natural Language Understanding and Logic Programming*, University of Rennes, September, 1985.

2195. MALUSZINSKI, J. and FULLSON, J. F., A Notion of Grammatical Unification Applicable to Logic Programming Languages, Technical Report, University of Denmark, 1981.

2196. MARTIN, P., APPELT, D. and PEREIRA, F. C. N., Transportability and Generality in a Natural-Language Interface System, *Proceedings of the International Joint Conference on Artificial Intelligence*, Karlsruhe, Germany, 1983.

2197. MARUYAMA, F. and YONEZAWA, A., A Prolog-Based Natural Language Front-End System, *New Generation Computing 2*, 1 (1984).

2198. MATSUMOTO, Y., KIYONO, M. and TANAKA, H., Facilities of the BUP Parsing System, *Proceedings of an International Workshop on Natural Language Understanding and Logic Programming*, University of Rennes, September, 1985.

2199. MATSUMOTO, Y., TANAKA, H., HIRAKAWA, H., MIYOSHI, H. and YASUKAWA, H., BUP: A Bottom-Up Parser Embedded in Prolog, *New Generation Computing 2*, (1983), Springer Verlag.

2200. MCCORD, M. C., Slot Grammars, *American Journal of Computational Linguistics 6*, 1 (1980), 255-286. Also available as a Technical Report from the University of Kentucky.

2201. MCCORD, M. C., Focalizers, the Scoping Problem, and Semantic Interpretation Rules in Logic Grammars, *Presented at Workshop on Logic Programming for Intelligent Systems*, Long Beach, California, 1982. Also Research Paper from University of Kentucky.

2202. MCCORD, M. C., Using Slots and Modifiers in Logic Grammars for Natural Language, *Artificial Intelligence 18*, (1983), 327-367. Also available as a Technical Report from the University of Kentucky.

2203. MCCORD, M. C., Modular Logic Grammars, *Proceedings of the 23rd Annual Meeting of the Association for Computational Linguistics*, American Association for Computational Linguistics, July, 1985.

2204. McSKIMIN, J. R. and MINKER, J., The Use of a Semantic Network in a Deductive Question-Answering System, *Proceedings of the International Conference on Artificial Intelligence*, Cambridge, Mass., 1977, 50-58.

2205. McSKIMIN, J. R. and MINKER, J., A Predicate Calculus Based Semantic Network for Question-Answering Systems, in *Associative Networks*, N. FINDLER, (ed.), Academic Press, New York, 1979, 205-238.

2206. MELLISH, C. S., Syntax-Semantics Interaction in Natural Language Parsing, Working Paper 31, Department of Artificial Intelligence, University of Edinburgh, 1978.

2207. MELLISH, C. S., Preliminary Syntactic Analysis and Interpretation of Mechanics Problems Stated in English, Working Paper 48, Department of Artificial Intelligence, University of Edinburgh, 1978.

2208. MELLISH, C. S., Some Problems In Early Noun Phrase Interpretation, *Proceedings of the Conference of the Society for the Study of Artificial Intelligence and Simulation of Behaviour*, S. HARDY, ed., 1980. Also available from Edinburgh as Research Paper 147.

2209. MELLISH, C. S., Coping With Uncertainty: Noun Phrase Interpretation and Early Semantic Analysis, Ph.D. Dissertation, Department of Artificial Intelligence, University of Edinburgh, 1981.

2210. MELLISH, C. S., Incremental Evaluation: An Approach to the Semantic Interpretation of Noun Phrases, Serial No CSRP 001, Computer Science Department, University of Sussex, 1982.

2211. MILNE, R., A Case for Deterministic Parsing Using Syntax, DAI Report 53, Department of Artificial Intelligence, University of Edinburgh, 1979.

2212. MILNE, R., A Framework for Deterministic Parsing Using Syntax and Semantics, DAI Report 64, Department of Artificial Intelligence, University of Edinburgh, 1980.

2213. MILNE, R., Using Determinism to Predict Garden Paths, *AISM Conference Proceedings*, 1980. Also available from Edinburgh as Research Paper 142.

2214. MILNE, R., Parsing Against Lexical Ambiguity, *Proceedings for COLING 80*, 1980. Also available from Edinburgh as Research Paper 144.

2215. MILNE, R., Resolving Lexical Ambiguity In A Deterministic Parser, PhD thesis, Department of Artificial Intelligence, University of Edinburgh, 1983.

2216. MINKER, J. and POWELL, P., Answer and Reason Extraction, Natural Language and Voice Output for Deductive Relational Data Bases, Technical Report TR-735, Department of Computer Science, University of Maryland, 1979.

2217. MINKER, J. and VANDERBRUG, G., Representations of the Language Recognition Problem for a Theorem Prover, *Journal of Computer and Information Science 3*, 3 (September, 1974), 217-250.

2218. MIYOSHI, H., MUKAI, K., HIRAKAWA, H., YASUKAWA, H. and FURUKAWA, K., Generation of Japanese Sentence Clause DCG in Prolog, Technical Memorandum TM-0010, ICOT - Institute for New Generation Computer Technology, Tokyo, Japan, 1983. In Japanese.

2219. NORTON, L. M., Automated Analysis of Instructional Text, *Artificial Intelligence 20*, 3 (May, 1983), 307-344.

2220. PASERO, R., Representation du Francais en Logique du Premier Ordre, en Vue de Dialoguer avec un Ordinateur., These de 3ieme Cycle, Groupe d'Intelligence Artificielle, Universite d'Aix-Marseille II, 1973.

2221. PASERO, R., A Dialogue in Natural Language, *Proceedings of the First International Logic Programming Conference*, Marseille, France, September, 1982.

2222. PEREIRA, F. C. N., Some Techniques for Writing Grammars in Logic, *Workshop on Logic Programming*, Long Beach, Los Angeles, September 1981.

2223. PEREIRA, F. C. N., Extraposition Grammars, *American Journal of Computational Linguistics* 7, 4 (October 1981), 243-256. Also in Proceedings of Workshop on Logic Programming held in Debrecen, Hungary by S-A. Tarnlund (editor), July 1980.

2224. PEREIRA, F. C. N., Ambiguity in Logic Grammars, *Presented at Workshop on Logic Programming for Intelligent Systems*, Long Beach, California, 1982.

2225. PEREIRA, F. C. N., Logic for Natural Language Analysis, Ph.D. thesis, University of Edinburgh, U.K., 1982. Reprinted as Technical Note 275, January 1983, Artificial Intelligence Center, SRI International, Menlo Park, California.

2226. PEREIRA, F. C. N., A Structure-Sharing Representation for Unification-Based Grammar Formalisms, *Proceedings of the 23rd Annual Meeting of the Association for Computational Linguistics*, American Association for Computational Linguistics, July, 1985.

2227. PEREIRA, F. C. N., Parsing and Deduction, *Proceedings of an International Workshop on Natural Language Understanding and Logic Programming*, University of Rennes, September, 1985.

2228. PEREIRA, F. C. N. and SHIEBER, S. M., The Semantics of Grammar Formalisms seen as Computer Languages, *Proceedings on the 10th International Conference on Computational Linguistics*, Stanford University, July, 1984.

2229. PEREIRA, F. C. N. and WARREN, D. H. D., Parsing as Deduction, *Proceedings of the 21st Annual Meeting of the Association for Computational Linguistics*, MIT, Cambridge, Massachusetts, June 15-17, 1983. Also available as a SRI Technical Report.

2230. PERICHAUD, L., Consultation en Francais d'une Banque de Donnees sur Fichiers et Mise en Place du Systeme Prolog Necessaire, These du 3ieme Cycle, Groupe Intelligence Artificielle, University Aix-Marseille, France, 1981.

2231. PIQUE, J. F., Sur un Modele Logique du Language Naturel et son Utilisation pour L'Interrogation des Banques de Donnees., These de 3ieme Cycle, Groupe d'Intelligence Artificielle, Universite d'Aix-Marseille II, 1982.

2232. PIQUE, J. F., On the Semantic Representation of Natural Language Sentences, *Proceedings of the First International Logic Programming Conference*, Marseille, France, September, 1982.

2233. PIQUE, J. F. and SABATIER, P., An Informative, Adaptable and Efficient Natural Language Consultable Database System, *Proceedings of the European Conference on Artificial Intelligence 1982*, Orsay, France, July 1982.

2234. POLLACK, J. and WALTZ, D., Parallel Interpretation of Natural Language, *International Conference On Fifth Generation Computer Systems*, November 1984.

2235. PORTO, A. and FILGUEIRAS, M., Natural Language Semantics: A Logic Programming Approach, *Proceedings of the International IEEE Conference on Logic Programming*, Atlantic City, 1984.

2236. PORTO, A. and FILGUEIRAS, M., Definite Clause Transition Grammars, *ISLP84*, Atlantic City, New Jersey, February 6-9, 1984, 228-233.

2237. POWERS, D. M. W., Neurolinguistics and Psycholinguistics as a Basis for Computer Acquisition of Natural Language, *SIGART Newsletter 84*, (June 1983), 29-34. Also DCS Report 8301, University of New South Wales.

2238. REYLE, U. and FREY, W., A Prolog Implementation of Lexical Functional Grammar, *Proceedings of the International Joint Conference on Artificial Intelligence*, Karlsruhe, Germany, 1983.

2239. RIDD, S., An Investigation of Prolog as an Aid to French Teaching and Language Translation, Technical Report, Department of Computer Science, Imperial College, London, 1982.

2240. SABATIER, P., Ellipsis, Grammaire Interpretative des Constructions Elliptiques du Francais, Technical Report, Groupe d'Intelligence Artificielle, Marseille, France, 1978.

2241. SABATIER, P., Dialogues en Francais avec un Ordinateur, These de 3ieme Cycle, Groupe d'Intelligence Artificielle, Universite d'Aix-Marseille II, 1980.

2242. SABATIER, P., Designing Transparant Natural Language Interfaces for Information Systems, Technical Report, LADL-CNRS, Universite de Paris, October, 1982.

2243. SABATIER, P., Contextual Grammars in Prolog, *Proceedings of Workshop on Logic Programming*, Algarve, Portugal, 1983.

2244. SABATIER, P., Puzzle Grammars, *Proceedings of an International Workshop on Natural Language Understanding and Logic Programming*, University of Rennes, September, 1985.

2245. SAINT-DIZIER, P., On Syntax and Semantics of Adjective Phrases in Logic Programming, Technical Report 247, Department of Computer Science, Universite de Rennes, France, 1985.

2246. SAINT-DIZIER, P., Quantifier Hierarchy in a Semantic Representation of Natural Languages Sentences, *Proceedings of an International Workshop on Natural Language Understanding and Logic Programming*, University of Rennes, September, 1985.

2247. SCHWIND, C. B., Natural Language Access to Prolog Database Systems, in *Report on the German Workshop on Artificial Intelligence 1982*, M. O'LEARY, (ed.), University of Hamburg, West Germany, 1982.

2248. SCHWIND, C. B., Logic Based Natural Language Processing, *Proceedings of an International Workshop on Natural Language Understanding and Logic Programming*, University of Rennes, September, 1985.

2249. SEDOGDO, C., A Meta-Grammar for Handling Coordination in Logic Grammars, *Proceedings of an International Workshop on Natural Language Understanding and Logic Programming*, University of Rennes, September, 1985.

2250. SILVA, G. and DWIGGINGS, D., Towards a Prolog Text Grammar, *SIGART Newsletter*, October 1980, 20-25.

2251. SILVA, G., MONTGOMERY, C. A. and DWIGGINGS, D., An Application of Automated Language Understanding Techniques to the Generation of Data Base Elements, *Proceedings 17th Annual Meeting of the Association of Computational Linguistics*, UCSD, San Diego, August, 1979.

2252. SIMMONS, R. F., Rule Based Computations on English, in *Pattern-Directed Inference Systems*, D. A. WATERMAN and F. HAYES-ROTH, (eds.), Academic Press, New York, 1978.

2253. SIMMONS, R. F., A Narrative Schema in Procedural Logic, in *Logic Programming*, K. L. CLARK and S. A. TARNLUND, (eds.), Academic Press, New York, 1982. A.P.I.C. Studies in Data Processing No. 16.

2254. SIMMONS, R. F., *Computations from the English*, Prentice-Hall, Englewood Cliffs, 1983.

2255. SIMMONS, R. F., A Text Knowledge Base for the AI Handbook, Technical Report TR-83-24, Department of Computer Science, University of Texas, Austin, 1983.

2256. SIMMONS, R. F. and CHESTER, D., Relating Sentences and Semantic Networks with Clausal Logic, Technical Report, Department of Computer Science, University of Texas, Austin, 1980. Also in CACM, August 1982.

2257. STABLER, E. P., Deterministic and Bottom-Up Parsing in Prolog, *Proceedings of the Third National Conference of the American Association for Artificial Intelligence*, 1983. AAAI.

2258. SZPAKOWICZ, S., Syntactic Analysis of Written Polish, in *Natural Language Communication with Computers*, L. BOLC, (ed.), Springer Verlag, 1978, 261-292. Lecture Notes in Computer Science No. 63.

2259. TANCIG, P. and BOJADZIEV, D., SOVA - An Integrated Question-Answering System Based on ATN (for Syntax) and Prolog (for Semantics) in a LISP Environment, in *Workshop on Logic Programming*, S. A. TARNLUND, (ed.), Debrecen, Hungary, July 1980.

2260. TAZI, S. and VIRBEL, J., Representation Formelle des Structures Textuelles pour un Editeur de Textes Intelligent, Technical Report, Department of Computer Science, INRIA, Toulouse, France, 1984. In French.

2261. TAZI, S. and VIRBEL, J., Formal Representation of Textual Structures for an Intelligent Text-Editing System, *Proceedings of an International Workshop on Natural Language Understanding and Logic Programming*, University of Rennes, September, 1985.

2262. TSENG, S. H., Questioning English Text with Clausal Logic: Case Studies of Three Texts, TR-84-08, University of Texas at Austin, Department of Computer Sciences, March 1984.

2263. TURNER, S. J., W-Grammars for Logic Programming, in *Implementations of Prolog*, J. A. CAMPBELL, (ed.), Ellis Horwood, 1984.

2264. UEHARA, K., OCHITANI, R., KAKUSHO, O. and TOYODA, J., A Bottom-Up Parser Based on Predicate Logic, *Proceedings of the International IEEE Conference on Logic Programming*, Atlantic City, 1984.

2265. UEHARA, K., OCHITANI, R., MIKAMI, O. and TOYODA, J., An Integrated Parser for text Understanding: Viewing Parsing as Passing Messages among Actors, *Proceedings of an International Workshop on Natural Language Understanding and Logic Programming*, University of Rennes, September, 1985.

2266. WALLACE, M., *Communicating with Databases in Natural Language*, Ellis Horwood Ltd., 1984.

2267. WARREN, D. H. D., Efficient Processing of Interactive Relational Database Queries Expressed in Logic, *Proceedings Seventh International Conference on Very Large Data Bases*, Cannes, France, 1981, 272-281.

2268. WARREN, D. H. D., Issues in Natural Language Access to Databases from a Logic Programming Viewpoint, *Proceedings of the 20th Annual Conference of the Association for Computational Linguistics*, Toronto, Canada, 1982.

2269. WARREN, D. H. D. and PEREIRA, F. C. N., Definite Clause Grammars for Language Analysis : A Survey of the Formalism and a Comparison with Augmented Transition Networks, *Artificial Intelligence 13*, 3 (1980), 231-278.

2270. WARREN, D. H. D. and PEREIRA, F. C. N., An Efficient Easily Adaptable System for Interpreting Natural Language Queries, DAI Research Paper No 155, Department of Artificial Intelligence, University of Edinburgh, February 1981.

2271. WARREN, D. S., Using Lambda-Calculus to Represent Meaning in Logic Grammars, *Proceedings of the 21th Annual Conference of the Association for Computational Linguistics*, MIT, 1983. Also Technical Report from SUNY at Stony Brook.

2272. WEISHEDEL, R. M., Mapping Between Semantic Representations using Horn Clauses, *Proceedings of the Third National Conference of the American Association for Artificial Intelligence*, 1983. AAAI.

2273. YASUKAWA, H., LFG in Prolog - Toward a Formal System for Representing Grammatical Relations, Technical Report TR-019, ICOT - Institute for New Generation Computer Technology, Tokyo, Japan, 1983.

2274. YU, Y. H., Translating Horn Clauses From English, Technical Report TR-84-29, Department of Computer Science, University of Texas, Austin, 1984.

CHAPTER 17

Knowledge Representation
Issues in Logic Programming

2275. AIDA, H., TANAKA, H. and MOTO-OKA, T., A Prolog Extension for Handling Negative Knowledge, *New Generation Computing 1*, (1983), Springer Verlag.

2276. ATTARDI, G. and SIMI, M., Consistency and Completeness of OMEGA, a Logic for Knowledge Representation, *Proceedings of the Seventh International Joint Conference on Artificial Intelligence*, Vancouver, Canada, 1981.

2277. BAINBRIDGE, S. and SKUCE, D., Knowledge Acquisition and Representation Using Logic, Set Theory and Natural Language Structures, *Proceedings of the Third National Conference of the Canadian Society for Computational Studies of Intelligence*, 1980.

2278. BIBEL, W., On First-Order Reasoning about Knowledge and Belief, in *Artificial Intelligence and Information-Control Systems of Robots*, I. PLANDER, (ed.), Elsevier, 1984.

2279. BLANNING, R., Management Applications of Logic Programming, Technical Report, Owen Graduate School of Management, Vanderbilt University, Nashville, Tennessee, 1983.

2280. CHOURAQUI, E., Construction of Data Structures for Representing Real World Knowledge, *Proceedings of the IFIP*, 1979.

2281. CLARK, M. J. N., HAYES, P. J., MARKS, J. O., PETTITT, P. and REEDER, M. W., Representation of Legislation & Aids for its Interpretation, *International Conference On Fifth Generation Computer Systems*, November 1984.

2282. DAHL, V., Logic Programming as a Representation of Knowledge, *Computer 16*, 10 (October 1983).

2283. DAVID, G., Problem Solving = Knowledge + Strategy, *Proceedings of the International Conference on Artificial Intelligence and Information Control Systems of Robots*, 1980.

2284. DAVIS, R. E., GALLAIRE, H. and LASSERRE, C., Controlling Knowledge Deduction in a Declarative Approach, *Proceedings Sixth Joint Conference on Artificial Intelligence*, 1979. International Joint Conference on Artificial Intelligence.

2285. DEBENHAM, J. K., Knowledge Base Design, *Australian Computer Journal 17*, 1 (February 1985).

2286. DIAS, V. and PEREIRA, L. M., A Survey of Knowledge Based Systems in Prolog, *Logic Programming Newsletter*, Universidade Nova de Lisboa, Winter 1984.

2287. DINCBAS, M., A Knowledge-Based Expert System for Automatic Analysis and Synthesis in CAD, *Proceedings IFIP 80*, 1980, 705-710. AFIPS Press.

2288. DWIGGINGS, D. and SILVA, G., A Knowledge-Based Automated Message Understanding Methodology for an Advanced Indications Systems, Technical Report R79-006, Operating Systems Division, Logicon, Woodland Hills, Ca, 1979.

2289. ELCOCK, E. W., How Complete are Knowledge-Representation Systems?, *Computer 16*, 10 (October 1983).

2290. ENOMOTO, H., YONEZAKI, N., SAEKI, M. and KUNIFUJI, S., Paradigms of Knowledge Based Software System and Its Service Image, Technical Report TR-030, ICOT - Institute for New Generation Computer Technology, Tokyo, Japan, 1983. Also in 3th Seminar on Software Engineering, Florence, Italy, 1983.

2291. FREY, W., REYLE, U. and ROHRER, C., Automatic Construction of a Knowledge Base by Analysing Texts in Natural Language, *Proceedings of the International Joint Conference on Artificial Intelligence*, Karlsruhe, Germany, 1983, 727-729.

2292. FURUKAWA, K. and FUCHI, K., Knowledge Engineering and the Fifth Generation Computers, *IEEE Database Engineering 6*, 4 (December 1983).

2293. FURUKAWA, K., KUNIFUJI, S., TAKEUCHI, A. and UEDA, K., The Conceptual Specification of the Kernel Language Version 1, *Draft Paper*, 1984.

2294. FURUKAWA, K., TAKEUCHI, A. and KUNIFUJI, S., Mandala: A Knowledge Programming Language based on Concurrent Prolog, ICOT Technical Memorandum TM-0028 (in Japanese) ICOT Technical Report TR-029 (in English), 1983.

2295. FURUKAWA, K., TAKEUCHI, A. and KUNIFUJI, S., Mandala: Knowledge Programming and System in the Logic-type Language, ICOT TR-043, February, 1984.

2296. FURUKAWA, K., TAKEUCHI, A., YASUKAWA, H. and KUNIFUJI, S., Mandala: A Logic Based Knowledge Programming System, *International Conference On Fifth Generation Computer Systems*, November 1984.

2297. FUTO, I., Combined Discrete/Continuous Modeling and Problem Solving, *SCS MultiConference on AI, Graphics and Simulation*, San Diego, California, January, 1985.

2298. FUTO, I. and GERGELY, T., Planning Activity Of Cooperative I-Actors, *IPAC International Symposium on AI*, Leningrad, USSR, October, 1983.

2299. FUTO, I. and GERGELY, T., A Logic Simulation Language For Modeling Cooperative Problem Solving System, *AFCNET Information Congress, Hardware and Software Components and Architecture for the 5th Generation*, Paris, France, March, 1985.

2300. GOEBEL, R. G., DLOG: A Logic-Based Data Model for the Machine Representation of Knowledge, Technical Report, Department of Computer Science, University of Waterloo,Canada, 1983. A Summary was published in SigArt 87, January 1984.

2301. GREEN, C. C. and WESFOLD, S. J., Knowledge-Based Programming Self-Applied, in *Introductory Readings in Expert Systems*, D. MICHIE, (ed.), Gordon and Breach, New York, 1982, 339-359.

2302. GRUMBACH, A., Knowledge Acquisition in Logic Programming, *Proceedings of the First International Logic Programming Conference*, Marseille, France, September, 1982.

2303. IRANI, K. B. and SHIH, Y., Implementation of Very Large Prolog-Based Knowledge Bases on Data Flow Architectures, *Proceedings of the First IEEE/AAAI Conference on Artificial Intelligence Applications*, Denver, Colorado, December, 1984.

2304. KAHN, K. M., The Implementation of Uniform: A Knowledge-Representation and Programming Language Based upon Equivalence of Descriptions, UPMAIL Technical Report 9, Uppsala University, 1982.

2305. KELLOG, C., Knowledge Management: A Practical Amalgam of Knowledge and Data Base Technology, *Proceedings of the National Conference on Artificial Intelligence*, Carnegie-Mellon University, August 1982.

2306. KITAKAMI, H. and OTHERS, A Method of Realizing a Knowledge Assimilation Mechanism, Technical Report TR-010, ICOT - Institute for New Generation Computer Technology, Tokyo, Japan, 1983. In Japanese.

2307. KITAKAMI, H., MIYACHI, T., KUNIFUJI, S. and FURUKAWA, K., A Methodology for Implementation of a Knowledge Acquisition System, Technical Memorandum TM-0024, ICOT - Institute for New Generation Computer Technology, Tokyo, Japan, 1983. Also in Proceedings of the International IEEE Logic Programming Conference, 1984.

2308. KOGAN, D. and FREILING, M., SIDUR-Structure Formalism For Knowledge Information Processing, *International Conference On Fifth Generation Computer Systems*, November 1984.

2309. KONAGAYA, A. and UNEMURA, M., Knowledge Information Processing Language: Shapeup, Technical Report, NEC Corporation, Japan, 1983.

2310. KUNIFUJI, S., ASOU, M., TAKEUCHI, A., MIYACHI, T., KITAKAMI, H., YOKOTA, H., YASAKUWA, H. and FURUKAWA, K., Amalgamation of Object Knowledge and Meta Knowledge by Prolog and Its Applications, *Knowledge Engineering and Artificial Intelligence Working Group of the Information Processing Society of Japan*, June, 1983. preprint 30-1, TR-009.

2311. KUNIFUJI, S., TAKEUCHI, A., FURUKAWA, K., UEDA, K. and KURUKAWA, T., A Logic Programming Language for Knowledge Utilization and Realization, *Proceedings of the Prolog Conference*, Tukuba, Japan, 1982. In Japanese.

2312. LEE, R. M., Applications Software and Organizational Change: Issues in the Representation of Knowledge, *Information Systems 8*, 3 (1983), 187-194.

2313. LIEBERMAN, H., Programming Descriptive Analogies By Example, *Internal Paper, AI Laboratory, MIT*, December 1983.

2314. MARKUSZ, Z. S., Knowledge Representation of Design in Many-Sorted Logic, *Proceedings Seventh International Joint Conference on Artificial Intelligence*, August 1981.

2315. MIYACHI, T., KUNIFUJI, S., KITAKAMI, H., FURUKAWA, K., TAKEUCHI, A. and YOKOTA, H., A Proposed Knowledge Assimilation Method for Logic Databases, Technical Memorandum TM-0004 (In Japanese), ICOT - Institute for New Generation Computer Technology, Tokyo, Japan, 1983. English Version in Proceedings of the International IEEE Logic Programming Conference, 1984.

2316. MIZOGUCHI, F., A Software Environment for Developing Knowledge-Based Systems, in *Computer Science and Technologies: 1982*, T. KITAGAWA, (ed.), Elsevier North-Holland, New-York, 1982, 334-349.

2317. MIZOGUCHI, F., KATAYAMA, Y. and OWADA, H., LOOKS: Knowledge Representation System For Designing Expert System In The Framework of Logic Programming, *International Conference On Fifth Generation Computer Systems*, November 1984.

2318. MOTODA, H., YAMADA, N. and YOSHIDA, K., A Knowledge Based System For Plant Diagnosis, *International Conference On Fifth Generation Computer Systems*, November 1984.

2319. MOZETIC, I., BRATKO, I. and NAVRAO, L., An Experiment in Automatic Synthesis of Expert Knowledge through Qualitative Modelling, *Proceedings of Workshop on Logic Programming*, Algarve, Portugal, 1983.

2320. NAKASHIMA, H., A Knowledge Representation System: Prolog/KR, Doctoral Dissertation, University of Tokyo, 1983.

2321. NAKASHIMA, H., Knowledge Representation in Prolog/KR, *Proceedings of the International IEEE Conference on Logic Programming*, Atlantic City, 1984.

2322. NILSSON, M., A Logical Model of Knowledge and Belief, UPMAIL Technical Report 28, Uppsala University, 1984.

2323. OGAWA, Y. and OTHERS, Knowledge Representation And The Inference Environment:KRINE, an Approach to Integration of Frame, Prolog and Graphics, *International Conference On Fifth Generation Computer Systems*, November 1984.

2324. OHSUGA, S., Knowledge-Based Systems as a New Interactive Computer System of the Next Generation, in *Computer Science and Technologies: 1982*, T. KITAGAWA, (ed.), Elsevier North-Holland, New-York, 1982, 227-249.

2325. PARSAYE, K., Database Management, Knowledge Base Management and Expert System Development in Prolog, *Proceedings of Workshop on Logic Programming*, Algarve, Portugal, 1983.

2326. RICH, C., Knowledge Representation Languages and Predicate Calculus: How to Have Your Cake and Eating it Too, *Proceedings of the National Conference on Artificial Intelligence*, Carnegie-Mellon University, August 1982. AAAI-82.

2327. SAKAI, K. and MIYACHI, T., Incorporating Naive Negation into Prolog, Technical Report TR-0028, ICOT - Institute for New Generation Computer Technology, Tokyo, Japan, 1983.

2328. SANDEWALL, E., PCF-2, A First-Order Calculus for Expressing Conceptual Information, Technical Report, Computer Science Department, Uppsala University, 1972.

2329. SCHOPPERS, M. J., Logic-programming production systems with Metalog, *Software Practice and Experience 13*, (1983).

2330. SCHOPPERS, M. J. and HARANDI, M. T., Metalog: a language for knowledge representation and manipulation, *Conference on Artificial Intelligence*, Rochester, Michigan, April, 1983.

2331. SHAPIRO, S. C., Representing and Locating Deduction Rules in a Semantic Network, *SIGART Newsletter*, June 1977.

2332. SHAPIRO, S. C., The SNePS Semantic Network Processing System, in *Associative Networks*, N. V. FINDLER, (ed.), Academic Press, 1979, 179-203.

2333. SHAPIRO, S. C., MCKAY, D. P., MARTINS, J. and MOGADO, E., SNePSLOG: A Higher Order Logic Programming Language, Technical Report No. 8, Computer Science Department, SUNY at Buffalo, Amherst, NY, 1981.

2334. SKUCE, D., Towards Communicating Qualitative Knowledge between Scientists and Machines, Ph.D. Dissertation, Department of Computer Science, McGill University , Montreal, 1977.

2335. SKUCE, D., An Approach to Defining and Communicating the Conceptual Structure of Data, Technical Report TR-79-05, Department of Computer Science, University of Ottawa, Canada, 1979.

2336. SKUCE, D., Expressing Qualitative Biomedical Knowledge Exactly Using the Language LESK, *International Journal of Computing in Biology and Medecine 15*, 1 (1982), 57-69.

2337. SKUCE, D., LESK: A Language Synthesizing Natural Language, Computer Language and Logic, *Proceedings Annual Conference on Computational Linguistics COLING-82*, Prague, July 1982.

2338. SKUCE, D., LESK Tutorial, Technical Report TR-83-12, Department of Computer Science, University of Ottawa, Canada, 1983.

2339. SKUCE, D., Expressing Academic Regulations in LESK, Technical Report TR-83-13, Department of Computer Science, University of Ottawa, Canada, 1983.

2340. SKUCE, D., Expressing UNIX Knowledge in LESK, Technical Report TR-83-14, Department of Computer Science, University of Ottawa, Canada, 1983.

2341. SKUCE, D., Formal Semantics of KNOWLOG, Technical Report TR-83-15, Department of Computer Science, University of Ottawa, Canada, 1983.

2342. SKUCE, D., KNOWLOG: A Prolog Extension for Implementing Expert Knowledge Systems, Technical Report TR-83-05, Department of Computer Science, University of Ottawa, Canada, 1983.

2343. STABLER, E. P. and ELCOCK, E. W., Knowledge Representation in an Efficient Deductive Inference System, *Proceedings of Workshop on Logic Programming*, Algarve, Portugal, 1983.

2344. STERLING, L., Logical Levels of Problem Solving, *Proceedings of the Second International Logic Programming Conference*, S. A. TARNLUND, ed., Uppsala University, Uppsala, Sweden, July 2-6, 1984, 231-242.

2345. STOLFO, S. J., Knowledge Engineering: Theory and Practice, *IEEE 1983 Proceedings of Trends and Applications in Artificial Intelligence*, 1983.

2346. SUGIYAMA, K., KAMEDA, M., AKIYAMA, K. and MAKINOUCHI, A., A Knowledge Representation System in Prolog, Technical Report TR-0024, ICOT - Institute for New Generation Computer Technology, Tokyo, Japan, 1983.

2347. SUWA, M. and OTHERS, Knowledge Base Mechanisms, in *Fifth Generation Computer Systems*, T. MOTO-OKA, (ed.), North-Holland, New York, 1981. Proceedings of the First International Conference on Fifth Generation Computer Systems.

2348. TOKORO, M., ISHIKAWA, Y., MARUICHI, T. and KAWAMURA, M., An Object Oriented Approach To Knowledge Systems, *International Conference On Fifth Generation Computer Systems*, November 1984.

2349. VASSILIOU, Y., CLIFFORD, J. and JARKE, M., Access to Specific Declarative Knowledge by Expert Systems: The Impact of Logic Programming, Technical Report, School of Business, University of New York, 1983.

2350. WALKER, A., SYLLOG: A Knowledge-Based Data Management System From Knowledge, 034-3481, Department of Computer Science, New York University, 1981.

2351. WALKER, A., Automatic Generation of Explanations of Results From Knowledge Bases, RJ-3481, IBM T.J. Watson Research Center, 1982.

CHAPTER 18

Logic Programming
in Learning Systems

2352. BANERJI, R. B., A Logic in Which One Learns Programs from Examples, *Presented at Workshop on Logic Programming for Intelligent Systems*, Long Beach, Los Angeles, September 1981.

2353. BECKER, J. M., AQ-Prolog User's Guide and Program Description, Technical Report, Department of Computer Science, University of Illinois, December 1983.

2354. BRATKO, I., Knowledge-Based Problem Solving in AL3, *ACM SIGART Newsletter*, April, 1982.

2355. BRAZDIL, P., Experimental Learning Model, *Proceedings of AISB-78*, Hamburg, 1978.

2356. BRAZDIL, P., Symbolic Derivations of Chess Patterns, *Proceedings of the European Conference on Artificial Intelligence 1982*, Orsay, France, 1982.

2357. BUNDY, A., *The Computer Modelling of Mathematical Reasoning*, Academic Press, 1983.

2358. BUNDY, A., Computer Modelling of Mathematical Reasoning, *Proceedings of the Annual Conference of The British Society For The Psychology of Learning Mathematics*, 1983. Also Research Paper 200, Department of Artificial Intelligence, Edinburgh, October 1983.

2359. BUNDY, A., Meta-Level Inference and Consciousness, DAI Research Paper No 187, Department of Artificial Intelligence, University of Edinburgh, 1983.

2360. BUNDY, A., BYRD, L., LUGER, G., MELLISH, C. S., MILNE, R. and PALMER, M. S., Mecho: A Program to Solve Mechanics Problems, Working Paper 50, Department of Artificial Intelligence, University of Edinburgh, 1979.

2361. BUNDY, A., LUGER, G., MELLISH, C. S. and PALMER, M. S., Knowledge about Knowledge: Making Decisions in Mechanics Problem Solving, *Proceedings of AISB-78*, University of Edinburgh, 1978, 71-82.

2362. BUNDY, A., LUGER, G., STONE, M. and WELHAM, B., Mecho: Year One, Working Paper 22, Department of Artificial Intelligence, University of Edinburgh, 1977. Also in Proceedings of AISB-76.

2363. BUNDY, A. and SILVER, B., A Critical Survey of Rule Learning Programs, Research Paper 169, Computer Science Department, Edinburgh University, 1982.

2364. BUNDY, A., SILVER, B. and PLUMMER, D., An Analytical Comparison Of Some Rule Learning Programs, *Third Annual Technical Conference of the British Computer Society's Expert Systems Specialist Group*, 1983. Also available as Research Paper 215, Department of Artificial Intelligence, University of Edinburgh.

2365. BYRD, L. and BORNING, A., Extending Mecho to Solve Statistics Problems, *Proceedings of AISB-80*, S. HARDY, ed., Amsterdam, Holland, 1980. Also available from University of Edinburgh as Department of Artificial Intelligence Research Paper No 137.

2366. COTTON, J., BYRD, L. and BUNDY, A., How Can Algebra Steps be Learned by Students with only Arithmetic Skills, Working Paper, Department of Artificial Intelligence, University of Edinburgh, 1981.

2367. DEAN, J. and MICHOL, J., Computer Assisted Learning In History: BOGBOD, A Detective Exercise Written In Prolog, *AISB Easter Conference on Artificial Intelligence and Education*, 1983.

2368. EMDE, W., HABEL, C. U. and ROLLINGER, C. R., The Discovery of the Equator or Concept Driven Learning, *Proceedings of the International Joint Conference on Artificial Intelligence*, Karlsruhe, Germany, 1983, 455-458.

2369. LUGER, G., Mathematical Model Building in the Solution of Mechanics Problems: Human Protocols and the Mecho Trace, *Cognitive Science 5*, (1981), 55-77.

2370. O'KEEFE, R. A., Concept Formation from Very Large Training Sets, *Proceedings of the International Joint Conference on Artificial Intelligence*, Karlsruhe, Germany, 1983.

2371. OHLSSON, S., On the Automated Learning of Problem Solving Rules, UPMAIL Technical Report 10, Uppsala University, 1982.

2372. PLUMMER, D., Two Techniques for Inductive Learning, Research Paper 186, Department of Artificial Intelligence, University of Edinburgh, March, 1983.

2373. PLUMMER, D. and BUNDY, A., Gazing: Identifying Potentially Useful Inferences, Working Paper 160, Department of Artificial Intelligence, University of Edinburgh, February, 1984.

2374. PORTER, B. W., Learning Problem Solving, Ph.D. Dissertation, Computer Science Department, University of California, Irvine, 1984.

2375. PORTER, B. W. and KIBLER, D. F., Learning Operator Transformations, *Proceedings of the Conference of the American Association for Artificial Intelligence*, Austin, Texas, 1984, 278-281. AAAI-84.

2376. SAMMUT, C. A., Learning Concepts by Performing Experiments, Ph.D. Dissertation, Department of Computer Science, University of New South Wales, 1981.

2377. SAMMUT, C. A. and BANERJI, R. B., Hierarchical Memories: An Aid to Concept Learning, *Proceedings of Machine Learning Workshop 83*, R. S. MICHALSKI, J. G. CARBONELL and T. M. MITCHELL, eds., 1983.

2378. SAMMUT, C. A. and COHEN, B., A Language for Describing Concepts as Programs, in *Language Design and Programming Methodology*, J. M. TOBIAS, (ed.), Springer Verlag, 1980. Lecture Notes in Computer Science - 79.

2379. DE SARAM, H., Prolog for Children and Teachers, *AISB Easter Conference on Artificial Intelligence and Education*, University of Exeter, U.K., April 1983.

2380. SHAPIRO, E. Y., An Algorithm that Infers Theorems from Facts, *Proceedings Seventh International Joint Conference on Artificial Intelligence*, August 1981. International Joint Conference on Artificial Intelligence.

2381. SHAPIRO, E. Y., *Algorithmic Program Debugging*, MIT Press, 1983. Ph.D. thesis, Yale University, May 1982.

2382. SILVER, B., Learning Algebraic Methods from Examples - A Progress Report, DAI Research Paper No 129, Department of Artificial Intelligence, University of Edinburgh, 1982.

2383. SILVER, B., An Algebra Learning Program - Thesis Proposal, DAI Working Paper No 111, Department of Artificial Intelligence, University of Edinburgh, 1982.

2384. SILVER, B., Learning Equation Solving Methods from Worked Examples, *Proceedings of Machine Learning Workshop 83*, R. S. MICHALSKI, J. G. CARBONELL and T. M. MITCHELL, eds., 1983.

2385. SILVER, B., Learning Equation Solving Methods from Worked Examples, *Proceedings of the International Machine Learning Workshop*, R. S. MICHALSKI, ed., June, 1983, 99-104. Also available from Edinburgh as Research Paper 188.

2386. SILVER, B., Precondition Analysis: Learning Equation Solving Strategies from Worked Examples, *Machine Learning 2*, R. S. MICHALSKI, R. S. CARBONELL and T. M. MITCHELL, eds., 1984. Earlier version available from Edinburgh as Research Paper 220.

2387. SKINNER, D., A Computer Program to Perform Integration by Parts, Working Paper 103, Department of Artificial Intelligence, Edinburgh, 1981.

2388. STERLING, L., IMPRESS - Meta-Level Concepts in Theorem Proving, DAI Research Paper No 119, Department of Artificial Intelligence, University of Edinburgh, 1983.

CHAPTER 19

Amalgamation of Object and Meta Level

2389. BOWEN, K. A., Reasoning about Programs in Amalgamated Logic, *Proceedings of the Prolog Programming Environments Workshop*, Linkoping University, Sweden, 1982.

2390. BOWEN, K. A. and KOWALSKI, R. A., Amalgamating Language and Metalanguage in Logic Programming, in *Logic Programming*, K. L. CLARK and S. TARNLUND, (eds.), Academic Press, New York, 1982, 153-173. A.P.I.C. Studies in Data Processing No. 16 (Also available as Technical Report from Syracuse University).

2391. BRAZDIL, P., Use Of Metalogical Primitives In Communication, *Sixth European Conference On Artificial Intelligence*, Pisa, September, 1984.

2392. BUNDY, A., Meta-Level Inference and Consciousness, DAI Research Paper No 187, Department of Artificial Intelligence, University of Edinburgh, 1983.

2393. BUNDY, A., Meta-Level Inference and Consciousness, in *The Mind and the Machine*, S. TORRANCE, (ed.), Ellis Horwood Publishing, 1984.

2394. BUNDY, A., BYRD, L., LUGER, G., MELLISH, C. S. and PALMER,
M. S., Solving Mechanics Problems Using Meta-Level Inference,
in *Expert Systems in the Microelectronic Age*, D. MICHIE, (ed.),
University of Edinburgh, Scotland, 1979, 153-167. Also in
Proceedings International Joint Conference on Artificial
Intelligence-79 and available as a Edinburgh Research Report.

2395. BUNDY, A. and STERLING, L., Meta-Level Inference in Algebra,
Research Paper 164, Department of Artificial Intelligence,
University of Edinburgh, Scotland, September, 1981. Presented
at the Workshop on Logic Programming for Intelligent Systems,
Long Beach, California, 1981.

2396. BUNDY, A. and WELHAM, B., Using Meta-Level Inference for
Selective Application of Multiple Rewrite Rules in Algebraic
Manipulation, *Artificial Intelligence 16*, 2 (1981), 189-212. Also
in Lecture Notes in Computer Science No. 87 by Springer-
Verlag.

2397. ESHGI, K., Application of Meta-Level Programming To Fault
Finding In Logic Circuits, *Proceedings Of The 1st International
Logic Programming Conference*, Marseilles, 1982, 240-246.

2398. GALLAIRE, H. and LASSERRE, C., A Control Metalanguage for
Logic Programming, *Workshop on Logic Programming*,
Debrecen, Hungary, 1980, 123-132. Also in Logic Programming,
Clark and Tarnlund, Academic Press, 1982.

2399. GALLAIRE, H. and LASSERRE, C., Metalevel Control for Logic
Programming, *Proceedings Logic Programming Workshop*, Long
Beach, CA, September 1981.

2400. KELLOG, C., Knowledge Management: A Practical Amalgam of
Knowledge and Data Base Technology, *Proceedings of the
National Conference on Artificial Intelligence*, Carnegie-Mellon
University, August 1982.

2401. KOWALSKI, R. A., *Logic for Problem Solving*, Elsevier North-Holland, New-York, 1979.

2402. KOWALSKI, R. A., The Use of Metalanguage to Assemble Object Level Programs and Abstract Programs, *Proceedings of the Prolog Programming Environments Workshop*, Linkoping University, Sweden, 1982.

2403. KUNIFUJI, S., ASOU, M., TAKEUCHI, A., MIYACHI, T., KITAKAMI, H., YOKOTA, H., YASAKUWA, H. and FURUKAWA, K., Amalgamation of Object Knowledge and Meta Knowledge by Prolog and Its Applications, *Knowledge Engineering and Artificial Intelligence Working Group of the Information Processing Society of Japan*, June, 1983. preprint 30-1, TR-009.

2404. STERLING, L., IMPRESS - Meta-Level Concepts in Theorem Proving, DAI Research Paper No 119, Department of Artificial Intelligence, University of Edinburgh, 1983.

2405. STERLING, L., Implementing Problem-Solving Strategies Using the Meta-level, *Proceedings of the Jerusalem Conference In Information Technology*, Jerusalem, Israel, 1984. Also available from Edinburgh as Research Paper 185.

2406. STERLING, L., Logical Levels of Problem Solving, *Proceedings of the Second International Logic Programming Conference*, S. A. TARNLUND, ed., Uppsala University, Uppsala, Sweden, July 2-6, 1984, 231-242.

2407. STERLING, L. and BUNDY, A., Meta-Level Inference and Program Verification, in *Lecture Notes in Computer Science 138: 6th Conference on Automated Deduction*, D. W. LOVELAND, (ed.), Springer-Verlag, 1982, 144-150. Also available from Edinburgh as DAI Research Paper no. 168.

2408. WEYRAUCH, R. W., Proglomena to a Theory of Mechanized Formal Reasoning, *Artificial Intelligence 13*, (1980).

PERMUTED SUBJECT INDEX

Metalanguage in Logic/	Amalgamating Language and	134
of Prolog for a CAD	Application /the Effectiveness	1619
Verification: Advances and	Application /and Program	1631
Expression du/ Systemes Expert -	Application a l'Electronique et	1835
Prolog:/ On a Possible	Application and Extension of	1652
/Retrieval: An Interesting	Application Area For The New/	1800
Automatique aux Manipulations/	Application de la Demonstration	1646
/Bases for Expert Systems: An	Application Driven Approach	1932
Systems Planning Language In/ An	Application of A Parallel	985
Language Understanding/ An	Application of Automated	2092
Machine And Its Architecture	Application Of Hash To Data Base	1175
Simultaneous Equations The	Application of Homogenization to	1746
Logic in Computer/ On the	Application of Mathematical	1766
Theorem Proving to Symbolic/	Application of Mechanical	1493
Programming To Fault Finding In/	Application of Meta-Level	2397
Rules/ /Inference for Selective	Application of Multiple Rewrite	1523
of Similar Substructures of/ The	Application of Prolog for Search	1687
/Contours of Integration: An	Application of Prolog in/	1488
Development of QA and DBM/ The	Application of Prolog to the	1600
Language Prolog for Panel/ The	Application of the Programming	1676
Language to the Design of/ The	Application of the Prolog	1472
to Problem Solving	Application of Theorem Proving	253
to Question-Answering Systems	Application of Theorem Proving	255
Abstract Prolog Machine and its	Application to Partial/ /of an	744
/of Rewriting Systems and its	Application to Prolog Processes	1200
/For Partial Evaluation And Its	Application To Source-to-Source/	2103
Of/ /Types And Rewriting Systems:	Application To The Programming	117
Goal Rewriting Model and Machine	Architecture /Engine PIE -	1171
To Data Base Machine And Its	Architecture /Of Hash	1175
The New Generation of Computer	Architecture	1193
and Demand-Driven Computer	Architecture Data-Driven	1194
Fifth Generation Computer	Architecture	1198
of Logic Programs On A Dataflow	Architecture Execution	1202
Concurrent Data Access	Architecture	1210
Studies of a Prolog Machine	Architecture Performance	1212
Design Philosophy and Machine	Architecture /Machine (PSI): Its	1236
Delta's Functionally-distributed	Architecture /Flow On RDBM	1243
DADO, A Large Parallel Computer/	Architecture and Applications of	1247
systolic/ Polymorphic arrays: an	architecture for a programmable	1214
Mechanisms New	Architecture for Knowledge Base	1151
DADO: A Tree Structured Machine	Architecture for Production/	1248
Execution of/ Towards a Computer	Architecture for the OR-Parallel	1205
Bases MPDC: Massive Parallel	Architecture for Very Large Data	1253
Mechanisms -/ Logic Machine	Architecture Inference	1227

Logic Machine	Architecture: Kernel Functions	1226
Inference Engine-PIE The	Architecture Of A Parallel	1234
Inference Computers The	Architecture Of Fifth Generation	1173
Languages An	Architecture of Parallel Logic	1208
A Large Parallel Computer for	Artificial Intelligence /DADO,	1247
/Programming Methodology, and	Artificial Intelligence	1644
framework for the techniques of	Artificial Intelligence) /(A	1927
Applications for Business	Artificial Intelligence	1907
Solving Algebraic Equations: An	Artificial Intelligence Approach	1789
Design of Drug Administration by	Artificial Intelligence Based/	1829
Software Engineering and	Artificial Intelligence in New/	1178
and Machines	Artificial Intelligence Language	1012
Practical Applications of an	Artificial Intelligence Language/	1599
Prolog Machines are/	Artificial Intelligence LISP and	757
/Simulation System Based on	Artificial Intelligence Methods	1606
Techniques In The Design/ Using	Artificial Intelligence	1501
Techniques and Applications	Artificial Intelligence: Tools,	1710
from the Super/ What Should	Artificial Intelligence Want	1213
Instructional Text	Automated Analysis of	1707
7th International Conference on	Automated Deduction /of the	463
Notes/ /of the 6th Conference on	Automated Deduction - Lecture	337
Notes/ /of the 5th Conference on	Automated Deduction - Lecture	123
Intelligent Backtracking for	Automated Deduction in FOL	358
Natural Question Answering and	Automated Deduction in the/	2063
Physical Plants Algorithms for	Automated Diagnosis of Faults in	1612
Techniques to/ An Application of	Automated Language Understanding	2092
Solving Rules On the	Automated Learning of Problem	2371
Methodology/ A Knowledge-Based	Automated Message Understanding	1564
Environment for Research in	Automated Reasoning A Portable	1080
Achievements in	Automated Reasoning	1793
	Automated Reasoning	1795
How They Work	Automated Reasoning Programs:	1794
	Automated Statistical Analysis	1709
	Automated Theorem Proving	122
Logical Basis	Automated Theorem Proving: A	336
Quartercentury Review	Automated Theorem Proving: A	338
Algorithms A New Class of	Automated Theorem-proving	1102
Programming Controlling	Backtrack in Horn Clause	320
Backtracking Finding	Backtrack Points for Intelligent	179
Search Problems by Intelligent	Backtracking /Combinatorial	149
Reasoning Through Intelligent	Backtracking /Top-Down Logical	150
Revision by Intelligent	Backtracking Deductive	151
Backtrack Points for Intelligent	Backtracking Finding	179
plans: A Basis for Intelligent	Backtracking Deduction	181
Logic Programs Using Selective	Backtracking An Interpreter of	414
Selective	Backtracking	415
An Algorithm for Intelligent	Backtracking	452
plan/ /improvement of exhaustive	backtracking: a strategy for	796
/Improvement of Exhaustive	Backtracking: A Strategy for/	417
Horn Clause/ Intelligent	Backtracking and Sidetracking in	791

Horn Clause/ Intelligent	Backtracking and Sidetracking in	412
/improvement of exhaustive	backtracking: data structure and/	761
AND-Parallelism with Intelligent	Backtracking for Annotated Logic/	1335
Deduction in FOL Intelligent	Backtracking for Automated	358
Selective	backtracking for logic programs	413
Symbols /Graphs for Intelligent	Backtracking in Deduction	193
AND/OR Trees	Backtracking Intelligently in	407
a Static Data/ Semi-Intelligent	Backtracking of Prolog Based on	855
Static Data/ Semi-Intelligent	Backtracking of Prolog Based on	679
Intelligent and Programmable	Backtracking Possibilities for/	1596
Compiling High-Level	Chip Descriptions into an/	1637
Theory to Aspects of Reactor and	Circuit Analysis /and Cutset	1571
Prolog in CMOS	Circuit Design	1726
Logic Programming is NOT	Circuit Design	20
VLSI Computer Assisted	Circuit Evaluation in Prolog for	1801
/and Reasoning of VLSI	Circuit in Temporal Logic	1215
Logic	Circuit Synthesis Using Prolog	1777
with Functions, Types and	Concurrency /Language	1140
a Connective Suitable to Express	Concurrency /Semantics of	1295
Logical Formalism for Specifying	Concurrency A	1341
Clause-Like Logic For Specifying	Concurrency A Horn	1345
in Prolog - A/ Mechanisms for	Concurrency Control and Recovery	673
Logic Representation of a	Concurrent Algorithm	279
Architecture	Concurrent Data Access	1210
Programs Associative	Concurrent Evaluation of Logic	1093
	Concurrent Execution of Logic	1274
	Concurrent Logic	1293
	Concurrent Logic Programming	1318
A New Method for Describing	Concurrent Problems Based on/	1294
Logic Allowing the Definition of	Concurrent Processes /Clause	1340
/System For The Verification of	Concurrent Processes Against/	1273
Prolog Interpreter Based on	Concurrent Programming	1308
Based on Predicate/ R-Maple: A	Concurrent Programming Language	1139
Quadtrees in	Concurrent Prolog	1301
Programming Language based on	Concurrent Prolog /A Knowledge	1309
A Note on Systems Programming in	Concurrent Prolog	1312
Mechanisms of Parallel and	Concurrent Prolog /Execution	1320
Chart Parsing in	Concurrent Prolog	1327
Optimizing System (POPS) in	Concurrent Prolog /OR-Parallel	1328
Bounded-Wait Merge in Shapiro's	Concurrent Prolog	1329
of Process Reduction in	Concurrent Prolog Serialization	1330
and Implementation of Flat	Concurrent Prolog Design	1337
Distributed Programming in	Concurrent Prolog	1358
Systems Programming in	Concurrent Prolog	1363
and Implementation in	Concurrent Prolog /Specification	1364
Object Oriented Programming in	Concurrent Prolog	1365
Complex Computer Hardware Using	Concurrent Prolog /of	1366
Interprocess Communication in	Concurrent Prolog	1369
of a Distributed Interpreter for	Concurrent Prolog The Design	1370
String Manipulation in	Concurrent Prolog	1375

Eager and Lazy Enumerations in	Concurrent Prolog	1396
A Unification Algorithm For	Concurrent Prolog	1406
Problems with	Concurrent Prolog	1409
/a Multiprocessor: A critique of	Concurrent Prolog and Comparison/ . .	1383
Interpreter A Subset of	Concurrent Prolog and Its	1359
Experiences in Transporting	Concurrent Prolog and the Bagel/ . . .	1398
Multiprocessor's Kernel/	Concurrent Prolog as a	1362
Efficient VLSI Design Language	Concurrent Prolog as an	1367
A Sequential Implementation of	Concurrent Prolog Based on the/ . . .	1338
Finding Algorithm A	Concurrent Prolog Based Region . . .	1394
Multi-Process Environment	Concurrent Prolog in a	1331
/Notes on the Bagel: A Systolic	Concurrent Prolog Machine	1360
Multiprocessor: A critique of/	Concurrent Prolog on a	1383
Algorithmic Programming in	Concurrent Prolog: the MAXFLOW/ .	1317
Passing Implementation of	Concurrent Prolog using Message . . .	1386
Algorithm = Logic +	Control	47
as Symbiosis of Meaning and	Control /Programming Languages . .	507
Programs More Explicit Making	Control and Data Flow of Logic	984
A/ Mechanisms for Concurrency	Control and Recovery in Prolog - . . .	673
Program The	Control Component of a Logic	165
Using Proof Plans to	Control Deduction	1780
The	Control Facilities of IC-Prolog	686
Understanding the	Control Flow of Prolog Programs . . .	852
Metalevel	Control for Logic Programming	2399
Automatic Generation of	Control for Logic Programs	950
Automating	Control for Logic Programs	953
Logic Program	Control in Logic	87
On the Implementation of	Control in Logic Programming/	709
Negation and	Control in PROLOG	1092
Language/ About the Role of	Control Information in Natural	2179
Prolog/ Nondeterministic	Control Mechanism in Dataflow	1319
Programming A	Control Metalanguage for Logic	2398
OR-Parallel Token Machine	Control of Activities in the	1280
/of a Complexity Measure for	Control of Design Errors in/	1647
Prolog-based Microcode/	Control Of Heuristic Search In A . . .	1903
A Primitive for the	Control of Logic Programs	296
Synchronisation in/ Meta	Control of process	1607
Logic Programs A	Control Regime for Horn Clause	147
Prolog	Control Rules	952
Memory Management for Flexible	Control Strategies /Prolog	833
User-Defined Parallel	Control Strategies	901
Programming	Control Strategies for Logic	297
Directed Search System	Control Structure of a Pattern	370
LOGAL: Algorithmic	Control Structures for Prolog	877
Prolog-Based Production System	Control Structures in a	1672
in the Design of Production	Control Systems /Programming . . .	1674
Constraints Intelligent	Control Using Integrity	306
Logic	Control with Logic	408
for the Analysis of Imprecise	Data /A Data-Driven System	1692
the Conceptual Structure of	Data /Defining and Communicating . .	1749

Does an Expert System Gets Its	Data How	1818
Directed by Problem Specific	Data /in Relational Databases	2029
	Data Abstraction in Prolog/KR	1098
Concurrent	Data Access Architecture	1210
DAL- A Logic For	Data Analysis	228
Logic For Representing	Data And Expertise	1862
A First Order Theory of	Data and Programs	168
of a Predicate-Calculus Oriented	Data Base /Tool for Management	1729
Medical Texts into a Deductive	Data Base Transformation of	2123
Comparison of Clark's Completed	Data Base and Reiter's Closed/ /A	461
How Should Clauses in a Logic	Data Base be Indexed	827
Horn Clauses And	Data Base Dependencies	1983
/Techniques to the Generation of	Data Base Elements	2092
Implementation Of The Relational	Data Base Engine Design And	1241
Unification for a Prolog	Data Base Machine	1952
Application Of Hash To	Data Base Machine And Its/	1175
A Relational Data Flow	Data Base Machine Based on/	1222
/Data in a Deductively Augmented	Data Base Management System	2018
The Partition Model: A Deductive	Data Base Model	472
and Co-Operativeness In A Logic	Data Base System Security	2053
An Experimental Relational	Data Base System Based on Logic	2033
An Introduction To Deductive	Data Base Systems	2028
Amalgam of Knowledge and	Data Base Technology /Practical	2016
An Axiomatic	Data Base Theory	2097
	Data Base Updates In Pure Prolog	2106
Architecture for Very Large	Data Bases /Massive Parallel	1253
Property Driven	Data Bases	1481
Natural Language Consultable	Data Bases /Design of Deductive	1970
Towards Constructive	Data Bases	1971
Impacts of Logic on	Data Bases	1993
Predicate Logic: A New Basis For	Data Bases	2012
and Pathfinding for Relational	Data Bases Deductive Planning	2017
Inferences over Recursive	Data Bases Performing	2050
to Co-operativeness in Logic	Data Bases An Approach	2056
A Logical Basis for	Data Bases	2096
Output for Deductive Relational	Data Bases /Language and Voice	2216
Answering Queries in Indefinite	Data Bases and the Null Value/	2002
Prolog	Data Bases, Expert Systems, and	1937
/Time and Negation in Logic	Data Bases Query-By-Example	2051
Security and Integrity in Logic	Data Bases using QB r	2107
Programs by Attribute/ Modelling	Data Dependencies in Logic	252
Inequalities	Data Dependencies on	365
/of Prolog Based on Static	Data Dependency Analysis	679
/of Prolog Based on a Static	Data Dependency Analysis	855
Logic for	Data Description	1656
for Combining Prolog with a	Data Driven Mechanism /Arguments	1145
Prolog: The Construction of a	Data Driven Model A Parallel	1144
Prolog-Based Knowledge Bases on	Data Flow Architectures /Large	2011
Combining/ EPILOG = Prolog +	Data Flow: Arguments for	1145
Based on/ A Relational	Data Flow Data Base Machine	1222

Prolog Machine Based on the	Data Flow Mechanism	1219
Based on The Generalized	Data Flow Model /Interpreter	1220
Explicit Making Control and	Data Flow of Logic Programs More . .	984
Data Base/ Reasoning with	Data in a Deductively Augmented . . .	2018
Graphs as	Data in Prolog Programs	978
Programming for a Generalized	Data Management System Logic . . .	1943
/and Meta-Data on a Generalized	Data Management System	1944
SYLLOG: A Knowledge-Based	Data Management System From/ . . .	1935
Expressive Power of the Logical	Data Model On the	2027
DLOG: A Logic-Based	Data Model for the Machine/	1846
/to Assess Security Risks in	Data Processing Systems Programs . .	1527
of exhaustive backtracking:	data structure and/ /improvement . .	761
Program Transformation by	Data Structure Mapping	265
Real World/ Construction of	Data Structures for Representing . . .	1529
/as a Means for Inferencing	Data Structures in an/	307
for Specification of Abstract	Data Types /with Clauses	1577
Developing and Reasoning about	Data Types /Environment for	913
Systems: Application/ Abstract	Data Types And Rewriting	117
/And The Logical Specification Of	Data Types As Unambiguous/	2115
/Of Algebraic Abstract	Data Types In Prolog	117
Programming A Logical Theory of	Data Types Motivated by	938
/Implementation Of Abstract	Data Types Specified By The/	1630
Interface between Users and a	Database On a Conversational	1965
The MU-Prolog Deductive	Database	2048
On Structuring a First Order	Database	2078
Questions Posed to a Prolog	Database /Interpreting English	2178
/in Logic of a Large Commercial	Database: A Methodology Put to/ . . .	1557
Descriptions of Programs for	Database Access Manipulating	1622
How Can we Combine A Relational	Database and a Prolog-Based/	840
/Dependencies in a Relational	Database and Propositional Logic . . .	1984
Designs for Question Answering/	Database and Theorem prover	2094
Horn Clauses and	Database Dependencies	1985
Equivalence Between Relational	Database Dependencies and a/ An . .	2082
EDD, An Expert System for	Database Design	1899
Texts and Facts in a Mixed	Database Environment Managing . . .	1948
Rapid Software Development in a	Database Framework - A Case/	1655
of Natural Language	Database Interrogation by Means . . .	1967
Logic as a	Database Language	2023
A New Approach to	Database Logic	2026
A Prolog	Database Machine	1953
A Relational	Database Machine DELTA	1245
Knowledge Base/ A Relational	Database Machine: First Step to	1235
	Database Management in Prolog . . .	1980
Base Management and Expert/	Database Management, Knowledge . .	1900
/Prolog and Relational	Database Management System	2030
Towards a Co-Operative	Database Management System	2054
Coupling Expert Systems with	Database Management Systems	1865
Towards an Integrated	Database Prolog System	2086
Logic /of Interactive Relational	Database Queries Expressed in	2104
Seasons Prolog: A	Database Query Language for All . . .	2112

Can/ /as a Relationally Complete	Database Query Language Which	. . . 2110
/to Integrity Constraints on	Database Relations	2058
Prolog A	Database Support System for	1964
Natural Language Consultable	Database System /and Efficient	2072
An Intelligent	Database System: AIDS	1986
for Constructive Expert	Database Systems /Programming . . .	1821
Tools for Expert	Database Systems	1847
a Unified Approach to Expert and	Database Systems Towards	1884
Transaction Restarts in Prolog	Database Systems	1942
in Expert Systems and	Database Systems /Optimization . . .	1960
Language Access to Prolog	Database Systems Natural	2247
Clause Indexing in Deductive	Database Systems Implementing . . .	750
in/ /the Use and Evolution of	Database Systems: A Case Study . . .	2041
Through Logic On	Database Systems Development	1972
Advances in	Database Theory	1998
Reconstruction of Relational	Database Theory /a Logical	2080
Deductive	Database Tools	2099
	Database Updates in Pure Prolog . . .	2105
Queries for a Linguistic	Database Using Prolog /Language . . .	2186
/and Select Operators in a Logic	Database Using Query-By-Example . .	2052
Extending A Relational	Database with Logic Programming/ . .	1955
Extending a Network	Database with Prolog	1987
Language for Virtual Relational	Databases LOFE: A	1038
and Inferences over Relational	Databases Set Operations	1089
Query Processing in Logic	Databases Parallel	1288
Non Monotonic Reasoning and	Databases	130
Domain Closure for first order	databases Equality and	1454
Natural Language Reports from	Databases /Generating	1662
Assimilation Method for Logic	Databases A Knowledge	1885
Logic Programming and Relational	Databases	1956
Logic Programming and	Databases On Integrating	1957
Logic Languages and Relational	Databases Interfacing Predicate . . .	1961
Natural Language and	Databases	1966
Prolog for	Databases	1968
Retrieval On Virtual Relational	Databases Deductive Information . . .	1981
Programs for Querying Relational	Databases Logic	1982
System On Relational	Databases /Question-answering	1990
Intelligent Access to Relational	Databases An	1991
Logic Databases versus Deductive	Databases	1994
Logic and	Databases	1996
and Introduction to Logic and	Databases An Overview	1997
New Applications of	Databases	2000
Logic, Algebra and	Databases	2004
Prolog Access to CODASYL and FDM	Databases Efficient	2005
Queries in Recursive First-Order	Databases On Compiling	2010
On the Equivalence of Logical	Databases	2025
Inferences over Relational	Databases Performing	2031
as an Aid to Analysis in Large	Databases Logical Inference	2035
On Deductive Relational	Databases	2037
of Definite and Indefinite	Databases On Theories	2038

On Recursive Axioms in Deductive Databases 2039
Assimilation Method for Logic Databases A Proposed Knowledge . . 2044
Integrity Checking in Relational Databases Logic for Improving 2059
of Workshop on Logical Bases for Databases Proceedings 2060
Integrity Checking in Deductive Databases 2064
Logic Programming and Databases 2066
On Closed World Databases 2076
Question-answering on Relational Databases Deductive 2077
Integrity of Typed First Order Databases On the 2079
Dependencies in Relational Databases Update 2081
of Logical Query Languages for Databases Implementation 2100
in Recursive First-Order Horn Databases /of Resolvents 271
Containing Static Calls to Databases /Prolog Programs 640
Logic and Databases: A Deductive Approach . . . 1999
Relational Databases a la Carte 2069
Prolog and Relational Databases: A Road to/ 2049
/Documents By Coupling Relational Databases And Prolog Expert/ 1792
Assumption On Indefinite Databases and the Closed World . . . 2036
Personal Information Deductive Databases and the Nature of 2098
Answering Queries in Indefinite Databases and the Null Value/ 2003
Deduction in Relational Databases Directed by Problem/ . . . 2029
Computer Prolog and Relational Databases for Fifth Generation 2024
in Natural Language Access to Databases from a Logic/ Issues 2268
Communicating with Databases in Natural Language 2266
Interpretation Databases: Theory Versus 1702
Databases Logic Databases versus Deductive 1994
/Algorithm For Relational Databases with Null Values 2075
Using Proof Plans to Control Deduction 1780
Parsing and Deduction 2227
Parsing as Deduction 2229
Logic Programs Based on Natural Deduction Evaluation of 268
Relations in Program-synthetic Deduction Special 352
A Strategy for Plan-based Deduction /Backtracking: 417
Conference on Automated Deduction /the 7th International . . . 463
a strategy for plan based deduction /backtracking: 796
A Note on Fuzzy Deduction 97
the 6th Conference on Automated Deduction - Lecture Notes in/ /of . . 337
the 5th Conference on Automated Deduction - Lecture Notes in/ /of . . 123
for logic programming Surface Deduction: a uniform mechanism . . . 1036
Modale Deduction Automatique en Logique . . 159
la/ Controle de Systemes de Deduction Automatique Fondes sur . . 225
Programming in a Natural Deduction Framework 260
Approach Controlling Knowledge Deduction in a Declarative 186
Backtracking for Automated Deduction in FOL Intelligent 358
Databases Directed by Problem/ Deduction in Relational 2029
/Question Answering and Automated Deduction in the System SYNTEX . . 2063
Intelligent Backtracking Deduction plans: A Basis for 181
Proof Procedure for the First/ Deduction Plans: A Graphical 177
Representing and Locating Deduction Rules in a Semantic/ 1126
for Intelligent Backtracking in Deduction Symbols /Graphs 193

Programming Based on a Natural	Deduction System Logic	267
Language Based on a Natural	Deduction System A Programming	495
Reasoning A Natural	Deduction System For Program	262
The Logical Definition of	Deduction Systems	2073
Automatic	Deduction with Hyper-resolution	437
Logic and Databases: A	Deductive Approach	1999
synthesis A	deductive approach to program	351
/of Medical Texts into a	Deductive Data Base	2123
The Partition Model: A	Deductive Data Base Model	472
An Introduction To	Deductive Data Base Systems	2028
The MU-Prolog	Deductive Database	2048
Implementing Clause Indexing in	Deductive Database Systems	750
	Deductive Database Tools	2099
Logic Databases versus	Deductive Databases	1994
On Recursive Axioms in	Deductive Databases	2039
Integrity Checking in	Deductive Databases	2064
Nature of Personal Information	Deductive Databases and the	2098
An Outline of BDGEN: a	Deductive DBMS	2065
/Representation in an Efficient	Deductive Inference System	2343
Computation and	Deductive Information Retrieval	208
On Virtual Relational Databases	Deductive Information Retrieval	1981
Fundamentals of Machine-Oriented	Deductive Logic	1909
Programming as a	Deductive Method	492
Processes: A First Example	Deductive Modelling of Cognitive	1626
Cognition	Deductive Modelling of Human	1627
Consultable/ Logical Design of	Deductive Natural Language	1970
Pathfinding for Relational Data/	Deductive Planning and	2017
Knowledge Representation from a	Deductive Point of View	121
System Dialog	Deductive Question Answering	2122
/Techniques for Rule Selection in	Deductive Question-answering	303
Relational Databases	Deductive Question-answering on	2077
System A	Deductive Question-answering	1011
/Use of a Semantic Network in a	Deductive Question-Answering/	2204
System On Relational/ A	Deductive Question-answering	1990
Function - The Mechanization of	Deductive Reasoning /Form and	442
/Language and Voice Output for	Deductive Relational Data Bases	2216
On	Deductive Relational Databases	2037
Optimization in a	Deductive Relational System	2001
Intelligent Backtracking	Deductive Revision by	151
Programs	Deductive Synthesis of Logic	276
Unification Algorithm	Deductive Synthesis of the	555
An Intelligent Router for VLSI	Design	1500
Information Handling and Drug	Design /Programming in Chemical	1547
Language Prolog for Panel House	Design /of the Programming	1676
Prolog in CMOS Circuit	Design	1726
Knowledge Base	Design	1826
Expert System for Logic	Design Prolog-based	1881
An Expert System for Database	Design EDD,	1899
Logic Programming is NOT Circuit	Design	20
Defense of Programming Language	Design In	284

Logic Based Program	Design	844
A Hardware Unification Unit:	Design and Analysis	586
LOGLISP: Motivation,	Design and Implementation	1115
Sequential Prolog Machine	Design and Implementation of a	690
Flat Concurrent Prolog	Design and Implementation of	1337
Personal Inference machine:/ The	Design and Implementation of the . . .	841
Personal Sequential/ Hardware	Design And Implementation Of The . .	1250
Relational Data Base Engine	Design And Implementation Of The . .	1241
Waterloo Prolog Environment	Design and Implementation of the . . .	680
Prolog: Some Thoughts on Prolog	Design by a LISP User Exeter	712
Fixture	Design by Prolog	1585
Microarchitecture for a Prolog/	Design Decisions Influencing the	1211
Programs /Measure for Control of	Design Errors in Logic Based	1647
A Rational	Design For Prolog Systems	1727
	Design in Logic	1679
Knowledge Representation of	Design in Many-Sorted Logic	1680
Prolog as an Efficient VLSI	Design Language Concurrent	1367
Programming A	Design Methodology in Prolog	1682
Interpreter for Concurrent/ The	Design of a Distributed	1370
Machine	Design of a High-Speed Prolog	777
Language Consultable/ Logical	Design of Deductive Natural	1970
Artificial Intelligence Based/	Design of Drug Administration by . . .	1829
Logic Programming in the	Design of Production Control/	1674
Overall	Design Of Simpos	1769
/of the Prolog Language to the	Design of Software and Hardware/ . .	1472
/Intelligence Techniques In The	Design Of Software For Digital/	1501
/Inference Machine (PSI): Its	Design Philosophy and Machine/ . . .	1236
Applications for Architectural	Design Problems /Method and Its . . .	1677
A Prolog-Based Drug	Design System	1545
Runnable Specification as a	Design Tool	1555
Prolog as a System	Design Tool	1563
DESIGN-PRO: A Multi-Model Schema	Design Tool in Prolog	2074
the Programming Language/ How to	Design Variants of Flats Using	1675
Drawing Systems and Knowledge	Engineering Dumb	1496
Symposia on Software Science and	Engineering /of the RIMS	1620
AI and Software	Engineering	1659
What Does It Bring To Software	Engineering ? /Programming:	933
Intelligence in New/ Software	Engineering and Artificial	1178
Generation Computers Knowledge	Engineering and the Fifth	1166
/at Work: The Case of a Civil	Engineering Environment	1538
Overview and/ /System for Civil	Engineering Legislation -	2151
Logic Programming	Engineering Shell	923
Knowledge	Engineering: Theory and Practice . . .	2345
Rule Based Computations on	English	1129
Computations from the	English	1131
of Formal Proofs into	English The Translation	2130
of Mechanics Problems Stated in	English /and Interpretation	2207
Translating Horn Clauses From	English	2274
Tidy French and	English Grammars and Their Use . . .	2187
Syntax and Formal Semantics of	English in PHLIQA1	2190

Prolog/ SHADOW: Interpreting	English Questions Posed to a	. . . . .	2178
Case Studies of/ Questioning	English Text with Clausal Logic:	. . .	2262
Questioning	English with Clausal Logic	. . . . . .	2191
Resolution by Unification and	Equality	. . . .	1436
of Complete Logic Programs With	Equality A Theory	. . . .	1442
in First Order Theories with	Equality /and Theorem Proving	. . .	1455
first order databases	Equality and Domain Closure for	. . .	1454
The Case For Using	Equality Axioms In Automatic/	. . . .	1446
	Equality for Prolog	. . . .	1074
Proving /for Back Chaining and	Equality in Resolution Theorem	. . . .	420
of Resolution to Include the	Equality Relation /Extension	. . . . .	1450
du Controle d'un Systeme	Expert /et Expression	. . . .	1835
Prolog-based Microcode Synthesis	Expert /Of Heuristic Search In A	. . .	1903
Prolog: The Rules to Become an	Expert	. . . .	36
l'Electronique et/ Systemes	Expert - Application a	. . . .	1835
Data-Independent Expert Systems/	EXPERT - The Implementation of	. .	1928
Towards a Unified Approach to	Expert and Database Systems	. . . . .	1884
Programming for Constructive	Expert Database Systems Logic	. . . .	1821
Tools for	Expert Database Systems	. . . . . .	1847
Planning in	Expert DB Systems by Using Rules	. .	2007
Reacteurs a Neutrons/ Un Systeme	Expert en Diagnostique sur	. . . . . .	1898
Utilisation des Systemes	Expert en Maintenance: Une/	. . . . .	1825
Information Systems	Expert Helpers to Data-Based	. . . . .	1842
Extension for Implementing	Expert Knowledge Systems /Prolog	. .	1924
/in Automatic Synthesis of	Expert Knowledge through/	. . . . .	1898
Lexikalische/ Ein Word	Expert Parser in Prolog: Die	. . . . .	2168
Semantische Komponente Ein Word	Expert Parser in Prolog: Die	. . . . .	2166
Integration von Syntax/ Ein Word	Expert Parser in Prolog:	. . . . . .	2167
Presentation/ Etude d'un Systeme	Expert pour la CAD -	. . . .	1831
Network Framework for	Expert System /Associative	. . . . .	1841
The Theory of CES: A Complete	Expert System	. . . .	1905
Meta-Interpreter	Expert System = Knowledge +	. . . .	1929
Implementation in/ MYCIN: The	Expert System and Its	. . . .	1099
Time Debugging An	Expert System Approach to Real	. . .	1849
Search/ A Front-End System: An	Expert System as an Online	. . . .	1904
Programs Developing	Expert System Builders in Logic	. . . .	1895
/Knowledge Base Management and	Expert System Development in/	. . . .	1900
Analysis and/ A Knowledge-Based	Expert System for Automatic	. . . . .	1833
Design EDD, An	Expert System for Database	. . . . .	1899
KARDIO-E: An	Expert System for/	. . . .	1875
Resource Evaluation/ ORBI, An	Expert System for Environmental	. . .	1902
Prolog-based	Expert System for Logic Design	. . . .	1881
in Regression/ A Logic-Based	Expert System for Model Building	. . .	1548
A Domestic Animal An	Expert System For The Ageing Of	. . .	1809
How Does an	Expert System Gets Its Data	. . . . .	1818
A Mycin-Like	Expert System in Prolog	. . . . . .	1668
of Logic/ /System For Designing	Expert System In The Framework	. . .	1691
Concept Development for	Expert System Knowledge Bases	. . .	1911
Meta-Interpreter as Medical	Expert System Shell A Prolog	. . . .	1827
YAPES: Yet Another Prolog-based	Expert System Shell	. . . .	1828

A Prolog Based	Expert System Shell	1861
GUESS-1: A General Purpose	Expert System Shell	1876
Manual APES (A Prolog	Expert System Shell): A User	1852
/of EMYCIN and APES (a Prolog	Expert System Shell for/	1859
An Experience of Building an	Expert System with Prolog	1815
Relational Databases And Prolog	Expert Systems /By Coupling	1792
A Language for Implementing	Expert Systems Prolog:	1817
A Short Introduction to	Expert Systems	1819
For Non-Monotonic Reasoning In	Expert Systems /Foundations	1845
Logic Programming for	Expert Systems	1851
A Language for Implementing	Expert Systems /to Prolog:	1854
Micro-Prolog For	Expert Systems	1858
Logic For	Expert Systems	1871
An Approach to Prolog-Based	Expert Systems	1882
Issues in Developing	Expert Systems	1883
Prolog Based	Expert Systems	1887
Controlling Prolog and	Expert Systems	1925
A Road to Data-Intensive	Expert Systems /Databases:	2049
Interface for a Polish Railway	Expert Systems Natural Language . .	2194
Logic Programming For	Expert Systems: A Two Day Course . .	1509
/Refinement in Rule Bases for	Expert Systems: An Application/ . . .	1932
Prolog For	Expert Systems: An Evaluation	1863
Semantic Query Optimization in	Expert Systems and Database/	1960
Data Bases,	Expert Systems, and Prolog	1937
Programming Developing	Expert Systems Builders in Logic . . .	1897
Applications	Expert Systems for Business	1934
Logic/ /Declarative Knowledge by	Expert Systems: The Impact of	1933
Management Systems Coupling	Expert Systems with Database	1865
/of Data-Independent	Expert Systems with/	1928
The Challenge of the	Fifth Generation	1152
Logic Programming for the	Fifth Generation	1177
and Software Technology in the	Fifth Generation /of Systems	1184
A View of the	Fifth Generation and its Impact	1196
/and Relational Databases for	Fifth Generation Computer	2024
Social/ What is Required of the	Fifth Generation Computer -	1174
Architecture	Fifth Generation Computer	1198
Project Towards a Western	Fifth Generation Computer System . .	1160
project Overview to the	fifth generation computer system . . .	1186
/and Symbol Manipulation in the	Fifth Generation Computer/	1161
a Preliminary Kernel Language of	Fifth Generation Computers /as . . .	1028
Preliminary Kernel Language of	Fifth Generation Computers /as . . .	1029
Knowledge Engineering and the	Fifth Generation Computers	1166
The Architectures In The	Fifth Generation Computers	1187
Project - A Trip Report Japan's	Fifth Generation Computers	1191
Computers The Architecture Of	Fifth Generation Inference	1173
Language: Version 0	Fifth Generation Kernel	1158
Conceptual Specification of the	Fifth Generation Kernel Language/ . .	1076
Begriffschrift - a	Fifth Generation Language	1183
The Unification of	Functional and Logic Languages	185
/Strategies for Integrating	Functional and Logic Programming . .	1136

Languages The Combination of	Functional and Logic Programming	. . 1046
Languages Avoiding Copying in	Functional and Logic Programming	. . 1441
Relational Database and/	Functional Dependencies in a	 1984
Prolog Implementation of Lexical	Functional Grammar A	 2238
/of a Prolog compatible	Functional Language	 111
Unification Qute: A	Functional Language Based On	 1118
Unification QUTE: A	Functional Language Based on	 451
Compiling the Graphical	Functional Language PROGRAPH	. . 1035
/Definition of HASL a Purely	Functional Language with/	 1002
Relationship between Logic and	Functional Languages On the	 1112
as the Operational Semantics of	Functional Languages Narrowing	. . . 428
Programming Language A	Functional plus Predicate Logic	 1010
/of Logic Programming and	Functional Programming	 1008
/Integration of Logic and	Functional Programming	 1134
/Logic Programming and	Functional Programming	 1135
/with Modules as Typed	Functional Programming	 1427
On Implementing Prolog in	Functional Programming	 1429
Programming for Telegram/	Functional Programming and Logic	. . 1462
Logical Variable	Functional Programming and the	. . . 1447
Style of Logic Programming	Functional Programming in the	 1110
A Combined Logical and	Functional Programming Language	. . 1101
/of Logic Programs into	Functional Programs	 1111
Using the Logical/ Real-Time	Functional Queue Operations	 1535
Software Specification by	Grammar Beyond Prolog:	 1143
Unification in	Grammar	 2183
of Lexical Functional	Grammar A Prolog Implementation	. . 2238
Towards a Prolog Text	Grammar	 2250
/for Unification-Based	Grammar Formalisms	 2226
Computer/ The Semantics of	Grammar Formalisms seen as	 2228
A	Grammar Kit in Prolog	 2182
Prolog's/ Parser Generation and	Grammar Manipulation Using	 249
On Gapping	Grammars	 1542
Structures and Attributes	Grammars /Structures, Program	. . . 1669
Definite Clause Translation	Grammars	 2114
As Unambiguous Context Free	Grammars /Of Data Types	 2115
Montagovian Definite Clause	Grammars	 2127
Metamorphosis	Grammars	 2144
Current Trends in Logic	Grammars	 2160
More On Gapping	Grammars	 2161
Treating Coordination in Logic	Grammars	 2163
Complete NP-Structures and Logic	Grammars	 2175
Slot	Grammars	 2200
Interpretation Rules in Logic	Grammars /Problem, and Semantic	. . 2201
Modular Logic	Grammars	 2203
Extraposition	Grammars	 2223
Ambiguity in Logic	Grammars	 2224
Definite Clause Transition	Grammars	 2236
Puzzle	Grammars	 2244
Handling Coordination in Logic	Grammars A Meta-Grammar for	. . . 2249
to Represent Meaning in Logic	Grammars Using Lambda-Calculus	. . 2271

Language Prolog with Two-Level	Grammars /the Logic Programming	349
Based on the Notion of Two-Level	Grammars A Version of Prolog	350
Analysis Lexicon	Grammars and Automatic Syntactic	2176
Definite Clause Translation	Grammars and Natural Language/	2116
Relational Equations,	Grammars and Programs	209
Definite Clause Translation	Grammars And The Logical/	2115
Tidy French and English	Grammars and Their Use	2187
A Survey of the/ Definite Clause	Grammars for Language Analysis :	2269
/Slots and Modifiers in Logic	Grammars for Natural Language	2202
Some Techniques for Writing	Grammars in Logic	2222
Restriction	Grammars in Prolog	2180
Contextual	Grammars in Prolog	2243
Integration of Frame, Prolog and	Graphics /an Approach to	2323
Logic Programming	Graphics and Infinite Terms	1568
	Graphics in Micro-Prolog	1639
Research/ PrologO: Turtle	Graphics in Micro-Prolog on the	1471
SeeLog: A Prolog	Graphics Interface	1714
with/ Temporal Logic Based	Hardware and its Verification	1591
Implementation Of The Personal/	Hardware Design And	1250
the Correctness of Digital	Hardware Designs Proving	1479
Proving Correctness of Digital	Hardware Designs /A Program for	1480
Efficient Synthesis/ Specifying	Hardware In Temporal Logic &	1592
to the Design of Software and	Hardware Objects /Language	1472
Design and Analysis A	Hardware Unification Unit:	586
/Verification of Complex Computer	Hardware Using Concurrent Prolog	1366
	Hardware Verification	1683
	Horn Clause Computability	493
Definition of/ An Extension to	Horn Clause Logic Allowing the	1340
A Control Regime for	Horn Clause Logic Programs	147
Goal Selection Strategies in	Horn Clause programming	201
Controlling Backtrack in	Horn Clause Programming	320
Parallel Execution of	Horn Clause Programs	1240
Parallel Execution Scheme for	Horn Clause Programs /AND/OR	1325
Recursive Functions	Horn Clause Programs for	1734
by Recursive Function	Horn Clause Programs Suggested	457
/Backtracking and Sidetracking in	Horn Clause Programs: The/	791
/Backtracking and Sidetracking in	Horn Clause Programs: The Theory	412
Generalizations	Horn Clause Queries and	160
Specifying Concurrency A	Horn Clause-Like Logic For	1345
Formal Semantics of Extended	Horn Clauses /Logic Programming:	1305
Formal Semantics of Generalized	Horn Clauses /Axiomatics and	227
Semantic Representations using	Horn Clauses Mapping Between	2272
Order Inductive Properties in	Horn Clauses On Proving First	281
Dependencies	Horn Clauses And Data Base	1983
Dependencies	Horn Clauses and Database	1985
The denotational semantics of	Horn Clauses as a Production/	612
/Theorem Prover for Negations of	Horn Clauses Based on/	1049
Translating	Horn Clauses From English	2274
On the Fixed Point Semantic of	Horn Clauses with Infinite Terms	226
in Recursive First-Order	Horn Databases /of Resolvents	271

Satisfiability of Propositional	Horn Formulae /for Testing the	196
Science: Initial Structures/ Why	Horn Formulas Matter in Computer	347
The Generalized Completeness of	Horn Predicate Logic as a/	93
Input and Unit Deductions for	Horn Sentences /Combination for	517
/for a Class Consisting of	Horn Sentences and Some Non-Horn/	516
Renaming a Set of Clauses as a	Horn Set	327
a Set of Clauses into the	Horn Set /Algorithm for Renaming	483
Semantic Resolution For	Horn Sets	273
LM-Prolog: The Language and Its	Implementation	1022
Logical Specification And	Implementation	1081
LOGLISP: Motivation, Design and	Implementation	1115
Prolog-C	Implementation	661
IC-Prolog Aspects of its	implementation	688
backtracking: data structure and	implementation /of exhaustive	761
in Horn Clause Programs: The	Implementation /and Sidetracking	791
Applied Logic - Its Use and	Implementation as Programming/	1784
Investigation LISP	Implementation Baseline	1124
Prolog: The Language and its	Implementation Compared with/	831
Nouvelle	Implementation De Metalog	1041
Nouvelle	Implementation de MetaLog	195
Prolog /Their Specification and	Implementation in Concurrent	1364
MYCIN: The Expert System and Its	Implementation in LOGLISP	1099
/Logic Elements and Its	Implementation in Prolog	1613
Graph-Theoretic Approach and Its	Implementation in Prolog /A	1634
Prolog /Language: a Theory and	Implementation in the Case of	307
Sense Reasoning Programs	Implementation Issues in Common	713
Some Reflections on	Implementation Issues of Prolog	663
Systems	Implementation Issues of Prolog	670
Waterloo Prolog	Implementation Manual	681
Theoretical Foundations/ On the	Implementation Methods and the	103
Acquisition/ A Methodology for	Implementation of a Knowledge	1869
on a Small Machine A Prolog	Implementation of a Large System	794
Independent Prolog	Implementation of a Machine	666
/to Structure-Sharing in the	Implementation of a Prolog/	764
Prolog Machine Design and	Implementation of a Sequential	690
Types Specified By/ Automatic	Implementation Of Abstract Data	1630
Prolog Based on/ A Sequential	Implementation of Concurrent	1338
Prolog using Message Passing	Implementation of Concurrent	1386
Logic Programming/ On the	Implementation of Control in	709
Data-Independent/ EXPERT - The	Implementation of	1928
Concurrent Prolog Design and	Implementation of Flat	1337
Hyper-resolution An	Implementation of	1104
Functional Grammar A Prolog	Implementation of Lexical	2238
Programming on HEP	Implementation of Logic	1352
Languages for Databases	Implementation of Logical Query	2100
The Transputer	Implementation of OCCAM	1228
An	Implementation of Prolog	801
An	Implementation of Prolog in C	707
Query-By-Example A Prolog	Implementation of	1470
Knuth-Rendix Reduction/ A Prolog	Implementation of the	1686

Inference/ The Design and	Implementation of the Personal	 841
Sequential/ Hardware Design And	Implementation Of The Personal	. . . 1250
Data Base Engine Design And	Implementation Of The Relational	. . . 1241
Prolog Environment Design and	Implementation of the Waterloo	 680
Cyclic Structures Efficient	Implementation of Unification of	. . . 269
Knowledge-Representation/ The	Implementation of Uniform: A	 1067
The	Implementation of UNSW-Prolog	. . . 804
Prolog-Based Knowledge Bases on/	Implementation of Very Large	 2011
Prolog An	implementation of Waterloo UNIX	. . . 778
Tail/ An Improved Prolog	Implementation which Optimises	. . . 829
in Recursive/ Representing	Infinite Sequences of Resolvents	 271
Logic Programming Graphics and	Infinite Terms	 1568
and Inequations on Finite and	Infinite Terms Equations	 175
Semantic of Horn Clauses with	Infinite Terms /the Fixed Point	. . . 226
Efficient Unification Over	Infinite Terms	 288
Prolog Interpreter Working with	Infinite Terms A	 710
Efficient Unification With	Infinite Terms In Logic/	 356
Manipulation Using Prolog's	Infinite Trees /and Grammar	 249
A Unification Algorithm for	Infinite Trees	 389
Prolog and	Infinite Trees	 695
in Prolog	Infinite Trees and Inequalities	 693
Parallel Computer for Artificial	Intelligence /of DADO, A Large	. . . 1247
Methodology, and Artificial	Intelligence /Programming	 1644
Robot	Intelligence	 1719
Business Artificial	Intelligence Applications for	 1907
Equations: An Artificial	Intelligence Approach /Algebraic	. . . 1789
/Administration by Artificial	Intelligence Based Computer/	 1829
/Engineering and Artificial	Intelligence in New Generation/	 1178
/of Theorem Proving Based Machine	Intelligence in Qsar	 1551
Machines Artificial	Intelligence Language and	 1012
/Applications of an Artificial	Intelligence Language Prolog	 1599
Machines are/ Artificial	Intelligence LISP and Prolog	 757
System Based on Artificial	Intelligence Methods /Simulation	. . . 1606
Design Of/ Using Artificial	Intelligence Techniques In The	 1501
and Applications Artificial	Intelligence: Tools, Techniques	 1710
What Should Artificial	Intelligence Want from the Super/	. . 1213
pour un Editeur de Textes	Intelligent /Textuelles	 2260
Databases An	Intelligent Access to Relational	. . . 1991
Backtracking Possibilities for/	Intelligent and Programmable	 1596
/Combinatorial Search Problems by	Intelligent Backtracking	 149
/Logical Reasoning Through	Intelligent Backtracking	 150
Deductive Revision by	Intelligent Backtracking	 151
Finding Backtrack Points for	Intelligent Backtracking	 179
Deduction plans: A Basis for	Intelligent Backtracking	 181
An Algorithm for	Intelligent Backtracking	 452
Sidetracking in Horn Clause/	Intelligent Backtracking and	 791
Sidetracking in Horn Clause/	Intelligent Backtracking and	 412
Annotated/ AND-Parallelism with	Intelligent Backtracking for	 1335
Automated Deduction in FOL	Intelligent Backtracking for	 358
Unification Graphs for	Intelligent Backtracking in/	 193

Integrity Constraints	Intelligent Control Using	306
AIDS An	Intelligent Database System:	1986
Computing	Intelligent Educational	1796
Retrieval: An Interesting/	Intelligent Information	1800
Interface	Intelligent Man-Machine	1771
In Portugese Language An	Intelligent Monitor Interaction	2193
Design An	Intelligent Router for VLSI	1500
/of Textual Structures for an	Intelligent Text-Editing System	2261
	Intelligent UNIX Shell project	1618
Compiler for Assertions: An	Introduction /An Incremental	1044
Prolog: A Tutorial	Introduction	70
Prolog: An	Introduction for Teachers	24
Measure for Control of Design/	Introduction of a Complexity	1647
Base Systems An	Introduction To Deductive Data	2028
A Short	Introduction to Expert Systems	1819
Databases An Overview and	Introduction to Logic and	1997
Programming An	Introduction to Logic	14
Programming	Introduction To Logic	39
An	Introduction to MU-Prolog	59
An	Introduction to Prolog	74
Programming	Introduction to Relational	344
Extension for Handling Negative	Knowledge A Prolog	1150
for Representing Real World	Knowledge /of Data Structures	1529
Study in Computer Utilization of	Knowledge /Advice: A Case	1574
A Logical Model of	Knowledge	1703
the Machine Representation of	Knowledge /Data Model for	1846
Approach to Geological	Knowledge A Rule-Based	1860
Data Management System From	Knowledge /A Knowledge-Based . . .	1935
as a Representation of	Knowledge Logic Programming	2282
Issues in the Representation of	Knowledge /Change:	2312
Expert System =	Knowledge + Meta-Interpreter	1929
Problem Solving =	Knowledge + Strategy	2283
Making Decisions in Mechanics/	Knowledge about Knowledge:	1519
Inference	Knowledge Acquisition and Meta . . .	1873
Representation Using Logic, Set/	Knowledge Acquisition and	1804
Programming	Knowledge Acquisition in Logic	1848
/for Implementation of a	Knowledge Acquisition System	1860
A Method of Realizing a	Knowledge Acquisition System	1874
A Logical Model of	Knowledge and Belief	1704
On First-Order Reasoning about	Knowledge and Belief	2278
/A Practical Amalgam of	Knowledge and Data Base/	2016
Prolog/ Amalgamation of Object	Knowledge and Meta Knowledge by . .	1180
A Method of Realizing a	Knowledge Assimilation Mechanism . .	1868
for Logic Databases A	Knowledge Assimilation Method	1885
for Logic Databases A Proposed	Knowledge Assimilation Method	2044
An Inferential Fuzzy Logic	Knowledge Base	1805
Shell for Representing a Medical	Knowledge Base) /Expert System . . .	1859
Automatic Construction of a	Knowledge Base by Analysing/	1589
	Knowledge Base Design	1826
Handbook A Text	Knowledge Base for the AI	2255

/Database Machine: First Step to	Knowledge Base Machine	1235
An Investigation for Building	Knowledge Base Machines	1941
Expert/ Database Management,	Knowledge Base Management and	1900
New Architecture for	Knowledge Base Mechanisms	1151
	Knowledge Base Mechanisms	1759
and Its Service/ Paradigms of	Knowledge Based Software System	1838
Diagnosis A	Knowledge Based System For Plant	1697
Prolog A Survey of	Knowledge Based Systems in	1830
Logic Programming Applied to	Knowledge Based Systems,/	1840
Development for Expert System	Knowledge Bases Concept	1911
of Explanations of Results From	Knowledge Bases /Generation	1936
van de Toekomst	Knowledge Bases: De Databanken	1190
/of Very Large Prolog-Based	Knowledge Bases on Data Flow/	2011
/Communicating Qualitative	Knowledge between Scientists and/	1748
Access to Specific Declarative	Knowledge by Expert Systems: The/	1933
/of Object Knowledge and Meta	Knowledge by Prolog and Its/	1180
Declarative/ Controlling	Knowledge Deduction in a	186
Dumb Drawing Systems and	Knowledge Engineering	1496
Fifth Generation Computers	Knowledge Engineering and the	1166
and Practice	Knowledge Engineering: Theory	2345
Language/ /Qualitative Biomedical	Knowledge Exactly Using the	1918
Expressing UNIX	Knowledge in LESK	1922
SIDUR-Structure Formalism For	Knowledge Information Processing	1653
Language: Shapeup	Knowledge Information Processing	1073
Systems Aiming for	Knowledge Information Processing	1163
Systems Challenge for	Knowledge Information Processing	1185
Implementing Dialogues in a	Knowledge Information System	2192
	Knowledge Inversion	981
Mechanics/ Knowledge about	Knowledge: Making Decisions in	1519
Practical Amalgam of Knowledge/	Knowledge Management: A	2016
CK-LOG: A Calculus for	Knowledge Processing in Logic	473
in the Logic-type/ Mandala:	Knowledge Programming and System	1169
based on Concurrent/ Mandala: A	Knowledge Programming Language	1309
Mandala: A Logic Based	Knowledge Programming System	1170
Bases for Expert Systems: An/	Knowledge Refinement in Rule	1932
/of OMEGA, a Logic for	Knowledge Representation	1005
/A Formal Semantics Approach to	Knowledge Representation	1878
Metalog: a language for	knowledge representation and/	1120
Inference Environment:KRINE, an/	Knowledge Representation And The	2323
Deductive Point of View	Knowledge Representation from a	121
Efficient Deductive Inference/	Knowledge Representation in an	2343
Prolog/KR	Knowledge Representation in	1097
Languages and Predicate/	Knowledge Representation	1722
Design in Many-Sorted Logic	Knowledge Representation of	1680
For Designing Expert/ LOOKS:	Knowledge Representation System	1691
in Prolog A	Knowledge Representation System	1930
Prolog/KR A	Knowledge Representation System:	1096
An Object Oriented Approach To	Knowledge Systems	1774
for Implementing Expert	Knowledge Systems /Extension	1924
/in Automatic Synthesis of Expert	Knowledge through Qualitative/	1698

A Logic Programming Language for Knowledge Utilization and/ 0
of the Equator or Concept Driven Learning The Discovery 1572
Two Techniques for Inductive Learning 2372
Memories: An Aid to Concept Learning Hierarchical 2377
Examples - A Progress Report Learning Algebraic Methods from . . . 1744
Experiments Learning Concepts by Performing . . . 2376
Methods from Worked Examples Learning Equation Solving 2384
Precondition Analysis: Learning Equation Solving/ 2386
Detective/ Computer Assisted Learning In History: BOGBOD, A . . . 1556
Experimental Learning Model 2355
Rules On the Automated Learning of Problem Solving 2371
Transformations Learning Operator 2375
Learning Problem Solving 2374
Proposal An Algebra Learning Program - Thesis 1745
A Critical Survey of Rule Learning Programs 1521
Comparison Of Some Rule Learning Programs An Analytical . . . 2364
Why Novices Will Find Learning Prolog Hard 77
En Prolog En Environnement Lisp LISLOG: Programmation 1017
A Logic Program Interpreter in LISP HCPRVR: 1027
Environment for Prolog in LISP QLOG - The Programming . . . 1072
A Prolog Interpreter written in LISP LP: 1084
Logic Programming in Lisp 1113
Prolog Compared with LISP 1440
A Pure Prolog Written in Pure Lisp 1642
Prolog System Written in LISP /Prolog: An Experimental . . . 711
Prolog versus LISP 78
its Implementation Compared with LISP Prolog: The Language and . . . 831
Prolog Compared with LISP ? 1451
The APPLOG Language: Prolog vs. LISP -- If you Can't Fight them/ . . . 1033
technique Embedding Prolog in LISP: an example of a LISP craft . . . 1071
Artificial Intelligence LISP and Prolog Machines are/ 757
Prolog in LISP: an example of a LISP craft technique Embedding . . . 1071
Prolog (for Semantics) in a LISP Environment /Syntax) and . . . 1138
Un Mariage Heureux Entre LISP et Prolog: Le Systeme/ 1056
Investigation LISP Implementation Baseline 1124
How To Implement Prolog On a Lisp Machine 1645
New Prolog Runs on LISP Machine 80
A Microcoded Unifier for Lisp Machine Prolog 677
Unique Features of Lisp Machine Prolog 733
A LISP Machine to Implement Prolog . . 1238
(Re)Implementing Prolog in LISP or YAQ - Yet Another QLISP . . 1021
A Partial Evaluator of Lisp Programs Written in Prolog . . . 1641
Thoughts on Prolog Design by a LISP User Exeter Prolog: Some 712
with Full First-Order Logic Programming 1018
First Order Programming Logic 1025
A Model Theory of Programming Logic 1065
Logic Programs and Many-Valued Logic 1091
for Extended Programming in Logic EPILOG: A Language 1107
A Narrative Schema in Procedural Logic 1130
Processes in First-Order Logic Applicative Communication . . . 114

PARLOG: Parallel Programming in	Logic	. . . .	1159
of VLSI Circuit in Temporal	Logic	Description and Reasoning . . .	1215
Concurrent Execution of	Logic	. . . .	1274
Programming in Predicate	Logic	Parallel	1276
Concurrent	Logic	. . . .	1293
Concurrent Problems Based on	Logic	/New Method for Describing . .	1294
about Programs in Amalgamated	Logic	Reasoning	132
Interpreter for Distributed	Logic	A Small	1342
New Presentation of Distributed	Logic	A	1343
for Distributed Programming in	Logic	A Proposal	1347
A Computational	Logic	. . . .	139
and LUCID Style Programming in	Logic	DataFlow, Flowcharts	142
On Embedding Function in	Logic	. . . .	1461
for the Mathematical	Logic	Software Applications	1476
a Decidable Subset of Default	Logic	A Theorem-Prover for	1495
A Resolution Principle in Modal	Logic	. . . .	158
with Prolog and Temporal	Logic	Verification	1590
Micro-Prolog: Programming in	Logic	. . . .	16
Prolog based on Mathematical	Logic	/the Programming Language . .	1675
Design in	Logic	. . . .	1679
of Design in Many-Sorted	Logic	Knowledge Representation . . .	1680
of ASPLE Using Predicate	Logic	A Formal Definition	1694
Languages Using Predicate	Logic	/of Programming	1695
for Doing Lazy Evaluation in	Logic	A Technique	1700
A Decision Method for Process	Logic	. . . .	1753
Programming Law in	Logic	. . . .	1864
Prolog-ELF Incorporating Fuzzy	Logic	. . . .	1867
of Machine-Oriented Deductive	Logic	Fundamentals	1909
Language, Computer Language and	Logic	/Synthesizing Natural	1919
Systems Development Through	Logic	On Database	1972
Database and Propositional	Logic	/in a Relational	1984
A New Approach to Database	Logic	. . . .	2026
Data Base System Based on	Logic	/Experimental Relational	2033
Programming with Resolution	Logic	. . . .	205
and a Subset of Propositional	Logic	/Database Dependencies	2082
Programming in Resolution	Logic	. . . .	210
Database Queries Expressed in	Logic	/of Interactive Relational	2104
About Natural	Logic	. . . .	2150
Spanish into Logic Through	Logic	Translating	2158
Questioning English with Clausal	Logic	. . . .	2191
for Writing Grammars in	Logic	Some Techniques	2222
Semantic Networks with Clausal	Logic	Relating Sentences and	2256
Parser Based on Predicate	Logic	A Bottom-Up	2264
Program Synthesis in Predicate	Logic	. . . .	278
System for First-Order	Logic	/Improved Theorem-Proving . .	311
Chaotic Semantics of Programming	Logic	. . . .	322
in the Semantics of Programming	Logic	Closures and Fairness	324
Programs in First Order	Logic	/of Recursive	361
Logic Control with	Logic	. . . .	408
for Knowledge Processing in	Logic	CK-LOG: A Calculus	473

Programming Language Predicate	Logic An Interpreter for the	489
from a Specification in	Logic /Unification Algorithms	510
Set Theoretic Interpretation for	Logic A	511
Sentences in Propositional	Logic /and Some Non-Horn	516
Programming in	Logic	56
Programming Language Based on	Logic On a High Level	75
Algorithms for Computational	Logic /Topics: Multiprocessing	755
Language Based on Predicate	Logic Prolog: A Very High Level	76
Logic Program Control in	Logic	87
Software Tools for First Order	Logic	873
Designed in First Order	Logic Evaluating Functions	89
with Full First-Order	Logic /Experiment in Programming	993
Algorithm =	Logic + Control	47
Specifying Hardware In Temporal	Logic & Efficient Synthesis Of/	1592
Implementation as/ Applied	Logic - Its Use and	1784
Tool Based on Mathematical	Logic - T-Prolog A Modelling	1611
Papers on Computational	Logic 1957-1966 /1: Classical	469
Papers on Computational	Logic 1967-1970 /2: Classical	470
Programs Predicate	Logic: A Calculus for Deriving	167
Specifying/ Distributed	Logic: A Logical System for	1339
Bases Predicate	Logic: A New Basis For Data	2012
	Logic Across the Curriculum	1580
An Extension to Horn Clause	Logic Allowing the Definition of/	1340
	Logic and Databases	1996
An Overview and Introduction to	Logic and Databases	1997
Approach	Logic and Databases: A Deductive	1999
can Link Diverse Subjects with	Logic and Fun Prolog	889
On the Relationship between	Logic and Functional Languages	1112
An(other) Integration of	Logic and Functional Programming	1134
	Logic and Programming	27
Methodologies	Logic and Programming	882
	Logic and Protocol Verification	1740
	Logic and Semantic Networks	1558
Principle Fuzzy	Logic and the Resolution	326
Formalism Predicate	Logic as a Computational	860
	Logic as a Computer Language	52
Children	Logic as a Computer Language for	50
Children - Term Two	Logic as a Computer Language for	886
Children: A One Year Course	Logic as a Computer Language for	23
Schools Teaching	Logic as a Computer Language in	1578
	Logic as a Database Language	2023
First-Order Predicate	Logic as a High-Level/	204
Programming Predicate	Logic as a Language for Parallel	1304
/of the Semantics of Predicate	Logic as a Programming Language	125
The Semantics of Predicate	Logic as a Programming Language	215
Predicate	Logic as a Programming Language	45
/Completeness of Horn Predicate	Logic as a Programming Language	93
Semantics of/ A Synchronization	Logic: Axiomatics and Formal	227
System A	Logic Based Chemical Information	1546
Verification with/ Temporal	Logic Based Hardware and its	1591

Programming System Mandala: A	Logic Based Knowledge	1170
Processing	Logic Based Natural Language	2248
description and two/ A predicate	logic based on indefinite	1004
Principle A Machine-Oriented	Logic Based on the Resolution	438
	Logic Based Program Design	844
Predicting Drug Interactions A	Logic Based Program System for	1550
and Its Applications for/	Logic Based Programming Method	1677
for Control of Design Errors in	Logic Based Programs /Measure	1647
Method LDM - A	Logic Based Software Development	988
/Signal Flow Model for Sequential	Logic Built from Combinatorial/	1613
Texts /English Text with Clausal	Logic: Case Studies of Three	2262
Prolog	Logic Circuit Synthesis Using	1777
Programming To Fault Finding In	Logic Circuits /of Meta-Level	2397
	Logic Control with Logic	408
How Should Clauses in a	Logic Data Base be Indexed	827
and Co-Operativeness In A	Logic Data Base System Security	2053
Approach to Co-operativeness in	Logic Data Bases An	2056
to Handle Time and Negation in	Logic Data Bases/ /Interpreter	2051
Security and Integrity in	Logic Data Bases using QB r	2107
and Select Operators in a	Logic Database Using/ /Aggregate	2052
Parallel Query Processing in	Logic Databases	1288
Assimilation Method for	Logic Databases A Knowledge	1885
Assimilation Method for	Logic Databases /Knowledge	2044
Databases	Logic Databases versus Deductive	1994
Prolog-based Expert System for	Logic Design	1881
/Logic Built from Combinatorial	Logic Elements and Its/	1613
Extending Logic Programming/	Logic Enhancement: A Method for	1569
	Logic for Compiler Writing	1785
DAL- A	Logic For Data Analysis	228
	Logic for Data Description	1656
	Logic For Expert Systems	1871
Checking in Relational/	Logic for Improving Integrity	2059
and Completeness of OMEGA, a	Logic for Knowledge/ Consistency	1005
Analysis	Logic for Natural Language	2225
Computer/ A Three-Valued	Logic for Natural Language	2157
Quantification in a Three-Valued	Logic for Natural Language/	2156
	Logic for Problem Solving	1657
Reference Mutual Belief	Logic for Processing Definite	2129
Expertise	Logic For Representing Data And	1862
A Horn Clause-Like	Logic For Specifying Concurrency	1345
Mechanization of Deductive/	Logic: Form and Function - The	442
Current Trends in	Logic Grammars	2160
Treating Coordination in	Logic Grammars	2163
Complete NP-Structures and	Logic Grammars	2175
Semantic Interpretation Rules in	Logic Grammars /Problem, and	2201
Modular	Logic Grammars	2203
Ambiguity in	Logic Grammars	2224
for Handling Coordination in	Logic Grammars A Meta-Grammar	2249
to Represent Meaning in	Logic Grammars /Lambda-Calculus	2271
Using Slots and Modifiers in	Logic Grammars for Natural/	2202

the Application of Mathematical	Logic in Computer Techniques On	1766
Programs from Examples A	Logic in Which One Learns	2352
	Logic Information Processing	490
and Negation in Logic Data/ A	Logic Interpreter to Handle Time	2051
An Inferential Fuzzy	Logic Knowledge Base	1805
An Architecture of Parallel	Logic Languages	1208
Unification of Functional and	Logic Languages The	185
Databases Interfacing Predicate	Logic Languages and Relational	1961
Inference Mechanisms - Layer 2/	Logic Machine Architecture	1227
Kernel Functions	Logic Machine Architecture:	1226
Some Aspects of a	Logic Machine Prototype	1217
Reasoning	Logic Modelling of Cognitive	1624
Database: A/ The Description in	Logic of a Large Commercial	1557
A Computational	Logic of Default Reasoning	1906
Impacts of	Logic on Data Bases	1993
for the OR-Parallel Execution of	Logic Progams /Architecture	1205
for OR-Parallel Execution of	Logic Progams Storage Models	1206
for OR-Parallel Execution of	Logic Progams Formal Models	1278
The British Nationality Act As A	Logic Program	1541
The Control Component of a	Logic Program	165
of DHSS Regulations as a	Logic Program Representation	1855
	Logic Program Control in Logic	87
LISP HCPRVR: A	Logic Program Interpreter in	1027
Numerical Integration	Logic Program Specification of	1532
Transformational	Logic Program Synthesis	453
A Fact Dependency System for the	Logic Programmer	1764
Static Type Checking in	Logic Programming /Declarative	100
of Adapting Resolution for	Logic Programming /Method	101
a uniform mechanism for	logic programming /Deduction:	1036
for List Processing and	Logic Programming /Environment	1061
- The Software for Prolog and	Logic Programming QLOG	1070
Algebra as a Typed Language for	Logic Programming /Relational	1087
Programming in the Style of	Logic Programming Functional	1110
A Prolog/LISP Type Language for	Logic Programming Qute:	1117
for Integrating Functional and	Logic Programming /Strategies	1136
/A Constructive Methodology In	Logic Programming	116
/and Abstraction in	Logic Programming	1168
Stream-Based Execution of	Logic Programming	1223
the Negation By Failure Rule in	Logic Programming /Notions for	126
Concurrent	Logic Programming	1318
Language and Metalanguage in	Logic Programming Amalgamating	134
Parallelism and Coroutining in	Logic Programming /Semantics of	1353
An Introduction to	Logic Programming	14
Types, Modules and Generics for	Logic Programming Equality,	1438
A Semantic Theory for	Logic Programming	144
	Logic Programming	1533
Incorporating Mutable Arrays in	Logic Programming	1584
System In The Framework of	Logic Programming /Expert	1691
Papers in	Logic Programming	1767
Teaching	Logic Programming	1788

Knowledge Acquisition in	Logic Programming	1848
Expert Systems Builders in	Logic Programming Developing	1897
by Expert Systems: The Impact of	Logic Programming /Knowledge . . .	1933
of Adjective Phrases in	Logic Programming /and Semantics . .	2245
W-Grammars for	Logic Programming	2263
Management Applications of	Logic Programming	2279
A Control Metalanguage for	Logic Programming	2398
Metalevel Control for	Logic Programming	2399
Cuttable Formulas for	Logic Programming	247
as a Complexity Measure for	Logic Programming Unification	287
Control Strategies for	Logic Programming	297
Foundations of	Logic Programming	329
Foundations Of	Logic Programming	331
and the Algebraic Semantics of	Logic Programming /Set of Trees . . .	353
With Infinite Terms In	Logic Programming /Unification . . .	356
Introduction To	Logic Programming	39
From Logic to	Logic Programming	445
The Practice of	Logic Programming	859
An Environment for	Logic Programming	896
Contributions to the Theory of	Logic Programming	95
and Trends for the Future of	Logic Programming Problems	974
Tool for the Architect of the/	Logic Programming - A Computing . .	1762
Approach	Logic Programming: A Parallel	1302
of E.Y./ Error Diagnosis in	Logic Programming, An Adaptation . .	1587
Interactive Approach Teaching	Logic Programming: An	1787
Dedicated High-Performance/	Logic Programming and a	1799
/to Diagnostics: Applications of	Logic Programming and Cutset/ . . .	1571
On Integrating	Logic Programming and Databases . .	1957
	Logic Programming and Databases . .	2066
On the Integration of	Logic Programming and Functional/ . .	1008
/Computational Model Integrating	Logic Programming and Functional/ . .	1135
Definition	Logic Programming and Inductive . . .	257
Applications	Logic Programming and Its	1525
processing	Logic programming and parallel	1296
Verification: Advances and/	Logic Programming and Program . . .	1631
Databases	Logic Programming and Relational . .	1956
of Key Distribution Protocols	Logic Programming and Validation . .	1741
Knowledge Based Systems,/	Logic Programming Applied to	1840
Natural Language Semantics: A	Logic Programming Approach	2235
Representation of Knowledge	Logic Programming as a	2282
Case of a Civil Engineering/	Logic Programming at Work: The . . .	1538
Natural Deduction System	Logic Programming Based on a	267
Inductive/ Foundation Of	Logic Programming Based on	258
A Mathematical Formalism for	Logic Programming Based on the/ . . .	379
	Logic Programming by Completion . .	1040
/Of A Unification Algorithm In a	Logic Programming Calculus	219
/of the First International	Logic Programming Conference	1524
Applicative Programming	Logic Programming Cum	191
Shell	Logic Programming Engineering	923
MYCIN in a	Logic Programming Environment . . .	1100

/A Relational Database with   Logic Programming Facilities   1955
Generalized Data Management/   Logic Programming for a   1943
APL Using   Logic Programming for Compiling   . . . 1560
Constructive Expert Database/ Logic Programming for   1821
Systems   Logic Programming for Expert   1851
Systems: A Two Day Course   Logic Programming For Expert   1509
Functional Programming and   Logic Programming for Telegram/   . . . 1462
Generation   Logic Programming for the Fifth   . . . 1177
                               Logic Programming for the Law   1916
Semantics of/ Synchronization in Logic Programming: Formal   1305
Infinite Terms   Logic Programming Graphics and   . . . 1568
Information Handling and Drug/ Logic Programming in Chemical   1547
                               Logic Programming in DADM   1068
                               Logic Programming in Lisp   1113
                               Logic Programming in NIAL   1052
of Production Control Systems Logic Programming in the Design   . . . 1674
Modelling of Machine Ports   Logic Programming in the   1673
Some Practical Properties of   Logic Programming Interpreters   143
Graph-Based   Logic Programming Interpreters   720
Design   Logic Programming is NOT Circuit   . . 20
A Note On The Set Abstraction In Logic Programming Language   1000
A Functional plus Predicate   Logic Programming Language   1010
Some Features of A New   Logic Programming Language   1050
Language Features of LPL, A   Logic Programming Language   1058
A Set-Oriented Predicate   Logic Programming Language   1088
DELTA-Prolog: A Distributed   Logic Programming Language   1105
SNePSLOG: A Higher Order   Logic Programming Language   1128
PARLOG: A Parallel   Logic Programming Language   1282
/Data Types Specified By The   Logic Programming Language   1630
Programming Law: LEGOL as a   Logic Programming Language   1913
Properties of a   Logic Programming Language   261
Prolog as a   Logic Programming Language   48
/Stream/Array Processing In   Logic Programming Language   992
Knowledge Utilization and/ A   Logic Programming Language for   . . .   0
Interpreter Based on/ SLOG: A Logic Programming Language   714
Prolog with/ A Comparison of the Logic Programming Language   349
Scheme A   Logic Programming Language   1443
a Reducibility/ Semantics of a Logic Programming Language with   . . 486
Functions, Types/ RF-Maple: A Logic Programming Language with   . . 1140
Combination of Functional and Logic Programming Languages The   . . 1046
/Copying in Functional and   Logic Programming Languages   . . .   1441
/A Method for Extending   Logic Programming Languages   1569
/Unification Applicable to   Logic Programming Languages   2195
the Implementation of Control in Logic Programming Languages On   . . 709
Case Study A Comparison of Two Logic Programming Languages: A   . . . 1137
A Model Theory of   Logic Programming Methodology   . . .   1758
Modular   Logic Programming of Compilers   . . .   899
Implementation of   Logic Programming on HEP   1352
machine   Logic Programming on the FFP   1133
Highly Parallel Machine   Logic Programming on ZMOB: A   . . .   1204

and Future	Logic Programming: Past, Present	. . . 69
An Overview of the HORNE	Logic Programming System	 1045
PARALOG: A Parallel	Logic Programming System	 1349
/Predicate Calculus As A	Logic Programming System	 455
/Measurement of the Parallel	Logic Programming System PARALOG	1268
History Teaching Applying	Logic Programming Techniques To	. . 1507
Associative Operations	Logic Programming Using Parallel	. . . 1372
/Access to Databases from a	Logic Programming Viewpoint	 2268
Bring To Software Engineering ?	Logic Programming: What Does It	. . . 933
Proceedings of the 1980	Logic Programming Workshop,/	 1772
for Proving Properties of	Logic Programs /Technique	 105
Proving Properties of	Logic Programs	 106
Concurrent Evaluation of	Logic Programs Associative	 1093
for Parallel Interpretation of	Logic Programs /Model	 1203
for Parallel Interpretation of	Logic Programs /Process Model	. . . 1285
Parallel Interpretation of	Logic Programs	 1287
AND Parallelism in	Logic Programs	 1289
and Nondeterminism in	Logic Programs AND Parallellism	. . . 1290
for Or-Parallel Execution of	Logic Programs A Formal Model	. . . 1315
Backtracking for Annotated	Logic Programs /with Intelligent	. . . 1335
Parallel Execution of	Logic Programs	 1376
Loop Trapping in	Logic Programs	 141
Semantics of	Logic Programs	 1448
A Control Regime for Horn Clause	Logic Programs	 147
to Improve the Behaviour of	Logic Programs /of Dependencies	. . . 148
Computer-based Synthesis of	Logic Programs	 1582
Properties of Non-Terminating	Logic Programs /to Proving	 163
Symmetry For The Derivation of	Logic Programs Using	 1638
Synthesis and Verification of	Logic Programs The	 166
for Representing the Law as	Logic Programs Prospects	 1736
A Query-The-User Facility for	Logic Programs	 1737
Trees and Transformation of	Logic Programs Computation	 1754
Production Systems and	Logic Programs Relational	 1889
Expert System Builders in	Logic Programs Developing	 1895
of Fair Computations of	Logic Programs /Semantics	 218
Tree Automata and	Logic Programs	 231
Deductive Synthesis of	Logic Programs	 276
Goal-Oriented Derivation of	Logic Programs	 277
A Primitive for the Control of	Logic Programs	 296
Unification-Free Execution of	Logic Programs	 308
Optimal Fixedpoints of	Logic Programs	 323
the Computational Complexity of	Logic Programs A Note on	 328
A Dataflow Interpreter for	Logic Programs	 384
Most Specific	Logic Programs	 394
an Algebra for Constructing	Logic Programs Towards	 399
Selective backtracking for	logic programs	 413
Process Specification Of	Logic Programs	 426
of Success Patterns in	Logic Programs Enumeration	 454
the Computational Complexity of	Logic Programs Alternation and	. . . 458
Computer-Based Synthesis of	Logic Programs	 462

Invertibility of	Logic Programs	465
Transformations of	Logic Programs	476
Specification and Derivation of	Logic Programs	478
Unfold/Fold Transformation of	Logic Programs	488
From Equational Programs Into	Logic Programs /Transformation . . .	497
of Resolution Strategies for	Logic Programs /Treatment	512
Unification Scheme for Systolic	Logic Programs A Distributed . . .	580
the Compilation of Annotated	Logic Programs Towards	723
Prolog - Compiling Predicate	Logic Programs. Implementing	826
Derivation of	Logic Programs	911
Generation of Control for	Logic Programs Automatic	950
Automating Control for	Logic Programs	953
Rational Debugging of	Logic Programs	964
An Interpreter for Predicate	Logic Programs : Part 1	659
Proposal Efficient	Logic Programs: A Research	870
Grammers Relating	Logic Programs and Attribute	190
Logic	Logic Programs and Many-Valued . . .	1091
Deduction Evaluation of	Logic Programs Based on Natural . . .	268
Modelling Data Dependencies in	Logic Programs by Attribute/	252
Relational Databases	Logic Programs for Querying	1982
Metacontrol of	Logic Programs in METALOG	1042
Programs Transformation of	Logic Programs into Functional	1111
Making Control and Data Flow of	Logic Programs More Explicit	984
Architecture Execution of	Logic Programs On A Dataflow	1202
Backtracking An Interpreter of	Logic Programs Using Selective	414
A Transformation System for	Logic Programs which Preserves/ . . .	1770
A Theory of Complete	Logic Programs With Equality	1442
/of the Static Semantics of	Logic Programs with Monadic/	590
Uncertainties: A Tool for/	Logic Programs With	1915
Concurrent Algorithm	Logic Representation of a	279
Digital	Logic Simulation in prolog	1632
Modeling Cooperative Problem/ A	Logic Simulation Language For	1311
Verification via Executable	Logic Specification Protocol	1742
Processes Against Temporal	Logic Specifications /Concurrent . . .	1273
Generating Correct Programs from	Logic Specifications	1554
Proof of Program/ Computational	Logic: Structure Sharing and	380
Computation Computational	Logic: the Unification	440
Translating Spanish into	Logic Through Logic	2158
From	Logic to Logic Programming	445
Tool Based on Mathematical	Logic: T-Prolog A Modelling	1610
	Logical Action Systems	423
Programming Language A Combined	Logical and Functional	1101
Integrity in Query-By-Example A	Logical Approach to Security and . . .	2055
A	Logical Approach to Simulation	1602
Proceedings of Workshop on	Logical Bases for Databases	2060
Automated Theorem Proving: A	Logical Basis	336
A	Logical Basis for Data Bases	2096
Assertion and Query The	Logical Basis of Programming by . . .	443
Financial Contracts CANDID: A	Logical Calculus for Describing	1877
On the Expressive Power of the	Logical Data Model	2027

On the Equivalence of	Logical Databases	2025
Systems The	Logical Definition of Deduction	2073
Interpreters	Logical Derivation Of Prolog	235
Natural Language Consultable/	Logical Design of Deductive	1970
Prolog: A Programming Tool for	Logical Domain Modelling	864
Reasoning Models within a	Logical Famework	1625
Problems in	Logical Form	381
Concurrency A	Logical Formalism for Specifying	1341
of Natural Language into	Logical Formulas Transformation	2124
to Integrity/ A Property of	Logical Formulas Corresponding	2058
A	Logical Foundation For Prolog II	291
Analysis in Large Databases	Logical Inference as an Aid to	2035
Solving	Logical Levels of Problem	2344
of the Semantic Features/ On a	Logical Method Serving the Proof	1473
A	Logical Model of Knowledge	1703
Belief A	Logical Model of Knowledge and	1704
The File System of a	Logical Operating System	1664
	Logical Program Synthesis	120
A	Logical Programming Language	98
The Meaning of	Logical Programs	359
Databases Implementation of	Logical Query Languages for	2100
The Declarative Semantics of	Logical Read-only Variables	1405
Revision of Top-Down	Logical Reasoning Through/	150
II A	Logical Reconstruction of Prolog	216
Relational Database/ Towards a	Logical Reconstruction of	2080
the IBM The	Logical Record Keeper: Prolog on	836
Implementation	Logical Specification And	1081
/Translation Grammars And The	Logical Specification Of Data/	2115
Cocurrency Distributed Logic: A	Logical System for Specifying	1339
Representation Problems	Logical Systems and	256
Motivated by Programming A	Logical Theory of Data Types	938
Functional Programming and the	Logical Variable	1447
Queue Operations Using the	Logical Variable /Functional	1535
Parsing with	Logical Variables	2174
LM-Prolog User	Manual	1023
ESP reference	manual	1030
Prolog/KR User's	Manual	1094
Theorem Prover (ITP) User's	Manual The Interactive	1121
- Layer 2 User Reference	Manual /Inference Mechanisms	1227
Micro-Prolog Reference	Manual	15
TUGA user's	manual	1536
Expert System Shell): A User	Manual APES (A Prolog	1852
APES: A User	Manual	1856
MU-Prolog 3.2db Reference	Manual	2047
Prolog Reference	Manual	29
T-Prolog User	Manual	30
Waterloo Unix Prolog Reference	Manual	34
Programmer's Reference	Manual Micro-Prolog,	57
Waterloo Prolog Implementation	Manual	681
Decsystem-10 Prolog User's	Manual	7

Prolog II -	Manual d'Utilisation	11
Subsystem/ A Preliminary User's	Manual of Debugging and Trace . . .	746
BS2000 Prolog User's Reference	Manual V2.4	44
C-Prolog User's	Manual Version 1.1	62
C Prolog User's	Manual Version 1.2	63
TPROLOG User	Manual Version 4.2	31
The HC	Manual: Virginia Tech prolog	68
Synchronisation in T-Prolog	Meta Control of process	1607
Predicate Simulate for Parallel	Meta Inference /- Meta	1181
Knowledge Acquisition and	Meta Inference	1873
Applications - Meta Predicate/	Meta Inference and Its	1181
/of Object Knowledge and	Meta Knowledge by Prolog and Its/ . .	1180
/Inference and Its Applications -	Meta Predicate Simulate for/	1181
The Personal Inference/ A	Microprogrammed Interpreter Of . . .	1148
Construction of a Data Driven	Model A Parallel Prolog: The	1144
on The Generalized Data Flow	Model /Prolog Interpreter Based . . .	1220
Power of the Logical Data	Model On the Expressive	2027
Experimental Learning	Model	2355
Model: A Deductive Data Base	Model The Partition	472
Model The Partition	Model: A Deductive Data Base	472
/Engine PIE - Goal Rewriting	Model and Machine Architecture . . .	1171
A Logic-Based Expert System for	Model Building in Regression/	1548
of Mechanics/ Mathematical	Model Building in the Solution	1670
Mechanical Theorem Proving by	Model Elimination	334
Theorem Provers Combining	Model Elimination And Resolution . . .	333
Implementations of/ A Formal	Model for Demand-Driven	1200
Correction A	Model for Error Detection and	1503
of a Prolog compatible/ A Formal	Model for Lazy Implementations . . .	111
of Logic Programs A Formal	Model for Or-Parallel Execution	1315
Interpretation of/ A Data-driven	Model for Parallel	1203
The AND/OR Process	Model for Parallel/	1285
A Specific QSAR	Model for Peptides	1553
from/ A Signal Flow	Model for Sequential Logic Built . . .	1613
DLOG: A Logic-Based Data	Model for the Machine/	1846
FUNLOG: A Computational	Model Integrating Logic/	1135
A Prolog-Based Framework for	Model Management	1949
A Logical	Model of Knowledge	1703
A Logical	Model of Knowledge and Belief	1704
ORBIT: a parallel computing	model of Prolog	1384
Programming Methodology A	Model Theory of Logic	1758
Logic A	Model Theory of Programming	1065
of Patterns From Abstract	Model to Efficient Compilation	703
Languages and Computational	Models /to Programming	285
of Logic Progams Storage	Models for OR-Parallel Execution . . .	1206
of Logic Progams Formal	Models for OR-Parallel Execution . . .	1278
Proving -/ Using Sophisticated	Models in Resolution Theorem	449
Formal Vienna Definition Method	Models of Prolog	397
Reasoning	Models within a Logical Famework . .	1625
Databases Non	Monotonic Reasoning and	130
of Logic Programs Based on	Natural Deduction Evaluation	268

Programming in a	Natural Deduction Framework	260
Logic Programming Based on a	Natural Deduction System	267
Programming Language Based on a	Natural Deduction System A	495
Program Reasoning A	Natural Deduction System For	262
Parallel Interpretation of	Natural Language	1354
Base by Analysing Texts in	Natural Language /of a Knowledge	1589
Resource Evaluation Through	Natural Language /Environmental	1902
Interrogation by Means of	Natural Language Database	1967
An Interesting Subset of	Natural Language	2146
Modifiers in Logic Grammars for	Natural Language /Slots and	2202
A Dialogue in	Natural Language	2221
for Computer Acquisition of	Natural Language /as a Basis	2237
Communicating with Databases in	Natural Language	2266
Databases from a/ Issues in	Natural Language Access to	2268
Prolog Database Systems	Natural Language Access to	2247
Logic for	Natural Language Analysis	2225
	Natural Language and Databases	1966
Answer and Reason Extraction,	Natural Language and Voice/	2216
/Clause Translation Grammars and	Natural Language Applications	2116
Programming in	Natural Language? At what Cost ?	2164
A Three-Valued Logic for	Natural Language Computer/	2157
LESK: A Language Synthesizing	Natural Language, Computer/	1919
Logical Design of Deductive	Natural Language Consultable/	1970
/Adaptable and Efficient	Natural Language Consultable/	2072
between a Program and/ Notes on	Natural Language Conversations	2135
A Prolog Way of Representing	Natural Language Fragments	2188
System A Prolog-Based	Natural Language Front-End	1684
A Kernel for a General	Natural Language Interface	2171
Polish Railway Expert Systems	Natural Language Interface for a	2194
Designing Transparant	Natural Language Interfaces for/	2242
Formulas Transformation of	Natural Language into Logical	2124
Syntax-Semantics Interaction in	Natural Language Parsing	2206
Logic Based	Natural Language Processing	2248
/System for Interpreting	Natural Language Queries	2270
Linguistic Database Using/	Natural Language Queries for a	2186
Role of Control Information in	Natural Language Question/ /the	2179
in a Three-Valued Logic for	Natural Language/ Quantification	2156
/for Automatically Generating	Natural Language Reports from/	1662
Logic Programming Approach	Natural Language Semantics: A	2235
the Semantic Representation of	Natural Language Sentences On	2232
/Using Logic, Set Theory and	Natural Language Structures	1804
Brief Description of Spiral: A	Natural Language Understanding/	2173
/in a Semantic Representation of	Natural Languages Sentences	2246
About	Natural Logic	2150
Towards the Provision of a	Natural Mechanism for Expressing/	1781
Compreensao de Linguagem	Natural por Computador: Uma/	2172
A	Natural Programming Calculus	1059
Automated Deduction in the/	Natural Question Answering and	2063
A System And When Is Failure A	Negation What Is Negation In	239
	Negation and Control in PROLOG	1092

Programs	Negation and Semantics of Prolog	450
	Negation as Failure	164
Comparison of Clark's Completed/	Negation As Failure: A	461
Parallellism	Negation as Failure and	1326
Completeness of the	Negation As Failure Rule	289
	Negation As Inconsistency	241
Two Completeness Notions for the	Negation By Failure Rule in/ /of	126
Failure A Negation What Is	Negation In A System And When Is	239
/Interpreter to Handle Time and	Negation in Logic Data Bases/	2051
Incorporating Naive	Negation into Prolog	1910
Two Solutions for the	Negation Problem	182
Knowledge by/ Amalgamation of	Object Knowledge and Meta	1180
Use of Metalanguage to Assemble	Object Level Programs and/ The	2402
Knowledge Systems An	Object Oriented Approach To	1774
Concurrent Prolog	Object Oriented Programming in	1365
Machine: From Sequential to	Parallel Inference	1264
Unification and other Complete/	Parallel Algorithms for	1377
/Based Execution Mechanisms of	Parallel and Concurrent Prolog	1320
Logic Programming: A	Parallel Approach	1302
Large Data Bases MPDC: Massive	Parallel Architecture for Very	1253
Logic Programming Using	Parallel Associative Operations	1372
Complexity Of Unification On	Parallel Computational	588
Reconfigurable General Purpose	Parallel Computer /A Dynamically	1224
/Applications of DADO, A Large	Parallel Computer for Artificial/	1247
Prolog ORBIT: a	parallel computing model of	1384
User-Defined	Parallel Control Strategies	901
Unification in a	Parallel Environment	817
/Reduction Machine for the	Parallel Evaluation of/	1209
Clause Programs	Parallel Execution of Horn	1240
Programs	Parallel Execution of Logic	1376
Horn/ A Process-Oriented AND/OR	Parallel Execution Scheme for	1325
Prolog Interpreter and its	Parallel Extension	1336
Goal Rewriting Model and/ Highly	Parallel Inference Engine PIE -	1171
The Architecture Of A	Parallel Inference Engine-PIE	1234
Problem Solving PRISM: A	Parallel Inference System for	1324
A Data-driven Model for	Parallel Interpretation of Logic/	1203
The AND/OR Process Model for	Parallel Interpretation of Logic/	1285
Programs	Parallel Interpretation of Logic	1287
Natural Language	Parallel Interpretation of	1354
Programs A Back-Up	Parallel Interpreter for Prolog	1307
An Architecture of	Parallel Logic Languages	1208
Language PARLOG: A	Parallel Logic Programming	1282
System PARALOG: A	Parallel Logic Programming	1349
Performance Measurement of the	Parallel Logic Programming/	1268
Programming on ZMOB: A Highly	Parallel Machine Logic	1204
/- Meta Predicate Simulate for	Parallel Meta Inference	1181
Coroutines and Networks of	Parallel Process	1323
Logic programming and	parallel processing	1296
A Relational Language for	Parallel Programming	1281
Applicative Language for Highly	Parallel Programming An	1300

Logic as a Language for	Parallel Programming Predicate	. . . 1304
of a simple language for	parallel programming /Semantics	. . . 1322
PARLOG:	Parallel Programming in Logic	 1159
Predicate Logic	Parallel Programming in	 1276
Based on The/ A Highly	Parallel Prolog Interpreter	 1220
Construction of a Data Driven/ A	Parallel Prolog: The	 1144
Segments on Shared-Memory Multi/	Parallel Prolog Using Stack	 1272
Assertion Set And	Parallel Prolog with Divided	 1350
Logic Databases	Parallel Query Processing in	 1288
/A Clause Representation for	Parallel Search	 1306
Prolog on the DADO Machine: A	Parallel System for High-Speed/	 1254
/and a New-principle Way Of	Parallel Systems, Description,/	 1368
Language In/ An Application of A	Parallel Systems Planning	 985
Logic/ The Semantics of	Parallelism and Coroutining in	 1353
AND	Parallelism in Logic Programs	 1289
and/ Knowledge Management: A	Practical Amalgam of Knowledge	. . . 2016
Language: Prolog	Practical Applications of an AI	 1549
Artificial Intelligence/	Practical Applications of an	 1599
Unification/ Description and	Practical Comparison of	 500
A	Practical Linear Algorithm	 109
Programming Interpreters Some	Practical Properties of Logic	 143
Prolog in	Practice	 1561
Engineering: Theory and	Practice Knowledge	 2345
The	Practice of Logic Programming	 859
for Telegram Analysis	Problem /and Logic Programming	. . 1462
a Long-Range Regional Planning	Problem Using T-Prolog for	 1609
A Prolog Program for the S-P	Problem	 1718
Two Solutions for the Negation	Problem	 182
Data Bases and the Null Value	Problem /Queries in Indefinite	 2002
Databases and the Null Value	Problem /Queries in Indefinite	 2003
of Horn/ The Satisfiability	Problem for a Class Consisting	 516
/of the Language Recognition	Problem for a Theorem Prover	 2217
/Investigations into the Decision	Problem For Relevant Logics: The/	. . 1085
A Solution to a CAD	Problem in Prolog	 1901
The Occur-Check	Problem in Prolog	 418
Chaining and Equality in/	Problem Representations for Back	. . . 420
A Forward Chaining	Problem Solver	 385
A Parallel Inference System for	Problem Solving PRISM:	 1324
Progress in Prolog-Based Robot	Problem Solving	 1487
Making Decisions in Mechanics	Problem Solving /Knowledge:	 1519
Discrete/Continuous Modeling and	Problem Solving Combined	 1598
Logic for	Problem Solving	 1657
Logical Levels of	Problem Solving	 2344
Learning	Problem Solving	 2374
of Theorem Proving to	Problem Solving Application	 253
Micro-Prolog For	Problem Solving	 54
Constraints for	Problem Solving	 853
Strategy	Problem Solving = Knowledge +	. . . 2283
Mechanisms	Problem Solving and Inference	 1165
Knowledge-Based	Problem Solving in AL3	 2354

/Simulation and	Problem Solving in TS-Prolog	1597
On the Automated Learning of	Problem Solving Rules	2371
• For Modeling Cooperative	Problem Solving System /Language	1311
Computer: Logo versus Prolog	Problem Solving with the	1665
/Simulation and Co-Operative	Problem Solvng on a Prolog Basis	1608
Relational Databases Directed by	Problem Specific Data /in	2029
Approach to the GUS Travel Agent	Problem Using Prolog An	1688
Object-Oriented Programming in	Prolog	1001
Une Extension de VLISP vers	Prolog LOVLISP:	1057
Equality for	Prolog	1074
Lambda	Prolog	1083
Negation and Control in	PROLOG	1092
The Versatility of	Prolog	110
LOGLISP: An Alternative to	Prolog	1114
Algebraic Abstract Data Types In	Prolog /To The Programming Of	117
A LISP Machine to Implement	Prolog	1238
des Structures du Controle de	Prolog Une Formalisation	124
en Iteration dans un Interprete	Prolog /de l'Appel Terminal	129
Quadtrees in Concurrent	Prolog	1301
Language based on Concurrent	Prolog /A Knowledge Programming	1309
Programming in Concurrent	Prolog A Note on Systems	1312
of Parallel and Concurrent	Prolog /Execution Mechanisms	1320
Chart Parsing in Concurrent	Prolog	1327
System (POPS) in Concurrent	Prolog /OR-Parallel Optimizing	1328
Merge in Shapiro's Concurrent	Prolog Bounded-Wait	1329
Process Reduction in Concurrent	Prolog Serialization of	1330
of Flat Concurrent	Prolog /and Implementation	1337
A Meta-Level Extension of	Prolog	135
Programming in Concurrent	Prolog Distributed	1358
Programming in Concurrent	Prolog Systems	1363
and Implementation in Concurrent	Prolog /Their Specification	1364
Programming in Concurrent	Prolog Object Oriented	1365
Hardware Using Concurrent	Prolog /of Complex Computer	1366
Communication in Concurrent	Prolog Interprocess	1369
Interpreter for Concurrent	Prolog /Design of a Distributed	1370
Manipulation in Concurrent	Prolog String	1375
for Prolog, Implemented in	PROLOG Coroutining Facilities	1379
a parallel computing model of	Prolog ORBIT:	1384
Lazy Enumerations in Concurrent	Prolog Eager and	1396
Algorithm For Concurrent	Prolog A Unification	1406
Problems with Concurrent	Prolog	1409
Algebraic Specification and	Prolog	1478
Teaching Mathematics with	Prolog	1506
How to Solve it with	Prolog	1537
How To Solve it with	Prolog	1539
Applications of an AI Language:	Prolog Practical	1549
A Detective Exercise Written In	Prolog /In History: BOGBOD,	1556
A Compiler Written in	Prolog	1566
Fixture Design by	Prolog	1585
Building Libraries in	Prolog	1588

and its Verification with	Prolog	/Logic Based Hardware	1591
Of State-diagrams Using	Prolog	/& Efficient Synthesis	1592
Artificial Intelligence Language	Prolog	/Applications of an	1599
and Its Implementation in	Prolog	/Logic Elements	1613
terms to embed descriptions in	Prolog	Using Hilbert	1617
Digital Logic Simulation in	prolog		1632
Handling of Bit Tables in	Prolog		1633
and Its Implementation in	Prolog	/Graph-Theoretic Approach	1634
Intermission - Actors in	Prolog		1640
of Lisp Programs Written in	Prolog	A Partial Evaluator	1641
with the Computer: Logo versus	Prolog	Problem Solving	1665
A Mycin-Like Expert System in	Prolog		1668
GUS Travel Agent Problem Using	Prolog	An Approach to the	1688
How to Define a Language Using	Prolog		1696
A Polymorphic Type System for	Prolog		1699
Programming in	Prolog		17
Trees and their Equations in	Prolog	Drawing	1715
et Realization d'un Systeme	Prolog	Etude	172
Les Bases Theoriques de	Prolog		173
Logic Circuit Synthesis Using	Prolog		1777
der Basis von Petri-Netzen und	Prolog	/Burosimulator auf	1791
	Prolog		18
Building an Expert System with	Prolog	An Experience of	1815
of Knowledge Based Systems in	Prolog	A Survey	1830
DNA Sequence Analysis System in	Prolog	BIOLOG - A	1880
Sistemas Periciais e	Prolog	/do Conhecimento:	1896
Tour of	Prolog		19
and Expert System Development in	Prolog	/Base Management	1900
A Solution to a CAD Problem in	Prolog		1901
Apple Orchard Management Using	Prolog	/Consultation System for	1908
Naive Negation into	Prolog	Incorporating	1910
Rule Support in	Prolog		1917
Production Systems and	Prolog		1926
Representation System in	Prolog	A Knowledge	1930
Data Bases, Expert Systems, and	Prolog		1937
A Database Support System for	Prolog		1964
Database Management in	Prolog		1980
a Network Database with	Prolog	Extending	1987
Systems: A Case Study in	Prolog	/Evolution of Database	2041
for an Imperative Complement to	Prolog	A Proposal	207
Schema Design Tool in	Prolog	/A Multi-Model	2074
Gegevensbank als Uitbreiding van	Prolog	/Eenvoudige Relationele	2102
Database Updates in Pure	Prolog		2105
Data Base Updates In Pure	Prolog		2106
to Parsing Conjunctions Using	Prolog	New Approaches	2118
Free Word Order Languages in	Prolog	Parsing	2121
Nothing more than	Prolog		2147
Restriction Grammars in	Prolog		2180
A Grammar Kit in	Prolog		2182
for a Linguistic Database Using	Prolog	Natural Language Queries	2186

A Bottom-Up Parser Embedded in	Prolog	BUP:	2199
Japanese Sentence Clause DCG in	Prolog	Generation of	2218
Contextual Grammars in	Prolog	. . . .	2243
and Bottom-Up Parsing in	Prolog	Deterministic	2257
Selective Depth-First Search in	Prolog	. . . .	275
and Denotational Semantics for	Prolog	/of Operational	293
Implementation in the Case of	Prolog	/Language: a Theory and . . .	307
A Study of	Prolog	. . . .	32
Towards a Theory of Types in	Prolog	. . . .	378
Theorem Proving Program in	Prolog	/Linear Resolution	390
Definition Method Models of	Prolog	Formal Vienna	397
The Occur-Check Problem in	Prolog	. . . .	418
A Note on Teaching	Prolog	. . . .	42
Modales et Temporelles en	Prolog	/pour des Logiques	456
Ascendante et Descendante en	Prolog	/Gauche et Analyse	496
Rules O.K.: Another Notation for	Prolog	Determinism	498
Opis Systemu	Prolog	. . . .	5
A Virtual Machine to Implement	Prolog	. . . .	637
User's Guide to DECsystem-10	Prolog	. . . .	64
du Langage de Programmation	Prolog	Interpreteur	641
Memoire pour les Interpreteurs	Prolog	/Machine de gestion de	643
Memoire dans les Interpreteurs	Prolog	Problemes de Gestion de . . .	646
of an Interpreter of a Modular	prolog	The Specification	653
En Iteration Dans Un Interprete	Prolog	/De L'appel Terminal	655
on Implementation Issues of	Prolog	Some Reflections	663
Implementatie van	Prolog	. . . .	664
of a Machine Independent	Prolog	Implementation	666
User's Guide to the EMAS	Prolog	. . . .	668
A Guide to Version 3 of Dec.-10	Prolog	. . . .	669
Unifier for Lisp Machine	Prolog	A Microcoded	677
The HC Manual: Virginia Tech	prolog	. . . .	68
Trees and Inequalities in	Prolog	Infinite	693
Last Steps Towards an Ultimate	Prolog	. . . .	696
Information about EMAS	Prolog	. . . .	699
Un Interpreteur de	Prolog	. . . .	708
Was ist	Prolog?	. . . .	71
A Prolog to	PROLOG	. . . .	72
Implantation de	Prolog	. . . .	722
Unique Features of Lisp Machine	Prolog	. . . .	733
An Introduction to	Prolog	. . . .	74
Tiny	Prolog	. . . .	762
implementation of Waterloo UNIX	Prolog	An	778
The Compilation Of Domain-Based	Prolog	On	779
La Memoire Dans Les Interpretes	Prolog	/Pour La Recuperation De . .	787
la Memoire dans les Interpretes	Prolog	/Pour la Recuperation de . . .	788
Real Time Garbage Collector for	Prolog	A	797
An Implementation of	Prolog	. . . .	801
The Programmer's Guide to IIUW	Prolog	. . . .	811
A Debugging System for	Prolog	. . . .	823
Utility Procedures In	Prolog	. . . .	849

et Utilisation du Language	Prolog Presentation	854
Multi-Version Structures In	Prolog	866
Eliminating Unwanted Loops in	Prolog	871
Control Structures for	Prolog LOGAL: Algorithmic	877
FOLL: Une Extension au Langage	Prolog	879
Eine Progammierumgebung fur	.Prolog	881
Children Programs in	Prolog	888
What The Naive User Wants From	Prolog	893
My Experience with	Prolog	9
Turtledove,Hurtle and	Prolog	909
Interconnection Languages and	Prolog Module	914
Programming Techniques in	Prolog Structured	915
Remarks On Coroutine in	Prolog	919
Very High Level Programming with	Prolog Features of	936
Declarative Input/Output in	Prolog	947
All Solutions Predicate In	Prolog	951
What Is A Variable In	Prolog?	954
Meta-logical Operations in	Prolog Programming	956
Updatable Arrays in	Prolog	957
A Worked Exercise in	Prolog Classification:	958
Reading Sentences In	Prolog	960
Two-Level	Prolog	968
Module Concepts for	Prolog	987
Solving Problems in	Prolog	999
Guest Private View: What is	Prolog ?	81
Control and Recovery in	Prolog - A Proposal /Concurrency	673
Logic Programs. Implementing	Prolog - Compiling Predicate	826
for Combining Prolog/ EPILOG =	Prolog + Data Flow: Arguments	1145
Komponente Parsing in	Prolog - Eine Semantische	2169
/Based on ATN (for Syntax) and	Prolog (for Semantics) in a/	1138
impossible	Prolog - Goto considered	971
l'Interpreteur et Exercices	Prolog - Mise en Route de	945
programming language	Prolog - Not just another	970
	Prolog - The wood for the trees	66
for Representing/ LFG in	Prolog - Toward a Formal System	2273
Language for All Seasons	Prolog: A Database Query	2112
The production systems and	Prolog (A framework for the/	1927
Language Comparison FIT -	Prolog: A Functional/Relational	1013
Implementing Expert Systems	Prolog: A Language for	1817
Implementing Expert/ Appendix to	Prolog: A Language for	1854
	Prolog: A Panacea?	43
Derivations de Programmes	Prolog a Partir de/	188
Generation of CAAD	Prolog: A Prelude to a New	1763
Logical Domain Modelling	Prolog: A Programming Tool for	864
McDermott on	Prolog: A Rejoinder	884
Ultimate Computer Language	Prolog: A Step Towards the	895
	Prolog: A Tutorial Introduction	70
Language Based on Predicate/	Prolog: A Very High Level	76
Databases Efficient	Prolog Access to CODASYL and FDM	2005
Programmiersprache	Prolog als Databank- und	1988

System Written in LISP Exeter	Prolog: An Experimental Prolog	711
Teachers	Prolog: An Introduction for	24
Which Unifies Much of LISP,	Prolog and Act 1 /Unification	1066
EPILOG /A critique of Concurrent	Prolog and Comparison with	1383
An Interface between	Prolog and Cyber-EDMS	1510
Controlling	Prolog and Expert Systems	1925
to Integration of Frame,	Prolog and Graphics /an Approach	2323
	Prolog and Inductive Definition	447
	Prolog and Infinite Trees	695
/Knowledge and Meta Knowledge by	Prolog and Its Applications	1180
A Subset of Concurrent	Prolog and Its Interpreter	1359
QLOG - The Software for	Prolog and Logic Programming	1070
	Prolog and Objects	1802
Management System Interfacing	Prolog and Relational Database	2030
A Road to Data-Intensive Expert/	Prolog and Relational Databases:	2049
for Fifth Generation Computer	Prolog and Relational Databases	2024
Verification with	Prolog and Temporal Logic	1590
to/ /in Transporting Concurrent	Prolog and the Bagel Simulator	1398
/Application and Extension of	Prolog: Applications Based on/	1652
	Prolog Applications in Hungary	1730
Higher-Order Extensions to	Prolog: Are They Needed ?	998
Prototyping of Information/	Prolog as a language for	1511
Language	Prolog as a Logic Programming	48
Kernel Language Concurrent	Prolog as a Multiprocessor's	1362
ESP - Extended Self-Contained	Prolog as a Preliminary Kernel/	1028
An Evaluation of	Prolog as a Prototyping System	1666
Complete Database Query/	Prolog as a Relationally	2110
	Prolog as a System Design Tool	1563
PROLOG Unifiers	Prolog As A Tool For Optimizing	1705
Teaching/ An Investigation of	Prolog as an Aid to French	1723
Design Language Concurrent	Prolog as an Efficient VLSI	1367
Modelierungswerkzeug	Prolog as Spezifikations- und	1732
A	Prolog Based Expert System Shell	1861
	Prolog Based Expert Systems	1887
Semi-Intelligent Backtracking of	Prolog Based on a Static Data/	855
/Using the Programming Language	Prolog based on Mathematical/	1675
Semi-Intelligent Backtracking of	Prolog Based on Static Data/	679
Two-Level Grammars A Version of	Prolog Based on the Notion of	350
/Implementation of Concurrent	Prolog Based on the Shallow/	1338
Algorithm A Concurrent	Prolog Based Region Finding	1394
System Simulation on	Prolog Basis	1601
Co-Operative Problem Solvng on a	Prolog Basis /Simulation and	1608
Oriented ? Should	Prolog be List or Record	156
	Prolog Benchmarking	83
with Logic and Fun	Prolog can Link Diverse Subjects	889
Code Words and Field/ Indexing	Prolog Clauses via Superimposed	2108
	Prolog Comments	1483
	Prolog Compared with LISP	1440
	Prolog Compared with LISP ?	1451
/for Lazy Implementations of a	Prolog compatible Functional/	111

A Portable	Prolog Compiler	657
Programs without the Use of a	Prolog Compiler /of Prolog	735
The Run-Time Environment for a	Prolog Compiler	832
Microcomputers	Prolog Compiler Due for	79
Computer The	Prolog Compiler for a CDC 6000	748
A	Prolog Compiler for the PLM	803
The Runtime Environment For A	Prolog Compiler Using A Copy/	834
/APL, LISP, MODULA-2, Smalltalk,	Prolog: Computer Languages for/	2
	Prolog Control Rules	952
Unification for a	Prolog Data Base Machine	1952
English Questions Posed to a	Prolog Database /Interpreting	2178
A	Prolog Database Machine	1953
Transaction Restarts in	Prolog Database Systems	1942
Natural Language Access to	Prolog Database Systems	2247
PROGRAPH As Environment For	Prolog DB applications	1106
Etude et Realisation en	Prolog de Problemes de Logique	416
	Prolog Debugging Facilities	851
Interpreter A	Prolog Demand Driven Computation	409
Exeter Prolog: Some Thoughts on	Prolog Design by a LISP User	712
Ein Word Expert Parser in	Prolog: Die Lexikalische/	2168
Ein Word Expert Parser in	Prolog: Die Semantische/	2166
Un Bel Example de	Prolog en Analyse et Synthese	1482
LISLOG: Programmation En	Prolog En Environnement Lisp	1017
Interpreteur De	Prolog En Pascal sous Multics	759
Implementation of the Waterloo	Prolog Environment Design and	680
Developing and Reasoning/ A	Prolog Environment for	913
	Prolog et Bases De Donnees	1995
Principles and/ Cooperation de	Prolog et d'un SGDB Generalise:	2057
Interface Entre	Prolog Et Un SGBD	1977
Interface entre	Prolog et un SGBD	1978
Cooperation entre une Machine	Prolog et une Base de Donnees/	785
User Manual APES (A	Prolog Expert System Shell): A	1852
/Comparison of EMYCIN and APES (a	Prolog Expert System Shell for/	1859
Relational Databases And	Prolog Expert Systems /Coupling	1792
Negative Knowledge A	Prolog Extension for Handling	1150
Implementing Expert/ KNOWLOG: A	Prolog Extension for	1924
/of the Effectiveness of	Prolog for a CAD Application	1619
/Re-interpreting and Extending	Prolog for a Multiprocessor/	1146
	Prolog for Children and Teachers	1731
	Prolog for Databases	1968
Evaluation	Prolog For Expert Systems: An	1863
Applications Enhanced	Prolog for Industrial	635
SYLLOG: An Approach to	Prolog for Nonprogrammers	1779
/of the Programming Language	Prolog for Panel House Design	1676
	Prolog For Programmers	920
	Prolog for Programmers	922
The Application of	Prolog for Search of Similar/	1687
	Prolog for SM-4	740
Verification and Simulation.	Prolog for Specification,	1623
Assisted Circuit Evaluation in	Prolog for VLSI Computer	1801

Predicate/ Derivation of Prolog From First Order 84
Query System An Optimizing Prolog Front-End to a Relational . . . 1635
GEOM: A Prolog Geometry Theorem Prover . . . 1540
Issues in Caching Prolog Goals 706
SeeLog: A Prolog Graphics Interface 1714
Why Novices Will Find Learning Prolog Hard 77
A Logical Reconstruction of Prolog II 216
A Logical Foundation For Prolog II 291
Prolog II - Manual d'Utilisation 11
Utilisation guide Prolog II VAX Installation and 721
L'environment De Prolog III 737
Waterloo Prolog Implementation Manual 681
System on a Small Machine A Prolog Implementation of a Large . . . 794
Functional Grammar A Prolog Implementation of Lexical . . . 2238
Query-By-Example A Prolog Implementation of 1470
Knuth-Rendix Reduction System A Prolog Implementation of the 1686
Optimises Tail/ An Improved Prolog Implementation which 829
The Memory Management of Prolog Implementations 660
/of Declarative Determinism in Prolog Implementations 781
Declarative Determinism in Prolog Implementations 782
Prolog in 10 Figures 868
Environment Concurrent Prolog in a Multi-Process 1331
An Implementation of Prolog in C 707
Prolog in CMOS Circuit Design 1726
Dwelling Houses Applications of Prolog in Designing Many-Storied . . . 1678
von Wissenbasen oder die Klasse prolog in einer/ /Organisation 1733
On Implementing Prolog in Functional Programming . . 1429
The Programming Environment for Prolog in LISP QLOG - 1072
LISP craft technique Embedding Prolog in LISP: an example of a 1071
Another QLISP (Re)Implementing Prolog in LISP or YAQ - Yet 1021
Prolog in Practice 1561
Integration: An Application of Prolog in Symbolic Computing /of . . 1488
An Abstract Prolog Instruction Set 1266
und/ Ein Word Expert Parser in Prolog: Integration von Syntax 2167
/of Distributed Systems using Prolog Interpreted Petri Nets 1469
The New Prolog Interpreter 667
/in the Implementation of a Prolog interpreter 764
FOOLOG - A Small and Efficient Prolog Interpreter 780
The World's Shortest Prolog Interpreter? 783
Parallel Extension Prolog Interpreter and its 1336
Concurrent Programming Prolog Interpreter Based on 1308
Generalized/ A Highly Parallel Prolog Interpreter Based on The . . . 1220
Infinite Terms A Prolog Interpreter Working with . . . 710
LISP LP: A Prolog Interpreter written in 1084
Logical Derivation Of Prolog Interpreters 235
Note On Garbage Collection In Prolog Interpreters A Short 642
A Memory Management Machine For Prolog Interpreters 645
A Note on Garbage Collection in Prolog Interpreters 662
Garbage Collection in Prolog Interpreters 665
Logicon: An Integration of Prolog into Icon 1077

Environment Integrating	Prolog into the POPLOG	1086
The Question? If	Prolog Is The Answer, What Is	6
	Prolog K/R - Language Features . . .	1095
Theoretical Foundations of the	Prolog Language /Methods and the . .	103
DURAL: An Extended	Prolog Language	1053
DURAL: A Modal Extension of	Prolog Language:	1054
AI Languages: The	Prolog Language	28
Software/ The Application of the	Prolog Language to the Design of . . .	1472
Un Mariage Heureux Entre LISP et	Prolog: Le Systeme LOVLISP	1056
the Microarchitecture for a	Prolog Machine /Influencing	1211
A Class of Architectures For A	Prolog Machine	1221
the Bagel: A Systolic Concurrent	Prolog Machine Lecture Notes on . . .	1360
Implementation of a Sequential	Prolog Machine Design and	690
The Berkeley	Prolog Machine	701
Rates Using the Warren Abstract	Prolog Machine /Achieveable LIPS . .	719
Design of a High-Speed	Prolog Machine	777
Abstract	Prolog Machine: A Specification	1229
A Specification of an Abstract	Prolog Machine and its/	744
Performance Studies of a	Prolog Machine Architecture	1212
reduction/ The proposal of	Prolog machine based on	1189
Flow Mechanism	Prolog Machine Based on the Data . .	1219
architectures Sequential	Prolog machine: image and host	1257
Sequential	Prolog Machine PEK	1252
/Control Mechanism in Dataflow	Prolog Machines	1319
Evaluation of Dataflow	Prolog Machines Simulating	1685
Collection Processing for	Prolog Machines On Garbage	724
Artificial Intelligence LISP and	Prolog Machines are/	757
d'Utilisation	Prolog: Manuel de Reference et	802
Flexible Control/ Efficient	Prolog Memory Management for . . .	833
Medical Expert System Shell A	Prolog Meta-Interpreter as	1827
Partial Evaluation And Its/ A	Prolog Meta-Interpreter For	2103
	Prolog Modulaire	905
/more Logically Or Writing	Prolog more Efficiently	1720
Making	Prolog More Expressive	332
System	Prolog na Maszynie CDC/Cyber 72 . .	731
et Mise en Place du Systeme	Prolog Necessaire /sur Fichiers	2070
How To Implement	Prolog On a Lisp Machine	1645
critique of/ Concurrent	Prolog on a Multiprocessor: A	1383
Machine Implementing	Prolog on a Multiprocessor	1251
	Prolog on Microcomputers	65
Parallel System for High-Speed/	Prolog on the DADO Machine: A . . .	1254
	Prolog on the DECsystem-10	828
The Logical Record Keeper:	Prolog on the IBM	836
/and Their Applications to	Prolog Optimization	805
The	Prolog Phenomenon	58
Systems and its Application to	Prolog Processes /of Rewriting	1200
An Overlapped	Prolog Processor	1255
Towards a Multiple Pipeline	Prolog Processor	1256
Towards a Pipelined	Prolog Processor	1258
Shell for Use with Any	Prolog Program A Menu-Driven . . .	904

Static Analyzer of Sequential	Prolog Program	962
Issues Tax Advisor: A	Prolog Program Analyzing Tax	1912
Entitlement to/ A Listing of a	Prolog Program Describing	1629
/Support Environment for	Prolog Program Development	925
the First n Formal Deratives/ A	Prolog Program for Generating	1651
Problem A	Prolog Program for the S-P	1718
Verify and Choose Method A	Prolog Program Illustrating a	1484
Problems in/ FAME: A	Prolog Program that Solves	1743
System The Documentation of a	Prolog Program Verification	1474
A Compendium of interesting	Prolog programmes	1721
A Design Methodology in	Prolog Programming	1682
Primlog: A Case of Augmented	Prolog Programming	918
Methodology of	Prolog Programming	979
Guide A Case-Study in	Prolog Programming - Railway . . .	990
	Prolog Programming Environments . .	1576
with SQL/DS PROSQL: A	Prolog Programming Interface	1528
	Prolog Programming Language . . .	1
The	Prolog Programming Language . . .	22
Kanji	Prolog Programming System	700
Interactive Program Verifier for	Prolog Programs On an	102
Prove Properties of Restricted	Prolog Programs /Technique to . . .	107
Back-Up Parallel Interpreter for	Prolog Programs A	1307
Algebraic Specifications to	Prolog Programs Translating	1562
of Mode Declarations in	Prolog Programs /Generation	1689
Algebraic Semantics of	Prolog Programs An Operational . . .	189
An Algorithm for Interpreting	Prolog Programs	213
An Interpreting Algorithm for	Prolog Programs	214
Negation and Semantics of	Prolog Programs	450
A Method for Producing Efficient	Prolog Programs /Programming: . . .	484
An Operational Semantics of	Prolog Programs	597
Associative Evaluation of	Prolog Programs	775
Analyzing	Prolog Programs	815
more Reliable and more Readable	Prolog Programs /to Obtain	848
the Control Flow of	Prolog Programs Understanding . . .	852
Environment for Large	Prolog Programs /a Programming . .	857
Improving	Prolog Programs	872
Graphs as Data in	Prolog Programs	978
Relations And The Inversion Of	Prolog Programs Directed	982
Finding Temporary Terms In	Prolog Programs	994
Static Calls to/ Optimizing	Prolog Programs Containing	640
Network Executing Distributed	Prolog Programs on a Broadcast . . .	835
Architectures On Compiling	Prolog Programs on Demand-Driven . .	1201
of a Prolog/ The Compilation of	Prolog Programs without the Use . . .	735
	Prolog Reference Manual	29
Waterloo Unix	Prolog Reference Manual	34
Security Benefit Regulations	Prolog Representation of Social	1853
New	Prolog Runs on LISP Machine	80
and Recursive Schemas to	Prolog Schemas /Flowchart	1648
An Executable	Prolog Semantics	589
Non-Procedural Software/ Glog: A	Prolog Semi-Compiler for	1614

Decision-Making in a Less/ A	Prolog Simulation of Migration	1725
by Grammar Beyond	Prolog: Software Specification	1143
The Pragmatics of	Prolog: Some Comments	202
Design by a LISP User Exeter	Prolog: Some Thoughts on Prolog	712
On the Treatment of Cuts in	Prolog Source-Level Tools	961
What Stories Should We Tell	Prolog Students?	10
Xp's: An Extended Or-Parallel	Prolog System	1269
Towards an Integrated Database	Prolog System	2086
A Direct Execution	Prolog System	728
The UNIX	Prolog System	765
University of York Portable	Prolog System - Release 1	809
Verification of Concurrent/ A	Prolog System For The	1273
(Second Edition) The UNIX	Prolog System Software Report 5	691
Preferred/ How To Obtain A	Prolog System With Your	21
Exeter Prolog: An Experimental	Prolog System Written in LISP	711
A Rational Design For	Prolog Systems	1727
Implementation Issues of	Prolog Systems	670
The comparison of several	Prolog systems	768
A Comparison of Several	Prolog Systems	769
Processes - An Unexploited	Prolog Technique Perpetual	1786
A	Prolog Technology Theorem Prover	480
Towards a	Prolog Text Grammar	2250
Data Driven Model A Parallel	Prolog: The Construction of a	1144
Implementation Compared with/	Prolog: The Language and its	831
/Programming in Concurrent	Prolog: the MAXFLOW experience	1317
Expert	Prolog: The Rules to Become an	36
Extension of	Prolog Through Matrix Reduction	155
in Data Processing/ Using	Prolog to Assess Security Risks	1527
Systems Some Applications of	Prolog to Decision Support	1660
A	Prolog to PROLOG	72
and DBM/ The Application of	Prolog to the Development of QA	1600
The Classroom	Prolog: Tomorrows Language For	4
A Portable	Prolog Tracing Package	1752
Meta-shifting	Prolog Transformation Through	487
Waterloo Unix	Prolog Tutorial	35
Waterloo UNIX	Prolog Tutorial Version 1.2	1303
Prolog As A Tool For Optimizing	PROLOG Unifiers	1705
Decsystem-10	Prolog User's Manual	7
C	Prolog User's Manual Version 1.2	63
V2.4 BS2000	Prolog User's Reference Manual	44
Implementation of Concurrent	Prolog using Message Passing	1386
Shared-Memory Multi/ Parallel	Prolog Using Stack Segments on	1272
	Prolog versus LISP	78
Fight them/ The APPLOG Language:	Prolog vs. LISP -- If you Can't	1033
Natural Language Fragments A	Prolog Way of Representing	2188
Flow: Arguments for Combining	Prolog with a Data Driven/ /Data	1145
	Prolog With A Dema Predicate	240
New-Prolog! An Extension Of	PROLOG With Causal Implications	1048
Set And Parallel	Prolog with Divided Assertion	1350
N-Prolog: An Extension of	Prolog with Hypothetical/	1047

/the Logic Programming Language	Prolog with Two-Level Grammars	349
	Prolog without Magic	867
A Pure	Prolog Written in Pure Lisp	1642
which Optimises Tail	Recursion /Prolog Implementation	829
Ascendante et/ Elimination de la	Recursion Gauche et Analyse	496
Language for Logic/ The	Relational Algebra as a Typed	1087
Algorithm On RDBM Delta's	Relational Algebra Processing	1244
/Mechansim for Generating	Relational Algebra Queries	2111
Design And Implementation Of The	Relational Data Base Engine	1241
Based on Logic An Experimental	Relational Data Base System	2033
Planning and Pathfinding for	Relational Data Bases Deductive	2017
and Voice Output for Deductive	Relational Data Bases /Language	2216
Machine Based on Hierarchical/ A	Relational Data Flow Data Base	1222
How Can we Combine A	Relational Database and a/	840
Functional Dependencies in a	Relational Database and/	1984
and a/ An Equivalence Between	Relational Database Dependencies	2082
DELTA A	Relational Database Machine	1245
First Step to Knowledge Base/ A	Relational Database Machine:	1235
System Interfacing Prolog and	Relational Database Management	2030
/Processing of Interactive	Relational Database Queries/	2104
/a Logical Reconstruction of	Relational Database Theory	2080
Programming/ Extending A	Relational Database with Logic	1955
LOFE: A Language for Virtual	Relational Databases	1038
Operations and Inferences over	Relational Databases Set	1089
Logic Programming and	Relational Databases	1956
/Predicate Logic Languages and	Relational Databases	1961
Information Retrieval On Virtual	Relational Databases Deductive	1981
Logic Programs for Querying	Relational Databases	1982
Question-answering System On	Relational Databases /Deductive	1990
An Intelligent Access to	Relational Databases	1991
Performing Inferences over	Relational Databases	2031
On Deductive	Relational Databases	2037
Improving Integrity Checking in	Relational Databases Logic for	2059
Deductive Question-answering on	Relational Databases	2077
Update Dependencies in	Relational Databases	2081
	Relational Databases a la Carte	2069
Data-Intensive/ Prolog and	Relational Databases: A Road to	2049
/Of Office Documents By Coupling	Relational Databases And Prolog/	1792
Problem Specific/ Deduction in	Relational Databases Directed by	2029
Generation Computer Prolog and	Relational Databases for Fifth	2024
/Query Evaluation Algorithm For	Relational Databases with Null/	2075
A	Relational Dataflow System	1286
and Programs	Relational Equations, Grammars	209
A fuzzy	relational inference language	1006
Programming A	Relational Language for Parallel	1281
	Relational Production Systems	505
and Logic Programs	Relational Production Systems	1889
Introduction to	Relational Programming	344
Overview of	Relational Programming	345
Illustrated by a Program for/	Relational Programming	1573

Optimizing Prolog Front-End to a	Relational Query System An	1635
Algebraic Semantics of Logic/	Relational Set of Trees and the	353
Optimization in a Deductive	Relational System	2001
Function for an Inferential	Relational System /and Selection	2034
Efficiency of Theorem Proving by	Resolution /the Completeness and	310
Combining Model Elimination And	Resolution Theorem Provers	333
A linear format for	resolution	335
Heterogeneous SLD	Resolution	392
Remarks on Fuzzy	Resolution	96
Theorem proving by	resolution as a basis for/	1055
Equality	Resolution by Unification and	1436
Le Systeme de	Resolution de Problemes METALOG	1832
Tendance/ Un Systeme de	Resolution de Problems a	2181
Semantic	Resolution For Horn Sets	273
/Alternative Method of Adapting	Resolution for Logic Programming	101
Programming with	Resolution Logic	205
Programming in	Resolution Logic	210
Automatique de Quelques/	Resolution par la Demonstration	1491
Fuzzy Logic and the	Resolution Principle	326
/Logic Based on the	Resolution Principle	438
Logic A	Resolution Principle in Modal	158
LogLisp Sequential Forms with	Resolution Semantics	1123
Programs A Unified Treatment of	Resolution Strategies for Logic	512
Filter for Literal Indexing in	Resolution Systems An Improved	2008
Some special purpose	resolution systems	317
/between Semantic Tableaux and	Resolution Theorem Provers	140
Back Chaining and Equality in	Resolution Theorem Proving /for	420
Using Sophisticated Models in	Resolution Theorem Proving -/	449
Program in/ An Ordered Linear	Resolution Theorem Proving	390
Goal Trees: Some Guidance from	Resolution Theory A Hole in	339
E-resolution: Extension of	Resolution to Include the/	1450
New/ A Linear Format for	Resolution with Merging and a	520
Two Results On Ordering For	Resolution with Merging and/	429
Function An Extension to Linear	Resolution with Selection	2040
Function Linear	Resolution with Selection	316
on Clausal Superposition and	Rewriting /Interpreter Based	714
/Inference Engine PIE - Goal	Rewriting Model and Machine/	1171
Graphs to Prove Theorems Using	Rewriting Rules for Connection	162
Demand-Driven Implementations of	Rewriting Systems and its/ /for	1200
To The/ Abstract Data Types And	Rewriting Systems: Application	117
Program/ From Term	Rewriting Systems to Distributed	1486
Inference-Driven	Semantic Analysis	1713
Phrase Interpretation and Early	Semantic Analysis /Noun	2209
	Semantic Code Analysis	1790
/Method Serving the Proof of the	Semantic Features of Programs	1473
Epistle System	Semantic Interpretation for the	363
Controlling Inference in the	Semantic Interpretation of/	367
/Evaluation: An Approach to the	Semantic Interpretation of Noun/	2210
Logic/ /the Scoping Problem, and	Semantic Interpretation Rules in	2201
Locating Deduction Rules in a	Semantic Network /and	1126

A Predicate Calculus Based	Semantic Network for/	2205
Question-Answering/ The Use of a	Semantic Network in a Deductive . . .	2204
System The SNePS	Semantic Network Processing	1127
Logic and	Semantic Networks	1558
Generating Sentences from	Semantic Networks	2126
Logic Relating Sentences and	Semantic Networks with Clausal . . .	2256
Infinite/ On the Fixed Point	Semantic of Horn Clauses with . . .`.	226
/A Discussion from a	Semantic Point of View	2136
Expert Systems and Database/	Semantic Query Optimization in . . .	1960
Graph-Theoretic/ External	Semantic Query Simplification: A . . .	1634
Natural Language/ On the	Semantic Representation of	2232
Quantifier Hierarchy in a	Semantic Representation of/	2246
Horn Clauses Mapping Between	Semantic Representations using	2272
Sets	Semantic Resolution For Horn	273
Theorem/ The Relation between	Semantic Tableaux and Resolution . .	140
and Links	Semantic Tableaux, Unification	515
Programming A	Semantic Theory for Logic	144
Sequential Forms with Resolution	Semantics LogLisp	1123
Parsing Using Syntax and	Semantics /for Deterministic	2212
An Executable Prolog	Semantics	589
Languages which Admit Initial	Semantics /Specification	618
connect? - Solving Problems in	Semantics Where to	623
which Strongly Admit Initial	Semantics /Institutions	630
(for Syntax) and Prolog (for	Semantics) in a LISP/ /on ATN . . .	1138
Approach Natural Language	Semantics: A Logic Programming . . .	2235
/and Financial Concepts: A Formal	Semantics Approach to Knowledge/ . .	1878
/of Operational and Denotational	Semantics for Prolog	293
with Functions The Call by Name	Semantics of a Clause Language	113
Suitable to/ A First-Order	Semantics of a Connective	1295
Language with a Reducibility/	Semantics of a Logic Programming . .	486
for parallel programming The	Semantics of a simple language	1322
in Logic/ On Syntax and	Semantics of Adjective Phrases	2245
On the	Semantics of Circumscription	375
Syntax and Formal	Semantics of English in PHLIQA1 . . .	2190
/in Logic Programming: Formal	Semantics of Extended Horn/	1305
of Logic Programs Top-Down	Semantics of Fair Computations	218
Narrowing as the Operational	Semantics of Functional/	428
/Logic: Axiomatics and Formal	Semantics of Generalized Horn/	227
seen as Computer Languages The	Semantics of Grammar Formalisms . .	2228
Production/ The denotational	semantics of Horn Clauses as a	612
Formal	Semantics of KNOWLOG	1923
/Set of Trees and the Algebraic	Semantics of Logic Programming . . .	353
	Semantics of Logic Programs	1448
Some Aspects of the Static	Semantics of Logic Programs with/ . .	590
Variables The Declarative	Semantics of Logical Read-only	1405
Coroutining in Logic/ The	Semantics of Parallelism and	1353
a Programming/ /Complexity of the	Semantics of Predicate Logic as	125
a Programming Language The	Semantics of Predicate Logic as	215
Chaotic	Semantics of Programming Logic . . .	322
Closures and Fairness in the	Semantics of Programming Logic . . .	324

An Operational Algebraic	Semantics of Prolog Programs	 189
Negation and	Semantics of Prolog Programs	 450
An Operational	Semantics of Prolog Programs	 597
An Axiomatic Approach to	Semantics of Specification/	 617
Parlog for Discrete Event	Simulation	1019
A Logical Approach to	Simulation	1602
Intelligence Based Computer	Simulation /by Artificial	1829
Based Systems, Modeling and	Simulation /Applied to Knowledge	. . 1840
Problem Solvng on a/ System	Simulation and Co-Operative	1608
Parallel Systems, Description,	Simulation and Planning /Way Of	. . 1368
in/ /Oriented Discrete/Continuous	Simulation and Problem Solving	1597
Digital Logic	Simulation in prolog	1632
Cooperative Problem/ A Logic	Simulation Language For Modeling	. . 1311
Decision-Making in a/ A Prolog	Simulation of Migration	1725
System	Simulation on Prolog Basis	1601
Artificial/ A Discrete	Simulation System Based on	1606
/Prolog Language to the Design of	Software and Hardware Objects	1472
Change: Issues in/ Applications	Software and Organizational	2312
Mathematical Logic	Software Applications for the	1476
Database Framework - A/ Rapid	Software Development in a	1655
LDM - A Logic Based	Software Development Method	988
AI and	Software Engineering	1659
/What Does It Bring To	Software Engineering ?	933
Artificial Intelligence in New/	Software Engineering and	1178
Developing Knowledge-Based/ A	Software Environment for	1690
Processing and Logic/ A New	Software Environment for List	1061
/Techniques In The Design Of	Software For Digital Switching/	1501
Programming QLOG - The	Software for Prolog and Logic	1070
Edition/ The UNIX Prolog System	Software Report 5 (Second	691
/of the RIMS Symposia on	Software Science and Engineering . . .	1620
Grammar Beyond Prolog:	Software Specification by	1143
Paradigms of Knowledge Based	Software System and Its Service/ . . .	1838
The Role of Systems and	Software Technology in the Fifth/ . . .	1184
Semi-Compiler for Non-Procedural	Software Tools Glog: A Prolog	1614
Logic	Software Tools for First Order	873
Inference System for	Solving PRISM: A Parallel	1324
in Prolog-Based Robot Problem	Solving Progress	1487
Matcher for Algebraic Equation	Solving A Powerful	1497
Matching in Algebraic Equation	Solving Using	1498
Decisions in Mechanics Problem	Solving /about Knowledge: Making	. . 1519
Modeling and Problem	Solving /Discrete/Continuous	1598
Logic for Problem	Solving	1657
Logical Levels of Problem	Solving	2344
Learning Problem	Solving	2374
of Theorem Proving to Problem	Solving Application	253
Micro-Prolog For Problem	Solving	54
Constraints for Problem	Solving	853
Problem	Solving = Knowledge + Strategy . . .	2283
Artificial Intelligence/	Solving Algebraic Equations: An	1789
Problem	Solving and Inference Mechanisms . . .	1165

Problems by Intelligent/	Solving Combinatorial Search	149
Problems A New method for	Solving Constraint Satisfaction	1735
Knowledge-Based Problem	Solving in AL3	2354
/Simulation and Problem	Solving in TS-Prolog	1597
Meta-Level Inference	Solving Mechanics Problems Using	1517
Examples Learning Equation	Solving Methods from Worked	2384
	Solving Problems in Prolog	999
Where to connect? -	Solving Problems in Semantics	623
Automated Learning of Problem	Solving Rules On the	2371
/Analysis: Learning Equation	Solving Strategies from Worked/	2386
PRESS	Solving Symbolic Equations with	1757
For Modeling Cooperative Problem	Solving System /Language	1311
versus Prolog Problem	Solving with the Computer: Logo	1665
Abstract Prolog Machine: A	Specification	1229
Imprecise Program	Specification	1477
via Executable Logic	Specification /Verification	1742
Logic Programs	Specification and Derivation of	478
Logical	Specification And Implementation	1081
in/ /Merge Operators: Their	Specification and Implementation	1364
Algebraic	Specification and Prolog	1478
of Complex/ Experience with	Specification and Verification	1366
of Distributed Systems using/	Specification and Verification	1469
Runnable	Specification as a Design Tool	1555
Beyond Prolog: Software	Specification by Grammar	1143
Gestion de Memoire pour les/	Specification d'une Machine de	644
/Unification Algorithms from a	Specification in Logic	510
/Approach to Semantics of	Specification Languages	617
Admit Initial/ Characterizing	Specification Languages which	618
Types /Compared with Clauses for	Specification of Abstract Data	1577
Prolog Machine and its/ A	Specification of an Abstract	744
of a Modular prolog The	Specification of an Interpreter	653
Insertion A Runnable	Specification of AVL-Tree	1575
/Grammars And The Logical	Specification Of Data Types As/	2115
Process	Specification Of Logic Programs	426
Integration Logic Program	Specification of Numerical	1532
Generation Kernel/ Conceptual	Specification of the Fifth	1076
Language Version/ The Conceptual	Specification of the Kernel	1167
LDM - A Program	Specification Support System	894
of Mechanical Theorem Proving to	Symbolic Calculus Application	1493
The Scope of	Symbolic Computation	294
An Application of Prolog in	Symbolic Computing /Integration:	1488
Patterns	Symbolic Derivations of Chess	1504
Solving	Symbolic Equations with PRESS	1757
and Reasoning of VLSI Circuit in	Temporal Logic Description	1215
Verification with Prolog and	Temporal Logic	1590
Specifying Hardware In	Temporal Logic & Efficient/	1592
and its Verification with/	Temporal Logic Based Hardware	1591
/of Concurrent Processes Against	Temporal Logic Specifications	1273
An LMA-based	Theorem Prover	1079
GEOM: A Prolog Geometry	Theorem Prover	1540

Recognition Problem for a	Theorem Prover /of the Language	. . 2217
A Prolog Technology	Theorem Prover	480
Question Answering/ Database and	Theorem prover Designs for	2094
Horn/ HORNLOG: A First-Order	Theorem Prover for Negations of . . .	1049
A Lemma Driven Automatic	Theorem Prover for Recursive/	138
Manual The Interactive	Theorem Prover (ITP) User's	1121
Semantic Tableaux and Resolution	Theorem Provers /between	140
Mechanism For Resolution-style	Theorem Provers An Inference	364
Elimination And Resolution	Theorem Provers Combining Model . .	333
Completely Non-Clausal	Theorem Proving	1090
Automated	Theorem Proving	122
Non-Resolution	Theorem Proving	127
IMPRESS - Meta-Level Concepts in	Theorem Proving	1755
and Equality in Resolution	Theorem Proving /Back Chaining . .	420
A review of automatic	theorem proving	439
in/ /Models in Resolution	Theorem Proving - Lecture Notes . . .	449
Automated	Theorem Proving: A Logical Basis . . .	336
Quartercentury Review Automated	Theorem Proving: A	338
Some Applications of	Theorem Proving Based Machine/ . . .	1551
Elimination Mechanical	Theorem Proving by Model	334
/Completeness and Efficiency of	Theorem Proving by Resolution	310
a basis for question-answering/	Theorem proving by resolution as . . .	1055
Theories/ Paramodulation and	Theorem Proving in First Order . . .	1455
An Ordered Linear Resolution	Theorem Proving Program in/	390
Solving Application of	Theorem Proving to Problem	253
Application of	Theorem Proving to/	255
Application of Mechanical	Theorem Proving to Symbolic/	1493
Prover for Recursive Function	Theory /Driven Automatic Theorem .	138
Advances in Database	Theory	1998
of Relational Database	Theory /a Logical Reconstruction . . .	2080
An Axiomatic Data Base	Theory	2097
unification in an equational	theory First-order	229
Some Guidance from Resolution	Theory A Hole in Goal Trees:	339
in Horn Clause Programs: The	Theory /and Sidetracking	412
/in an Applicative Language: a	Theory and Implementation in the/ . .	307
Representation Using Logic, Set	Theory and Natural Language/ /and .	1804
Knowledge Engineering:	Theory and Practice	2345
A Semantic	Theory for Logic Programming	144
Extended Dempster and Shafer's	Theory For Problems With/ /On . . .	286
System The	Theory of CES: A Complete Expert . .	1905
Programs With Equality A	Theory of Complete Logic	1442
` A First Order	Theory of Data and Programs	168
by Programming A Logical	Theory of Data Types Motivated . . .	938
Contributions to the	Theory of Logic Programming	95
Methodology A Model	Theory of Logic Programming	1758
Reasoning Proglomena to a	Theory of Mechanized Formal	1142
A Model	Theory of Programming Logic	1065
Logic Programming Based on the	Theory of Relations /for	379
Towards a	Theory of Types in Prolog	378
/of Logic Programming and Cutset	Theory to Aspects of Reactor and/ . .	1571

Databases:	Theory Versus Interpretation	1702
A Functional Language Based On	Unification Qute:	1118
PUNIFY: An AI-Machine for	Unification	194
On The Sequential Nature Of	Unification	198
Associative-Commutative	Unification	222
Algebraic Aspects of	Unification	283
A New Linear Algorithm for	Unification	299
Linear	Unification	406
Fast	Unification	441
A Functional Language Based on	Unification QUTE:	451
Computational Complexity Of	Unification On Parallel	588
An Efficient	Unification Algorithm	108
A Rehabilitation of Robinson's	Unification Algorithm	527
Deductive Synthesis of the	Unification Algorithm	555
Associative-Commutative/ A	Unification Algorithm for	479
Concurrent Prolog A	Unification Algorithm For	1406
Infinite Trees A	Unification Algorithm for	389
A Systolic	Unification Algorithm for VLSI	1230
Programming/ Synthesis Of A	Unification Algorithm In a Logic	219
/and Practical Comparison of	Unification Algorithms	500
Deriving Different	Unification Algorithms from a/	510
of Equational/ Universal	Unification and a Classification	468
Resolution by	Unification and Equality	1436
Semantic Tableaux,	Unification and Links	515
/A Higher-Order Language with	Unification and Multiple Results	1458
Parallel Algorithms for	Unification and other Complete/	1377
A Notion of Grammatical	Unification Applicable to Logic/	2195
Measure for Logic Programming	Unification as a Complexity	287
Purely Functional Language with	Unification Based Conditional/ /a	1002
Computational Logic: the	Unification Computation	440
Base Machine	Unification for a Prolog Data	1952
Intelligent Backtracking in/	Unification Graphs for	193
Environment	Unification in a Parallel	817
theory First-order	unification in an equational	229
	Unification in Grammar	2183
Space	Unification in Linear Time and	354
	Unification of Commutative Terms	467
Efficient Implementation of	Unification of Cyclic Structures	269
Logic Languages The	Unification of Functional and	185
Efficient	Unification Over Infinite Terms	288
State of the Art in Matching and	Unification Problems /on the	427
A Modified	Unification Procedure	382
Logic Programs A Distributed	Unification Scheme for Systolic	580
Analysis A Hardware	Unification Unit: Design and	586
Uniform: A Language Based Upon	Unification Which Unifies Much/	1066
In Logic Programming Efficient	Unification With Infinite Terms	356
Unification Algorithm for	VLSI A Systolic	1230
of Test Structures for	VLSI Rule Based Generation	1671
Circuit Evaluation in Prolog for	VLSI Computer Assisted	1801
Description and Reasoning of	VLSI Circuit in Temporal Logic	1215

An Intelligent Router for VLSI Design 1500
Prolog as an Efficient VLSI Design Language Concurrent . . 1367
Knowledge-Based VLSI Routing System-WIREX- 1232

AUTHOR INDEX

Abramson, H. 1465, 1002, 2114, 2116, 2115, 1542, 518

Acharya, S. 1942

Adiba, M. 1944, 1943

Ahamed, M. 835

Ahmad, S. 87

Aida, H. 1150, 1268, 1234

Aiello, L. 89, 842

Aiso, H. 1198

Aitchison, I.E. 1619

Akita, K. 635

Akiyama, K. 1930

Akutagawa, T. 635

Albert, P. 1802

Allen, J.F. 1466, 1045, 1003

Allison, L. 589

Alps, R.A. 1004

Alvey, P. 1859

Amamiya, M. 1151

Amsterdam, J. 2

Anderson, R. 520

Anderson, S.O. 1470, 1467, 2107

Andreka, H. 93

Aoki, T. 1249

Aponte, M.V. 94, 1468

Appelt, D. 2196

Apt, K.R. 95

Aronson, A. 97, 96

Ashcroft, E. 98

Asirelli, P. 590, 100

Asou, M. 1180, 962, 1269

Attardi, G. 1005, 842

Avenhaus, J. 1630

Azema, P. 1469

Babb, E. 101

Backhouse, R.C. 1470

Bainbridge, S. 1804

Baldwin, J.F. 1006, 1805

Ball, D. 1471

Ballieu, G. 637

Balogh, K. 988, 844, 1473, 102, 103, 1476, 1472, 1474, 653

Balzer, R.M. 1477

Bancilhon, F. 1948

Bandes, R.G. 1478, 1007

Banerji, R.B. 2352, 2377

Banning, R.W. 1949

Barath, E. 1609

Barberye, G. 639

Barbuti, R. 1009, 107, 1008, 106, 105, 100

Barrow, H.G. 1479, 1480

Bartha, F. 1652

Barthes, J.P. 1481

Battani, G. 641, 2117, 640, 1482

Baxter, L.D. 108, 109, 1484, 1483, 110

Becker, J.M. 1485

Bein, K. 1548

Bekkers, Y. 645, 642, 643, 646, 644

Bell, W. 4

Bellia, M. 1200, 111, 1010, 114, 1486, 1009, 1201, 1008, 115, 113

Belovari, G. 1488, 1487

Bendl, J. 1489, 651, 650, 652, 653

Berger-Sabbatel, G. 1953, 1954, 1951, 1490, 1952

Bergman, M. 117, 116, 1493, 298, 1491, 1494

Berwick, R. 2118

Besnard, P. 1495

Bibel, W. 122, 155, 121, 120, 2278, 119, 118, 123

Bic, L. 1203, 1202

Bidoit, M. 527

Bien, J.S. 2120, 5, 2119, 2121

Bijl, A. 1764, 1496

Billaud, M. 124

Black, F. 1011

Blair, H.A. 125, 126

Blanning, R. 2279

Bledsoe, W.W.   520, 127, 128
Bloss, A.   1441
Bobrow, D.G.   6
Boizumault, P.   129, 655
Bojadziev, D.   1138
Bolc, L.   2122, 2123, 2124
Boley, H.   1012, 1013
Bonkowski, B.   1271
Borgault, S.   1014
Borgwardt, P.   1272
Borning, A.   1497, 1814, 1498
Bosc, P.   1806
Bosco, P.G.   1273
Bossu, G.   466, 130, 2125
Bouchon, P.   1500
Bourgault, S.   1015, 1016, 1017, 1501
Bowen, D.L.   657, 7
Bowen, K.A.   134, 135, 131, 1274, 1956, 1018, 8, 132
Boyer, M.   2126
Boyer, R.S.   139, 138, 136, 137
Boyle., J.   1147
Brainbridge, A.   2127
Brandin, D.H.   1152
Bratko, I.   1698, 1875, 1502, 2354
Brazdil, P.   1503, 2355, 1504, 1505
Brecht, H.   1153
Briggs, J.H.   1507, 1508, 1580, 27, 1509, 26, 1506, 893
Broda, K.   1019, 140
Brodie, M.   1957
Brough, D.R.   1809, 1880, 142, 141, 143, 893
Brown, F.M.   144
Brownbridge, D.R.   1194
Bruynooghe, M.   147, 848, 148, 1510, 659, 662, 797, 151, 665, 664, 146, 1276, 661, 1511, 150, 149, 663, 145, 660
Buckley, G.   1942
Bundy, A.   1521, 2364, 153, 2373, 1520, 1820, 666, 154, 1519, 1513, 1812, 1813, 1514, 1756, 1522, 9, 1516, 1517, 1757, 1518, 152, 1515, 1498, 1523, 1811, 849, 10, 1512
Burstall, R.M.   1037, 1020, 1427
Byrd, L.   669, 657, 63, 7, 1814, 1820, 666, 1812, 851, 1517, 1757, 1518, 667, 852, 668, 1811
Caferra, R.   155
Campbell, J.A.   1488, 156
Canet, B.   645, 642, 643, 646, 644
Cao, D.   1204
Carey, M.   673
Carlsson, M.   1021, 677, 853, 1645, 1022, 1023, 1429, 735
Carre, F.   1024
Carre, M.F.   1526
Carroll, J.M.   1527
Cartwright, R.   1025
Cercek, B.   1875
Cerro, L.F.   158
Chabrier, J.   854
Chakravarthy, U.S.   1961, 1204, 1960
Chandra, A.   160
Chang, C.L.   1815, 1528, 161, 162
Chang, J.   855
Chang, J.H.   679
Chapleau, S.   1077
Chen, T.Y.   526
Chen-Ellis, G.   1671
Cheng, M.H.M.   680, 681, 34
Chester, D.   2256, 1026
Chester, D.L.   1027, 2130
Chikayama, T.   1338, 1396, 992, 1028, 1029, 1030, 1158, 1769, 1031
Chin, M.Y.   1816
Cho, J.W.   1222
Cholnoky, E.   1549, 1599
Chomicki, J.   857, 2041

Chomicki, L.	1964	Cowie, J.R.	2153	
Chouraqui, E.	1529	Cox, P.T.	1034, 1035, 181,	
Chow, K.P.	1568		177, 179, 178,	
Chu, B.T.	2081		1036	
Ciancarini, P.	163	Crammond, J.A.	1208	
Ciepielewski, A.	1315, 1314, 1280,	Creelman, P.	872	
	1207, 1278, 1206,	Cross, M.	765	
	1205	Cunningham, R.J.	873	
Clark, K.L.	168, 1530, 685,	Dahl, V.	183, 2157, 2148,	
	14, 1281, 1531,		2160, 1970, 2282,	
	687, 688, 1532,		1821, 2161, 1972,	
	15, 164, 1032,		1542, 2156, 2159,	
	1276, 1282, 1159,		1971, 2158, 2163,	
	167, 860, 1817,		182, 2154	
	165, 686, 859,	Daladier, A.	2164	
	166, 689	Damas, A.	699	
Clark, M.J.N.	1534	Dameri, E.	1200, 111, 114,	
Cleary, J.G.	1386		1486	
Clifford, J.	1933, 1635, 1819,	Dang, W.	1952	
	1934, 1818	Darlington, J.	1530, 1209, 1037,	
Clocksin, W.F.	657, 690, 17, 18,		185	
	1535, 691	Darronnat, Y.	1822	
Coelho, H.	2140, 2137, 2136,	Darvas, F.	1548, 1546, 1550,	
	1967, 1540, 1537,		1543, 1545, 1553,	
	1539, 1538, 2139,		1544, 1552, 1547,	
	1966, 2135, 1965,		1549, 1599, 1551,	
	864, 1968, 1536		1600	
Coeur, A.	1951	Dasai, T.	635, 700	
Cohen, B.	2378	Dausman, M.	1294, 1293, 510	
Cohen, J.	249	David, G.	2283	
Cohen, S.	866, 1430, 1033	David, J.M.	1825	
Colmerauer, A.	2150, 2146, 2148,	Davis, R.E.	186, 1554, 20,	
	175, 172, 693,		1555	
	696, 173, 2143,	DeGroot, D.	1298, 1296, 1297	
	2141, 2144, 2147,	DeOliveira, E.	1902	
	2142, 869, 174,	DeSaram, H.	1731	
	695, 868, 867,	Dean, J.	1556, 1701	
	2187, 171, 2145,	Debenham, J.K.	1826, 1038, 1557	
	2149	Debray, S.	835	
Conery, J.S.	1289, 1290, 1286,	Degano, P.	1295, 1200, 111,	
	870, 1287, 1288,		1010, 163, 114,	
	1285		1486, 107, 106,	
Constable, R.L.	176		113, 105	
Corbin, J.	527	Dekeyser, L.	1827, 1828	
Cortesi, D.E.	19	DelCerro, L.F.	159	
Cory, H.T.	1541	Deliyanni, A.	1558	
Cotta, J.C.	2151, 1539	Dembinski, P.	1335	
Cotton, J.	1820	Demoen, B.	21	
Courant, M.	2152, 1806	Demolombe, R.	1559, 1977, 1978	
Covington, M.A.	871	Deransart, P.	117, 189, 597,	

	188, 252, 190		882, 202
Derby, H.	1560	Elsinger, N.	203
Dershowitz, N.	1040, 191	Emanuelson, P.	703
Despain, A.M.	1211, 1212, 855,	Emde, W.	1572
	679, 701	Ennals, J.R.	685, 25, 888,
Deutsch, T.	1829		1580, 27, 886, 23,
Dewitt, D.	673		26, 24, 889, 1579,
Dias, V.	1830		1578, 893, 689
Didur, P.	1271, 1299	Enomoto, H.	1182, 1838
Diel, H.	1210	Eriksson, L.	1582, 462, 1584,
Digricoli, V.J.	1436		1581, 219, 1583
Dilger, W.	194, 193	Ernst, C.	1825
Dincbas, M.	1833, 1831, 1836,	Eshgi, K.	2397
	1832, 1015, 1014,	Fages, F.	222, 220, 221
	1017, 1042, 1041,	Fagin, B.	706
	195, 1835, 1834,	Fagin, R.	2082, 1984, 1983,
	1501		1985
Diomedi, S.	1295	Fahmi, A.	225
Dobry, T.	1212	Falaschi, M.	227, 226, 1305
Dobry, T.P.	1211	Farinas, L.	228
Dodson, D.C.	877	Farkas, Z.	1585, 988, 894
Doedens, C.F.J.	1955	Fay, M.J.	229
Doman, A.	1300	Feigenbaum, E.A.	1161, 1162
Domolki, B.	1561	Ferguson, R.J.	707, 895
Donz, P.	879	Fernandez, J.A.	94, 1468
Doshita, S.	517	Ferrand, G.	1587
Dowling, W.	196	Feuer, A.	1588
Doyle, J.	1213	Feuerstein, D.	1015, 1014
Draker, C.R.	1908	Fiat, A.	1214
Drosten, K.	1562	Field, A.J.	185
Dunin-Keplicz, B.	22	Fieschi, D.	1839
Durand, J.	197	Fieschi, M.	1866, 1839
Dwiggings, D.	1564, 2092, 1563,	File, G.	231
	2250	Fileman, J.	1585
Dwork, C.	198	Filgueiras, M.	2171, 710, 2173,
Dworkis, C.	1837		2172, 2236, 2235,
Edelman, S.	1301		709, 2069, 708
Eder, E.	155, 199	Finin, T.W.	2174
Eder, G.	200, 1565	Fishman, D.H.	1986, 1306, 1960
Edgar, G.A.	1566	Fogelholm, R.	711, 712
Edman, A.	1567	Fong, S.	2118
Eggert, P.R.	1569, 1568	Forbus, K.	713
Ehrich, H.D.	1562	Foster, A.	1044
Ehrlich, S.M.	1570, 1571	Fowler, G.S.	68
Eimermacher, M.	881, 2168, 2166,	Francez, N.	896
	2167, 2169	Frank, A.	1987
Eisenstadt, M.	1710	Freeman, M.W.	1841, 1840, 405
Eisinger, N.	1302	Freiling, M.	1653
Elcock, E.W.	1043, 1044, 1980,	French, P.	1509
	201, 2289, 2343,	Frey, W.	2238, 1589, 2175

Fribourg, L.	1437, 714	Gelenbe, E.	2000
Frisch, A.M.	234, 1045, 1003	Gelernter, D.	1312
Fronhoefer, B.	155	Genesereth, M.R.	2093
Fuchi, K.	1163, 1166, 235, 1187, 1164	Gergely, T.	1602, 1311, 247, 1310, 1050, 1601
Fuenmayor, M.E.	640	Giandonato, G.	1273
Fuhlrott, O.	1988	Giannesini, F.	249
Fujita, M.	1683, 1232, 1592, 1591, 1590	Gibson, J.	1051, 1132
		Giovanetti, E.	1273
Fullson, J.F.	349, 2195	Giraud, C.	1615, 1616
Furbach, U.	1046	Glasgow, J.I.	1052, 901
Furtado, A.L.	1842	Glover, D.	1880
Furukawa, K.	1307, 1990, 1885, 1180, 1874, 1869, 1991, 390, 2044, 1396, 2218, 1328, 1369, 1873, 1166, 1309, 1170, 1169, 1181, 1168, 1165, 1336, 1308, 1375, 1167	Goebel, R.	1332
		Goebel, R.G.	1846, 1618, 33, 1576, 1617, 681, 34, 35, 1303
		Goguen, J.A.	1438
		Goldenberg, S.	896
		Goldreich, O.	252
		Golshani, F.	1847
		Gonen, A.	1571
Fusaoka, A.	1215	Gonzalez, J.C.	1619
Futo, I.	1368, 1606, 28, 1602, 1550, 1311, 1611, 1610, 1598, 1829, 1552, 1597, 1596, 1607, 102, 103, 1310, 1549, 1599, 29, 1551, 1608, 1601, 30, 1600, 1474, 31, 1609	Goodall, A.	36
		Goto, S.	1054, 1053, 1171, 1232, 1620
		Grad, A.	1875
		Graefe, G.	673
		Grant, J.	2002, 2003, 2001
		Grau, B.	1621
		Gray, P.M.D.	2005, 2004, 1622
		Green, C.C.	253, 255, 2301, 1055
Futumura, Y.	237	Green, T.R.	37
Gabanyi, Z.	1548	Greenbaum, S.	420
Gabbay, D.	241, 1048, 240, 1845, 239	Greenwood, S.	904
		Gregory, S.	1281, 942, 1313, 1032, 1282, 1159, 1019, 1623, 723
Gabbay, D.M.	1047		
Gabriel, J.R.	1612, 719, 1613, 1570, 1571	Greussay, P.	1057, 1056
		Gross, M.	2176
Gallaire, H.	2398, 1998, 1997, 32, 320, 186, 1702, 1993, 1996, 1999, 1994, 2399, 1995	Grumbach, A.	1848
		Grundzinski, T.	1964
		Guiliano, M.	1045, 1003
		Guizol, J.	905, 2177
Gallier, J.	720	Gupta, N.K.	1849
Gallier, J.H.	1049, 196	Gust, H.	38
Ganzinger, H.	899	Gutierrez, C.	1440
Gardarin, G.	2000	H.Minsky, N.	857
Garreta, H.	721	Habata, S.	724
Garrett, R.	1614	Habel, C.U.	256, 1572

Author Index

Hadley, R.	2178	Holldobler, S.	1046
Hagert, G.	1626, 1627, 1624, 1625	Honda, M.	1628
		Honma, Y.	1882
Hagino, T.	1628	Horn, A.	280
Hagiya, N.	258, 257	Horster, P.J.	1064
Hammond, P.	1859, 1629, 1852, 1857, 1856, 1854, 1861, 1860, 1880, 1862, 1851, 1858, 1853, 1855, 1541	Horstmann, P.W.	1632
		Horvat, M.	1875
		Howarth, R.	1860
		Hsiang, J.	913, 281
		Hsu, L.S.	728
Han, J.	2007	Huai-Min, S.	1065
Hansson, A.	259, 262, 1059, 1058, 1624, 260, 1060, 265, 261, 1625, 1217	Hudak, P.	1441
		Huet, G.	283, 284
		Hustler, A.	1864
		Ianeselli, J.C.	1953, 1952
Hanus, M.	899	Ida, T.	285
Harandi, M.T.	266, 1120	Igusa, H.	700
Hardy, S.	1061, 1086, 1132, 1062, 156	Iima, Y.	1182
		Ince, D.C.	914
Harel, D.	160	Irani, K.B.	2011
Haridi, S.	1315, 1316, 1314, 1280, 269, 268, 1207, 1278, 1058, 267, 260, 261, 1217, 1206	Ishii, A.	1633
		Ishikawa, Y.	1774
		Ishizuka, M.	286, 1867
		Itai, A.	287
		Ito, N.	1320, 1319, 1219, 1685, 1189
Hattori, T.	1172, 1158, 1769		
Hawley, R.	909	Jacobs, B.	97, 96
Hayashi, K.	1881	Jaffar, J.	291, 1443, 1442, 289, 288
Hayes, P.J.	1534		
Heck, N.	1630	Jananaming, M.	2012
Hellerstein, L.	1394, 1317	Janson, A.	193
Helm, R.A.	1863	Jarke, M.	1933, 1635, 1819, 1865, 1934, 1634, 1636, 1818, 1957
Henschen, L.J.	2008, 2010, 2050, 271, 2009		
Herath, J.	1267	Jenkins, L.E.	1637
Hertzberger, L.O.	1173	Jenkins, M.A.	901
Hess, M.	2179	Johansson, A.L.	262, 1582, 462, 1581, 2012, 1583, 1638
Heuschen, L.J.	273		
Hill, D.D.	1726		
Hill, R.	274	John, C.C.	1790
Hines, L.M.	128	Jomier, G.	2030
Hirakawa, H.	2199, 1396, 2218	Jones, N.D.	293
Hirata, K.	1234	Jones, S.	915
Hirata, M.	517	Josephson, N.A.	1040
Hirschman, L.	1841, 1840, 2180, 275	Joubert, M.	1866, 1839, 2181
		Joubert, T.	759, 639
Hoare, C.A.R.	1063	Juanole, G.	1469
Hogger, C.J.	1318, 276, 911, 277, 39, 1631, 279, 278	Julien, S.	1639
		Jurkiewics, Z.	731
		Kacsuk, P.	1220

Kahn, G.	1323, 294, 1322	Koch, G.	2188
Kahn, K.M.	2182, 1641, 296,	Kofalusi, V.	1651, 1652
	1642, 1398, 1645,	Koga, A.	1628
	1640, 1023, 1644,	Kogan, D.	1653
	735, 1067, 1066,	Kohli, M.	306, 1204, 1324
	733	Kohoutek, H.	1176
Kakuda, T.	1881	Komorowski, H.J.	744, 1071, 1654,
Kakusho, O.	2264		923, 307, 1072,
Kakuta, T.	1235, 1245, 1244		1070, 1655, 1069,
Kale, L.V.	1221, 297, 835		308
Kameda, M.	1930	Konagaya, A.	1073
Kanai, N.	1867	Kornfeld, W.A.	1074
Kaneda, Y.	1251, 1252	Kosa, M.	651, 653
Kanellakis, P.C.	198	Kouloumdjian, J.	2022
Kanoui, H.	1646, 1493, 298,	Koves, P.	746, 925, 44, 747,
	737, 696, 869,		652
	1494, 2149	Kowalski, R.A.	1659, 47, 134,
Kaposi, A.A.	1682, 1647, 918		311, 312, 316,
Kapur, D.	299		1558, 52, 50,
Karatsu, H.	1174		2023, 1656, 1871,
Kasif, S.	1648, 1302, 1204,		1657, 1658, 1177,
	1324		54, 45, 123, 48,
Katayama, Y.	1691		240, 1178, 310,
Katuta, T.	1941		1541, 1446, 215,
Kawamura, M.	1774		2402
Kawato, N.	1777, 1881	Kowlaski, R.	1075
Kay, M.	2183	Kramer, J.	806
Keddis, T.	2099	Krekels, B.	1827, 1828
Kellog, C.	2017, 2016, 1068,	Krishnamoorty, M.S.	299
	2018	Kriwaczek, F.R.	1661, 1660, 1541
Khabaza, T.	1325, 1326	Kubota, K.	1249
Kibler, D.F.	1289, 1290, 1286,	Kuchnir, L.	1571
	302, 870, 2375,	Kuehner, D.	316, 317
	1287, 1288	Kukich, K.	1662
Kim, J.I.	1222	Kunifuji, S.	1885, 1180, 1874,
Kirakawa, H.	1327, 1328		1869, 2111, 2044,
Kishi, M.	1320		1076, 1873, 1309,
Kisz, Z.	2185		1170, 1169, 1181,
Kitagawa, T.	1649		1838, 2024, 1375,
Kitakami, H.	1885, 1180, 1874,		1167
	1868, 1869, 2044,	Kuno, E.	1320
	1873	Kuper, G.M.	2026, 2025, 2027
Kitsuregawa, M.	1175	Kurokawa, T.	1769
Kittredge, R.	2186, 2187	Kurukawa, T.	0, 1182, 933
Kiyono, M.	2198	Kusalik, A.J.	1329, 1330, 1664
Klahr, P.	2017, 303	LaPalme, G.	2126
Kleene, S.C.	304, 305	Labadi, K.	102, 103, 1476,
Kluzniak, F.	42, 739, 742, 41,		1474
	43, 920, 922, 740,	Landsbergen, S.P.	2190
	919, 1650, 741	Lapalme, G.	1077

Lartigue, A.	787, 788		333
Lasserre, C.	2398, 320, 186, 2399	Lowry, A.	815, 1372, 1225, 753, 752
Lassez, C.	1665, 1863	Lozinski, E.L.	2029
Lassez, J.L.	291, 1443, 325, 1442, 512, 1183, 322, 324, 289, 526, 394, 323, 612, 321	Lubonski, P.	2194
		Lucena, G.J.	1304
		Luckham, D.	1466
		Luger, G.	1519, 1670, 1812, 1813, 1517
Laus-Maczynska, K.	2121	Lugosi, G.	1489
Lavrac, N.	1875	Lundberg, B.	340
Lazinski, M.	748	Lusk, ,E.L.	1147
LeGloan, A.	722	Lusk, E.	756, 343
LePape, J.P.	1017, 1042, 1041, 195	Lusk, E.L.	1079, 1080, 719, 1078, 1352, 1226, 1227, 755
Lee, N.S.	1876		
Lee, R.	1332, 161	Lyall, A.	1880
Lee, R.C.T.	326	MacLennan, B.J.	344, 345
Lee, R.K.S.	1331	MacQueen, D.	1323
Lee, R.M.	2312, 1877, 1878	MacQueen, D.B.	1020
Lehman, M.M.	1184	Maekawa, S.	1252
Leibrandt, U.	1666	Maeng, S.R.	1222
Lengauer, C.	935	Magee, J.	806
Levi, G.	1200, 111, 1010, 114, 227, 1486, 1009, 107, 1201, 226, 1008, 115, 106, 1305, 113, 1405, 105, 100	Maguire, G.	815
		Maher, M.J.	291, 1443, 325, 1442, 512, 1183, 322, 324, 323, 1448, 612, 321
		Mahr, B.	617, 618
Levine, S.H.	2191	Maibaum, T.S.	938, 1577, 1081
Levy, J.	1406	Maio, C.	1254
Lewis, H.R.	327	Makinouchi, A.	1930
Li-Guo, W.	1065	Makowsky, J.A.	617, 618, 287, 347
Lichtman, B.M.	936		
Lieberman, H.	1667	Malachi, Y.	1082
Lima, I.G.	1195	Malcolm, M.A.	1271, 1299
Lindholm, T.G.	719	Malpas, J.	56
Lindstrom, G.	1447, 1333, 1223	Maluszinski, J.	349, 2195, 350
Lingas, A.	328	Maluszynski, J.	1335, 252, 190, 308
Lioupis, D.	1224		
Littleford, A.	1668	Mangir, T.	1672, 1671
Lloyd, J.W.	216, 2028, 289, 799, 329, 331, 750, 332, 751, 800	Manna, Z.	351, 555, 352, 1082
		Mano, T.	1881
		Manuel, T.	757
Logrippo, L.	1669	Maquire, G.	1372
Lopata, A.	1553	Marayuma, T.	1234
Lopes, G.P.	2193, 2192	Mark, L.	2081
Loveland, D.W.	339, 335, 336, 338, 334, 337,	Marks, J.O.	1534
		Markus, A.	1585, 1674, 1673

Markusz, Z.S. 1682, 1489, 1678, 1679, 1585, 1675, 1647, 1680, 1677, 918, 1676
Marque-Pucheu, G. 2030, 353
Marriot, K.G. 1863
Martelli, A. 1200, 355, 356, 1486, 354
Martelli, M. 111, 114, 1009, 1201, 1008, 115
Martin, M. 759, 639, 758
Martin, P. 2196
Martin-Gallausiaux, J. 2030
Martins, J. 357, 1128
Maruichi, T. 1774
Maruyama, F. 1684, 1683, 1881
Masuda, K. 1319, 1219, 1685, 962, 1189
Matos, A. 1686
Matrai, G. 1553, 1687
Matsuda, H. 1252
Matsumoto, Y. 1307, 2199, 2198, 1336, 1308
Matwin, S. 417, 796, 761, 358, 742
May, D. 1228
Mayor, B. 359
McCabe, F.G. 1229, 685, 942, 687, 688, 1083, 57, 15, 1817, 686, 762, 689
McCarthy, J. 362, 1025, 361
McCord, M.C. 2201, 1084, 2203, 363, 2200, 2163, 2202
McCorduck, P. 1162
McCrosky, C.D. 901
McCume, W.W. 364, 1226
McDermott, D.V. 365, 982, 981, 58
McGrath, G.M. 1038, 1557
McKay, D.P. 357, 2088, 1841, 1840, 275, 1128, 366
McKeeman, W.M. 983, 1532
McMahon, G.B. 1721
McRobbie, M.A. 1085
McSkimin, J.R. 2205, 2204
McWeeny, P.A. 1299
Mellish, C.S. 764, 1688, 1689, 367, 2209, 2210,

Meloni, H. 641, 2117, 945, 905, 1482
Merret, T.H. 1087
Meseguer, J. 1438
Meyer, R.K. 1085
Miaczynska, M. 1481
Michoguchi, F. 1882
Michol, J. 1556
Mierowsky, C. 1337, 1364
Mikami, O. 2265
Miller, C.D.F. 1208
Miller, F. 1840
Mills, P. 1230
Milne, R. 2211, 2212, 1812, 2214, 2215, 2213
Minker, J. 1998, 2033, 2040, 97, 1997, 2216, 2002, 2003, 376, 2205, 1088, 370, 306, 1961, 1883, 2035, 1996, 1999, 1302, 1204, 2037, 2036, 2039, 2038, 375, 2001, 2031, 1306, 1324, 96, 2217, 2034, 1960, 1089, 2204
Minsky, N. 2041
Miranker, D. 1247, 1231
Mishra, P. 378
Missikoff, M. 1884
Mitchell, J.C. 198
Mitsumoto, K. 1232
Mitta, K. 1307
Miwa, K. 1882
Miyachi, T. 1885, 1180, 1874, 1869, 2044, 1910, 1873
Miyazaki, N. 2111, 1941, 1235, 1245, 1244
Miyazaki, T. 1338
Miyoshi, H. 2199, 2218
Mizoguchi, F. 1690, 1691, 1887
Moffat, D.S. 1622
Mogado, E. 1128
Molnar, E. 1674, 1673

1086, 1519, 1812, 2207, 17, 1517, 2208, 1518, 2206, 765, 691

Montanari, U.   355, 354
Monteiro, L.F.   1345, 1341, 379,
                        1343, 1340, 1347,
                        1342, 1339, 1353,
                        1346
Montgomery, C.A.   2092, 1692
Moore, J.S.   139, 138, 380,
                        137
Moore, R.C.   381
Mori, H.   1232
Morisawa, Y.   1462
Morokhovets, M.K.   382
Morris, J.B.   1450
Morris, P.H.   384, 385, 870,
                        1889, 1693
Moss, C.   947
Moss, C.D.   769, 1694, 388,
                        1696, 768, 1695
Moto-Oka, T.   1175, 1150, 1185,
                        1188, 1171, 1268,
                        1592, 1591, 1590
Moto-oka, T.   1186, 1234, 1187
Motoda, H.   1697
Moura, C.M.O.   1842
Mozetic, I.   1698, 1875
Mukai, K.   390, 389, 2218,
                        700
Muller, J.P.   1349, 194
Murakami, K.   2111, 1941, 1235,
                        1244
Murray, N.V.   1090
Mycroft, A.   1699, 1091, 293
Naish, L.   951, 59, 950, 953,
                        392, 394, 2047,
                        1092, 952, 2048
Nait-Abdallah, M.A.   218
Nakagawa, H.   1350
Nakajima, R.   1628, 1168
Nakamura, K.   1093, 775
Nakasawa, O.   1182
Nakashima, H.   1096, 1098, 1097,
                        1094, 1095, 954
Nakazaki, R.   777
Nakzaki, Y.   724
Naqvi, S.A.   2008, 1986, 2010,
                        2050, 2049, 271,
                        2009
Narain, S.   1700, 1099, 1100
Narendran, P.   299
Nasr, R.   1105

Navrao, L.   1698
Neely, R.   1623
Nemeti, I.   93
Neveln, R.C.   1004
Neves, J.C.   2055, 2051, 2056,
                        1470, 1467, 2053,
                        2107, 2054, 2052
Newton, M.O.   1101
Ng, P.   778
Nguyen, G.T.   1953, 2057, 1944,
                        1954, 1943, 1952
Nichol, J.   1701
Nicolas, J.M.   1998, 2065, 1997,
                        2058, 2062, 2061,
                        1702, 2064, 1999,
                        2059, 2063, 2039,
                        2060
Niehuis, S.   1791
Nilsson, J.F.   350, 397, 779
Nilsson, M.   1703, 1704, 782,
                        780, 1705, 781,
                        783
Nishikawa, H.   1250, 1265, 841,
                        1236
Nitadori, K.   1384
Nitta, K.   1336, 1308
Noelke, U.   1706
Noguchi, S.   497
Nordstrom, B.   398
Norton, L.M.   1707, 275
O'Keefe, R.A.   1699, 1708, 1709,
                        958, 1894, 959,
                        961, 956, 1451,
                        960, 1757, 399,
                        957
O'Shea, T.   1710
Ochitani, R.   2264, 2265
Ogawa, Y.   2323
Ogino, T.   635
Ohlbach, H.J.   400
Ohlsson, S.   2371
Ohsuga, S.   1711
Olivares, J.   2057, 785
Oliveira, E.   1895, 1897, 1896
Omori, S.   923
Onai, R.   1328, 1219, 962,
                        1189, 1269
Orlowska, E.   228
Overbeek, ,R.A.   1147
Overbeek, R.A.   1102, 1104, 1079,

	1080, 719, 756,		2232, 2231
	1078, 1352, 1226,	Pitchumani, V.	993
	1227, 343, 755	Pittombils, E.	797
Owada, H.	1691	Plaisted, D.	191
Oxley, D.	1134	Plaisted, D.A.	1716, 419, 420,
Pagello, E.	404		418
Pakalns, J.L.	1712	Plummer, D.	2364, 2373, 2372
Palamidessi, C.	227, 226, 1305,	Poe, M.	1903
	1405	Pollack, J.	1354
Palmer, M.	1841, 275	Pollard, G.H.	1240
Palmer, M.S.	1713, 1519, 1812,	Pollit, A.S.	1904, 1717
	2174, 1517, 623	Poole, D.L.	1906, 2073, 1905
Panangden, P.	1223	Port, G.S.	526
Pape, J.P.L.	1016	Porter, B.W.	2375, 2374
Parcy, J.P.	1898	Porto, A.	1939, 965, 414,
Parfitt, N.	1809		794, 1718, 1108,
Parker, D.S.	2066		2236, 1107, 791,
Parsaye, K.	1900, 1899, 2068		412, 423, 2235,
Pasero, R.	2221, 2220, 2149		415, 413, 968
Pasztorne-Varga, K.	1901		
Paterson, M.S.	406	Potter, W.D.	2074
Patt, Y.N.	701	Poutain, D.	65
Percebois, C.	1238, 787, 788	Powell, P.	2216
Pereira, F.C.N.	1764, 669, 2224,	Powers, D.M.W.	1721, 2108, 2237,
	2270, 2226, 62,		1720, 971, 970,
	963, 63, 7, 2269,		66, 1719
	2223, 2225, 2227,	Pratt, Y.N.	1211, 1212
	2229, 831, 1714,	Prawitz, ,D.	425
	2222, 2228, 2196,	Prini, G.	842
	64	Proszely, G.	2185
Pereira, L.M.	965, 414, 409,	Puder, K.	2180
	794, 1830, 407,	Pull, H.	185
	63, 7, 151, 1105,	Quiniou, R.	1495
	1540, 1539, 791,	Quinton, P.	1495
	412, 408, 1902,	Raatz, S.	720
	831, 964, 2069,	Radenski, A.	1110
	150, 415, 413,	Rae, R.	666
	1353, 64	Ramamohanarao, K.	799, 751, 800
Perichaud, L.	2070	Ramanujam, R.	426
Perlis, D.	376, 375	Raulefs, P.	427
Perrot, E.	416	Rayner, M.	1584
Persch, G.	1294, 1293, 510	Reddy, U.	428
Petersson, K.	398	Reddy, U.S.	1112, 1111
Pettitt, P.	1534	Reeder, M.W.	1534
Piertrzykowski, T.	1036	Reeve, M.	1209
Pietrzykowski, T.	181, 417, 796,	Reiter, R.	2075, 434, 2077,
	761, 358, 1106		1454, 2076, 2078,
Pilsworth, B.W.	1805		2079, 2080, 429
Pinter, R.	896	Reitman, W.	1907
Pique, J.F.	2150, 2072, 1715,	Reyle, U.	2238, 1589, 1047,
			1048

Rich, C.	1722	Sanchis, E.	1469
Richard, P.	1948	Sandewall, E.	1729, 1116
Ridd, S.	1723	Sandford, D.M.	449
Ridoux, O.	645, 642, 643, 644	Sansonnet, J.P.	1238
		Santane-Toth, E.	988, 894, 1730
Riet, R.P.V.	1190	Saraswat, V.	1409
Ringwood, G.	1623	Sato, H.	700
Roach, J.W.	1725, 1876, 1908, 68	Sato, M.	450, 1118, 451, 574, 575, 1117
Roberts, G.M.	801	Sato, T.	452, 1770, 454, 487, 453, 488
Roberts, P.R.	1613		
Robin, S.	2152, 1806	Savory, S.	1706
Robinson, G.	1455	Sawamura, J.	805
Robinson, J.A.	438, 439, 437, 440, 441, 1909, 442, 69, 1113, 1114, 1115, 974, 443	Schlobohm, D.	1912
		Schnupp, P.	1666, 1733, 1732, 71
		Schoppers, M.J.	266, 1119, 1120
		Schorre, D.V.	1569
Rohrer, C.	1589	Schorre, V.	1121
Rokusawa, K.	1320	Schrag, R.C.	1125, 1124, 1123, 1122
Rollinger, C.R.	1572		
Roscoe, A.W.	1063	Schultz, J.W.	455
Rossi, G.	356	Schwind, C.B.	2248, 2247, 456
Roussel, P.	1468, 802, 2149	Sciore, E.	2087, 2086
Roussopoulos, N.	2081	Sebelik, J.	978, 1734, 457
Roux, M.	1866, 1839	Sedogdo, C.	2249
Roy, S.	1726	Seidel, R.	1735
Rozenshtein, D.	2041	Seki, H.	1215
Ruspini, E.H.	1692	Sergot, M.J.	1861, 1737, 1862, 54, 241, 1913, 1736, 1541
Saasat, S.	806		
Sabatier, P.	2072, 2243, 2242, 2241, 2240, 1902, 2244		
		Seviora, R.E.	1849
		Shafrir, A.	1358
Sadler, M.R.	1081	Shamir, A.	1214
Sadri, F.	1541	Shapiro, E.	1388
Saeki, M.	1838	Shapiro, E.Y.	1738, 1317, 458, 2380, 1727, 1359, 1362, 1358, 1364, 1191, 1360, 1242, 1915, 979, 1365, 1739, 1214, 1301, 1363
Safra, M.	1727		
Sagiv, Y.	2082, 2083, 1728		
Sahlin, D.	1316, 269, 268		
Saint-Dizier, P.	1728, 2245, 2246		
Sakai, H.	1241		
Sakai, K.	1910, 1769		
Sakurai, T.	258, 447, 1118, 451, 574, 575, 1117	Shapiro, S.C.	357, 2088, 1126, 1128, 1127, 366
		Sharpe, W.P.	1916
Salle, P.	1024, 1526	Shaw, D.E.	1247, 1248, 1254
Sambuc, R.	2148	Sheperdson, J.C.	461
Sammut, C.A.	2378, 1011, 2377, 2376, 70, 804	Shepherd, R.	1228
		Shibayama, E.	1628
Sammut, R.A.	70, 804	Shibayama, S.	2111, 1941, 1235,

	1245, 1244, 1243	Srivas, M.	913, 281
Shidu, D.P.	1740, 1741, 1742	Srivastava, A.	1134
Shieber, S.M	2228	Stabler, E.P.	2094, 1980, 2257, 2343
Shih, Y.	2011		
Shimizu, H.	1320, 1219, 1685, 1189	Stafford, G.	1271
		Steele, B.D.	1928, 1509
Shmueli, O.	1917	Steels, L.	475
Shoham, Y.	982, 1743, 981	Stefanek, P.	978, 1734, 457
Shortliffe, E.H.	462	Stein, J.	1121
Shostak, R.E.	463	Stepanek, P.	1754, 476
Shyamasundar, R.K.	426	Stepankova, O.	1753, 1754, 476
Sibert, E.E.	1113, 1114, 1115	Sterling, L.	1929, 2405, 1755,
Sickel, S.	464, 983, 465, 1532, 167		2344, 1756, 1522, 1751, 1757
Sidhu, D.	1840	Stickel, M.E.	339, 480, 479, 478
Siegel, P.	466, 130		
Siekmann, J.	427, 469, 470, 467, 468	Stolfo, S.J.	815, 1247, 1248, 2345, 1372, 753, 752, 1254, 817
Silva, G.	1564, 2092, 2250		
Silver, B.	1521, 1745, 2364, 1520, 1744, 2384, 2386, 1757, 1746	Stone, H.S.	1188
		Stone, M.	1813
		Strzalkowski, P.	2123, 2124
Simi, M.	1005	Subrahmanyam, P.A.	1136, 1135, 1461
Simizu, H.	1319	Sugiyama, K.	1930
Simmons, R.F.	1130, 2255, 1131, 2256, 1129	Sugiyama, Y.	1462
		Sun, H.	1758
Simons, R.A.	1377	Suwa, M.	1759
Sintzoff, M.	471	Suzuki, K.	700
Sivasankaran, T.	1636	Suzuki, N.	1367, 1098, 1366, 1249
Skinner, D.	2387		
Skuce, D.	1749, 1921, 1918, 1922, 1669, 1923, 1804, 1924, 1919, 1920, 1750, 1748	Swidzinski, M.	990
		Swinson, P.S.G.	1764, 74, 1762, 1761, 1763
		Sykora, O.	483
Slagle, J.	162	Sylla, K.H.	1733
Sloman, A.	1132, 1062	Syre, J.C.	2063
Sloman, M.	806	Szabo, P.	427, 468
Smith, B.	1133	Szafran, K.	811
Smith, D.E.	2093	Szalo, P.	1609
Smith, P.	1751	Szelke, E.	1674
Smolka, G.	1458, 984	Szenes, K.	1368, 1611, 1610, 985
Soeterman, B.	1672		
Sommella, D.T.	1020	Szeredi, J.	1368, 1606, 28, 1611, 1610, 988, 894, 1607, 484, 987, 75, 1766, 76, 29, 1608, 30, 1600, 31, 1609
Soulhi, S.	2129		
Sowa, J.F.	72		
Spacek, L.	73, 1752, 1925, 1926, 1927		
Spivey, J.M.	809		
Spyratos, N.	472	Szeredi, P.	1550, 925, 651, 1552, 103, 1730,
Srinivasan, C.V.	473		

	1561, 1551, 652	Toan, N.G.	1951
Szots, M.	1137, 247, 1050	Toda, K.	1267
Szpakowicz, S.	990, 42, 742,	Todd, S.	1773
	1767, 41, 43, 922,	Togashi, A.	497
	2258, 811, 22	Tojo, S.	1182
Szuba, T.	1768	Tokoro, M.	1774
Tagaki, S.	1769	Tomura, S.	954
Takahashi, K.	1215	Topor, R.W.	2099, 332
Takeshima, T.	805	Torii, K.	1462
Takeuchi, A.	1180, 2044, 1338,	Toth, L.	2185
	1369, 1309, 1170,	Townsend, H.R.A.	498
	1169, 1181, 1365,	Toyoda, J.	2264, 2265
	1375, 1167	Tran, D.	1961
Takeuti, G.	485	Travis, L.	2017, 2018
Taki, K.	1250, 1265, 841,	Treleaven, P.C.	1194, 1195, 1192,
	1236		1193
Tam, C.M.	1370	Trilling, L.	1806
Tamaki, H.	580, 1770, 454,	Trum, P.	500, 499
	487, 486, 453,	Tseng, S.H.	2262
	488	Tsuji, J.	1182, 1769
Tamas, G.	1829	Tsur, S.	1917
Tamura, N.	1251, 1376, 1252	Turner, S.J.	2263
Tamura, T.	635	Tzoar, D.	817
Tanaka, H.	1175, 1150, 2199,	Tzur, S.	896
	2198, 1171, 1771,	Uchida, S.	1250, 1264, 1263,
	1592, 1591, 1234,		1265, 1769, 841,
	1590		1236
Tanaka, Y.	1253	Ueda, K.	992, 1181, 1375,
Tancig, P.	1138		1167, 954
Tarlecki, A.	630	Uehara, K.	2264, 2265, 1776
Tarnlund, S.A.	168, 2096, 1059,	Uehara, T.	1777, 1881
	2097, 489, 495,	Ukkonen, E.	994
	1626, 1627, 493,	Ullman, J.D.	2083, 2100, 2025,
	1058, 490, 1567,		2101
	2012, 492, 1060,	Umeyama, S.	1376
	265, 261, 1217,	Umrigar, Z.D.	993
	1583	Unemura, M.	1073
Taylor, J.	77	Ungaro, L.	645, 642, 643,
Taylor, S.	815, 1372, 1225,		646, 644
	753, 752, 1254,	Unvericht, E.	427
	817	Valentini, S.	404
Tazi, S.	496, 2261, 2260	Valtorta, M.	1932, 1931
Tector, A.L.	877	Van Caneghem, M.	671, 672, 696,
Temine, G.	2125		869, 11, 1959
Thistlewaite, P.B.	1085	Van Emden, M.H.	216, 213, 214,
Thom, J.A.	2098, 800, 2048		207, 1575, 1574,
Thorne, P.G.	2098		208, 1531, 95,
Tick, E.	1255, 1257, 1256,		142, 1981, 1577,
	1258		204, 1982, 884,
Tiomkin, M.	896		1304, 210, 205,

	212, 1576, 209,		2271
	1573, 215, 218,	Weaver, M.J.	1908
	1160, 206, 885,	Weber, Y.	1825
	35, 1303	Wegman, M.N.	406
Van Gelder, A.	246, 2101	Weinberg, T.	135
Van Roy, P.	803	Weiner, J.L.	836
Vanderbrug, G.	2217	Weir, D.	1580, 1788, 1787
Vardi, M.Y.	2026, 2025, 2027	Weishedel, R.M.	2272
Varga, K.	653	Welham, B.	1813, 1523, 849
Vassey, P.	1778	Welham, R.	82, 1789, 999
Vassiliou, Y.	1933, 1635, 1819,	Wesfold, S.J.	2301
	1865, 1934, 1818	Weyrauch, R.W.	1142
Vataja, P.	994	Wiederhold, G.	1884
Vayssade, M.	1481	Wilk, P.F.	83
Veloso, P.A.S.	938	Willems, J.L.	1827, 1828
Venken, R.	823, 2103, 2102,	Willems, Y.D.	1827, 1828
	1511	Williams, M.H.	2055, 2056, 1470,
Vere, S.	504, 505		1819, 1467, 2107,
Verity, J.W.	78		2054
Viccari, R.M.	2193	Wilson, W.G.	1790
Victor, F.	1791	Wilson, W.W.	1143
Vidal, J.	1500	Winniger, P.	2057, 1951
Virbel, J.	2261, 2260	Winterstein, G.	1294, 1293, 510,
Virkar, R.S.	1908		500, 1464
Vitter, J.S.	1377	Wise, M.J.	1144, 511, 1383,
Voda, P.J.	507, 1139, 1140		84, 1146, 1145,
Wada, K.	1252		2108
Wadge, B.	98	Wisskirchen, P.	1791
Waldinger, R.	351, 555, 352,	Woehl, K.	1792
	1082	Wolfram, D.A.	512
Walker, A.	1939, 1936, 1937,	Woo, N.	586
	1938, 1528, 143,	Wos, ,L.	1147
	1935, 1779	Wos, L.	1793, 1795, 1794,
Wallace, M.	2266		1455
Wallace, R.S.	1141	Wright, D.J.	2110
Wallen, L.A.	1781, 1780	Wright, D.W.	2099
Waller, L.	80, 79	Wrightson, G.	469, 470, 515
Waltz, D.	1354	Wu, O.	1527
Wang, L.	1758	Wyatt, D.	1980
Warren, D.H.D.	669, 1266, 2270,	Yamada, N.	1697
	829, 1784, 1196,	Yamaguchi, Y.	1267
	1379, 63, 7, 2269,	Yamamoto, A.	1250, 1265, 841,
	2104, 1783, 81,		1236
	998, 827, 826,	Yamasaki, S.	517, 516
	2268, 1785, 2229,	Yasakuwa, H.	1180
	1786, 831, 828,	Yasuhara, H.	1384
	1258, 64, 1782	Yasukawa, H.	2199, 2218, 2273,
Warren, D.S.	1221, 2105, 2106,		1170
	833, 835, 832,	Yasuura, H.	588
	834, 2087, 2086,	Yazdani, M.	1796, 85, 1797,

	1798
Yazdanian, K.	2065, 2064
Yokoi, T.	1197, 1172, 1799, 1769
Yokomori, T.	1000
Yokota, H.	1180, 2111, 1941, 2044, 1235, 1245, 840, 1244, 2024
Yokota, M.	1148, 1158, 1250, 1265, 841, 1236
Yonezaki, N.	1838
Yonezawa, A.	1684, 1168
Yoshida, K.	1697
Yoshida, M.	517, 516
You, J.H.	1136, 1135, 1461
Young, A.	1980
Young, J.D.	18
Young, T.	1271
Yu, B.	1140
Yu, Y.H.	2274
Yuasa, T.	1628
Yuba, T.	1267
Zaniolo, C.	1001, 2112
Zanon, G.	2040, 1149
Zappacosta-Amboldi, S.	873
Zarri, G.P.	1800
Zaumen, W.T.	1801
Zfirah, H.	1917
Zhou, S.Q.	1006
de Rougemont, M.	445
del Cerro, L.F.	2129
van Emde Boas, P.	1955
van Emde Boas-Lubsen, H.	1955